Figures of Resistance

FIGURES OF RESISTANCE

Essays in Feminist Theory

Teresa de Lauretis

Edited and with an
Introduction by **Patricia White**

UNIVERSITY OF ILLINOIS PRESS
URBANA AND CHICAGO

Library of Congress
Cataloging-in-Publication Data
de Lauretis, Teresa.
Figures of resistance : essays in
feminist theory / Teresa de Lauretis ;
edited and with an introduction
by Patricia White.
p.   cm.
Includes bibliographical
references and index.
ISBN-13: 978-0-252-03197-7
(cloth : alk. paper)
ISBN-10: 0-252-03197-0
(cloth : alk. paper)
ISBN-13: 978-0-252-07439-4
(pbk. : alk. paper)
ISBN-10: 0-252-07439-4
(pbk. : alk. paper)
1. Feminist theory. 2. Lesbianism.
I. White, Patricia, 1964– II. Title.
HQ1190.D4   2007
306.76'6301—dc22   2006029388

Contents

Acknowledgments

This book would not exist without the work and the enthusiasm of many, to whom I am deeply grateful. Joan Catapano first suggested the idea of a feminist theory "reader" and saw it through to publication. Judith Mayne and B. Ruby Rich persuaded me that a collection of hard-to-find, older and newer articles would still have value for today's readers as sea-change interventions in feminist and film studies. I thank the doctoral students in my fall 2003 History of Consciousness seminar in feminist theory, with whom I developed my thoughts for the title essay; Anu Koivunen, who introduced me when I presented a lecture version of the title essay at the University of Stockholm and who also edited a collection of my writings in Finnish translation; Maryann Valiulis, who invited me to speak at Trinity College, Dublin, on the felicitous occasion of the centenary of women's entrance into the college; and Mary McDermott, who kindly acted as my guide in Dublin. Most of all, I am grateful to Patricia White for her perfect pitch in the selection, her painstaking editing, and unerring advice. Working with her has always been a privilege and a joy. Finally,

· ACKNOWLEDGMENTS ·

I thank Zoe Leonard for generously sharing her art with us and allowing her photographs to converse with our writings.

TERESA DE LAURETIS

» » »

For their helpful comments on the introduction, I would like to thank Nora Johnson, Homay King, Bakirathi Mani, Judith Mayne, B. Ruby Rich, Bethany Schneider, Cynthia Schneider, Kate Thomas, and Catina Yervasi. Thanks to Joan Catapano for her vision of this book, and to project editor Angela Burton, copyeditor Julie Gay, cover designer Carrie House, and book designer Cope Cumpston for so ably realizing it. And above all, thanks to Teresa de Lauretis, whose intellectual generosity is evident on every page.

PATRICIA WHITE

Introduction:
Thinking Feminist

Patricia White

Teresa de Lauretis is among the foremost feminist theorists of the past several decades; her thought has set terms of debate at key junctures, and it helps renew the relevance of feminist theory for our current moment. Just as her background bridges Europe and America, her work links continental theories with U.S. feminism in mutually productive ways. Having edited and introduced the 1991 special issue of *differences* entitled "Queer Theory," she is a founder of that academic discourse who has nevertheless remained an astute critic of the status of feminist and lesbian theory within it.[1] Her writing, evoking that of such feminist prose stylists as Virginia Woolf even while analyzing it, is at once demanding and thrillingly precise.

The eleven essays in this collection, written over the two-decade span from 1985 to 2005, demonstrate the scope and impact of Teresa de Lauretis's thought and its ongoing promise. Organized into three parts, "Representations," "Readings," and "Epistemologies," the book includes benchmark pieces as well as harder-to-find interventions. The essays have been gathered and contextualized to illuminate their interconnections, with an emphasis on the constitution of subjectivity within representation, sexuality, and epistemology. While the volume will be welcome to readers familiar with de Lauretis's work, it can also serve as a introduction for teachers and students of women's studies and lesbian/gay/bisexual/transgender (LGBT) studies, as well as for the many readers from a variety of disciplines and from outside the academy who will find de Lauretis's thinking and writing uniquely stimulating. The selections consider representations of women and lesbianism, present readings of texts that theorize and invite desire and fantasy, and construct ways of thinking about feminism and subjectivity. Sometimes they double back on each other, detour to discuss related developments (while inevitably neglecting others), and introduce concerns adjacent to feminism and theory. Taken together, they show a writer and thinker who, despite her indisputable originality and a sometimes almost intimidating command of language and concepts, is deeply dialogic.

These essays invite the reader to join in a process of revisiting and revising that de Lauretis has demonstrated is central to the project of feminist theory. In keeping with two central discourses in her ongoing work—semiotics and psychoanalysis—the concepts and practices of feminism and theory in which she engages are reciprocal and open-ended. In her work, as in the work of such contemporary feminist theorists as Donna Haraway and Chandra Mohanty, no single, static notion of feminism will do. Moreover, as feminism cannot be circumscribed in object, scope, or period, the concept of postfeminism makes little sense. Neither does de Lauretis use the term "theory" as a scientist might, as a proven postulate, "a set of statements or principles devised to explain a group of facts";[2] rather, she refers to her writing and the theories she critiques as "passionate fictions."[3] This designation, with its evocation of desire and narrative, demonstrates one way in which, for de Lauretis, feminism cannot be defined in isolation from theory or the speculative. Indeed, as I will argue, feminist specificity lies in a *subjective* way of knowing.

Poststructuralist theories of the subject—psychoanalytic and linguistic, cinematic and semiotic—are key to her work and to that of many of her peers, and they resonate with the feminist insight "the personal is political." This resonance is perhaps clearest in de Lauretis's concept of "the subject of feminism." The term implies "an understanding of the (female) subject as not only distinct from Woman . . . the *represen-*

tation of an essence inherent in all women, . . . but also distinct from women, the real historical beings and social subjects who are defined by the technology of gender and actually engendered in social relations."[4] That Woman and women are distinct from each other—and that therefore, despite and within the mythology of Woman, women can indeed be subjects of speech and desire, can even begin to represent Woman otherwise—is an insight eloquently elaborated in de Lauretis's transformative 1984 book *Alice Doesn't: Feminism, Semiotics, Cinema*. It is in her next book, *Technologies of Gender: Essays on Theory, Film and Fiction* (1987), that she introduces the "subject of feminism" as a third, conceptual figure, representing the tensions between idealized representation (Woman) and actual experience (women), and in particular the *consciousness* of this tension.

The mode of definition de Lauretis uses ("not only distinct from . . . , but also distinct from . . .") can frustrate some readers' and students' desire for an affirmative feminism. And yet the method enacts the thought: de Lauretis's concepts move in and out of contexts where they take on meaning in tension with other formulations. For example, the essay "The Technology of Gender" ends with a paradox. The subject of feminism is spatially and temporally located "here and now. That is to say, elsewhere."[5] The contradiction here, possible in language if not in space, reformulates de Lauretis's assertion that the subject of feminism is both "inside *and* outside the ideology of gender."[6] That is, women are constructed through gender (and other forms of) ideology, and feminism is the practice and consciousness of that ideology's limits, a "de-re-construction."[7] The category of the subject, entailing the knowledge and the experience of being (constructed as) a woman, is central to de Lauretis's theoretical project. And the subject, as in *topic*, of feminism is her domain as a theorist.

The histories and itineraries of feminism shape de Lauretis's work and have in turn been shaped by it. Born in Italy in 1938 and educated there in literature, classics, and modern languages, de Lauretis emigrated as a young mother to the United States in the mid-1960s, where she taught in various Italian departments before moving to the University of Wisconsin–Milwaukee in 1968. The Milwaukee campus was an epicenter of the U.S. reception of French and British film theory and a favorable environment for her first publications in film and feminist theory.[8] The book that emerged from this period, *Alice Doesn't*, made an important intervention in both feminist theory and the male-dominated academy with its erudition (a few of the many discourses engaged are narratology, experimental cinema, and psychoanalysis) and its graceful rhetoric, which often delivered withering critiques of masculinist theory. *Alice Doesn't* brought wide visibility to emergent feminist theoretical work on film, articulating such concepts as the male gaze and "woman-as-image" together with narrative theory and semiotics in a way that is still authoritative. De Lauretis pushed debates beyond the rigorous but circumscribed work on language and textuality being undertaken by Anglo-American feminist psychoanalytic scholars in the 1980s, and feminist film theory quickly found a place at the cutting edge of feminist thought.[9] Just as important, through theorizing such apparent givens as "experience," she ensured that the political concerns of women's cultural production and women's studies programs remained pertinent to a sometimes insular feminist film theory. The very title of *Alice Doesn't*—drawn from a piece of ephemera, a feminist banner dated October 29, 1975—is provocative.[10] It joins the concrete and the abstract, conjuring a heroine (Lewis Carroll's, or perhaps another Alice) and a gesture of unspecified, ebullient refusal. For me, the slogan anticipates one of de Lauretis's most important formulations about feminism: "[T]he critical negativity of its theory, and the affirmative positivity of its politics—is both [its] historical condition of existence and its theoretical condition of possibility."[11] This interdependence of theory and activism, history and potential, describes a (women's) *movement* rather than a condition of stasis.

In 1985 de Lauretis herself moved, accepting her second long-term academic position. She joined other sui generis thinkers such as Haraway, James Clifford, and Hayden White in the interdisciplinary History of Consciousness program at the University of California, Santa Cruz. De Lauretis has taught at UCSC ever since, with increasingly frequent, significant sojourns in Europe. *Technologies of Gender,* published a few years after this move, is informed by Santa Cruz's multicultural feminist inquiry and activism. In this collection and in such influential essays from the late 1980s and early 1990s as "Eccentric Subjects" and "Sexual Indifference and Lesbian Representation," which appear in the present volume, de Lauretis, in her inimitable and inspiring prose, recasts feminist histories of cultural production, reframes debates around sexual difference that had seemed exhausted, and generates far-reaching concepts—the subject of feminism, the technology of gender—that keep sharp the revolutionary edge of feminist theory as it abuts other, crucial discourses.[12] Work by lesbians and women of color, burgeoning in U.S. feminist culture and thought of the 1980s, is central to her redefinition of gender "beyond sexual difference," the difference of woman from man that is precisely *indifferent* to divisions of race, class, and sexuality. Foucault's concept of a social technology, in which subjects are en-gendered (he would say produced) differentially but not oppositionally or (purely) oppressively, is rethought by de Lauretis in feminist terms that emphasize gender and experience. Her insistence on "differences among women as differences within women"[13] bypasses the impasse of identity politics premised on coherent, volitional social agents by emphasizing multiple alliances and notions of division. It is lesbianism in particular that allows de Lauretis to specify the condition of being at once inside and outside the ideology of gender, constructed within and as the blind spot of sexual difference (that is, the institution of heterosexuality), constrained by its definitions yet critical of its precepts. Finally, the book's readings of women's texts demonstrate that feminist de- and re-constructions are themselves technologies of gender, thereby envisioning change as a local process of resignification and shifting consciousness, but one with global implications.

De Lauretis's *The Practice of Love: Lesbian Sexuality and Perverse Desire* appeared in 1994 when lesbian scholarship found contexts not only within the women's studies curricula that had first fostered it but also in the antihomophobic literary and cultural criticism of Eve Sedgwick, the gender philosophy of Judith Butler, and other works of queer theory.[14] In this book de Lauretis aims to think through lesbian subjectivity with and against psychoanalysis. She accounts for what she calls sexual structuring, akin to the process of engendering outlined in *Technologies of Gender,* which engages and shapes private fantasies and practices in relation to public representations ranging from the patriarchal family to the movies. The book challenges and refreshes feminist and queer theory alike with its insistence on retaining feminist concepts of gender in its primary consideration of sexuality.

In more recent published work and work-in-progress, de Lauretis continues to think through psychoanalytic concepts—notably, that of the drives—to understand the relationship between psychic structuring and the possibilities and practices of a given social context and moment.[15] While these concerns are not explicitly those of feminist theory, which de Lauretis defines as "a controlled reflection and self-reflection, not on women in general but rather on feminism itself as a historico-political formation,"[16] they share a feminist epistemology, or way of knowing, with earlier work. It is this quality of *thinking feminist* that makes de Lauretis's contribution vital at the current juncture, both for queer and psychoanalytic theory in particular, and for early twenty-first century feminism in general, as it approaches issues of human rights, globalization, and new media technologies.

The recent history of the concept of gender—a historical reconceptualization to which this current volume contributes—helps us map some important shifts in feminist theory since it was first practiced in the academy, by de Lauretis and many others, in the 1970s. At that point gender was likely to be deployed as synonymous with sexuality, defined by Catharine MacKinnon as "that which is most one's own, yet most taken away."[17] Alternatively, gender was the organizing term of social constructionism, as elaborated in Gayle Rubin's concept of the sex/gender system.[18] But accounting for race and ethnicity and, more recently, postcolonial and transnational positions in feminism complicated assumptions of gender as a common bond—either of victimhood or sisterly solidarity—with the realization that "the experience of gender is itself shaped by race relations, and that must be the case, however different the outcome, for all women."[19] A definition of gender as simply sexual difference or complementarity also failed to grasp the institutional nature of heterosexuality, what Monique Wittig ironically calls that "core of nature within culture."[20] De Lauretis suggests a more Foucauldian understanding of the "technology of gender," one that in some ways complies, and in others competes, with the theories that gained prominence in the 1990s of gender as a performative effect. Certainly the accounts share an emphasis on discursive construction; however, de Lauretis insists on gender's rootedness in the experience of the body and in a social subjectivity at once constrained by ideology and capable of creativity.

It seems to me that the current vitality of gender as an analytical and activist category testifies to the usefulness of de Lauretis's conceptualization. Such diverse formations as, for example, Muslim women's participation in democratic government and the rap music of Missy Elliot do not conform to universalizing definitions, nor are their effects purely performative. They exemplify de Lauretis's sense of the "movement in and out of gender as ideological representation . . . between the positions made available by hegemonic discourses and . . . the elsewhere . . . those other spaces both discursive and social that exist, since feminist practices have (re)constructed them . . . in the interstices of institutions, in counter-practices and new forms of community."[21]

Another key dimension of de Lauretis's under-construction definition of gender is the way it is experienced in her writing. Across contributions to feminism, film, literary, cultural, and semiotic theory, Teresa de Lauretis's prose is at once dense and lucid, syntactically complex and tropically vivid. Even casual contact with her work lets the reader know that the language is irreducible; the work of thought takes place in and through writing, as concepts evolve from sentence to sentence. Teaching de Lauretis entails teaching ideas, but also, crucially, reading. Of course, she shares an attention to rhetoric and the figural with other prominent feminist thinkers—literary scholars Shoshana Felman, Barbara Johnson, and Jane Gallop, and film and cultural theorists Kaja Silverman, Mary Ann Doane, and Rey Chow, to name just a few who are based in the United States. Language-oriented French feminists Luce Irigaray and Julia Kristeva influenced this work, and the European connection runs deep in de Lauretis's case. She sometimes writes in her native Italian and remains engaged with Italian and wider European feminist theory, and her work is widely translated. But beyond a complexity of syntax one may be tempted to attribute to her facility with romance languages, the lack of linearity in de Lauretis's arguments and other distinctive features of her writing are structural manifestations of her feminist project that set it apart from the work of her colleagues. Writing is what she identifies as a "self-analyzing practice,"[22] germane to feminist thought, and the effects of her essays are experienced cumulatively.

"What if, once Oedipus reached his destination, he found that Alice didn't live there anymore?"[23] When the reader encounters this rhetorical question toward the end of "Desire in Narrative," she might chuckle, or even feel jubilant, as if she's made an ingenious but somehow inevitable chess move. De Lauretis's sentences often mix metaphors and embed examples, qualifiers, and cognates. The process of revision enacted in the course of an argument (for example, in "The Technology of Gender" the reader finds italicized restatements of core propositions, with a twist of key phrases)[24] means that there is often no easily citable thesis.

Instead, whole paragraphs are quotable. Passages from other writers or from her own earlier work are often adduced, and her argument proceeds through reading these citations. Far from excluding the work of others, her prose introjects and makes it over. This dialogism extends to her own positions. De Lauretis will frequently call attention to her earlier thinking, layering or complicating it, and she often remarks on her rhetorical strategies. Finally, she has a distinctive tendency to conclude on an open-ended image (exemplified in the "elsewhere" in the punch line of "The Technology of Gender" quoted above; the rhetorical question; the fragment—*Alice Doesn't;* or the ellipsis, which concludes two essays collected here). As de Lauretis writes about Virginia Woolf's *A Room of One's Own,* "the text actually produces the representation of its contradiction."[25] Contradiction, paradox, tension: these are (im)possible figures of feminism. De Lauretis exemplifies writing—and perforce reading—as what she might call, in a favorite phrase borrowed from Monique Wittig, a "subjective, cognitive practice" a writing-toward what is known but not fully articulated.[26] Changes—of emphasis in key phrases, of subject in dependent clauses, of parallel tracks from essay to essay—recall the "habit changes," the result of experience, that she suggests engender the subject of feminism.[27] Habit changes come about through the consciousness, and unconscious apperception, of changes in material and discursive reality as well as in internal fantasies. I will elaborate on some of these ideas and terms below in the context of the essays that develop them; what I want to stress here is that the form and the substance of argument are indivisible. Even as it is singular, a subject's writing, this prose demands a dialogue, an answering subject.

In the organization of this volume and the introductions to individual essays that follow in the next section, I have tried to maximize this dialogue. Collecting and juxtaposing the essays changes their terms of address, allowing them to speak to each other. Previously published essays have not been revised for this volume beyond minor formatting changes and the occasional addition of references; instead, each is preceded by de Lauretis's note on its original context. Although I would characterize all of the materials presented here as timely, they are often quite specifically "dated," or at least marked by shifters—"recent," "now," "currently." Updating these, an editor would obscure how de Lauretis's work proceeds through interventions, and also how it predicts or anticipates shifts in terrain theoretical and cultural. But even more to the point, their deictic function—which the dictionary defines as "of or relating to a word, the determination of whose referent is dependent on the context in which it is said or written"—is consistent with de Lauretis's theory and practice, in which it matters "who says that sentence, and where, when, and of whom it is said."[28]

The essays within each of the three parts, "Representations," "Readings," and "Epistemologies," are chronologically arranged. Inevitably, there are repetitions and redoublings, yet these iterations often put concepts to work in new ways. And while the essay groupings have strong rationales, other orderings using the same rubrics are plausible. "Representations" gathers essays on the cinema, literature, and theory that illuminate the process of self-representation in conjunction with these practices. "Readings" includes close analyses of specific texts: a passage in a novel, a case history, a film. "Epistemologies" generates figures of feminist consciousness and sexual subjectivity, among them "eccentric subjects," "habit changes," and "figures of resistance."

In light of the emphasis I have placed on style, it may not be surprising that the concept of the figural makes an explicit appearance in the previously unpublished essay that gives this volume its title—de Lauretis's most recent piece, and the last in the book. The phrase "figures of resistance" captures the way certain figures—the thinkers and writers discussed in the essay—refuse to accede to prevailing orders and modes of knowing, as well as the way the figural properties of language (or representation more generally) *always* resist a purely referential approach to the world. This is how, de Lauretis figures, feminist theory takes place, here and now.

» » »

"Rethinking Women's Cinema" is the first and earliest work included in this volume. Here de Lauretis shifts the terrain of feminist film theory from the groundwork of Laura Mulvey's 1974 essay "Visual Pleasure and Narrative Cinema" to conceive of the female spectator who had been polemically and rhetorically excluded by Mulvey's account of the male gaze constructed in and by classical cinema. More specifically, de Lauretis speaks of (and to) a viewer addressed *as a woman* by certain women's films. "Rethinking Women's Cinema" was originally published in *New German Critique* just after *Alice Doesn't* appeared, and it expands that text's recognition of the "surplus of pleasure" the female spectator might find at the movies.[29] The essay shares questions about authorship and aesthetics, and certain canonical film texts (Chantal Akerman's sublime *Jeanne Dielman* [1975] among them), with much of the compelling work by other feminist film scholars in the mid-1980s. But, crucially, de Lauretis finds the work of Audre Lorde as useful as that of Jacques Lacan. She is able to overcome the terms of a stalemate in theories of female spectatorship by insisting on the social as well as psychic forces at play in processes of desire and identification. Finally, she sidesteps the pitfalls of political modernism's prescriptive aesthetics (avant-garde films produce radical responses in spectators), as well as cultural studies' often voluntaristic politics of reception (we make of texts what we will). Instead, she recommends that we "rethink the problem of a specificity of women's cinema and aesthetic forms . . . in terms of address—who is making films for whom, who is looking and speaking, how, where, and to whom" (35)—in other words, as "the production of a feminist social vision" (34). The importance of "reformulation—re-vision, rewriting, rereading, rethinking, 'looking back at *ourselves*,'" arises from the understanding that this social vision is far from homogenous; rather, it is shaped by "differences among women as *differences within women*" (39). Such differences—of race, ethnicity, generation, experience, and consciousness—de Lauretis sees figured in Lizzie Borden's collaboratively scripted, multiracial independent feature *Born in Flames* (1983). The essay exemplifies de Lauretis's contribution to feminist theory in the 1980s: intervening in technologies of representation, including theory; foregrounding the cinema as an arena of transformation; theorizing a multiple subjectivity shaped by sexuality and race, as well as gender; and recasting the apparent split between theory and practice as "the very strength, the drive and productive heterogeneity of feminism" (35).[30] Finally, the understanding of reception found here anticipates feminist interest in the public sphere and calls for further theorization of the public sphere of feminism itself.

The second essay in part 1, "Sexual Indifference and Lesbian Representation," first published in *Theatre Journal*, brought de Lauretis's work to the wider attention of LGBT scholars and communities when it was anthologized in *The Lesbian and Gay Studies Reader*.[31] Its publication here allows readers to see connections to her other work on representation. The first essay de Lauretis published from a lesbian

perspective, "Sexual Indifference" is an expansive and provocative interrogation of lesbian literary and filmic figures that challenge the norms
of visibility of hom(m)osexuality. Borrowing this pun, along with the
term sexual (in)difference, from Luce Irigaray to underscore how a
masculine imaginary excludes women from the position of desiring
subject, de Lauretis sets an agenda for theorizing lesbian subjectivity
by critiquing an impasse in straight feminist theory. Literary texts by
Radclyffe Hall, Djuna Barnes, and Cherríe Moraga, and films in whose
address de Lauretis finds an echo of her own relationship to desire and
the gaze, provide figures (both characters and textual forms) of excess
and contradiction.

No one states the contradiction of lesbian subjectivity more concisely
than the widely mourned novelist, playwright, and theorist Monique
Wittig (1935–2003). "Lesbians are not women," Wittig famously de-
clared.[32] This flatly contradictory but intuitively resonant statement
stakes necessary ground for lesbian theorizing, de Lauretis argues in
"When Lesbians Were Not Women," the final essay of part 1. Written
for a French conference on Wittig in 2001, the essay includes and builds
on passages from de Lauretis's previously published work in which she
engages with Wittig's thought (chapters 2 and 7 of this volume). But the
synthesis achieved warrants its inclusion here. Wittig's critique of the
institution of heterosexuality is a strong materialist account of gender,
de Lauretis points out, despite current (mis)readings that characterize the French theorist's assertion of lesbian difference as humanist or
identitarian. But beyond this, Wittig's definition of consciousness of
gender and its limits as "a subjective, cognitive practice" provides a
crucial component of de Lauretis's own understanding of subjectivity as
paradoxically en-gendered. "Lesbians are not women" is a conceptual
figure, a representation of what can be known through and despite
the limits of gender. De Lauretis returns frequently in this collection
to key passages and phrases from Wittig's essays "The Straight Mind"
and "One Is Not Born a Woman," finding in the French writer's brief
theoretical texts, in her circumscribed yet influential oeuvre, a generative representation of reading (as a) lesbian.

Part 2, "Readings," comprises three close analyses of cultural
texts—Radclyffe Hall's classic novel of *lesbianisme damnée, The Well
of Loneliness,* Freud's case of homosexuality in a woman, and David Cronenberg's 1993 film adaptation of David Henry Hwang's play

M. Butterfly—readings that engage with psychoanalysis, particularly the concepts of fantasy and fetishism, and supplement and extend de Lauretis's important, densely argued, and passionately invested book, *The Practice of Love*. What might be characterized as de Lauretis's "return to Freud" in this work is perhaps the most challenging aspect of her recent thinking. Yet, de Lauretis stresses, her interest in and use of Freud is quite literally perverse, and readers will find much that is new, critical, and enabling here.

As in earlier work, de Lauretis rejects Lacanian orthodoxies—the dogma of sexual (in)difference—that would render unimaginable an account of lesbian sexual subjectivity. Far from defining psychoanalysis as inimical to lesbian theory, de Lauretis asserts a special relationship. No other discourse concerns itself so centrally with gender, sexuality, and their interaction with and shaping by the social. Furthermore, we must grapple with psychoanalysis's widely circulating accounts of us. As de Lauretis notes, feminists have demonstrated that there are "very good reasons for reading and rereading Freud himself" and this is "[a]ll the more so for lesbians . . . whose self-definition, self-representation, and political as well as personal identity, are not only grounded in the sphere of the sexual, but actually constituted in relation to our sexual difference from socially dominant, institutionalized, heterosexual forms."[33] She is certainly not alone in returning to psychoanalysis in the elucidation of queer theory, though she is arguably unique in how she does so.[34]

The Practice of Love is a resolutely personal work; despite the density of its argument, de Lauretis describes it as all but autobiographical.[35] Its ambition and modesty are equally striking: it aims to construct what she calls "a formal model of perverse desire" (xiii) by reading against Freud's normative account and to develop a theory of "sexual structuring" (xix) through readings of literary, filmic, and theoretical texts that speak to her own fantasies and experiences. Painstakingly worked out in *The Practice of Love*, though easy enough to grasp intuitively, the concept of perverse desire goes against—turns away from, in the literal sense of perversion—heteronormative desire. De Lauretis retains in her account of desire certain concepts in Freud's theory (and its Lacanian revision) that might seem inimical to her task, namely castration and the phallus. Yet her revisions are significant. She keeps the concept of castration/lack—for its corollary is desire itself—and the notion of the phallus as signifier of desire, which structurally links desire (and the sense of self that attends it) to representation.[36] No mere efflorescence of passion, desire is tied to objects—fantasy objects. But unlike a number of other feminist psychoanalytic thinkers, de Lauretis attempts to rewrite the law of the father by defining the signifier of desire in lesbianism not as the *paternal* phallus, but more on the order of a fetish. The fetish or fantasy phallus is an erotically invested figure of the loss of the original object (a woman's body—the mother's and one's own). What's the difference? Refusing the paternal signifier, the concept of fetish or fantasy-phallus no longer forces gender and desiring subjectivity to line up in complementary ways, no longer requires a masculine position of desire. De Lauretis thus restores desire's perverseness, a welcome turn, and her argument mimics this mobility, displacing or perverting the notion of the phallus with that of the fetish.

The three essays in part 2 (together with "Habit Changes" in part 3) develop these quite complex arguments, even as they engage specific texts, and can serve as a point of entry to *The Practice of Love*. In "The Lure of the Mannish Lesbian," de Lauretis outlines the central concept of perverse desire in relation to a scene from *The Well of Loneliness*, a scene of mourning and masturbation. She argues that the "fantasy of bodily dispossession," of an "unlovable body," is marked or signified here by Stephen's scar; the character's pursuit of the perfect masculine trousers and a woman to love accompanies a kind of impaired narcissism.[37] This is a somewhat surprising fantasy to detect in a text that seems so invested in female masculinity, to borrow Judith Halberstam's term.[38] Yet the possible perverseness of de Lauretis's reading makes it all the more illustrative of the particularity of subjective fantasy, which can be sustained even in works created for public consumption, as the fact that Hall's novel continues to strike a responsive chord today suggests.

In chapter 5, "Letter to an Unknown Woman," de Lauretis elaborates on the theory of perverse desire in relation to the young female patient discussed in Freud's "Psychogenesis of a Case of Homosexuality in a Woman." More precisely, she elaborates on this theory in relation to Freud's *text*. De Lauretis demonstrates that because his normative notion of the (positive) Oedipus complex does not apply in this case, Freud does not "get" what is at stake in the young woman's desire; she remains unknown. Rather than attempting to set the record straight, de Lauretis uncovers Freud's misreadings, their stakes and consequences, and makes room for a story of desire featuring a new protagonist.

It is also misreading that fascinates de Lauretis in David Cronenberg's *M. Butterfly* (1993)—the white male hero's misreading not only of the gender but also of the desire of his lover, as well as the auteur's singular interpretation of the desire at work in the text (that is, Cronenberg identifies with the duped hero). The perversion at issue in chapter 6, "Public and Private Fantasies in David Cronenberg's *M. Butterfly*," is fetishism, and especially femininity as fetish, redoubled and inflected through Orientalism. Reading the film as "at once the public representation of a fantasy and an exploration of the effects of public fantasies on the private fantasies of individuals" (140–41), de Lauretis further demonstrates how a subject's fantasy can be sustained by a text—that is, a film, novel, or opera might serve as the mise-en-scène of one's desire—despite one's politics, and despite the absence of any strict correspondence between its characters and one's identity or sexual orientation. In this reading, opera as a form of "public fantasy" is extended in the contemporary function of cinema.[39] The Canadian director's vision of a Chinese-American playwright's deconstruction of an Italian opera classic based on both concrete and diffuse versions of the story of the West's love affair with (its construction of) subservient "Oriental" femininity is intertextually rich, illustrating Gramsci's account (so central to British cultural studies and cited here by de Lauretis) of popular culture as "something deeply felt and experienced."[40] René Gallimard (Jeremy Irons)'s love for Song Liling (John Lone) is nothing if not deeply felt, with his own suicide demanded by his identification with his version of the fantasy. Yet this film's staging indicates new possibilities of the subject, de Lauretis suggests, in our identification of and with Song Liling as an active agent of desire.

"Fantasy is the psychic mechanism that structures subjectivity by reworking or translating social representations into subjective representations and self-representations" (123). Lucidly addressing the intersections of private and public fantasy, this essay foregrounds one of de Lauretis's most exciting theoretical contributions to cinema studies. The insistence on the specificity of a subject's fantasy does not mean it is unmotivated by or unconnected to the text or intertext in question; on the contrary, specific characters and textual features elicit it. But it is engaged through one's personal history and identifications, both personal and political. In this way, the piece illustrates, psychoanalysis can enrich cultural criticism's sometimes prescriptive views of readers and viewers' encounters with texts.

The psychoanalytic concept of the fetish, like that of fantasy, has broader implications for de Lauretis's theory and practice of cultural interpretation. The fetish substitutes for a lost object that was never really there (Butterfly, for example), potentially devaluing that originary position or definitive meaning (and with it, phallic authority). Fetishism is a condition of desire based on knowledge and its suspension/disavowal, a paradox homologous with the series of contradictions upheld as productive in de Lauretis's thought. In the essays in this section, de Lauretis has detached the concept of fetish from the paternal phallus to understand the circulation of desire within these texts and between texts and readers. In a sense, she has deployed the concept of fetishism in relation to reading itself. The fetish's mobility figures the open-endedness and particularity of readings, the doubleness of language, and in turn the possibility of sustaining a fantasy of oneself as the subject of desire (the very fantasy she sees as operative in *M. Butterfly*). This possibility is crucial to lesbianism, and it is finally why psychoanalysis has such an important place in de Lauretis's work. In the distinct but not detached projects of lesbian and feminist theory pursued in the final section of this book, the relationship between the subjects of desire and knowledge is key.

In part 3, "Epistemologies," five essays written from 1990 to 2005 demonstrate how central the feminist subject of knowledge is to de Lauretis's work. Once again, the phrase reads both ways; the periphrastic genitive (the use of "of") urges us to understand the *topic* of knowledge as decidedly a feminist one—feminism is an epistemological as well as a political project. At the same time, subjectivity *in* knowledge, de Lauretis argues, is feminism's contribution to, and shifting of the ground of, epistemology itself. Joining the twentieth-century critiques mounted by existentialism, phenomenology, and deconstruction, feminism shakes the foundations of the Cartesian cogito's definition of thought as separate from body ("I think, therefore I am"). But it goes further to conceive of embodied consciousness in (the political and subjective) terms of women's experience. Such a consciousness is excessive to the status quo; it is a consciousness of difference, not absolute, but socially constructed and subjectively assumed. Further, it is assumed as split and dislocated, divided between objectification and subjectivity, defined in terms of prevailing notions of femininity and lived through identifications—some unconscious—outside the gender (heterosexual) matrix.

De Lauretis pursues this avowedly epistemological project in chapter 7, "Eccentric Subjects,"[41] reprinted for the first time since its original publication in 1990. Written just after *Technologies of Gender*, "Eccentric Subjects" continues that book's theoretical concerns, with the term "ex-centric" echoing the spatial figure of an "elsewhere" that is also "here and now." The concept conveys "a critical, distanced, and eccentric position in relation to the ideology of gender, . . . not immune or external to gender, but self-critical, distanced, ironic, exceeding—eccentric."[42] This position is a product of displacement and self-displacement. In a genealogy of feminist (takes on) consciousness, de Lauretis first argues that the theories of femininity offered by such powerful writers as Simone de Beauvoir and Catharine MacKinnon are finally eloquent demonstrations of the same "paradox of woman"[43] that led her to insist, in *Alice Doesn't* and elsewhere, that the social subjects *women* remain distinct from, yet overlap, the representation *Woman*. Consciousness of object-status belies that status—the very movement or turn through which these formidable women theorize Woman exceeds the confines of that representation.

In order to displace the paradox, de Lauretis writes:

> I propose that a point of view, or an eccentric discursive position outside the male (hetero)sexual monopoly of power/knowledge— which is to say, a point of view excessive to, or not contained by, the sociocultural institution of heterosexuality—is necessary to feminism at this point in history, that such a position exists in feminist consciousness as personal-political practice and can be found in certain feminist critical texts. (163)

Her essay proceeds by reading such texts, by women of color and lesbians—including Gloria Anzaldúa, Minnie Bruce Pratt, Chandra Mohanty and Biddy Martin, and Monique Wittig—for their formulations of a subject of displacement, disidentification, and self-consciousness that indeed characterize her own position. For de Lauretis, the critique of heterosexuality, "the macroinstitution that subtends all technologies of gender,"[44] by no means privileges "lesbian" as a pure position outside patriarchy. "Lesbian" is one of several figures of the eccentric subject, whose existence within and beyond the ideology of gender it has been feminist critical theory's task to outline. De Lauretis unravels the paradox of woman in what she calls historical consciousness in

"Eccentric Subjects," only to end with what is for her the more generative paradox discussed earlier in this introduction: Wittig's "lesbians
are not women."

Precisely the valence of "woman" in the history of feminism—as imputed essence in so-called cultural feminism or category under erasure
in the poststructuralist variant—is interrogated in chapter 8, "Upping
the Anti [sic] in Feminist Theory," also written in 1990. This essay asserts that pervasive and reflexive accusations of "essentialism" raised
in quite theoretically sophisticated feminist critiques actually divert attention from the more pressing question of feminism's "essential difference"—that which makes its epistemological project and political praxis
unique. More polemical than many of the pieces included here, "Upping
the Anti" suggests that rather than dwelling on polarizing "conflicts
in feminism" (the title of the volume in which this version of the essay
first appeared),[45] "conflict" or tension—in the form of debate and in
that of an epistemological irreducibility between the known and the
imagined—should be seen as of the essence to feminism. The agonistic
framing of cultural versus poststructuralist positions simply revives stale
theory/practice disputes, fuels the so-called "sex wars," and magnifies
oppositions between lesbians and heterosexual feminists, and women
of color and white women. Yet the passion involved indicates high
stakes, which de Lauretis formulates as concurrent "erotic, narcissistic"
and "ethical" drives—the former enhancing a self-image of feminism
as rebellious, the later urging community and accountability.[46] As she
notes, this formulation builds on her earlier characterization of theory
and politics that I have already had occasion to quote: "the tension of
a twofold pull in contrary directions . . . [that] is both the historical
condition of existence of feminism and its theoretical condition of possibility" (quoted on 197). At the essay's conclusion, de Lauretis defines
feminist theory as "a developing theory of the female-sexed or female-
embodied social subject, whose constitution and whose modes of social
and subjective existence include most obviously sex and gender, but also
race, class, and any other significant sociocultural divisions and representations" (198). That subject's "specific, emergent, and conflictual
history" is constitutive of that developing theory, she continues: this is
feminist historical consciousness.

The "female-sexed or female-embodied" subject is essential to de
Lauretis's definition and informs the turn from consciousness to epis-

temological questions raised by the unconscious (think of her use of the metaphor of the drives), in the next essay included here. Interestingly, in light of chapter 8's navigation of (the question of) debates in feminism, chapter 9, "Habit Changes," a reflection on the preoccupations of *The Practice of Love* and a response to critiques and concerns it provoked, originally appeared in a 1994 special issue of *differences* entitled "Feminism Meets Queer Theory," where it was preceded by a substantive review of *The Practice of Love* by lesbian philosopher Elizabeth Grosz. In her contribution, de Lauretis declined to engage the special issue's framework directly, but I would argue that it is precisely the requirement of female embodiment that distinguishes her work in lesbian theory as grounded in feminist thought. In "Habit Changes," de Lauretis elaborates not only on her book's model of perverse desire, but also on Freud's concept of "a body-ego," which she deploys to insist on subjectivity's ongoing constitution on the border between external and internal.[47] The importance of this conception cannot be overestimated; for, as de Lauretis notes, the subject, and the body as it grounds her notion of subjectivity, are often no more present in queer theory than in metaphysics. Such abstraction, she asserts, is in part a legacy of the influence of Michel Foucault's early work, with its strong opposition to psychoanalysis and its emphasis on the exercise of power in subjection. It is finally de Lauretis's insistence on the embodied subject that centers her work on lesbian sexuality in the project of feminist epistemology.

In the final chapter of *The Practice of Love,* summarized in "Habit Changes," de Lauretis explicitly brings together Freud and Foucault, the two major thinkers in the epistemology of sex, with a feminist insistence on the possibility of change. The unlikely candidate for facilitating this rapprochement is nineteenth-century American philosopher C. S. Peirce, whose account of semiosis first influenced de Lauretis through Umberto Eco's work. For Peirce, "a sign . . . is something which stands to somebody for something in some respect or capacity," and it is that *somebody,* the "subject of semiotics" in the formulation made popular by Kaja Silverman, who is so strikingly compatible with feminism's epistemology of the self, and, in de Lauretis's argument, with Freud's body-ego.[48] It is at this join that external social discourses, institutions, and representations are not only made sense of cognitively by a specific subject, but also unconsciously incorporated into one's ongoing fantasies, identifications, experiences and activities—one's habits, in Peirce's term.

Psychoanalysis, from its concern with how the social becomes subjective, is extended to envision how the subject can change the social. *Practice of Love* aims to outline, through readings of Freud and various cinematic, literary, and feminist critical texts, a theory of sexual structuring, an account of the shaping of one's sexual desire, persona, and fantasies, through interactions with representations. This process works in tandem with the en-gendering of subjectivity through the "technology of gender"—ideology, institutions, and practices including feminism. That one might be en-gendered in an ex-centric way parallels the possibility of sexual structuring according to a "perverse" model (again, the spatial figures are congruent). De Lauretis stresses Foucault's conceptualization of power in the social field, making her "return to Freud" a devious one. In later volumes of his *History of Sexuality,* she observes, Foucault uses surprisingly homologous language to Peirce's in speaking of the subject's interaction with social systems (of power or signs). Foucault advocates "self-analysis" (while admittedly bypassing psychoanalysis); it was Peirce's notion of "self-analyzing habit" that gave de Lauretis, in the final chapter of *Alice Doesn't,* a way to talk about change that is specific to a feminist epistemology.[49] The subject is the starting point, but change is not willed or simply intellectual. It is, again, embodied.[50] As the formulations in this short essay on the *Practice of Love* demonstrate, that book is undoubtedly a work of theory, but it is one that shows that "thinking feminist" need not exclude desiring.

First published in Italian, and translated for English publication in 2002, "The Intractability of Desire" (chapter 10) lucidly revisits key terms—"gender and sexual difference, identity and politics, sexuality and desire" (217)—in the unfolding of de Lauretis's work on subjectivity, putting them in the context of current debates in Italian feminist theory while hinting at new directions in her thought. Looking closely at recent Italian feminist writings in which theorizing takes place in the very subjective modes of dialogues and published notebooks, de Lauretis observes that their formulations of subjectivity tend to rely on identity, community, and politics rather than on a strong concept of sexuality. She argues that this bypasses the negativity, the intractability, of a desire that cannot be trained, directed, disciplined at will, but that is essential to a subjectivity conceived as corporeal and psychic as well as social. Identity and politics cannot constrain fantasy, in other words. The irreducible "twofold pull" of feminism I have repeatedly invoked must be sustained *as tension:* "if to live the contradiction [between the positivity of politics, the negativity of theory] is the condition of existence of a feminist subjectivity, to analyze it is the condition of a feminist politics" (221). Negativity comes to the fore in de Lauretis's current work on the death drive,[51] elaborated not simply as a deconstructionist impulse but as the division of desire that cuts across the female-embodied social subject.

The insistence on the constitutive relation of tensions or contradictions to feminist epistemology leads de Lauretis to an explicit consideration of the irreducibility of the figural itself in the final chapter, which gives this volume its title: "Figures of Resistance." Speculating that feminist argumentation must frequently be undertaken through works of imagination precisely because it calls for something that does not (yet) exist, de Lauretis points out that this duality is a property of figural language itself: to say more than the grammatical sense; to cross a boundary of silence though connotation. De Lauretis turns to particular writer/theorists to explore her claim, but first she traces a feminist genealogy of the contradictory relationship of women to knowledge.

The essay opens with the stories, prompted by de Lauretis's own transnational itinerary as a lecturer, of several pioneering women who attended European universities during the Renaissance and gave their names to the feminist institutions or occasions that enabled her own work centuries later. Not authors in the traditional sense, they left no written accounts of their lives. Yet the quest for knowledge of the seventeenth-century Italian noblewoman Elena Lucrezia Cornaro Piscopia and others—silenced or muted by enforced chastity, early death, or madness—make them precursors of such writers as Virginia Woolf, who so eloquently spoke of and embodied the internal division in the female speaking subject, while indicting its institutional causes, in that most famous of all feminist lectures, published as *A Room of One's Own.* Woolf's terms of address are so insistently dialogic (the text opens, "But, you may ask. . . .") that they seem to overcome displacements in history and geography and the limits of her own historical consciousness.[52] When de Lauretis introduced her notion of "habit change" in the final chapter of *Alice Doesn't,* it built upon a close reading of Woolf's text, of her ironic, subjective version of "the truth about W." (the shorthand deflates and ruefully acknowledges the paradox of Woman). In this context, more than two decades later, de Lauretis re-reads *A Room of One's Own,* a canonical, anticanonical text, as an exemplary work of feminist theory, even—especially—when it can only talk about silence.

The silence inscribed in Woolf's figures—the hypothetical Judith Shakespeare who died before writing a word; the "vast chamber" begging for illumination—figures the silence inscribed in women's speech when they speak "the language of man," argues de Lauretis. "Given the persistent association between women and silence, the question then arises: what is the relation of women to language and writing, including the writing of feminist theory?" (241). "Figures of Resistance" addresses this question in its account of de Lauretis's teaching feminist theory by way of women's literary texts. Works by Djuna Barnes, Toni Morrison, Joanna Russ, and Jeanette Winterson *figure* resistance, not only through characters and situations, but also and especially through qualities of language that exceed the literal. De Lauretis's return to works she has discussed before or that she suggests we reread—such as the literary theory of Paul de Man—can be seen as dialogical. Not only do other writers speak in this essay, but the students in her class, through citations and references to their critical practice, do as well. She addresses the current political moment by speaking of the resistance *of* theory, to alter de Man's term in his essay "The Resistance to Theory" and to expand his sense to the feminist context. This strategy of *address* revisits her concerns in the first essay of this volume, to ask of feminism anew, and not just rhetorically: "who is . . . speaking: how, when, where, and to whom"?

As her essay ends with reference to the classroom, it seems appropriate for me to acknowledge my own debt to de Lauretis's generous pedagogy. A college student in 1984 when de Lauretis came to lecture, I asked for an inscription in my already talismanic copy of *Alice Doesn't.* She wrote: "I don't know what to say that will be meaningful to you forever, so I just wish you happiness and lots of satisfaction in thinking feminist." The words delight me when I teach from the now-ragged book, but I also get a little embarrassed, for the line break in the inscription called out for the assertion of an indefinite article, and I put one there. However (literally) sophomoric, "(a) thinking feminist" felicitously linked the epistemological and the amorous. I ultimately found my thinking feminist, but first I went to graduate school to study with Teresa de Lauretis. The satisfactions of thinking feminist were palpable there—in the here of the words on the page, the now of classroom exchange—and on the horizon, the elsewhere de Lauretis evoked so memorably. Introducing these essays, some of them written during that time, is for me an experience of return, and a new departure.

I

Representations

BORN IN FLAMES (LIZZIE BORDEN, 1983, USA)

Chapter 1

Rethinking
Women's Cinema

hen Silvia Bovenschen in 1976 posed the question "Is there a feminine aesthetic?" the only answer she could give was, yes and no: "Certainly there is, if one is talking about aesthetic awareness and modes of sensory perception. Certainly not, if one is talking about an unusual variant of artistic production or about a painstakingly constructed theory of art."[1] If this contradiction seems familiar to anyone even vaguely acquainted with the development of feminist thought over the past fifteen years, it is because it echoes a contradiction specific to, and perhaps even constitutive of, the women's movement itself: a twofold pressure, a simultaneous pull in opposite directions, a tension toward the positivity of politics, or affirmative action in behalf of women as social subjects, on one front, and the negativity inherent in the radical critique of patriarchal, bourgeois culture, on the other. It is also the contradiction of women in language, as we attempt to speak as subjects of discourses which negate or objectify us through their representations. As Bovenschen put it, "We are in a terrible bind. How do we speak? In what categories do we think? Is even logic a bit of virile trickery? . . . Are our desires and notions of happiness so far removed from cultural traditions and models?" (119).

Not surprisingly, therefore, a similar contradiction was also central to the debate on women's cinema, its politics and its language, as it was articulated within Anglo-American film theory in the early 1970s in relation to feminist politics and the women's movement, on the one hand, and to artistic avant-garde practices and women's filmmaking, on the other. There, too, the accounts of feminist film culture produced in the mid- to late seventies tended to emphasize a dichotomy between two concerns of the women's movement and two types of film work that seemed to be at odds with each other: one called for immediate documentation for purposes of political activism, consciousness raising, self-expression, or the search for "positive images" of woman; the other insisted on rigorous, formal work on the medium—or, better, the cinematic apparatus, understood as a social technology—in order to analyze and disengage the ideological codes embedded in representation.

Thus, as Bovenschen deplores the "opposition between feminist demands and artistic production" (131), the tug of war in which women artists were caught between the movement's demands that women's art portray women's activities, document demonstrations, etc., and the formal demands of "artistic activity and its concrete work with material and media"; so does Laura Mulvey set out two successive moments of feminist film culture. First, she states, there was a period marked by the effort to change the *content* of cinematic representation (to present realistic images of women, to record women talking about their real-life experiences), a period "characterized by a mixture of consciousness-raising and propaganda."[2] It was followed by a second moment, in which the concern with the language of representation as such became predominant, and the "fascination with the cinematic process" led filmmakers and critics to the "use of and interest in the aesthetic principles and terms of reference provided by the avant-garde tradition" (7).

In this latter period, the common interest of both avant-garde cinema and feminism in the politics of images, or the political dimension of aesthetic expression, made them turn to the theoretical debates on language and imaging that were going on outside of cinema, in semiotics, psychoanalysis, critical theory, and the theory of ideology. Thus, it was argued that, in order to counter the aesthetic of realism, which was hopelessly compromised with bourgeois ideology, as well as Hollywood cinema, avant-garde and feminist filmmakers must take an oppositional stance against narrative "illusionism" and in favor of formalism. The assumption was that "foregrounding the process itself, privileging the signifier, necessarily disrupts aesthetic unity and forces the spectator's attention on the means of production of meaning" (7).

While Bovenschen and Mulvey would not relinquish the political commitment of the movement and the need to construct other representations of woman, the way in which they posed the question of expression (a "feminine aesthetic," a "new language of desire") was couched in the terms of a traditional notion of art, specifically the one propounded by modernist aesthetics. Bovenschen's insight that what is being expressed in the decoration of the household and the body, or in letters and other private forms of writing, is in fact women's aesthetic needs and impulses, is a crucial one. But the importance of that insight is undercut by the very terms that define it: the "*pre*-aesthetic realms." After quoting a passage from Sylvia Plath's *The Bell Jar*, Bovenschen comments:

> Here the ambivalence once again: on the one hand we see aesthetic activity deformed, atrophied, but on the other we find, even within this restricted scope, socially creative impulses which, however, have no outlet for aesthetic development, no opportunities for growth. . . . [These activities] remained bound to everyday life, feeble attempts to make this sphere more aesthetically pleasing. But the price for this was narrowmindedness. The object could never leave the realm in which it came into being, it remained tied to the household, it could never break loose and initiate communication. (132–33)

Just as Plath laments that Mrs. Willard's beautiful home-braided rug is not hung on the wall but put to the use for which it was made, and thus quickly spoiled of its beauty, so would Bovenschen have "the object" of artistic creation leave its context of production and use value in order to enter the "artistic realm" and so to "initiate communication"; that is to say, to enter the museum, the art gallery, the market. In other words, art is what is enjoyed publicly rather than privately, has an exchange value rather than a use value, and that value is conferred by socially established aesthetic canons.

Mulvey, too, in proposing the destruction of narrative and visual pleasure as the foremost objective of women's cinema, hails an established
tradition, albeit a radical one: the historic left avant-garde tradition that
goes back to Eisenstein and Vertov (if not Méliès) and through Brecht
reaches its peak of influence in Godard, and on the other side of the
Atlantic, the tradition of American avant-garde cinema.

> The first blow against the monolithic accumulation of traditional
> film conventions (already undertaken by radical filmmakers) is
> to free the look of the camera into its materiality in time and
> space and the look of the audience into dialectics, passionate
> detachment.[3]

But much as Mulvey and other avant-garde filmmakers insisted that
women's cinema ought to avoid a politics of emotions and seek to
problematize the female spectator's identification with the on-screen
image of woman, the response to her theoretical writings, like the reception of her films (codirected with Peter Wollen), showed no consensus.
Feminist critics, spectators, and filmmakers remained doubtful. For
example, Ruby Rich:

> According to Mulvey, the woman is not visible in the audience,
> which is perceived as male; according to Johnston, the woman
> is not visible on the screen. . . . How does one formulate an un-
> derstanding of a structure that insists on our absence even in the
> face of our presence? What is there in a film with which a woman
> viewer identifies? How can the contradictions be used as a critique?
> And how do all these factors influence what one makes as a woman
> filmmaker, or specifically as a feminist filmmaker?[4]

The questions of identification, self-definition, the modes or the very
possibility of envisaging oneself as subject—which the male avant-garde
artists and theorists have also been asking, on their part, for almost
one hundred years, even as they work to subvert the dominant representations or to challenge their hegemony—are fundamental questions
for feminism. If identification is "not simply one psychical mechanism
among others, but the operation itself whereby the human subject is
constituted," as Laplanche and Pontalis describe it, then it must be all
the more important, theoretically and politically, for women who have
never before represented ourselves as subjects, and whose images and

subjectivities—until very recently, if at all—have not been ours to shape, to portray, or to create.[5]

There is indeed reason to question the theoretical paradigm of a subject-object dialectic, whether Hegelian or Lacanian, that subtends both the aesthetic and the scientific discourses of Western culture; for what that paradigm contains, what those discourses rest on, is the unacknowledged assumption of sexual difference: that the human subject, Man, is the male. As in the originary distinction of classical myth reaching us through the Platonic tradition, human creation and all that is human—mind, spirit, history, language, art, or symbolic capacity—is defined in contradistinction to formless chaos, *phusis* or nature, to something that is female, matrix and matter; and on this primary binary opposition, all the others are modeled. As Lea Melandri states,

> Idealism, the oppositions of mind to body, of rationality to matter, originate in a twofold concealment: of the woman's body and of labor power. Chronologically, however, even prior to the commodity and the labor power that has produced it, the matter which was negated in its concreteness and particularity, in its "relative plural form," is the woman's body. Woman enters history having already lost concreteness and singularity: she is the economic machine that reproduces the human species, and she is the Mother, an equivalent more universal than money, the most abstract measure ever invented by patriarchal ideology.[6]

That this proposition remains true when tested on the aesthetic of modernism or the major trends in avant-garde cinema from visionary to structural-materialist film, on the films of Stan Brakhage, Michael Snow, or Jean-Luc Godard, but is not true of the films of Yvonne Rainer, Valie Export, Chantal Akerman, or Marguerite Duras, for example; that it remains valid for the films of Fassbinder but not those of Ottinger, the films of Pasolini and Bertolucci but not Cavani's, and so on, suggests to me that it is perhaps time to shift the terms of the question altogether.

To ask of these women's films: What formal, stylistic, or thematic markers point to a female presence behind the camera? and hence to generalize and universalize, to say: This is the look and sound of women's cinema, this is its language—finally only means complying, accepting a certain definition of art, cinema, and culture, and obligingly showing how women can and do "contribute," pay their tribute, to "society." Put another way, to ask whether there is a feminine or female aesthetic, or a specific language of women's cinema, is to remain caught in the master's house and there, as Audre Lorde's suggestive metaphor warns us, to legitimate the hidden agendas of a culture we badly need to change. Cosmetic changes, she is telling us, won't be enough for the majority of women—women of color, black women, and white women as well; or, in her own words, "assimilation within a solely western-european herstory is not acceptable."[7]

It is time we listened. Which is not to say that we should dispense with rigorous analysis and experimentation on the formal processes of meaning production, including the production of narrative, visual pleasure, and subject positions, but rather that feminist theory should now engage precisely in the redefinition of aesthetic and formal knowledges, much as women's cinema has been engaged in the transformation of vision.

Take Akerman's *Jeanne Dielman* (1975), a film about the routine daily activities of a Belgian middle-class and middle-aged housewife, and a film where the pre-aesthetic is already fully aesthetic. That is not so, however, because of the beauty of its images, the balanced composition of its frames, the absence of the reverse shot, or the perfectly calculated editing of its still-camera shots into a continuous, logical, and obsessive narrative space; it is so because it is a woman's actions, gestures, body, and look that define the space of our vision, the temporality and rhythms of perception, the horizon of meaning available to the spectator. So that narrative suspense is not built on the expectation of a "significant event," a socially momentous act (which actually occurs, though unexpectedly and almost incidentally, one feels, toward the end of the film), but is produced by the tiny slips in Jeanne's routine, the small forgettings, the hesitations between real-time gestures as common and "insignificant" as peeling potatoes, washing dishes, or making coffee—and then not drinking it. What the film constructs—formally and artfully, to be sure—is a picture of female experience, of duration, perception, events, relationships, and silences, which feels immediately and unquestionably true. And in this sense the "pre-aesthetic" is *aesthetic* rather than *aestheticized,* as it is in films such as Godard's *Two or Three Things I Know About Her* (1967), Polanski's *Repulsion* (1965), or Antonioni's *Eclipse* (1962). To say the same thing in another way, Akerman's film addresses the spectator as female.

The effort, on the part of the filmmaker, to render a presence in the feeling of a gesture, to convey the sense of an experience that is subjective yet socially coded (and therefore recognizable), and to do so formally, working through her conceptual (one could say, theoretical) knowledge of film form, is averred by Chantal Akerman in an interview on the making of *Jeanne Dielman*:

> I *do* think it's a feminist film because I give space to things which were never, almost never, shown in that way, like the daily gestures of a woman. They are the lowest in the hierarchy of film images. . . . But more than the content, it's because of the style. If you choose to show a woman's gestures so precisely, it's because you love them. In some way you recognize those gestures that have always been denied and ignored. I think that the real problem with women's films usually has nothing to do with the content. It's that hardly any women really have confidence enough to carry through on their feelings. Instead the content is the most simple and obvious thing. They deal with that and forget to look for formal ways to express what they are and what they want, their own rhythms, their own way of looking at things. A lot of women have unconscious contempt for their feelings. But I don't think I do. I have enough confidence in myself. So that's the other reason why I think it's a feminist film—not just what it says but *what* is shown and *how* it's shown.[8]

This lucid statement of poetics resonates with my own response as a viewer and gives me something of an explanation as to why I recognize in those unusual film images, in those movements, those silences, and those looks, the ways of an experience all but unrepresented, previously unseen in film, though lucidly and unmistakably apprehended here. And so the statement cannot be dismissed with commonplaces such as authorial intention or intentional fallacy. As another critic and spectator points out, there are "two logics" at work in this film, "two modes of the feminine": character and director, image and camera, remain distinct yet interacting and mutually interdependent positions. Call them femininity and feminism; the one is made representable by the critical work of the other; the one is kept at a distance, constructed, "framed," to be sure, and yet "respected," "loved," "given space" by the other.[9] The two "logics" remain separate:

> The camera look can't be construed as the view of any character. Its interest extends beyond the fiction. The camera presents itself, in its evenness and predictability, as equal to Jeanne's precision. Yet the camera continues its logic throughout; Jeanne's order is disrupted, and with the murder the text comes to its logical end since Jeanne then stops altogether. If Jeanne has, symbolically, destroyed the phallus, its order still remains visible all around her.[10]

Finally, then, the space constructed by the film is not only a textual or filmic space of vision, in frame and off—for an off-screen space is still inscribed in the images, although not sutured narratively by the reverse shot but effectively reaching toward the historical and social determinants which define Jeanne's life and place her in her frame. But beyond that, the film's space is also a critical space of analysis, a horizon of possible meanings which includes or extends to the spectator ("extends beyond the fiction") insofar as the spectator is led to occupy at once the two positions, to follow the two "logics," and to perceive them as equally and concurrently true.

In saying that a film whose visual and symbolic space is organized in this manner *addresses its spectator as a woman,* regardless of the gender of the viewers, I mean that the film defines all points of identification (with character, image, camera) as female, feminine, or feminist. However, this is not as simple or self-evident a notion as the established film-theoretical view of cinematic identification, namely, that identification with the look is masculine, and identification with the image is feminine. It is not self-evident precisely because such a view—which indeed correctly explains the working of dominant cinema—is now accepted: that the camera (technology), the look (voyeurism), and the scopic drive itself partake of the phallic and thus somehow are entities or figures of a masculine nature.

How difficult it is to "prove" that a film addresses its spectator as female is brought home time and again in conversations or discussions between audiences and filmmakers. After a screening of *Redupers* in Milwaukee (in January 1985), Helke Sander answered a question about the function of the Berlin wall in her film and concluded by saying, if I may paraphrase: "but of course the wall also represents another division that is specific to women." She did not elaborate, but again, I felt that what she meant was clear and unmistakable. And so does at least one other critic and spectator, Kaja Silverman, who sees the wall as a division other in kind from what the wall would divide—and can't, for things do "flow through the Berlin wall (TV and radio waves, germs, the writings of Christa Wolf)," and Edda's photographs show the two Berlins in "their quotidian similarities rather than their ideological divergences."

> All three projects are motivated by the desire to tear down the wall, or at least to prevent it from functioning as the dividing line between two irreducible opposites. . . . *Redupers* makes the wall a signifier for psychic as well as ideological, political, and geographical boundaries. It functions there as a metaphor for sexual difference, for the subjective limits articulated by the existing symbolic order both in East and West. The wall thus designates the discursive boundaries which separate residents not only of the same country and language, but of the same partitioned space.[11]

Those of us who share Silverman's perception must wonder whether in fact the sense of that other, specific division represented by the wall in *Redupers* (sexual difference, a discursive boundary, a subjective limit) is in the film or in our viewers' eyes. Is it actually there on screen, in the film, inscribed in its slow montage of long takes and in the stillness of the images in their silent frames; or is it, rather, in our perception, our insight, as—precisely—a subjective limit and discursive boundary (gender), a horizon of meaning (feminism) which is projected into the images, onto the screen, around the text?

I think it is this other kind of division that is acknowledged in Christa Wolf's figure of "the divided heaven," for example, or in Virginia Woolf's "room of one's own": the feeling of an internal distance, a contradiction, a space of silence, which is there alongside the imaginary pull of cultural and ideological representations without denying or obliterating them. Women artists, filmmakers, and writers acknowledge this division or difference by attempting to express it in their works. Spectators and readers think we find it in those texts. Nevertheless, even today, most of us would still agree with Silvia Bovenschen.

"For the time being," writes Gertrud Koch, "the issue remains whether films by women actually succeed in subverting this basic model of the camera's construction of the gaze, whether the female look through the camera at the world, at men, women and objects will be an essentially different one."[12] Posed in these terms, however, the issue will remain fundamentally a rhetorical question. I have suggested that the emphasis must be shifted away from the artist behind the camera, the gaze, or the text as origin and determination of meaning, toward the wider public sphere of cinema as a social technology: we must develop our understanding of cinema's implication in other modes of cultural representation, and its possibilities of both production and counterproduction of social vision. I further suggest that, even as filmmakers are confronting the problems of transforming vision by engaging all of the codes of cinema, specific and non-specific, against the dominance of that "basic model," our task as theorists is to articulate the conditions and forms of vision for another social subject, and so to venture into the highly risky business of redefining aesthetic and formal knowledge.

Such a project evidently entails reconsidering and reassessing the early feminist formulations or, as Sheila Rowbotham summed it up, "look[ing] back at ourselves through our own cultural creations, our actions, our ideas, our pamphlets, our organization, our history, our theory."[13] And if we now can add "our films," perhaps the time has come to re-think women's cinema as the production of a feminist social vision. As a form of political critique or critical politics, and through the specific consciousness that women have developed to analyze the subject's relation to sociohistorical reality, feminism not only has invented new strategies or created new texts, but, more important, it has conceived a new social subject, women: as speakers, writers, readers, spectators, users, and makers of cultural forms, shapers of cultural processes. The project of women's cinema, therefore, is no longer that of destroying or disrupting man-centered vision by representing its blind spots, its gaps, or its repressed. The effort and challenge now are how to effect another vision: to construct other objects and subjects of vision, and to formulate the conditions of representability of another social subject. For the time being, then, feminist work in film seems necessarily focused on those subjective limits and discursive boundaries that mark women's division as gender-specific, a division more elusive, complex, and contradictory than can be conveyed in the notion of sexual difference as it is currently used.

The idea that *a film may address the spectator as female*, rather than portray women positively or negatively, seems very important to me in the critical endeavor to characterize women's cinema as a cinema for, not only by, women. It is an idea not found in the critical writings I mentioned earlier, which are focused on the film, the object, the text. But rereading those essays today, one can see, and it is important to stress it, that the question of a filmic language or a feminine aesthetic has been articulated from the beginning in relation to the women's movement: "the new grows only out of the work of confrontation" (Mulvey, "Feminism," 4); women's "imagination constitutes the movement itself" (Bovenschen, 136); and in Claire Johnston's non-formalist view of women's cinema as counter-cinema, a feminist political strategy should reclaim, rather than shun, the use of film as a form of mass culture: "In order to counter our objectification in the cinema, our collective fantasies must be released: women's cinema must embody the working through of desire: such an objective demands the use of the entertainment film."[14]

Since the first women's film festivals in 1972 (New York, Edinburgh) and the first journal of feminist film criticism (*Women and Film*, published in Berkeley from 1972 to 1975), the question of women's expression has been one of both self-expression and communication with other women, a question at once of the creation/invention of new images and of the creation/imaging of new forms of community. If we rethink the problem of a specificity of women's cinema and aesthetic forms in this manner, in terms of address—who is making films for whom, who is looking and speaking, how, where, and to whom—then what has been seen as a rift, a division, an ideological split within feminist film culture between theory and practice, or between formalism and activism, may appear to be the very strength, the drive and productive heterogeneity of feminism. In their introduction to *Re-vision: Essays in Feminist Film Criticism*, Mary Ann Doane, Patricia Mellencamp, and Linda Williams point out:

> If feminist work on film has grown increasingly theoretical, less oriented towards political action, this does not necessarily mean that theory itself is counter-productive to the cause of feminism, nor that the institutional form of the debates within feminism have simply reproduced a male model of academic competition. . . . Feminists sharing similar concerns collaborate in joint authorship and editorships, cooperative filmmaking and distribution arrange-

ments. Thus, many of the political aspirations of the women's movement form an integral part of the very structure of feminist work in and on film.[15]

The "re-vision" of their title, borrowed from Adrienne Rich ("Re-vision—the act of looking back, of seeing with fresh eyes," writes Rich, is for women "an act of survival"), refers to the project of reclaiming vision, of "seeing difference differently," of displacing the critical emphasis from "images of" women "to the axis of vision itself—to the modes of organizing vision and hearing which result in the production of that 'image.'"[16]

I agree with the *Re-vision* editors when they say that over the past decade, feminist theory has moved "from an analysis of difference as oppressive to a delineation and specification of difference as liberating, as offering the only possibility of radical change" (12). But I believe that radical change requires that such specification not be limited to "sexual difference," that is to say, a difference of women from men, female from male, or Woman from Man. Radical change requires a delineation and a better understanding of the difference of women from Woman, and that is to say as well, *the differences among women*. For there are, after all, different histories of women. There are women who masquerade and women who wear the veil; women invisible to men, in their society, but also women who are invisible to other women, in our society.[17]

The invisibility of black women in white women's films, for instance, or of lesbianism in mainstream feminist criticism, is what Lizzie Borden's *Born in Flames* (1983) most forcefully represents, while at the same time constructing the terms of their visibility as subjects and objects of vision. Set in a hypothetical near-future time and in a place very much like lower Manhattan, with the look of a documentary (after Chris Marker) and the feel of contemporary science-fiction writing (the post-new-wave s-f of Samuel Delany, Joanna Russ, Alice Sheldon, or Thomas Disch), *Born in Flames* shows how a "successful" social democratic cultural revolution, now into its tenth year, slowly but surely reverts to the old patterns of male dominance, politics as usual, and the traditional Left disregard for "women's issues." It is around this specific gender oppression, in its various forms, that several groups of women (black women, Latinas, lesbians, single mothers, intellectuals, political activists, spiritual and punk performers, and a Women's Army) succeed in mobilizing and joining together not by ignoring but, paradoxically, by acknowledging their differences.

Like *Redupers* and *Jeanne Dielman*, Borden's film addresses the spectator as female, but it does not do so by portraying an experience which feels immediately one's own. On the contrary, its barely coherent narrative, its quick-paced shots and sound montage, the counterpoint of image and word, the diversity of voices and languages, and the self-conscious science-fictional frame of the story hold the spectator across a distance, projecting toward her its fiction like a bridge of difference. In short, what *Born in Flames* does for me, woman spectator, is exactly to allow me "to see difference differently," to look at women with eyes I've never had before and yet my own; for, as it remarks the emphasis (the words are Audre Lorde's) on the "interdependency of different strengths" in feminism, the film also inscribes the differences among women as *differences within women*.

Born in Flames addresses me as a woman and a feminist living in a particular moment of women's history, the United States today. The film's events and images take place in what science fiction calls a parallel universe, a time and a place elsewhere that look and feel like here and now, yet are not, just as I (and all women) live in a culture that is and is not our own. In that unlikely, but not impossible, universe of the film's fiction, the women come together in the very struggle that divides and differentiates them. Thus, what it portrays for me, what elicits my identification with the film and gives me, spectator, a place in it, is the contradiction of my own history and the personal/political difference that is also within myself.

"The relationship between history and so-called subjective processes," says Helen Fehervary in a recent discussion of women's film in Germany, "is not a matter of grasping the truth in history as some objective entity, but in finding the truth of the experience. Evidently, this kind of experiential immediacy has to do with women's own history and self-consciousness."[18] That, how, and why our histories and our consciousness are different, divided, even conflicting, is what women's cinema can analyze, articulate, reformulate. And, in so doing, it can help us create something else to be, as Toni Morrison says of her two heroines:

Because each had discovered years before that they were neither white nor male, and that all freedom and triumph was forbidden to them, they had set about creating something else to be.[19]

In the following pages I will refer often to *Born in Flames*, discussing some of the issues it has raised, but it will not be with the aim of a textual analysis. Rather, I will take it as the starting point, as indeed it was for me, of a series of reflections on the topic of this essay.

Again it is a film, and a filmmaker's project, that bring home to me with greater clarity the question of difference, this time in relation to factors other than gender, notably race and class—a question endlessly debated within Marxist feminism and recently rearticulated by women of color in feminist presses and publications. That this question should reemerge urgently and irrevocably now is not surprising, at a time when severe social regression and economic pressures (the so-called "feminization of poverty") belie the self-complacency of a liberal feminism enjoying its modest allotment of institutional legitimation. A sign of the times, the recent crop of commercial, man-made "woman's films" (*Lianna* [1983], *Personal Best* [1982], *Silkwood* [1983], *Frances* [1982], *Places in the Heart* [1984], etc.) is undoubtedly "authorized," and made financially viable, by that legitimation. But the success, however modest, of this liberal feminism has been bought at the price of reducing the contradictory complexity—and the theoretical productivity—of concepts such as sexual difference, the personal is political, and feminism itself to simpler and more acceptable ideas already existing in the dominant culture. Thus, to many today, "sexual difference" is hardly more than sex (biology) or gender (in the simplest sense of female socialization) or the basis for certain private "life styles" (homosexual and other nonorthodox relationships); "the personal is political" all too often translates into "the personal instead of the political"; and "feminism" is unhesitantly appropriated, by the academy as well as the media, as a discourse—a variety of social criticism, a method of aesthetic or literary analysis among others, and more or less worth attention according to the degree of its market appeal to students, readers, or viewers. And, yes, a discourse perfectly accessible to all men of good will. In this context, issues of race or class must continue to be thought of as mainly sociological or economic, and hence parallel to but not dependent on gender, implicated with but not determining of subjectivity, and of little relevance to this "feminist discourse" which, as such, would have no competence in the matter but only, and at best, a humane or "progressive" concern with the disadvantaged.

The relevance of feminism (without quotation marks) to race and class, however, is very explicitly stated by those women of color, black, and white who are not the recipients but rather the "targets" of equal opportunity, who are outside or not fooled by liberal "feminism," or who understand that feminism is nothing if it is not at once political and personal, with all the contradictions and difficulties that entails. To such feminists it is clear that the social construction of gender, subjectivity, and the relations of representation to experience do occur within race and class as much as they occur in language and culture, often indeed across languages, cultures, and sociocultural apparati. Thus, not only is it the case that the notion of gender, or "sexual difference," cannot be simply accommodated into the preexisting, ungendered (or male-gendered) categories by which the official discourses on race and class have been elaborated; but it is equally the case that the issues of race and class cannot be simply subsumed under some larger category labeled femaleness, femininity, womanhood, or, in the final instance, Woman. What is becoming more and more clear, instead, is that all the categories of our social science stand to be reformulated *starting from* the notion of gendered social subjects. And something of this process of reformulation—re-vision, rewriting, rereading, rethinking, "looking back at *ourselves*"—is what I see inscribed in the texts of women's cinema but not yet sufficiently focused on in feminist film theory or feminist critical practice in general. This point, like the relation of feminist writing to the women's movement, demands a much lengthier discussion than can be undertaken here. I can do no more than sketch the problem as it strikes me with unusual intensity in the reception of Lizzie Borden's film and my own response to it.

What *Born in Flames* succeeds in representing is this feminist understanding: that the female subject is en-gendered, constructed and defined in gender across multiple representations of class, race, language, and social relations; and that, therefore, differences among women are differences *within* women, which is why feminism can exist despite those differences and, as we are just beginning to understand, cannot continue to exist without them. The originality of this film's project is its representation of woman as a social subject and a site of differences;

differences which are not purely sexual or merely racial, economic, or (sub)cultural, but all of these together and often enough in conflict with one another. What one takes away after seeing this film is the image of a heterogeneity in the female social subject, the sense of a distance from dominant cultural models and of an internal division within women that remain, not in spite of but concurrently with the provisional unity of any concerted political action. Just as the film's narrative remains unresolved, fragmented, and difficult to follow, heterogeneity and difference within women remain in our memory as the film's narrative image, its work of representing, which cannot be collapsed into a fixed identity, a sameness of all women as Woman, or a representation of Feminism as a coherent and available image.

Other films, in addition to the ones already mentioned, have effectively represented that internal division or distance from language, culture, and self that I see recur, figuratively and thematically, in recent women's cinema (it is also represented, for example, in Gabriella Rosaleva's *Il Processo a Caterina Ross* [1982] and in Lynne Tillman and Sheila McLaughlin's *Committed* [1984]). But *Born in Flames* projects that division on a larger social and cultural scale, taking up nearly all of the issues and putting them all at stake. As we read on the side of the (stolen) U-Haul trucks which carry the free women's new mobile radio transmitter, reborn as Phoenix-Regazza (girl phoenix) from the flames that destroyed the two separate stations, the film is "an adventure in moving." As one reviewer saw it,

> An action pic, a sci-fi fantasy, a political thriller, a collage film, a snatch of the underground: *Born in Flames* is all and none of these. . . . Edited in 15-second bursts and spiked with yards of flickering video transfers . . . *Born in Flames* stands head and shoulders above such Hollywood reflections on the media as *Absence of Malice*, *Network*, or *Under Fire*. This is less a matter of its substance (the plot centers on the suspicious prison "suicide," à la Ulrike Meinhoff, of Women's Army leader Adelaide Norris) than of its form, seizing on a dozen facets of our daily media surroundings.[20]

The words of the last sentence, echoing Akerman's emphasis on form rather than content, are in turn echoed by Borden in several printed statements. She, too, is keenly concerned with her own relation as filmmaker to filmic representation ("Two things I was committed to with the film were questioning the nature of narrative . . . and creating a process whereby I could release myself from my own bondage in terms of class and race").[21] And she, too, like Akerman, is confident that vision can be transformed because hers has been: "Whatever discomfort I might have felt as a white filmmaker working with black women has been over for so long. It was exorcized by the process of making the film." Thus, in response to the interviewer's (Anne Friedberg) suggestion that the film is "progressive" precisely because it "demands a certain discomfort for the audience, and forces the viewer to confront his or her own political position(s) (or lack of political position)," Borden flatly rejects the interviewer's implicit assumption.

> I don't think the audience is solely a white middle-class audience. What was important for me was creating a film in which that was *not* the only audience. The problem with much of the critical material on the film is that it assumes a white middle-class reading public for articles written about a film that they assume has only a white middle-class audience. I'm very confused about the discomfort that reviewers feel. What I was trying to do (and using humor as a way to try to do it) was to have various positions in which everyone had a place on some level. Every woman—with men it is a whole different question—would have some level of identification with a position within the film. Some reviewers over-identified with something as a privileged position. Basically, none of the positioning of black characters was *against* any of the white viewers but more of an invitation: come and work with us. Instead of telling the viewer that he or she could *not* belong, the viewer was supposed to be a repository for all these different points of view and all these different styles of rhetoric. Hopefully, one would be able to identify with one position but be able to evaluate all of the various positions presented in the film. Basically, I feel this discomfort only from people who are deeply resistant to it.[22]

This response is one that, to my mind, sharply outlines a shift in women's cinema from a modernist or avant-garde aesthetic of subversion to an emerging set of questions about filmic representation to which the term *aesthetic* may or may not apply, depending on one's definition of art, one's definition of cinema, and the relationship between the two. Similarly, whether or not the terms *postmodern* or *postmodernist aes-*

thetic would be preferable or more applicable in this context, as Craig Owens has suggested of the work of other women artists, is too large a topic to be discussed here.[23]

At any rate, as I see it, there has been a shift in women's cinema from an aesthetic centered on the text and *its* effects on the viewing or reading subject—whose certain, if imaginary, self-coherence is to be fractured by the text's own disruption of linguistic, visual, and/or narrative coherence—to what may be called an aesthetic of reception, where the spectator is the film's primary concern—primary in the sense that it is there from the beginning, inscribed in the filmmaker's project and even in the very making of the film.[24] An explicit concern with the audience is of course not new either in art or in cinema, since Pirandello and Brecht in the former, and it is always conspicuously present in Hollywood and TV. What is new here, however, is the particular conception of the audience, which now is envisaged in its heterogeneity and otherness from the text.

That the audience is conceived as a heterogeneous community is made apparent, in Borden's film, by its unusual handling of the function of address. The use of music and beat in conjunction with spoken language, from rap singing to a variety of subcultural lingos and nonstandard speech, serves less the purposes of documentation or cinema vérité than those of what in another context might be called characterization: they are there to provide a means of identification of and with the characters, though not the kind of psychological identification usually accorded to main characters or privileged "protagonists." "I wanted to make a film that different audiences could relate to on different levels—if they wanted to ignore the language they could," Borden told another interviewer, "but not to make a film that was anti-language."[25] The importance of "language" and its constitutive presence in both the public and the private spheres is underscored by the multiplicity of discourses and communication technologies—visual, verbal, and aural—foregrounded in the form as well as the content of the film. If the wall of official speech, the omnipresent systems of public address, and the very strategy of the women's takeover of a television station assert the fundamental link of communication and power, the film also insists on representing the other, unofficial social discourses, their heterogeneity, and *their* constitutive effects vis-à-vis the social subject.

In this respect, I would argue, both the characters and the spectators of Borden's film are positioned in relation to social discourses and representations (of class, race, and gender) within particular "subjective limits and discursive boundaries" that are analogous, in their own historical specificity, to those which Silverman saw symbolized by the Berlin wall in *Redupers*. For the spectators, too, are limited in their vision and understanding, bound by their own social and sexual positioning, as their "discomfort" or diverse responses suggest. Borden's avowed intent to make the spectator a locus ("a repository") of different points of view and discursive configurations ("these different styles of rhetoric") suggests to me that the concept of a heterogeneity of the audience also entails a heterogeneity of, or in, the individual spectator.

If, as claimed by recent theories of textuality, the Reader or the Spectator is implied in the text as an effect of its strategy—either as the figure of a unity or coherence of meaning which is constructed by the text (the "text of pleasure"), or as the figure of the division, dissemination, incoherence inscribed in the "text of jouissance"—then the spectator of *Born in Flames* is somewhere else, resistant to the text and other from it. This film's spectator is not only *not* sutured into the "classic" text by narrative and psychological identification; nor is it bound in the time of repetition, "at the limit of any fixed subjectivity, materially inconstant, dispersed in process," as Stephen Heath aptly describes the spectator intended by avant-garde (structural-materialist) film.[26] What happens is, this film's spectator is finally not liable to capture by the text.

And yet one is engaged by the powerful erotic charge of the film; one responds to the erotic investment that its female characters have in each other, and the filmmaker in them, with something that is neither pleasure nor *jouissance,* oedipal nor pre-oedipal, as they have been defined for us; but with something that is again (as in *Jeanne Dielman*) a recognition, unmistakable and unprecedented. Again the textual space extends to the spectator, in its erotic and critical dimensions, addressing, speaking-to, making room, but not (how very unusual and remarkable) cajoling, soliciting, seducing. These films do not put me in the place of the female spectator, do not assign me a role, a self-image, a positionality in language or desire. Instead, they make a place for what I will call me, knowing that I don't know it, and give "me" space to try to know, to see, to understand. Put another way, by addressing me as *a* woman, they do not bind me or appoint me as Woman.

The "discomfort" of Borden's reviewers might be located exactly in this dis-appointment of spectator and text: the disappointment of not finding oneself, not finding oneself "interpellated" or solicited by the film, whose images and discourses project back to the viewer a space of heterogeneity, differences and fragmented coherences that just do not add up to one individual viewer or one spectator-subject, bourgeois or otherwise. There is no one-to-one match between the film's discursive heterogeneity and the discursive boundaries of any one spectator. We are both invited in and held at a distance, addressed intermittently and only insofar as we are able to occupy the position of addressee; for example, when Honey, the Phoenix Radio disc jockey, addresses to the audience the words: "Black women, be ready. White women, get ready. Red women, stay ready, for this is our time and all must realize it."[27] Which individual member of the audience, male or female, can feel singly interpellated as spectator-subject or, in other words, unequivocally addressed?

There is a famous moment in film history, something of a parallel to this one, which not coincidentally has been "discovered" by feminist film critics in a woman-made film about women, Dorothy Arzner's *Dance, Girl, Dance* (1940): it is the moment when Judy interrupts her stage performance and, facing the vaudeville audience, steps out of her role and speaks to them as a woman to a group of people. The novelty of this direct address, feminist critics have noted, is not only that it breaks the codes of theatrical illusion and voyeuristic pleasure, but also that it demonstrates that no complicity, no shared discourse, can be established between the woman performer (positioned as image, representation, object) and the male audience (positioned as the controlling gaze); no complicity, that is, outside the codes and rules of the performance. By breaking the codes, Arzner revealed the rules and the relations of power that constitute them and are in turn sustained by them. And sure enough, the vaudeville audience in her film showed great discomfort with Judy's speech.

I am suggesting that the discomfort with Honey's speech has also to do with codes of representation (of race and class as well as gender) and the rules and power relations that sustain them—rules which also prevent the establishing of a shared discourse, and hence the "dream" of a common language. How else could viewers see in this playful, exuberant, science-fictional film a blueprint for political action which, they claim, wouldn't work anyway? ("We've all been through this before. As a man I'm not threatened by this because we know that this doesn't work. This is infantile politics, these women are being macho like men used to be macho. . . .")[28] Why else would they see the film, in Friedberg's phrase, "as a *prescription* through fantasy"? Borden's opinion is that "people have not really been upset about class and race. . . . People are really upset that the women are gay. They feel it is separatist."[29] My own opinion is that people are upset with all three, class, race, and gender—lesbianism being precisely the demonstration that the concept of gender is founded across race and class on the structure which Adrienne Rich and Monique Wittig have called, respectively, "compulsory heterosexuality" and "the heterosexual contract."[30]

The film-theoretical notion of spectatorship has been developed largely in the attempt to answer the question posed insistently by feminist theorists and well summed up in the words of Ruby Rich already cited above: "How does one formulate an understanding of a structure that insists on our absence even in the face of our presence?" In keeping with the early divergence of feminists over the politics of images, the notion of spectatorship was developed along two axes: one starting from the psychoanalytic theory of the subject and employing concepts such as primary and secondary, conscious and unconscious, imaginary and symbolic processes; the other starting from sexual difference and asking questions such as, How does the female spectator see? With what does she identify? Where/How/In what film genres is female desire represented? and so on. Arzner's infraction of the code in *Dance, Girl, Dance* was one of the first answers in this second line of questioning, which now appears to have been the most fruitful by far for women's cinema. *Born in Flames* seems to me to work out the most interesting answer to date.

For one thing, the film assumes that the female spectator may be black, white, "red," middle-class or not middle-class, and wants her to have a place within the film, some measure of identification—"identification with a position," Borden specifies. "With men [spectators] it is a whole different question," she adds, obviously without much interest in exploring it (though later suggesting that black male spectators responded to the film "because they don't see it as just about women. They see it as empowerment").[31] In sum, the spectator is addressed as female in gender and multiple or heterogeneous in race and class; which is to say, here too all points of identification are female or feminist, but rather than the "two logics" of character and filmmaker, like *Jeanne Dielman, Born in Flames* foregrounds their different discourses.

Second, as Friedberg puts it in one of her questions, the images of women in *Born in Flames* are "unaestheticized": "you never fetishize the body through masquerade. In fact the film seems consciously de-aestheticized, which is what gives it its documentary quality."[32] Nevertheless, to some, those images of women appear to be extraordinarily beautiful. If such were to be the case for most of the film's female spectators, however socially positioned, we would be facing what amounts to a film-theoretical paradox, for in film theory the female body is construed precisely as fetish or masquerade.[33] Perhaps not unexpectedly, the filmmaker's response is amazingly consonant with Chantal Akerman's, though their films are visually quite different, and the latter's is in fact received as an "aesthetic" work.

> Borden: "The important thing is to shoot female bodies in a way that they have never been shot before. . . . I chose women for the stance I liked. The stance is almost like the gestalt of a person."[34]
>
> And Akerman (cited above): "I give space to things which were never, almost never, shown in that way. . . . If you choose to show a woman's gestures so precisely, it's because you love them."

The point of this cross-referencing of two films that have little else in common beside the feminism of their makers is to remark the persistence of certain themes and formal questions about representation and difference which I *would* call aesthetic, and which are the historical product of feminism and the expression of feminist critical-theoretical thought.

Like the works of the feminist filmmakers I have referred to, and many others too numerous to mention here, *Jeanne Dielman* and *Born in Flames* are engaged in the project of transforming vision by inventing the forms and processes of representation of a social subject, women, that until now has been all but unrepresentable; a project already set out (looking back, one is tempted to say, programmatically) in the title of Yvonne Rainer's *Film about a Woman Who . . .* (1974), which in a sense all of these films continue to reelaborate. The gender-specific division of women in language, the distance from official culture, the urge to imagine new forms of community as well as to create new images ("creating something else to be"), and the consciousness of a "subjective factor" at the core of all kinds of work—domestic, industrial, artistic, critical, or political work—are some of the themes articulating the particular relation of subjectivity, meaning, and experience which en-genders the social subject as female. These themes, encapsulated in the phrase "the personal is political," have been formally explored in women's cinema in several ways: through the disjunction of image and voice, the reworking of narrative space, the elaboration of strategies of address that alter the forms and balances of traditional representation. From the inscription of subjective space and duration inside the frame (a space of repetitions, silences, and discontinuities in *Jeanne Dielman*) to the construction of other discursive social spaces (the discontinuous but intersecting spaces of the women's "networks" in *Born in Flames*), women's cinema has undertaken a redefinition of both private and public space that may well answer the call for "a new language of desire" and actually have met the demand for the "destruction of visual pleasure," if by that one alludes to the traditional, classical and modernist, canons of aesthetic representation.

So, once again, the contradiction of women in language and culture is manifested in a paradox: most of the terms by which we speak of the construction of the female social subject in cinematic representation bear in their visual form the prefix *de-* to signal the deconstruction or the destructuring, if not destruction, of the very thing to be represented. We speak of the deaestheticization of the female body, the desexualization of violence, the deoedipalization of narrative, and so forth. Rethinking women's cinema in this way, we may provisionally answer Bovenschen's question thus: There is a certain configuration of issues and formal problems that have been consistently articulated in what we call women's cinema. The way in which they have been expressed and developed, both artistically and critically, seems to point less to a "feminine aesthetic" than to a feminist *deaesthetic*. And if the word sounds awkward or inelegant . . .

Written initially as a contribution to the catalogue of *Kunst mit Eigen-Sinn,* an international exhibition of art by women at the Museum des 20. Jahrhunderts in Vienna, 1985. First published in the present, expanded version, and with the title "Aesthetic and Feminist Theory: Rethinking Women's Cinema," in *New German Critique* 34 (Winter 1985).

Chapter 2

Sexual Indifference and Lesbian Representation

If it were not lesbian, this text would make no sense.
—Nicole Brossard, *L'Amer*

There is a sense in which lesbian identity could be assumed, spoken, and articulated conceptually as political through feminism—and, current debates to wit, against feminism; in particular through and against the feminist critique of the Western discourse on love and sexuality, and therefore, to begin with, the rereading of psychoanalysis as a theory of sexuality and sexual difference. If the first feminist emphasis on sexual difference as gender (woman's difference from man) has rightly come under attack for obscuring the effects of other differences in women's psychosocial oppression, nevertheless that emphasis on sexual difference did open up a critical space—a conceptual, representational, and erotic space—in which women could address themselves to women. And in the very act of assuming and speaking from the position of subject, a woman could concurrently recognize women as subjects and as objects of female desire.

It is in such a space, hard-won and daily threatened by social disapprobation, censure, and denial, a space of contradiction requiring constant reaffirmation and painful renegotiation, that the very notion of sexual difference could then be put into question, and its limitations be assessed, both vis-à-vis the claims of other, not strictly sexual, differences, and with regard to sexuality itself. It thus appears that "sexual difference" is the term of a conceptual paradox corresponding to what is in effect a real contradiction in women's lives: the term, at once, of a sexual *difference* (women are, or want, something different from men) and of a sexual *indifference* (women are, or want, the same as men). And it seems to me that the racist and class-biased practices legitimated in the notion of "separate but equal" reveal a very similar paradox in the liberal ideology of pluralism, where social difference is also, at the same time, social indifference.

The psychoanalytic discourse on female sexuality, wrote Luce Irigaray in 1975, outlining the terms of what here I will call sexual (in)difference, tells "that *the feminine occurs only within models and laws devised by male subjects.* Which implies that there are not really two sexes, but only one. A single practice and representation of the sexual."[1] Within the conceptual frame of that *sexual indifference,* female desire for the self-same, an other female self, cannot be recognized. "That a woman might desire a woman 'like' herself, someone of the 'same' sex, that she might also have auto- and homosexual appetites, is simply incomprehensible" in the phallic regime of an asserted sexual difference between man and woman which is predicated on the contrary, on a complete indifference for the "other" sex, woman's. Consequently, Irigaray continues, Freud was at a loss with his homosexual female patients, and his analyses of them were really about male homosexuality. "The object choice of the homosexual woman is [understood to be] determined by a *masculine* desire and tropism"—that is, precisely, the turn of so-called sexual difference into sexual indifference, a single practice and representation of the sexual.

> So there will be no female homosexuality, just a hommo-sexuality in which woman will be involved in the process of specularizing the phallus, begged to maintain the desire for the same that man has, and will ensure at the same time, elsewhere and in complementary and contradictory fashion, the perpetuation in the couple of the pole of "matter."[2]

With the term *hommo-sexuality* [*hommo-sexualité*]—at times also written *hom(m)osexuality* [*hom(m)osexualité*]—Irigaray puns on the

French word for man, *homme*, from the Latin *homo* (meaning "man"), and the Greek *homo* (meaning "same"). In taking up her distinction between homosexuality (or homo-sexuality) and "hommosexuality" (or "hom(m)osexuality"), I want to remark the conceptual distance between the former term, homosexuality, by which I mean lesbian (or gay) sexuality, and the diacritically marked hommo-sexuality, which is the term of sexual indifference, the term (in fact) of heterosexuality; I want to remark both the incommensurable distance between them and the conceptual ambiguity that is conveyed by the two almost identical acoustic images. Another paradox—or is it perhaps the same?

>> >> There is no validation for sodomy found in the teaching of the
ancient Greek philosophers Plato or Aristotle.
—Michael Bowers, Petitioners brief in *Bowers v. Hardwick*

To attempt to answer that question, I turn to a very interesting reading of Plato's *Symposium* by David Halperin which (1) richly resonates with Irigaray's notion of sexual indifference (see also her reading of "Plato's Hystera" in *Speculum*), (2) emphasizes the embarrassing ignorance of the present Attorney General of the State of Georgia in matters of classical scholarship, which he nevertheless invokes,[3] and (3) traces the roots of the paradoxes here in question to the very philosophical foundation of what is called Western civilization, Plato's dialogues. For in those master texts of hommo-sexuality, as Halperin proposes, it is the female, reproductive body that paradoxically guarantees true eros between men, or as Plato calls it, "correct paederasty."[4]

"Why is Diotima a Woman?" Halperin argues, is a question that has been answered only tautologically: because she is not or cannot be a man. It would have been indecorous to imply that Socrates owed his knowledge of erotic desire to a former paederastic lover. But there is a reason more stringent than decorum why Socrates's teacher should have been a woman. Plato wanted to prescribe a new homoerotic ethos and a model of "correct paederasty" based on the reciprocity of erotic desire and a mutual access to pleasure for both partners, a reciprocity of eros whose philosophical import found ultimate expression in the dialogue form. His project, however, ran against the homoerotic sexual ethos and practices of the citizens of classical Athens, "accustomed as they were to holding one another to an aggressively phallic norm of sexual conduct—and, consequently, to an ethic of sexual domination in their relations with males and females alike" (133). For an adult male citizen of Athens could have legitimate sexual relations only with his social inferiors: boys, women, foreigners, and slaves. Plato repudiated such erotic asymmetry in relations between men and boys and, through the teaching of Socrates/Diotima, sought to erase "the distinction between the 'active' and the 'passive' partner . . . according to Socrates, both members of the relationship become active, desiring lovers; neither remains a merely passive object of desire" (132).

Hence the intellectual and mythopoetic function of Diotima: her discourse on erotic desire, unlike a man's, could appear directly grounded in the experiential knowledge of a non-hierarchical, mutualistic and reproductive sexuality, i.e., female sexuality as the Greeks construed it. It is indeed so grounded in the text, both rhetorically (Diotima's language systematically conflates sexual pleasure with the reproductive or generative function) and narratively, in the presumed experience of a female character, since to the Greeks female sexuality differed from male sexuality precisely in that sexual pleasure for women was intimately bound up with procreation. Halperin cites many sources from Plato's *Timaeus* to various ritual practices which represented, for example, "the relation of man to wife as a domestic form of cultivation homologous to agriculture whereby women are tamed, mastered, and made fruitful. . . . [I]n the absence of men, women's sexual functioning is aimless and unproductive, merely a form of rottenness and decay, but by the application of male pharmacy it becomes at once orderly and fruitful" (141).

After remarking on the similarity between the Greek construction and the contemporary gynecological discourses on female eroticism, Halperin raises the question of Plato's politics of gender, noting that "the interdependence of sexual and reproductive capacities is in fact a feature of male, not female, physiology," and that male sexuality is the one in which "reproductive function cannot be isolated from sexual pleasure (to the chagrin of Augustine and others)" (142). His hypothesis is worth quoting at length:

> Plato, then, would seem to be . . . interpreting as "feminine" and allocating to men a form of sexual experience which is masculine to begin with and which men had previously alienated from

themselves by defining it as feminine. In other words, it looks as if what lies behind Plato's erotic doctrine is a double movement whereby men project their own sexual experience onto women only to reabsorb it themselves in the guise of a "feminine" character. This is particularly intriguing because it suggests that in order to facilitate their own appropriation of what they take to be the feminine men have initially constructed "femininity" according to a male paradigm while creating a social and political ideal of "masculinity" defined by their own putative ability to isolate what only women can *actually* isolate—namely, sexual pleasure and reproduction, recreative and procreative sex. (142–43; emphasis in the original)

Let me restate the significance of Halperin's analysis for my own argument here. Plato's repudiation of asymmetrical paederasty and of the subordinate position in which that placed *citizen* boys who, after all, were the future rulers of Athens, had the effect of elevating the status of all male *citizens* and thus of consolidating *male citizen* rule. It certainly was no favor done to women or to any "others" (male and female foreigners, male and female slaves). But his move was yet more masterful: the appropriation of the feminine for the erotic ethos of a male social and intellectual elite (an ethos that would endure well into the twentieth century, if in the guise of "heretical ethics" or in the femininity [*dévenir-femme*] claimed by his most deconstructive critics)[5] had the effect not only of securing the millenary exclusion of women from philosophical dialogue, and the absolute excision of non-reproductive sexuality from the Western discourse on love. The construction and appropriation of femininity in Western erotic ethos has also had the effect of securing the heterosexual social contract by which all sexualities, all bodies, and all "others" are bonded to an ideal/ideological hierarchy of males.[6]

The intimate relationship of sexual (in)difference with social (in)difference, whereby, for instance, the defense of the mother country and of (white) womanhood has served to bolster colonial conquest and racist violence throughout Western history, is nowhere more evident than in "the teaching of the ancient Greek philosophers," *pace* Attorney General Bowers. Hence the ironic rewriting of history, in a female-only world of mothers and amazons, by Monique Wittig and Sande Zeig in *Lesbian Peoples: Material for a Dictionary.*[7] And hence, as well, the crucial emphasis in current feminist theory on articulating, specifying, and historicizing the position of the female social subject in the intricate experiential nexus of (often contradictory) heterogeneous differences, across discourses of race, gender, cultural, and sexual identity, and the political working through those differences toward a new, global, yet historically specific and even local, understanding of community.[8]

» » Pardon me, I must be going!
 — Djuna Barnes, *The Ladies Almanack*

Lesbian representation, or rather, its condition of possibility, depends on separating out the two contrary undertows that constitute the paradox of sexual (in)difference, on isolating but maintaining the two senses of homosexuality and hommo-sexuality. Thus the critical effort to dislodge the erotic from the discourse of gender, with its indissoluble knot of sexuality and reproduction, is concurrent and interdependent with a rethinking of what, in most cultural discourses and sociosexual practices, is still, nevertheless, a gendered sexuality. In the pages that follow, I will attempt to work through these paradoxes by considering how lesbian writers and artists have sought variously to escape gender, to deny it, transcend it, or perform it in excess, and to inscribe the erotic in cryptic, allegorical, realistic, camp, or other modes of representation, pursuing diverse strategies of writing and of reading the intransitive and yet obdurate relation of reference to meaning, of flesh to language.

Gertrude Stein, for example, "encrypted" her experience of the body in obscure coding, her "somagrams" are neither sexually explicit or conventionally erotic, nor "radically visceral or visual," Catharine Stimpson argues.[9] Stein's effort was, rather, to develop a distinguished "anti-language" in which to describe sexual activity, her "delight in the female body" (38) or her ambivalence about it, as an abstract though intimate relationship where "the body fuses with writing itself" (36), an act "at once richly pleasurable and violent" (38). But if Stein does belong to the history of women writers, claims Stimpson, who also claims her for the history of lesbian writers, it is not because she wrote out of femaleness "as an elemental condition, inseparable from the body" (40), the way some radical feminist critics would like to think; nor because her writing sprung from a preoedipal, maternal body, as others would have it. Her language was not "female" but quite the contrary, "as genderless as an atom of platinum" (42), and strove to obliterate the boundaries of gender identity.

Djuna Barnes's *Nightwood*, which Stimpson calls a "parable of damnation,"[10] is read by others as an affirmation of inversion as homosexual difference. In her "Writing Toward *Nightwood*: Djuna Barnes's Seduction Stories," Carolyn Allen reads Barnes's "little girl" stories as sketches or earlier trials of the sustained meditation on inversion that was to yield in the novel the most suggestive portrait of the invert, the third sex.

> In that portrait we recognize the boy in the girl, the girl in the Prince, not a mixing of gendered behaviors, but the creation of a new gender, "neither one and half the other." . . . In their love of the same sex [Matthew, Nora and Robin] admire their non-conformity, their sexual difference from the rest of the world.[11]

That difference, which for the lesbian includes a relation to the self-same ("a woman is yourself caught as you turn in panic; on her mouth you kiss your own," says Nora), also includes her relation to the child, the "ambivalence about mothering one's lover," the difficult and inescapable ties of female sexuality with nurture and with violence. In this light, Allen suggests, may we read Barnes's personal denial of lesbianism and her aloofness from female admirers as a refusal to accept and to live by the homophobic categories promoted by sexology: man and woman, with their respective deviant forms, the effeminate man and the mannish woman—a refusal that in the terms of my argument could be seen as a rejection of the hommo-sexual categories of gender, a refusal of sexual (in)difference.

Thus the highly metaphoric, oblique, allusive language of Barnes's fiction, her "heavily embedded and often appositional" syntax, her use of the passive voice, indirect style, and interior monologue techniques in narrative descriptions, which Allen admirably analyzes in another essay, are motivated less by the modernist's pleasure in formal experimentation than by her resistance to what *Nightwood* both thematizes and demonstrates, the failure of language to represent, grasp, and convey her subjects: "The violation [of reader's expectation] and the appositional structure permit Barnes to suggest that the naming power of language is insufficient to make Nora's love for Robin perceivable to the reader."[12]

>> >> "Dr. Knox," Edward began, "my problem this week is chiefly
concerning restrooms."
– Judy Grahn, "The Psychoanalysis of Edward the Dyke"

Ironically, since one way of escaping gender is to so disguise erotic
and sexual experience as to suppress any representation of its specificity, another avenue of escape leads the lesbian writer fully to embrace
gender, if by replacing femaleness with masculinity, as in the case of
Stephen Gordon in *The Well of Loneliness,* and so risk to collapse
lesbian homosexuality into hommo-sexuality. However, representation is related to experience by codes that change historically and,
significantly, reach in both directions: the writer struggles to inscribe
experience in historically available forms of representation, the reader
accedes to representation through her own historical and experiential
context; each reading is a rewriting of the text, each writing a rereading of (one's) experience. The contrasting readings of Radclyffe Hall's
novel by lesbian feminist critics show that each critic reads from a
particular position, experiential but also historically available to her,
and, moreover, a position chosen, or even politically assumed, from the
spectrum of contemporary discourses on the relationship of feminism
to lesbianism. The contrast of interpretations also shows to what extent
the paradox of sexual (in)difference operates as a semiotic mechanism
to produce contradictory meaning effects.

The point of contention in the reception of a novel that by general
agreement was the single most popular representation of lesbianism in
fiction, from its obscenity trial in 1928 to the 1970s, is the figure of
its protagonist Stephen Gordon, the "mythic mannish lesbian" of the
title of Esther Newton's essay, and the prototype of her more recent
incarnation, the working-class butch.[13] Newton's impassioned defense
of the novel rests on the significance of that figure for lesbian self-definition, not only in the 1920s and 1930s, when the social gains in gender
independence attained by the New Woman were being reappropriated
via sexological discourses within the institutional practices of heterosexuality, but also in the 1970s and 1980s, when female sexuality has
been redefined by a women's movement "that swears it is the enemy of
traditional gender categories and yet validates lesbianism as the ultimate
form of femaleness" (558).

Newton argues historically, taking into account the then available discourses on sexuality which asserted that "normal" women had at best a reactive heterosexual desire, while female sexual deviancy articulated itself in ascending categories of inversion marked by increasing masculinization, from deviant—but rectifiable—sexual orientation (or "homosexuality" proper, for Havelock Ellis) to congenital inversion. Gender crossing was at once a symptom and a sign of sexual degeneracy.[14] In the terms of the cultural representations available to the novelist, since there was no image of female sexual desire apart from the male, Newton asks, "Just how was Hall to make the woman-loving New Woman a sexual being? . . . To become avowedly sexual, the New Woman had to enter the male world, either as a heterosexual on male terms (a flapper) or as—or with—a lesbian in male body drag (a butch)" (572–73). Gender reversal in the mannish lesbian, then, was not merely a claim to male social privilege or a sad pretense to male sexual behavior, but represented what may be called, in Foucault's phrase, a "reverse discourse": an assertion of sexual agency and feelings, but autonomous from men, a reclaiming of erotic drives directed toward women, of a desire for women that is not to be confused with woman identification.

While other lesbian critics of *The Well of Loneliness* read it as an espousal of Ellis's views, couched in religious romantic imagery and marred by a self-defeating pessimism, aristocratic self-pity, and inevitable damnation, what Newton reads in Stephen Gordon and in Radclyffe Hall's text is the unsuccessful attempt to represent a female desire not determined by "masculine tropism," in Irigaray's words, or, in my own, a female desire not hommo-sexual but homosexual. If Radclyffe Hall herself could not envision homosexuality as part of an autonomous female sexuality (a notion that has emerged much later, with the feminist critique of patriarchy as phallic symbolic order), and if she therefore did not succeed in escaping the hommo-sexual categories of gender ("Unlike Orlando, Stephen is trapped in history; she cannot declare gender an irrelevant game," as Newton remarks [570]), nevertheless the figure of the mannish female invert continues to stand as the representation of lesbian desire against both the discourse of hommo-sexuality and the feminist account of lesbianism as woman identification. The context of Newton's reading is the current debate on the relationship of lesbianism to feminism and the reassertion, on the one hand, of the historical and political importance of gender roles (e.g., butch-femme) in lesbian self-definition and representation, and on the other, of the demand for a separate understanding of sex and gender as distinct areas of social practice.

The latter issue has been pushed to the top of the theoretical agenda by the polarization of opinions around the two adverse and widely popularized positions on the issue of pornography taken by Women Against Pornography (WAP) and by S/M lesbians (Samois). In "Thinking Sex," a revision of her earlier and very influential "The Traffic in Women," Gayle Rubin wants to challenge the assumption that feminism can contribute very much to a theory of sexuality, for "feminist thought simply lacks angles of vision which can encompass the social organization of sexuality."[15] While acknowledging some (though hardly enough) diversity among feminists on the issue of sex, and praising "pro-sex" feminists such as "lesbian sadomasochists and butch-femme dykes," adherents of "classic radical feminism," and "unapologetic heterosexuals" for not conforming to "movement standards of purity" (303), Rubin nonetheless believes that a "theory and politics specific to sexuality" must be developed apart from the theory of gender oppression, that is feminism. Thus she goes back over her earlier feminist critique of Lacan and Lévi-Strauss and readjusts the angle of vision:

> "The Traffic in Women" was inspired by the literature on kin-based systems of social organization. It appeared to me at the time that gender and desire were systematically intertwined in such social formations. This may or may not be an accurate assessment of the relationship between sex and gender *in tribal organizations*. But it is surely not an adequate formulation for sexuality *in Western industrial societies*. (307, emphasis added)

In spite of Rubin's rhetorical emphasis (which I underscore graphically in the above passage), her earlier article also had to do with gender and sexuality in Western industrial societies, where indeed Rubin and several other feminists were articulating the critique of a theory of symbolic signification that elaborated the very notion of desire (from psychoanalysis) in relation to gender as symbolic construct (from anthropology)—a critique that has been crucial to the development of feminist theory. But whereas "The Traffic in Women" (a title directly borrowed from Emma Goldman) was focused on women, here her interest has shifted toward a non-gendered notion of sexuality concerned, in Foucault's terms "with the sensations of the body, the quality of pleasures, and the nature of impressions."[16]

Accordingly, the specificity of either female or lesbian eroticism is no longer a question to be asked in "Thinking Sex," where the term "homosexual" is used to refer to both women and men (thus sliding inexorably, it seems, into its uncanny hommo-sexual double), and which concludes by advocating a politics of "theoretical as well as sexual pluralism" (309). At the opposite pole of the debate, Catharine MacKinnon argues:

> If heterosexuality is the dominant gendered form of sexuality in a society where gender oppresses women through sex, sexuality and heterosexuality are essentially the same thing. This does not erase homosexuality, it merely means that sexuality in that form may be no less gendered.[17]

I suggest that, despite or possibly because of their stark mutual opposition and common reductivism, both Rubin and MacKinnon collapse the tension of ambiguity, the semantic duplicity, that I have tried to sort out in the two terms homosexual and hommo-sexual, and thus remain caught in the paradox of sexual (in)difference even as they both, undoubtedly, very much want to escape it, one by denying gender, the other by categorically asserting it. As it was, in another sense, with Radclyffe Hall, Newton's suggestive reading notwithstanding. I will return to her suggestions later on.

>> >> A theory in the flesh
   — Cherríe Moraga, *This Bridge Called My Back*

It is certain, however, as Rubin notes, that "lesbians are *also* oppressed as queers and perverts" (308, emphasis added), not only as women; and it is equally certain that some lesbians are also oppressed as queers and perverts, and also as women of color. What cannot be elided in a politically responsible theory of sexuality, of gender, or of culture is the critical value of that "also," which is neither simply additive nor exclusive but signals the nexus, the mode of operation of *interlocking* systems of gender, sexual, racial, class, and other, more local categories of social stratification.[18] Just a few lines from *Zami,* Audre Lorde's "biomythography," will make the point, better than I can.

> But the fact of our Blackness was an issue that Felicia and I talked about only between ourselves. Even Muriel seemed to believe that as lesbians, we were all outsiders and all equal in our outsiderhood. "We're all niggers," she used to say, and I hated to hear her say it. It was wishful thinking based on little fact; the ways in which it was true languished in the shadow of those many ways in which it would always be false.
>
> It was hard enough to be Black, to be Black and female, to be Black, female, and gay. To be Black, female, gay, and out of the closet in a white environment, even to the extent of dancing in the Bagatelle, was considered by many Black lesbians to be simply suicidal. And if you were fool enough to do it, you'd better come on so tough that nobody messed with you. I often felt put down by their sophistication, their clothes, their manners, their cars, and their femmes.[19]

If the black/white divide is even less permeable than the gay/straight one, it does not alone suffice to self-definition: "Being Black dykes together was not enough. We were different. . . . Self-preservation warned some of us that we could not afford to settle for one easy definition, one narrow individuation of self" (226). Neither race nor gender nor homosexual difference alone can constitute individual identity or the basis for a theory and a politics of social change. What Lorde suggests is a more complex image of the psycho-socio-sexual subject ("our place was the very house of difference rather [than] the security of any one particular difference") which does not deny gender or sex but transcends them. Read together with the writings of other lesbians of color or those committed to antiracism (see note 8 above), Lorde's image of the house of difference points to a conception of community not pluralistic but at once global and local—global in its inclusive and macro-political strategies, and local in its specific, micro-political practices.

I want to propose that, among the latter, not the least is the practice of writing, particularly in that form which the *québécoise* feminist writer Nicole Brossard has called *"une fiction théorique,"* fiction/theory: a formally experimental, critical and lyrical, autobiographical and theoretically conscious, practice of writing-in-the-feminine that crosses genre boundaries (poetry and prose, verbal and visual modes, narrative and cultural criticism), and instates new correlations between signs and meanings, inciting other discursive mediations between the symbolic and the real, language and flesh.[20] And for all its specific cultural, historical, and linguistic variation—say between francophone and anglophone contemporary Canadian writers, or between writers such as Gloria Anzaldúa, Michelle Cliff, Cherríe Moraga, Joanna Russ, Monique Wittig, or even the Virginia Woolf of *Three Guineas* and *A Room of One's Own*—the concept of fiction/theory does make the transfer across borderlines and covers a significant range of practices of lesbian (self-)representation.

» » Lesbians are not women.
    — Monique Wittig, "The Straight Mind"

In a superb essay tracing the intertextual weave of a lesbian imagination throughout French literature, the kind of essay that changes the landscape of both literature and reading irreversibly, Elaine Marks proposes that to undomesticate the female body one must dare reinscribe it in excess—as excess—in provocative counterimages sufficiently outrageous, passionate, verbally violent and formally complex to both destroy the male discourse on love and redesign the universe.[21] The undomesticated female body that was first *concretely* imaged in Sappho's poetry ("she is suggesting equivalences between the physical symptoms of desire and the physical symptoms of death, not between Eros and Thanatos," Marks writes [372]) has been read and effectively recontained within the male poetic tradition—with the very move described by Halperin above—as phallic or maternal body. Thereafter, Marks states, no "sufficiently challenging counterimages" were produced in French literature until the advent of feminism and the writing of a lesbian feminist, Monique Wittig.

"Only the women's movement," concurred the writer in her preface to the 1975 English edition of *The Lesbian Body*, "has proved capable of producing lesbian texts in a context of total rupture with masculine culture, texts written by women exclusively for women, careless of male approval."[22] If there is reason to believe that Wittig would no longer have accepted the designation lesbian-feminist in the 1980s (her latest published novel in English, *Across the Acheron*, more than suggests as much), Marks's critical assessment of *The Lesbian Body* remains, to my way of seeing, correct:

> In *Le corps lesbien* Monique Wittig has created, through the incessant use of hyperbole and a refusal to employ traditional body codes, images sufficiently blatant to withstand reabsorption into male literary culture. . . . The j/e of *Le corps lesbien* is the most powerful lesbian in literature because as a lesbian-feminist she reexamines and redesigns the universe. (375–76)

Like Djuna Barnes's, Wittig's struggle is with language, to transcend gender. Barnes, as Wittig reads her, succeeds in "universalizing the feminine" because she "cancels out the genders by making them obsolete. I find it necessary to suppress them. That is the point of view of a lesbian."[23] And indeed, from the impersonal *on* [one] in *L'Opoponax*, to the feminine plural *elles* [they] replacing the generic masculine *ils* [they] in *Les guérillères*, to the divided, linguistically impossible *j/e* [*I*], lover and writing subject of *The Lesbian Body*, Wittig's personal pronouns work to "lesbianize" language as impudently as her recastings of both classical and Christian myth and Western literary genres (the Homeric heroes and Christ, *The Divine Comedy* and *Don Quixote*, the epic, the lyric, the *Bildungsroman*, the encyclopedic dictionary) do to literary history.[24] What will not do, for her purposes, is a "feminine writing" [*écriture féminine*] which, for Wittig, is no more than "the naturalizing metaphor of the brutal political fact of the domination of women" (63) and so complicit in the reproduction of femininity and of the female body as Nature.

Thus, as I read it, it is in the garbage dump of femininity, "In this dark adored adorned gehenna," that the odyssey of Wittig's *j/e-tu* in *The Lesbian Body* begins: "Fais tes adieux m/a très belle," "say your farewells m/y very beautiful . . . strong . . . indomitable . . . learned . . . ferocious . . . gentle . . . best beloved to what they call affection tenderness or gracious abandon. No one is unaware of what takes place here, it has no name as yet."[25] Here where?—in this book, this journey into the body of Western culture, this season in hell. And what takes place here?—the dismemberment and slow decomposition of the *female* body limb by limb, organ by organ, secretion by secretion. No one will be able to stand the sight of it, no one will come to aid in this awesome, excruciating and exhilarating labor of love: dis-membering and re-membering, reconstituting the body in a new erotic economy, relearning to know it ("it has no name as yet") by another semiotics, reinscribing it with invert/inward desire, rewriting it otherwise, otherwise: *a lesbian* body.

The project, the conceptual originality and radical import of Wittig's lesbian as subject of a "cognitive practice" that enables the reconceptualization of the social and of knowledge itself from a position eccentric to the heterosexual institution, are all there in the first page of *Le corps lesbien*.[26] A "subjective cognitive practice" and a practice of writing as consciousness of contradiction ("the language you speak is made up of words that are killing you," she wrote in *Les guérillères);* a consciousness of writing, living, feeling, and desiring in the noncoincidence of experience and language, in the interstices of representation, "in the intervals that your masters have not been able to fill with their words of proprietors."[27] Thus, the struggle with language to rewrite the body beyond its precoded, conventional representations is not and cannot be a reappropriation of the female body as it is, domesticated, maternal, oedipally or preoedipally engendered, but is a struggle to transcend both gender and "sex" and recreate the body otherwise: to see it perhaps as monstrous, or grotesque, or mortal, or violent, and certainly also sexual, but with a material and sensual specificity that will resist phallic idealization and render it accessible to women in another sociosexual economy. In short, if it were not lesbian, this body would make no sense.

>> >> Replacing the Lacanian slash with a lesbian bar
—Sue-Ellen Case, "Towards a Butch-Femme Aesthetic"

At first sight, the reader of *The Lesbian Body* might find in its linguistically impossible subject pronoun several theoretically possible valences that go from the more conservative (the slash in *j/e* represents the division of the Lacanian subject) to the less conservative (*j/e* can be expressed by writing but not by speech, representing Derridean *différance*), and to the radical feminist ("*j/e is* the symbol of the lived, rending experience which is *m/y* writing, of this cutting in two which throughout literature is the exercise of a language which does not constitute m/e as subject," as Wittig is reported to have said in Margaret Crosland's introduction to the Beacon paperback edition I own). Another reader, especially if a reader of science fiction, might think of Joanna Russ's brilliant lesbian-feminist novel, *The Female Man,* whose protagonist is a female genotype articulated across four spacetime probabilities in four characters whose names all begin with J—Janet, Jeannine, Jael, Joanna—and whose sociosexual practices cover the spectrum from celibacy and "politically correct" monogamy to live toys and the 1970s equivalent of s/m.[28] What Wittig actually said in one of her essays in the 1980s is perhaps even more extreme:

> The bar in the *j/e* of *The Lesbian Body* is a sign of excess. A sign that helps to imagine an excess of "I," an "I" exalted. "I" has become so powerful in *The Lesbian Body* that it can attack the order of heterosexuality in texts and assault the so-called love, the heroes of love, and lesbianize them, lesbianize the symbols, lesbianize the gods and the goddesses, lesbianize the men and the women. This "I" can be destroyed in the attempt and resuscitated. Nothing resists this "I" (or this *tu* [you], which is its name, its love), which spreads itself in the whole world of the book, like a lava flow that nothing can stop.[29]

Excess, an exaltation of the "I" through costume, performance, mise-en-scène, irony, and utter manipulation of appearance, is what Sue-Ellen Case sees in the discourse of camp. If it is deplorable that the lesbian working-class bar culture of the 1950s "went into the feminist closet" during the 1970s, when organizations such as the Daughters of Bilitis encouraged lesbian identification with the more legitimate feminist dress codes and upwardly mobile lifestyles, writes Case, "yet the closet, or the bars, with their hothouse atmosphere [have] given us camp—the style, the discourse, the *mise-en-scène* of butch-femme roles." In these roles, "recuperating the space of seduction,"

> the butch-femme couple inhabit the subject position together. . . . These are not split subjects, suffering the torments of dominant ideology. They are coupled ones that do not impale themselves on the poles of sexual difference or metaphysical values, but constantly seduce the sign system, through flirtation and inconstancy into the light fondle of artifice, replacing the Lacanian slash with a lesbian bar.[30]

The question of address, of who produces cultural representations and for whom (in any medium, genre, or semiotic system, from writing to performance), and of who receives them and in what contexts, has been a major concern of feminism and other critical theories of cultural marginality. In the visual arts, that concern has focused on the notion of spectatorship, which has been central to the feminist critique of representation and the production of different images of difference, for example in women's cinema.[31] Recent work in both film and performance theory has been elaborating the film-theoretical notion of spectatorship with regard to what may be the specific relations of homosexual subjectivity, in several directions. Elizabeth Ellsworth, for one, surveying the reception of *Personal Best* (1982), a commercial man-made film about a lesbian relationship between athletes, found that lesbian feminist reviews of the film adopted interpretive strategies which rejected or altered the meaning carried by conventional (Hollywood) codes of narrative representation. For example, they redefined who was the film's protagonist or "object of desire," ignored the sections focused on heterosexual romance, disregarded the actual ending and speculated, instead, on a possible extratextual future for the characters beyond the ending. Moreover, "some reviewers named and illicitly eroticized moments of the film's 'inadvertent lesbian verisimilitude' . . . codes of body language, facial expression, use of voice, structuring and expression of desire and assertion of strength in the face of male domination and prerogative."[32]

While recognizing limits to this "oppositional appropriation" of dominant representation, Ellsworth argues that the struggle over interpretation is a constitutive process for marginal subjectivities, as well as an important form of resistance. But when the marginal community is directly addressed, in the context of out-lesbian performance such as the WOW Cafe or the Split Britches productions, the appropriation seems to have no limits, to be directly "subversive," to yield not merely a site of interpretive work and resistance but a representation that requires no interpretive effort and is immediately, univocally legible, signalling "the creation of new imagery, new metaphors, and new conventions that can be read, or given new meaning, by a very specific spectator."[33]

The assumption behind this view, as stated by Kate Davy, is that such lesbian performance "undercut[s] the heterosexual model by implying a spectator that is not the generic, universal male, not the cultural construction 'woman,' but lesbian—a subject defined in terms of sexual similarity . . . whose desire lies outside the fundamental model or underpinnings of sexual difference" (47). Somehow, this seems too easy a solution to the problem of spectatorship, and even less convincing as a representation of "lesbian desire." For, if sexual similarity could so unproblematically replace sexual difference, why would the new lesbian theatre need to insist on gender, if only as "the residue of sexual difference" that is, as Davy herself insists, worn in the "stance, gesture, movement, mannerisms, voice, and dress" (48) of the butch-femme play? Why would lesbian camp be taken up in theatrical performance, as Case suggests, to recuperate that space of seduction which historically has been the lesbian bar, and the Left Bank salon before it—spaces of daily-life performance, masquerade, cross-dressing, and practices constitutive of both community and subjectivity?

In an essay on "The Dynamics of Desire" in performance and pornography, Jill Dolan asserts that the reappropriation of pornography in lesbian magazines ("a visual space meant at least theoretically to be free of male subordination") offers "liberative fantasies" and "representations of one kind of sexuality based in lesbian desire," adding that the "male forms" of pornographic representation "acquire new meanings when they are used to communicate desire for readers of a different gender and sexual orientation."[34] Again, as in Davy, the question of lesbian desire is begged; and again the ways in which the new context would produce new meanings or "disrupt traditional meanings" (173) appear to be dependent on the presumption of a unified lesbian viewer/reader, gifted with undivided and non-contradictory subjectivity, and every bit as generalized and universal as the female spectator both Dolan and Davy impute (and rightly so) to the anti-pornography feminist performance art. For, if all lesbians had one and the same definition of "lesbian desire," there would hardly be any debate among us, or any struggle over interpretations of cultural images, especially the ones we produce.

What is meant by a term so crucial to the specificity and originality claimed for these performances and strategies of representation, is not an inappropriate question, then. When she addresses it at the end of her essay, Dolan writes: "Desire is not necessarily a fixed, male-owned commodity, but can be exchanged, with a much different meaning, between women" (173). Unless it can be taken as the ultimate camp representation, this notion of lesbian desire as commodity exchange is rather disturbing. For, unfortunately—or fortunately, as the case may be—commodity exchange does have the same meaning "between women" as between men, by definition—that is, by Marx's definition of the structure of capital. And so, if the "aesthetic differences between cultural feminist and lesbian performance art" are to be determined by the presence or absence of pornography, and to depend on a "new meaning" of commodity exchange, it is no wonder that we seem unable to get it off (our backs) even as we attempt to take it on.

» » The king does not count lesbians.
     – Marilyn Frye, *The Politics of Reality*

The difficulty in defining an autonomous form of female sexuality and desire in the wake of a cultural tradition still Platonic, still grounded in sexual (in)difference, still caught in the tropism of hommo-sexuality, is not to be overlooked or willfully bypassed. It is perhaps even greater than the difficulty in devising strategies of representation which will, in turn, alter the standard of vision, the frame of reference of visibility, of *what can be seen*. For, undoubtedly, that is the project of lesbian performance, theatre and film, a project that has already achieved a significant measure of success, not only at the WOW Cafe but also, to mention just a few examples, in Cherríe Moraga's *teatro, Giving Up the Ghost* (1986), Sally Potter's film *The Gold Diggers* (1983), or Sheila McLaughlin's *She Must Be Seeing Things* (1987). My point here is that redefining the conditions of vision, as well as the modes of representing, cannot be predicated on a single, undivided identity of performer and audience (whether as "lesbians" or "women" or "people of color" or any other single category constructed in opposition to its dominant other, "heterosexual women," "men," "whites," and so forth).

Consider Marilyn Frye's suggestive Brechtian parable about our culture's conceptual reality ("phallocratic reality") as a conventional stage play, where the actors—those committed to the performance/maintenance of the Play, "the phallocratic loyalists"—visibly occupy the foreground, while stagehands—who provide the necessary labor and framework for the material (re)production of the Play—remain invisible in the background. What happens, she speculates, when the stagehands (women, feminists) begin thinking of themselves as actors and try to participate visibly in the performance, attracting attention to their activities and their own role in the play? The loyalists cannot conceive that anyone in the audience may see or focus their attention on the stagehands' projects in the background, and thus become "disloyal" to the Play, or, as Adrienne Rich has put it, "disloyal to civilization."[35] Well, Frye suggests, there are some people in the audience who do see what the conceptual system of heterosexuality, the Play's performance, attempts to keep invisible. These are lesbian people, who can see it because their own reality is not represented or even surmised in the Play, and who therefore reorient their attention toward the background, the spaces, activities and figures of women elided by the performance. But "attention is a kind of passion" that "fixes and directs the application of one's physical and emotional work":

> If the lesbian sees the women, the woman may see the lesbian seeing her. With this, there is a flowering of possibilities. The woman, feeling herself seen, may learn that she *can be* seen; she may also be able to know that a woman can see, that is, can author perception. . . . The lesbian's seeing undercuts the mechanism by which the production and constant reproduction of heterosexuality for women was to be rendered *automatic.* (172)

And this is where we are now, as the critical reconsideration of lesbian history past and present is doing for feminist theory what Pirandello, Brecht, and others did for the bourgeois theater conventions, and avantgarde filmmakers have done for Hollywood cinema; the latter, however, have not just disappeared, much as one would wish they had. So, too, have the conventions of seeing, and the relations of desire and meaning in spectatorship, remained partially anchored or contained by a frame of visibility that is still heterosexual, or hommo-sexual, and just as persistently color blind.

For instance, what are the "things" the Black/Latina protagonist of McLaughlin's film imagines seeing, in her jealous fantasies about her white lover (although she does not "really" see them), if not those very images which our cultural imaginary and the whole history of cinema have constructed as the visible, *what can be seen,* and eroticized? The originality of *She Must Be Seeing Things* is in its representing the *question* of lesbian desire in these terms, as it engages the contradictions and complicities that have emerged subculturally, in both discourses and practices, through the feminist-lesbian debates on sex-radical imagery as a political issue of representation, as well as real life. It may be interestingly contrasted with a formally conventional film like Donna Deitch's *Desert Hearts* (1986), where heterosexuality remains off screen, in the diegetic background (in the character's past), but is actively present nonetheless in the spectatorial expectations set up by the genre (the love story) and the visual pleasure procured by conventional casting, cinematic narrative procedures, and commercial distribution. In sum, one film works *with and against* the institutions of heterosexuality and cinema, the other works *with* them. A similar point could be made about certain films with respect to the novels they derive from, such as *The Color Purple* (1985) or *Kiss of the Spider Woman* (1985), where the critical and formal work of the novels against the social and sexual indifference built into the institution of heterosexuality is altogether suppressed and rendered invisible by the films' compliance with the apparatus of commercial cinema and its institutional drive to, precisely, commodity exchange.

So what *can* be seen? Even in feminist film theory, the current "impasse regarding female spectatorship is related to the blind spot of lesbianism," Patricia White suggests in her reading of Ulrike Ottinger's film *Madame X: An Absolute Ruler* (1977).[36] That film, she argues, on the contrary, displaces the assumption "that feminism finds its audience 'naturally'" (95); it does so by addressing the female spectator through specific scenarios and "figures of spectatorial desire" and "trans-sex identification," through figures of transvestism and masquerade. And the position the film thus constructs for its spectator is not one of essential femininity or impossible masculinization (as proposed by Mary Ann Doane and Laura Mulvey, respectively), but rather a position of marginality or "deviance" *vis-à-vis* the normative heterosexual frame of vision.[37]

Once again, what *can* be seen? "When I go into a store, people see a black person and only incidentally a woman," writes Jewelle Gomez, a writer of science fiction and author of vampire stories about a black lesbian blues singer named Gilda. "In an Upper West Side apartment building late at night when a white woman refuses to get on an elevator with me, it's because I am black. She sees a mugger as described on the late night news, not another woman as nervous to be out alone as she is."[38] If my suspicion that social and sexual indifference are never far behind one from the other is not just an effect of paranoia, it is quite possible that, in the second setting, the elevator at night, what a white woman sees superimposed on the black image of the mugger is the male image of the dyke, and both of these together are what prevents the white woman from seeing the other one like herself. Nevertheless, Gomez points out, "I can pass as straight, if by some bizarre turn of events I should want to . . . but I cannot pass as white in this society." Clearly, the very issue of passing, across any boundary of social division, is related quite closely to the frame of vision and the conditions of representation.

"Passing demands quiet. And from that quiet—silence," writes Michelle Cliff.[39] It is "a dual masquerade—passing straight/passing lesbian [that] enervates and contributes to speechlessness—to speak might be to reveal."[40] However, and paradoxically again, speechlessness can only be overcome, and her "journey into speech" begin, by "claiming an identity they taught me to despise"; that is, by passing black "against a history of forced fluency," a history of passing white.[41] The dual masquerade, her writing suggests, is at once the condition of speechlessness and of overcoming speechlessness, for the latter occurs by recognizing and representing the division in the self, the difference and the displacement from which any identity that needs to be claimed derives, and hence can be claimed only, in Lorde's words, as "the very house of difference."

Those divisions and displacements in history, memory, and desire are the "ghost" that Moraga's characters want to but cannot altogether give up. The division of the Chicana lesbian Marisa/Corky from the Mexican Amalia, whose desire cannot be redefined outside the heterosexual imaginary of her culture, is also the division of Marisa/Corky from herself, the split produced in the girl Corky by sexual and social indifference, and by her internalization of a notion of hommo-sexuality which Marisa now lives as a wound, an infinite distance between her female body and her desire for women. If "the realization of shared oppression on the basis of being women and Chicanas holds the promise of a community of Chicanas, both lesbians and heterosexual," Yvonne Yarbro-Bejarano states, nevertheless "the structure of the play does not move neatly from pain to promise," and the divisions within them remain unresolved.[42] The character Marisa, however, I would add, has moved away from the hommo-sexuality of Corky (her younger self at age 11 and 17); and with the ambiguous character of Amalia, who loved a man almost as if he were a woman and who can love Marisa only when she (Amalia) is no longer one, the play itself has moved away from any simple opposition of "lesbian" to "heterosexual" and into the conceptual and experiential continuum of a female, Chicana subjectivity from where the question of lesbian desire must finally be posed. The play ends with that question—which is at once its outcome and its achievement, its *éxito*.

>> >> What to do with the feminine invert?
　　　 —Esther Newton, "The Mythic Mannish Lesbian"

Surveying the classic literature on inversion, Newton notes that Rad-clyffe Hall's "vision of lesbianism as sexual difference and as mascu-linity," and her "conviction that sexual desire must be male," both assented to and sought to counter the sociomedical discourses of the early twentieth century. "The notion of a feminine lesbian contradicted the congenital theory that many homosexuals in Hall's era espoused to counter the demands that they undergo punishing 'therapies'" (575). Perhaps that counter-demand led the novelist further to reduce the typol-ogy of female inversion (initially put forth by Krafft-Ebing as comprised of four types, then reduced to three by Havelock Ellis) to two: the invert and the "normal" woman who misguidedly falls in love with her. Hence the novel's emphasis on Stephen, while her lover Mary is a "forgettable and inconsistent" character who in the end gets turned over to a man. However, unlike Mary, Radclyffe Hall's real-life lover Una Troubridge "did not go back to heterosexuality even when Hall, late in her life, took a second lover," Newton points out. Una would then represent what *The Well of Loneliness* elided, the third type of female invert, and the most troublesome for Ellis: the "womanly" women "to whom the actively inverted woman is most attracted. These women differ in the first place from normal or average women in that . . . they seem to possess a genuine, though not precisely sexual, preference for women over men."[43] Therefore, Newton concludes, "Mary's real story has yet to be told" (575), and a footnote after this sentence refers us to "two impressive beginnings" of what could be Mary's real story, told from the perspective of a self-identified, contemporary femme.[44]

The discourses, demands, and counter-demands that inform lesbian identity and representation in the 1980s are more diverse and socially heterogeneous than those of the first half of the century. They include, most notably, the political concepts of oppression and agency developed in the struggles of social movements such as the women's movement, the gay liberation movement, and third world feminism, as well as an awareness of the importance of developing a theory of sexuality that takes into account the working of unconscious processes in the construction of female subjectivity. But, as I have tried to argue, the discourses, demands, and counter-demands that inform lesbian representation are still unwittingly caught in the paradox of socio-sexual (in)difference, often unable to think homosexuality and hommo-sexuality at once separately *and* together. Even today, in most representational contexts, Mary would be either passing lesbian or passing straight, her (homo)sexuality being in the last instance what can not be seen. Unless, as Newton and others suggest, she enter the frame of vision *as or with* a lesbian in male body drag.

Written at the invitation of Sue-Ellen Case, then editor of *Theatre Journal*, and first published in *Theatre Journal*, vol. 40, no. 2 (May 1988), 155–77.

Chapter 3

When Lesbians
Were Not Women

There was a time, in discontinuous space—a space dispersed across the continents—when lesbians were not women. I don't mean to say that now lesbians are women, although a few do think of themselves that way, while others say they are butch or femme; many prefer to call themselves queer or transgender; and others identify with female masculinity—there are lots of self-naming options for lesbians today. But during that time, what lesbians were was that one thing: not women. And it all seemed so clear, at that time.

It would be perhaps appropriate, in [an essay] on Monique Wittig, to mourn her passing and honor her memory with a story, a fiction in the style of *Les guérillères,* an allegory after *Paris-la-politique,* or an epic poem remade like *Virgil, non.* Wittig herself is something of a legend now. But I will not tell you a story—or, not exactly a story. I will reflect on what her work meant for me in the 1980s when I was working in feminist and lesbian studies and how it still intersects with the critical questions that concern me now.

In the 1980s, it was reading Wittig, and the few but wonderfully intense conversations I had with her in northern California, that first started me on the project of writing lesbian theory as distinct from feminist theory. The distinction became clear in my mind only after I read three crucial texts: "The Straight Mind," "One Is Not Born a Woman," and *The Lesbian Body*. In retrospect, it seems to me that a new figure—a conceptual figure—emerged from those works and was encapsulated in the statement "lesbians are not women."[1] Generally misunderstood and criticized from many quarters, nevertheless that statement did fire the imagination and, indeed, from the vantage point of today has proved to be prophetic. As I said a moment ago, today's lesbians are many other things—and only rarely women. But at that time the statement "lesbians are not women" had the power to open the mind and make visible and thinkable a *conceptual* space that until then had been rendered unthinkable by, precisely, the hegemony of the straight mind—as the space called "the blind spot" is rendered invisible in a car's rear-view mirror by the frame or chassis of the car itself. Wittig's writing opened up a conceptual, virtual space that was foreclosed by all discourses and ideologies left and right, including feminism.

In that conceptual virtual space, a different kind of woman appeared to me, if I may say so, after the title of a book we read at that time.[2] I called her the "eccentric subject."[3] For if lesbians are not women and yet lesbians are, like me, flesh and blood, thinking and writing beings who live in the world and with whom I interact every day, then lesbians are social subjects and, in all likelihood, psychic subjects as well. I called that subject "eccentric" not only in the sense of deviating from the conventional, normative path but also eccentric in that it did not center itself in the institution that both supports and produces the straight mind, that is, the institution of heterosexuality. Indeed, that institution did not foresee such a subject and could not contemplate it, could not envision it.

What characterizes the eccentric subject is a double displacement: first, the psychic displacement of erotic energy onto a figure that exceeds the categories of sex and gender, the figure Wittig called "the lesbian," and, second, the self-displacement or disidentification of the subject from the cultural assumptions and social practices attendant upon the categories of gender and sex. Here is how Wittig defined that figure:

Lesbian is the only concept I know of which is beyond the categories of sex (woman and man), because the designated subject (lesbian) is *not* a woman, either economically, or politically, or ideologically. For what makes a woman is a specific social relation to a
man, a relation that we have previously called servitude, a relation
which implies personal and physical obligation as well as economic
obligation ("forced residence," domestic corvée, conjugal duties,
unlimited production of children, etc.), a relation which lesbians
escape by refusing to become or to stay heterosexual. (20)

To refuse the heterosexual contract, not only in one's practice of living
but also in one's practice of knowing—what Wittig called a "subjective, cognitive practice"—constitutes an epistemological shift in that it
changes the conditions of possibility of both knowing and knowledge,
and this constitutes a shift in historical consciousness.[4]

Consciousness of oppression [Wittig wrote] is not only a reaction
to (fight against) oppression. It is also the whole conceptual reevaluation of the social world, its whole reorganization with new
concepts, from the point of view of oppression . . . call it a subjective, cognitive practice. The movement back and forth between
the levels of reality (the conceptual reality and the material reality
of oppression, which are both social realities) is accomplished
through language. (18–19)

The work of language in that movement back and forth is inscribed
in the very title of Wittig's 1980 essay, "On ne naît pas femme." If de
Beauvoir the philosopher had said, "One is not *born* but *becomes* a
woman" (and so, in his way, had Freud), Wittig the writer said, "One
is not born a *woman*" (emphasis added). Almost the same words and
yet such a difference in meaning—not to say such a sexual difference. In
shifting the emphasis from the word *born* to the word *woman,* Wittig's
citation of de Beauvoir's phrase invoked or mimicked the heterosexual
definition of woman as "the second sex," at once destabilizing its meaning and displacing its affect.

Such a shift entails displacement and self-displacement: leaving or giving up a place that is known, that is "home"—physically, emotionally,
linguistically, epistemologically—for another place that is unknown,
that is not only emotionally but also conceptually unfamiliar, a place
from which speaking and thinking are at best tentative, uncertain, un-

authorized. But the leaving is not a choice because one could not live there in the first place. Thus all aspects of the displacement, from the geopolitical to the epistemological and the affective, are painful and risky, for they entail a constant crossing back and forth, a remapping of boundaries between bodies and discourses, identities and communities. At the same time, however, they enable a reconceptualization of the subject, of the relations of subjectivity to social reality, and a position of resistance and agency that is not outside but rather eccentric to the social cultural apparati of the heterosexual institution.

I remember thinking at that time that the possibility to imagine an eccentric subject constituted through disidentification and displacement was somehow related to one's geographical, linguistic, and cultural dislocation—Wittig's, from France to the United States; my own, from Italy to the United States. Only later did I find that a similar conception of the subject was emerging in postcolonial theory and would be subsequently articulated in Homi Bhabha's notion of cultural hybridity and the recent studies on the transnational subject.[5] However, already back then, in the 1980s, I noted the kinship of Wittig's "lesbian" with other figures of eccentric subjects that emerged from the writings of women or lesbians of color such as Trinh T. Minh-ha, Gloria Anzaldúa, Barbara Smith, and Chandra Mohanty. I would argue, therefore, that Wittig's critical writings anticipated some of the emphases of today's postcolonial feminism.

With de Beauvoir and with other feminists of our generation in France, Italy, Britain, and the Americas, Wittig shared the premise that women are not a "natural group" whose oppression would be a consequence of their physical nature but rather a social and political category, an ideological construct, and the product of an economic relation. Most of us, at that time, shared a Marxist understanding of class and a materialist analysis of exploitation, although in Europe that understanding preceded feminism whereas in anglophone America it often followed and resulted from the feminist analysis of gender. I need not tell you about the theory of materialist feminism, because others have done so.[6] I will only say that the definition of gender oppression as a political and subjective category—one arrived at from the specific standpoint of the oppressed, in the struggle, and as a form of consciousness—was distinct from the economic, objective category of exploitation. And that redefinition was also shared by others in North America, such as the black feminist group the Combahee River Collective, for whom gender oppression was indissociable from racist domination.[7]

But Wittig went further: If women are a social class whose specific condition of existence is gender oppression and whose political consciousness affords them a standpoint, a position of struggle, and an epistemological perspective based in lived experience, then what Wittig saw as the goal of feminism was the disappearance of women (as a class). A curious paradox has occurred in the history of feminism since the 1970s in relation to this idea. I will come back to it in a moment, but first allow me to continue with my account of the argument.

In order to imagine what female people would be like in such a classless (i.e., genderless) society, Wittig did not offer a myth or a fiction but referred to the actual existence of a "lesbian society," which, however marginally, did function in a certain way autonomously from heterosexual institutions. In this sense, she claimed, lesbians are not women: "The refusal to become (or to remain) heterosexual always meant to refuse to become a man or a woman, consciously or not. For a lesbian this goes further than the refusal of the *role* 'woman.' It is the refusal of the economic, ideological, and political power of a man."[8] Well, the phrase "lesbian society" had everyone in an uproar. They took it to be descriptive of a type of social organization, or a blueprint for a futuristic, utopian, or dystopian society like the amazons of *Les guérillères* or the all-female communities imagined in Joanna Russ's science fiction novel *The Female Man*. They said Wittig was a utopist, an essentialist, a dogmatic separatist, even a "classic idealist." You cannot be a Marxist, people said, and speak of a lesbian society. You can speak of lesbian society only in the liberal political perspective of free choice, according to which anyone is free to live as they like, and that, of course, is a capitalist myth.

In effect, Wittig mobilized both the discourse of historical materialism and that of liberal feminism in an interesting strategy, one against the other and each against itself, proving them both inadequate to conceiving the subject in feminist materialist terms.[9] To this end, she argued, the Marxist concept of class consciousness and the feminist concept of individual subjectivity must be articulated together. Their joining is what she called a "subjective, cognitive practice," which implies the reconceptualization of the subject and the relations of subjectivity to sociality from a position that is eccentric to the institution of heterosexuality and therefore exceeds its discursive-conceptual horizon: the position of the subject lesbian. Here, then, is the sense in which Wittig proposed the disappearance of women as the goal of feminism.

Critiques came from all quarters of feminism, including many lesbian quarters; for example, those lesbians who wanted to reclaim femininity for women and rehabilitate its traits of nurturing, compassion, tenderness, and caring as equal in value to so-called masculine gender traits; these were the same critics who indicted Wittig's already famous book *The Lesbian Body* for what they called its violence. Critiques came from those who wanted to promote a women's culture, conceived not as a class but as a community of woman-identified women, and from those who favored the idea of a "lesbian continuum" to which any woman who, for whatever reason, had refused or resisted the institution of marriage could rightfully belong—and be considered a lesbian regardless of sexual choice, behavior, or desire. And critiques also came from those who, on the one hand, considered sexuality and desire central to lesbian subjectivity while on the other maintained that heterosexuality necessarily defines homosexuality and dictates the very forms of lesbian and gay sexualities, however subversive or parodic they may be.

These critiques mainly failed to see that Wittig's "lesbian" was not just an individual with a personal "sexual preference" or a social subject with a simply "political" priority but the term or conceptual figure for the subject of a cognitive practice and a form of consciousness that are not primordial, universal, or coextensive with human thought, as de Beauvoir would have it, but historically determined and yet subjectively assumed—an eccentric subject constituted in a process of struggle and interpretation; of translation, detranslation, and retranslation (as Jean Laplanche might put it); a rewriting of self in relation to a new understanding of society, of history, of culture.

Similarly, her critics did not understand that Wittig's "lesbian society" did not refer to some collectivity of gay women but was the term for a conceptual and experiential space carved out of the social field, a space of contradictions in the here and now that need be affirmed and not resolved. When she concluded, "It is *we* who historically must undertake the task of defining the individual subject in materialist terms," that "we" was not the privileged women of de Beauvoir, "qualified to elucidate the situation of woman."[10] Wittig's "we" was the point of articulation from which to rethink both Marxism and feminism; it was, or so it seemed to me, the term of a particular form of feminist consciousness which, at that historical moment, could only exist as the consciousness of a something else; it was the figure of a subject that exceeds its conditions of subjection, a subject in excess of its discursive construction, a subject of which we only knew what it was not: not-woman. Reread the second sentence of *Le corps lesbien:* "Ce qui a cours ici, pas une ne l'ignore, n'a pas de nom pour l'heure."[11]

There is, as I said, a curious paradox in the history of feminism since the 1970s with regard to Wittig's call for the disappearance of women. In a certain sense, women have disappeared from the current lexicon of feminist studies, at least in the anglophone world. It began in the late 1980s, in the wake of identity politics and with the increasing participation of women of color, lesbians and straight, in academic studies, when the word *women* came to be subjected to the same critique that had dismantled the notion of Woman (capital *W, la femme*) by the early 1980s.[12] In the 1990s, then, to speak of women without racial, ethnic, or other geopolitical modifiers was to take for granted a common and equal oppression based on gender or sex, which disregarded concomitant forms of oppression based on racial, ethnic, class, and other differences.[13] The notion of sexual difference was especially targeted and discarded—not without good reasons—as inadequate, insufficient, Eurocentric, and class-centered. Moreover, in the version of poststructuralist feminism that has become popular in academic feminist and queer theory (where the term *poststructuralist* references almost exclusively the influence of the early Foucault and Derrida), women are understood to be simulacra of the social imaginary, with no inherent physical or psychic substance. Women, like gender, sexuality, the subject, and the body itself, according to this view, are all discursive constructs, sites of convergence of the performative effects of power. In this perspective, a concept such as Wittig's "subjective, cognitive practice" and the notion of lived experience, which was central to feminist theory in the 1970s and 1980s, have been dismissed as essentialist, naturalizing, ideological,[14] or, worse, as humanist—which, in the context of the "posthumanist" or postmodern vogue of the 1990s, was definitely a derogatory word. So, in a way, one could say that women *have* disappeared.[15]

The paradox is this: Wittig, who had first proposed the disappearance of women, was herself cast in the essentialist, passé, or humanist camp. In the words of one poststructuralist feminist philosopher, "Wittig calls for a position beyond sex that returns her theory to a problematic humanism based in a problematic metaphysics of presence."[16] The phrase *metaphysics of presence,* a sign of the influence of Jacques Derrida's early work, recurs several times in Judith Butler's *Gender Trouble* (1990), the book that brought Wittig to the attention of nonlesbian and nonfeminist readers, and for this reason will be briefly referred to here. Marketed as a feminist intervention in the field of French philosophy, the book was widely cited and translated and became an authoritative text of gender studies and queer theory. Its extensive discussion of Wittig's work in the disciplinary context of philosophy effectively mainstreamed Monique Wittig as a French feminist theorist (next to the two others whose names circulated widely in North American universities, Luce Irigaray and Julia Kristeva). Butler, however, objected to Wittig's radical stance, which she mistook for what she called a "separatist prescriptivism"—as if Wittig had been arguing that all women should become lesbians or that only lesbians could be feminist.

Like the other critics, Butler failed to understand the figural, theoretical character of Wittig's "lesbian" and its epistemological valence. The subject of a cognitive practice based in the lived experience of one's body, one's desire, one's conceptual and psychical disidentification from the straight mind, Wittig's "lesbian" was well aware of the power of discourse to shape one's social and subjective (and, I would add, psychic) reality: "If the discourse of modern theoretical systems and social science exert[s] a power upon us, it is because it works with concepts which closely touch us," Wittig had written in "The Straight Mind" (26–27). Butler, however, referred to Wittig's lesbian subject as the "cognitive subject," endowing it with strong Cartesian connotations, and tossed her theory in the dump of surpassed and discarded philosophies. To the reader of *Gender Trouble,* Wittig appears to be an existentialist who believes in human freedom, a humanist who presumes the ontological unity of Being prior to language, an idealist masquerading as a materialist, and, most paradoxically of all, an unintentional, unwitting collaborator with the regime of heterosexual normativity.[17] This, in my opinion, may account for the relative disregard or condescension in which Wittig's work has been typically held in gender and queer studies until now. Until, that is, the renewed attention to Wittig's work on the part of a new generation may perhaps reopen another virtual space of lesbian thought and writing.

The conceptual originality and radical import of Wittig's theory are inscribed in her fiction prior to *The Straight Mind*. In *Les guérillères*, the figure of the lesbian as subject of a cognitive practice that enables the reconceptualization of the social and of knowledge itself from a position eccentric to the heterosexual institution is figured in the practice of writing as consciousness of contradiction ("the language you speak is made up of words that are killing you"), a consciousness of writing, living, feeling, and desiring in the noncoincidence of experience and language, in the interstices of representation, "in the intervals that your masters have not been able to fill with their words of proprietors."[18] And it is also already there in the first page of *Le corps lesbien*.

One of the first to grasp this was Elaine Marks, who in "Lesbian Intertextuality" (1979) wrote: "In *Le corps lesbien* Monique Wittig has created, through the incessant use of hyperbole and a refusal to employ traditional body codes, images sufficiently blatant to withstand reabsorption into male literary culture."[19] Indeed, the thematic topos of the voyage in Wittig's fiction corresponds to her formal journey as a writer. Both are voyages without fixed destination, without end, more like a self-displacement that in turn displaces the textual figurations of classical and Christian mythologies, the Homeric heroes and Christ, in Western literary genres and reinscribes them otherwise: *The Divine Comedy* (*Virgil, non*) and *Don Quixote* (*Voyage sans fin*), the epic (*Les guérillères*), the lyric (*Le corps lesbien*), the Bildungsroman (*L'Opoponax*), the encyclopedic dictionary (*Brouillon pour un dictionnaire des amantes*), and later the satire (*Paris-la-politique*), the political manifesto and the critical essay (*The Straight Mind*).

In *Le corps lesbien*, the odyssey of the lesbian subject *j/e* is a journey into language, into the body of Western culture, a season in hell. "Ce qui a cours ici, pas une ne l'ignore, n'a pas de nom pour l'heure." *Ici* refers at once to the events described in the diegesis and to the process of their inscription, the process of writing. The dismemberment of the female body limb by limb, organ by organ, secretion by secretion, is at the same time the deconstruction term by term of the anatomical female body as represented or mapped by patriarchal discourse. The journey and the writing ignore that map, exceed the words of the masters to expose the intervals between them, the gaps of representation, and trespass into the interstices of discourse to reimagine, re-learn, and rewrite the body in another libidinal economy. And yet the journey and the writing do not produce an alternative map, a whole, coherent, healthy female body or a teleological narrative of love between women with a happy ending, till death do us part. On the contrary, death is assumed in the lesbian body; inscribed in it from the beginning. "Fais tes adieux m/a très belle." "Ce qui a cours ici" is death, the slow decomposition of the body, the stench, the worms, the open skull. Death is here and now, because it is the inseparable companion and the condition of desire.

Time and again, over the years, I have returned to this extraordinary text that will not let itself ever be read at one time or "consumed" once and for all. That the book is about desire (nonphallic desire, to be sure) was always clear to me. If Virginia Woolf's *Orlando* has been called the longest love letter in history (to Vita Sackville-West), *Le corps lesbien*, I thought, might be called the longest love poem in modern literature. But what has become clear to me only lately is that *Le corps lesbien* is not about love. It is an extended poetic image of *sexuality*, a canto or a vast fresco, brutal and thrilling, seductive and awe-inspiring.

Let me be clear: I do not mean sexuality in Foucault's sense of a technology that produces "sex" as the truth of proper bourgeois subjects. I mean it in the sense of Freud's conception of sexuality as a psychic drive that disrupts the coherence of the ego; a pleasure principle that opposes, shatters, resists, or compromises the logic of the reality principle. The latter is none other than the symbolic logic of the name of the father, the family, the nation, and all the other institutions of society that are based on the macroinstitution, and the presumption, of heterosexuality. Freud saw these two forces, the pleasure principle and the reality principle, as active concurrently in the psyche and at war with each other. When he later reconfigured them on a scale beyond the individual, he named one Eros and the other death drive. But it is the latter, the death drive and not the Platonic Eros, that is the agent of disruption, unbinding, negativity, and resistance that he had first identified in the sexual drive. It is the death drive, and not Eros, that is most closely, structurally associated with sexuality in Freud's metapsychology, his theory of the psyche.[20]

This warring of two psychic forces is what I now see in Wittig's text: its inscription of the enigma of sexuality and of nonphallic, non-Oedipal desire. And this is perhaps what has always provoked my fascination with *Le corps lesbien* and the urge to return to it time and time again: the enigma that it poses and the enigma that it is.

Written as a contribution to the Symposium *Autour de l'oeuvre politique, théorique et littéraire de Monique Wittig,* Paris, June 2001, and published in French translation in *Parce que les lesbiennes ne sont pas des femmes,* eds. Marie-Hélène Bourcier and Suzette Robichon (Paris: Editions Gaies et Lesbiennes, 2002), 35–53. First published in English in *On Monique Wittig: Theoretical, Political, and Literary Essays,* ed. Namascar Shaktini (Urbana: University of Illinois Press, 2005), 51–62.

II

Readings

M. BUTTERFLY (DAVID CRONENBERG, 1993, USA)

Chapter 4

The Lure of the
Mannish Lesbian

Lesbian scholarship has not had much use for psychoanalysis. Developing in the political and intellectual context of feminism over the past two decades, in the Eurowestern "First World," lesbian critical writing has typically rejected Freud as the enemy of women and consequently avoided consideration of Freudian and neo-Freudian theories of sexuality. Certainly, the feminist mistrust of psychoanalysis as both a male-controlled clinical practice and a popularized social discourse on the "inferiority" of women has excellent, and historically proven, practical reasons. Nevertheless, some feminists have persistently argued that there are also very good theoretical reasons for reading and rereading Freud himself. All the more so for lesbians, I suggest, whose self-definition, self-representation, and political as well as personal identity are not only grounded in the sphere of the sexual, but actually constituted in relation to our sexual difference from socially dominant, institutionalized, heterosexual forms.[1]

One direction of my work, of which this paper presents a small but pivotal fragment, is to reread Freud's writings against the grain of the dominant interpretations that construct a positive, "normal," hetero-sexual and reproductive sexuality, and to look instead for what I would call Freud's negative theory of perversion. For it seems to me that, in his work from the *Three Essays on the Theory of Sexuality* (1905) on, the very notions of a normal sexuality, a normal psychosexual develop-ment, a normal sexual act are inseparable—and indeed derive—from the detailed consideration of their aberrant, deviant or perverse manifesta-tions and components. And we may recall, furthermore, that the whole of Freud's theory of the human psyche, the sexual instincts and their vicissitudes, owes its foundations and development to psychoanalysis, his clinical study of the psychoneuroses; that is to say, those cases in which the mental apparatus and instinctual drives reveal themselves in their processes and mechanisms, which are "normally" hidden or unre-markable otherwise. The normal, in this respect, is only conceivable by approximation, more in the order of a projection than an actual state of being.

What is the advantage of such a project to a lesbian theorist? For one thing, in the perspective of a theory of perversion, lesbian sexual-ity would no longer have to be explained by Freud's own concept of the masculinity complex, which not only recasts homosexuality in the mold of normative heterosexuality, thus precluding all conceptualiza-tion of a female sexuality autonomous from men; but it also fails to account for the non-masculine lesbian, that particular figure that since the nineteenth century has consistently baffled both sexologists and psychoanalysts, and that Havelock Ellis named "the womanly woman," the feminine invert.[2] Secondly, if perversion is understood with Freud as a deviation of the sexual drive (*Trieb*) from the path leading to the reproductive object, that is to say, if perversion is merely another path taken by the drive in its cathexis or choice of object, rather than a pa-thology (although, like every other aspect of sexuality it may involve pathogenic elements), then a theory of perversion would serve to articu-late a model of perverse desire, where perverse means not pathological but rather non-heterosexual or non-normatively heterosexual.[3]

In one of the rare attempts to look at lesbianism in a feminist and psychoanalytic perspective, an article by Diane Hamer suggests that lesbianism, for some women, may be "a psychic repudiation of the category 'woman,'" and sees a direct correspondence between feminism as "a political movement based on a refusal to accept the social 'truth' of men's superiority over women" and lesbianism as "a psychic refusal of the 'truth' of women's castration." In this context, she remarks, "it is interesting to note that Freud referred to both his homosexual women patients as 'feminists.'"[4] Even more interesting, to me, is to see a lesbian theorist decisively and explicitly reappropriate, in feminist perspective, this most contended of Freud's notions, the masculinity complex in women. For, once taken, this step—a very important one, in my opinion, without which our theorizing may just keep on playing in the pre-Oedipal sandbox—Hamer has left behind years of debates on Freud's sexism and feminist outrage, and volumes on Freud's historical limitations and feminist exculpation (debates and volumes, I may add, to which I have myself contributed in some measure). But when she then attempts to define lesbian desire, in Lacanian terms, she runs aground of the corollary to the masculinity complex, namely, the castration complex. This latter, she states, we must refuse:

> Classically, lesbians are thought to pretend possession of the phallus . . . and are thus aligned, albeit fraudulently, on the side of masculinity. In this rather simplistic account lesbian desire becomes near impossible; desire cannot exist *between lesbians,* since they are both on the same side of desire, or, if a lesbian does experience desire, it is bound to be towards a feminine subject who could only desire her back as though she were a man. However, as I have suggested, lesbianism is less a claim to phallic possession (although it may be this too) than it is a refusal of the meanings attached to castration. As such it is a refusal of any easy or straightforward allocation of masculine and feminine positions around the phallus. Instead it suggests a much more fluid and flexible relationship to the positions around which desire is organized. (147)

The problem with this solution—the "refusal of the meanings attached to castration"—is that it begs the question: in the Lacanian framework, symbolic castration is the condition of desire and what constitutes the paternal phallus as the 'allocator' of positions in desire. In other words, castration and the phallus as signifier of desire go hand in hand, one cannot stir without the other. Thus, to reject the notion of castration (to refuse to rethink its terms) is to find ourselves without symbolic means to signify desire.

In this paper, I will up Hamer's defiant gesture and, just as she reappropriates the masculinity complex, I want to reappropriate castration and the phallus for lesbian subjectivity, but in the perspective of Freud's negative theory of perversion. I will propose *a model of perverse desire* based on the one perversion that Freud insisted was not open to women—fetishism.

I take as my starting point a classic text of lesbianism, the classic novel of female sexual inversion, Radclyffe Hall's *The Well of Loneliness*, which, from its obscenity trial in London in 1928 to well into the 1970s, has been the most popular representation of lesbianism in fiction.[5] Thus, it needs no other introduction, except a word of warning: my reading of a crucial passage in the text—crucial because it inscribes a certain fantasy of the female body that works against the grain of the novel's explicit message—is likely to appear far-fetched. This is so, I suggest, because my reading also works against the heterosexual coding of sexual difference (masculinity and femininity) which the novel itself employs and in which it demands to be read.

The Scene at the Mirror

The passage I selected occurs during Stephen's love affair with Angela Crosby, at the height of her unappeased passion and jealousy for the woman who, Stephen correctly suspects, is having an affair with Roger, her most loathed rival. The only things in which Stephen is superior to Roger are social status and, even more relevant to Angela, wealth: Stephen is an independently rich woman at age 21 and some day will be even richer. Though bothered by this "unworthy" thought, Stephen nevertheless seeks to use her money and status to advantage; to impress Angela, she buys her expensive presents and orders herself "a rakish red car" as well as several tailor-made suits, gloves, scarves, heavy silk stockings, toilet water and carnation-scented soap. "Nor could she resist," remarks the narrator, "the lure of pyjamas made of white crêpe de Chine [which] led to a man's dressing-gown of brocade—an amazingly ornate garment" (186). And yet, "on her way back in the train to Malvern, she gazed out of the window with renewed desolation. Money could not buy the one thing that she needed in life; it could not buy Angela's love." Then comes the following short section (book II, chapter 24, section 6):

That night she stared at herself in the glass; and even as she did so she hated her body with its muscular shoulders, its small compact breasts, and its slender flanks of an athlete. All her life she must drag this body of hers like a monstrous fetter imposed on her spirit. This strangely ardent yet sterile body that must worship yet never be worshipped in return by the creature of its adoration. She longed to maim it, for it made her feel cruel; it was so white, so strong and so self-sufficient; yet withal so poor and unhappy a thing that her eyes filled with tears and her hate turned to pity. She began to grieve over it, touching her breasts with pitiful fingers, stroking her shoulders, letting her hands slip along her straight thighs—Oh, poor and most desolate body!

Then, she, for whom Puddle was actually praying at that moment, must now pray also, but blindly; finding few words that seemed worthy of prayer, few words that seemed to encompass her meaning—for she did not know the meaning of herself. But she loved, and loving groped for the God who had fashioned her, even unto this bitter loving. (186–87)

The typographical division that separates the last sentence of the first paragraph, describing the movement of Stephen's hands and fingers on her own body, from the first sentence of the second paragraph cannot disguise the intensely erotic significance of the scene. At face value, the paragraph division corresponds to the ideological division between body and mind, or "spirit," announced in the first paragraph ("all her life she must drag this body of hers like a monstrous fetter imposed on her spirit"), so that the physical, sexual character of Stephen's unappeased love and thwarted narcissistic desire is displaced onto an order of language which excludes her—the prayer to a distant, disembodied God by one who can pray to him because she also has no body, i.e., Puddle, Stephen's tutor and companion, and her desexualized double. While in the first paragraph Stephen "stares" at her own body in the mirror, in the second she is blind, groping—a sudden reversal of the terms of vision which recalls the "nothing to see" of the female sex in psychoanalysis and, in a rhetorical sleight-of-hand, forecloses its view, its sensual perception, denying its very existence.

But a few words belie the (overt) sublimation and the (covert) negation of the sexual that the second paragraph would accomplish: "Then," the first word in it, temporally links the movement of the hands in the preceding paragraph to the final words of the second, "even unto this bitter loving," where the shifter "this" relocates the act of loving in a present moment that can only refer to the culmination or conclusion of the scene interrupted by the paragraph break, the scene of Stephen in front of the mirror "touching her breasts with pitiful fingers, stroking her shoulders, letting her hands slip along her straight thighs (and, if we might fantasize along with the text, watching in the mirror her own hands move downward on her body) . . . even unto this bitter loving." No wonder the next paragraph must rush in to deny both her and us the vision of such an intolerable act.

The message of the novel is clear: Stephen's groping blind and wordless toward an Other who should provide the meaning, but does not, only leads her back to the real of her body, to a "bitter" need which cannot accede to symbolization and so must remain, in Lady Gordon's words, "this *unspeakable* outrage that you call love" (200, emphasis added). As the passage anticipates, the narrative resolution can only be cast in terms of renunciation and salvation, in an order of language that occludes the body in favor of spirit and, with regard to women specifically, forecloses the possibility of any autonomous and non-reproductive female sexuality. Stephen's "sacrifice" of her love for Mary—and, more gruesome still, of Mary's love for her—which concludes Radclyffe Hall's "parable of damnation" (in Catharine Stimpson's words) will ironically reaffirm not just the repression, but indeed the foreclosure or repudiation of lesbianism as such; that is to say, the novel cannot conceive of an autonomous female homosexuality and thus can only confirm Stephen's view of herself as a "freak," a "mistake" of nature, a masculine woman.[6]

The passage, however, contains another, ambiguous message. The scene represents a fantasy of bodily dispossession, the fantasy of an unlovely/unlovable body—a body not feminine or maternal, not narcissistically cherished, fruitful or productive, nor, on the other hand, barren (as the term goes) or abject, but simply imperfect, faulty and faulted, dispossessed, inadequate to bear and signify desire. Because it is not feminine, this body is inadequate as the object of desire, to be desired by the other, and thus inadequate to signify the female subject's desire in its feminine mode; however, because it is masculine but not male, it is also inadequate to signify or bear the subject's desire in the masculine mode. Stephen's body is not feminine, on the stereotypical Victorian model of femininity that is her mother Anna. It is "ardent and sterile," and its taut muscular strength, whiteness and phallic self-sufficiency make Stephen wish to "maim" it, to mark it with a physical, indexical sign of her symbolic castration, her captivity in gender and her semiotic dispossession ("she did not know the meaning of herself") by the Other, the God who made her "a freak of a creature." For she can "worship" the female body in another but "never be worshipped in return." If she hates her naked body, it is because that body is masculine, "so strong and so self-sufficient," so phallic. The body she desires, not only in Angela but also autoerotically for herself, the body she can make love to, is a feminine, female body. Paradoxical as it may seem, the "mythic mannish lesbian" (in Esther Newton's wonderful phrase) wishes to have a feminine body, the kind of female body she desires in Angela and later in Mary—a femme's body. How to explain such a paradox?

The Fantasy of Castration

I want to argue that this fantasy of bodily dispossession is subtended by an original fantasy of castration, in the sense elaborated by Laplanche and Pontalis, with the paternal phallus symbolically present and visible in the muscular, athletic body of Stephen who "dares" to look so like her father.[7] It is that paternal phallus, inscribed in her very body, which imposes the taboo that renders the female body (the mother's, other women's, and her own) forever inaccessible to Stephen, and thus signifies her castration. But before I discuss in what ways, and in what sense, the notion of castration may be reformulated in relation to lesbian subjectivity, I want to point out how the paradox in the passage cited above contradicts, or at least complicates, the more immediate reading of Stephen's masculinity complex. For on the one hand, Stephen's sense of herself depends on a strong masculine identification; yet, on the other hand, it is precisely her masculine, phallic body which bears the mark of castration and frustrates her narcissistic desire in the scene at the mirror. So, in this case, it is not possible simply to equate the phallic with the masculine and castration with the feminine body, as psychoanalysis would have it. And hence the question, What does castration mean in relation to lesbian subjectivity and desire?

The difficulty of the psychoanalytic notion of castration for feminist theory is too well known to be rehearsed once again. To sum it up in one sentence, the problem lies in the definition of female sexuality as *complementary* to the physiological, psychic, and social needs of the male, and yet as a *deficiency* vis-a-vis his sexual organ and its symbolic representative, the phallus—a definition which results in the exclusion of women not from sexuality (for, on the contrary, women are the very locus of the sexual), but rather from the field of desire. There is another paradox in this theory, for the very effectiveness of symbolic castration consists precisely in allowing access to desire, the phallus representing at once the mark of difference and lack, the threat of castration, and the signifier of desire. But access to desire through symbolic castration, the theory states, is only for the male. The female's relation to symbolic castration does not allow her entry into the field of desire as subject, but only as object.

This is so, Freudians and Lacanians join forces in saying, because women lack the physical property that signifies desire: not having a penis (the bodily representative and support of the libido, the physical referent which in sexuality, in fantasy, becomes the signifier, or more properly the sign-vehicle, the bearer, of desire), females are effectively castrated, symbolically, in the sense that they lack—they do not have and will never have—the paternal phallus, the means of symbolic access to the first object of desire that is the mother's body. It is the potential for losing the penis, the *threat* of castration, that subjects the male to the law of the father and structures the male's relation to the paternal phallus as one of insufficiency; and it is that potential for loss which gives the penis its potential to attain the value or the stature of the paternal phallus. Having nothing to lose, the theory goes, women cannot desire; having no phallic capital to invest or speculate on, as men do, women cannot be investors in the marketplace of desire but are instead commodities that circulate in it.[8]

Feminist theorists, following Lacan, have sought to disengage the notion of castration from its reference to the penis by making it purely a condition of signification, of the entry into language, and thus the means of access to desire. Silverman, for example, states: "One of the crucial features of Lacan's redefinition of castration has been to shift it away from this obligatory anatomical referent [the penis] to the lack induced by language."[9] Yet the semiotic bond between the signification of the phallus and the "real" penis remains finally indissoluble: "No one has the phallus but the phallus is the male sign, the man's assignment . . . The man's masculinity, his male world, is the assertion of the phallus to support his having it."[10]

In all such arguments, however, nearly everyone fails to note that the Lacanian framing of the question in terms of having or being the phallus is set in the perspective of normative heterosexuality (which both analysis and theory seek to reproduce in the subject), with the sexual difference of man and woman clearly mapped out and the act of copulation firmly in place.[11] But what if, I ask, we were to reframe the question of the phallus and the fantasy of castration in the perspective provided by Freud's negative theory of perversion?

With regard to the passage from *The Well of Loneliness* (but it could be shown of other lesbian texts as well), let me emphasize that, if it does inscribe a fantasy of castration, it also, and very effectively, speaks desire, and thus is fully in the symbolic, in signification. Yet the desire it speaks is not masculine, not simply phallic. But, if the phallus is both the mark of castration and the signifier of desire, then the question is: What manner of desire is this? What acts as the phallus in this lesbian fantasy? I will propose that it is not the paternal phallus, or a phallic symbol, but something of the nature of a fetish, something which signifies at once the absence of the object of desire (the female body) and the subject's wish for it.

A Model of Perverse Desire

In the clinical view of fetishism, the perversion is related to the subject's disavowal of the mother's castration, which occurs by a splitting of the ego as a defense from the threat of castration. Disavowal implies a contradiction, a double or split belief: on the one hand, the recognition that the mother does not have a penis as the father does; and yet, on the other hand, the refusal to acknowledge the absence of the penis in the mother. As a result of this disavowal, the subject's desire is metonymically displaced, diverted onto another object, part of the body, clothing, etc., which acts as "substitute" (Freud says) for the missing maternal penis. In this way, Freud writes, to the child who is to become a fetishist "the woman has got a penis, in spite of everything, but this penis is no longer the same as it was before. Something else *has* taken its place, has been appointed its substitute, as it were, and now inherits the interest which was formerly directed to its predecessor."[12] In this diversion consists, for Freud, the *perversion* of the sexual instinct, which is thus diverted or displaced from its legitimate object and reproductive aim. But since the whole process, the disavowal (*Verleugnung*) and the displacement (*Verschiebung*), is motivated by the subject's fear of his own possible castration, what it brings into evidence is the fundamental role in fetishism of the paternal phallus (that which is missing in the mother). And this is why, Freud states, fetishism does not apply to women: they have nothing to lose, they have no penis, and thus disavowal would not defend their ego from an already accomplished "castration."

However, argues an interesting essay by Leo Bersani and Ulysse Dutoit, Freud placed too much emphasis on the paternal phallus. "The fetishist can see the woman as she is, without a penis, because he loves her with a penis somewhere else," they say:

> The crucial point—which makes the fetishistic object different from the phallic symbol—is that the success of the fetish depends on its being seen as authentically different from the missing penis. With a phallic symbol, we may not be consciously aware of what it stands for, but it attracts us because, consciously or unconsciously, we perceive it as the phallus. In fetishism, however, the refusal to see the fetish as a penis-substitute may not be simply an effect of repression. The fetishist has displaced the missing penis from the woman's genitals to, say, her underclothing, but we suggest that if he doesn't care about the underclothing resembling a penis it is because: (1) he knows that it is not a penis; (2) he doesn't want it to be only a penis; and (3) he also knows that *nothing* can replace the lack to which in fact he has resigned himself.[13]

Thus, to the fetishist, the fetish does much more than *replace* the penis, "since it signifies something which was never anywhere": it "derange[s] his *system of desiring*," even as far as "deconstructing and mobilizing the self." Unlike a phallic symbol, which stands for the perceived penis, the fetish is a "fantasy-phallus," "an inappropriate object precariously attached to a desiring fantasy, unsupported by any perceptual memory." Fetishism, they conclude, outlines a model of desire dependent on "an ambiguous negation of the real. . . . This negation creates an interval between the new object of desire and an unidentifiable first object, and as such it may be the model for all substitutive formations in which the first term of the equation is lost, or unlocatable, and in any case ultimately unimportant." And they suggest that "the process which *may* result in pathological fetishism can also have a permanent psychic validity of a formal nature" (71, emphasis added).

I will follow up their argument and propose that if—and admittedly it's a big if, but not a speculation alien to or unprecedented in psychoanalytic theory[14]—if the psychic process of disavowal that detaches desire from the paternal phallus in the fetishist can *also* occur in other subjects, and have enduring effects or formal validity as a psychic process, then this "formal model of desire's mobility," which I prefer to call *perverse desire*, is eminently applicable to lesbian sexuality.

The Fetish as Fantasy-Phallus

Consider the following three statements from their essay cited above, with the word lesbian in lieu of the word fetishist: 1) the lesbian can see the woman as she is, without a penis, because she loves her with a penis somewhere else; 2) the lesbian also knows that nothing can replace the lack to which in fact she has resigned herself; 3) lesbian desire is sustained and signified by a fetish, a fantasy-phallus, an inappropriate object precariously attached to a desiring fantasy, unsupported by any perceptual memory. In other words, what the lesbian desires in a woman and in herself ("the penis somewhere else") is indeed not a penis but the whole or perhaps a part of the female body, or something metonymically related to it, such as physical, intellectual or emotional attributes, stance, attitude, appearance, self-presentation, and hence the importance of performance, clothing, costume, etc. She knows full well she is not a man, she doesn't have the paternal phallus, but that does not necessarily mean she has no means to signify desire: the fantasy-phallus is at once what signifies her desire and what she desires in a woman. As Joan Nestle put it,

> For me, the erotic essence of the butch-femme relationship was the external difference of women's textures and the bond of knowledgeable caring. I loved my lover for how she stood as well as for what she did. Dress was a part of it: the erotic signal of her hair at the nape of her neck, touching the shirt collar; how she held a cigarette; the symbolic pinky ring flashing as she waved her hand. I know this sounds superficial, but all these gestures were a style

of self-presentation that made erotic competence a political statement in the 1950s . . . Deeper than the sexual positioning was the
overwhelming love I felt for [her] courage, the bravery of [her]
erotic independence.[15]

The object and the signifier of desire are not anatomical entities,
such as the female body or womb and the penis respectively; they are
fantasy entities, objects or signs that have somehow become "attached
to a desiring fantasy" and for that very reason may be "inappropriate"
(to signify those anatomical entities) and precarious, not fixed or the
same for every subject, and even unstable in one subject. But if there is
no privileged, founding object of desire, if "the objects of our desires
are always substitutes for the objects of our desires" (as Bersani and
Dutoit put it), nevertheless desire itself, with its movement between
subject and object, between the self and an other, is founded on difference and dependent on "the sign which describes both the object and
its absence" (Laplanche and Pontalis).

This is why a notion of castration and a notion of phallus as signifier
of desire are necessary to signify lesbian desire and subjectivity, although
they must be redefined in reference to the female body, and not the penis.
It is not just that fantasies of castration have a central place in lesbian
texts, subjectivity and desire. It is also that what I have called the fetish
or fantasy-phallus, in contradistinction to the paternal penis-phallus,
serves as the bearer, the signifier, of difference and desire. Without it,
the lesbian lovers would be merely two women in the same bed. The
lesbian fetish, in other words, is any object, any "inappropriate object
precariously attached to a desiring fantasy," any sign whatsoever, that
marks the difference and the desire between the lovers—for instance,
again in Nestle's words, "the erotic signal of her hair at the nape of her
neck, touching the shirt collar," or "big-hipped, wide-assed women's
bodies."

The Wound and the Scar

Returning, then, to the text I started from, it may now be possible to
see its fantasy of bodily dispossession as related to a somewhat different
notion of castration. Let me recall for you the passage in *The Well of
Loneliness* where, in describing Stephen's purchase of clothes intended

to impress Angela—and they are, as we know, masculine-cut or mannish clothes—the narrator tells us: "Nor could she resist the lure of pyjamas made of crêpe de Chine [which] led to a man's dressing-gown of brocade—an amazingly ornate garment". Now, we can be almost sure that Angela would never see those pyjamas and dressing gown. And yet Stephen *could not resist their lure.* Just as she hates her masculine body naked, so does she respond to the lure of masculine clothes; and we may remember, as well, the intensity with which both Stephen Gordon and her author Radclyffe Hall yearned to cut their hair quite short, against all the contemporary appearance codes. What I am driving at, is that masculine clothes, the insistence on riding astride, and all the other accoutrements and signs of masculinity, up to the war scar on her face, are Stephen's fetish, her fantasy-phallus. This does explain the paradox of the scene at the mirror, in which she hates her *naked* body and wants to "maim" it (to inscribe it with the mark of castration) precisely because it is masculine, "ardent and sterile . . . so strong and so self-sufficient," so phallic, whereas the body she desires and wants to make love to, another's or her own, is a feminine, female body.

Consider, if you will, this scene at the mirror as the textual reenactment of the Lacanian mirror stage which, according to Laplanche and Pontalis, constitutes the matrix or first outline of the ego.

> The establishment of the ego can be conceived of as the formation of a psychical unit paralleling the constitution of the bodily schema. One may further suppose that this unification is precipitated by the subject's acquisition of an image of himself founded on the model furnished by the other person—this image being the ego itself. Narcissism then appears as the amorous captivation of the subject by this image. Jacques Lacan has related this first moment in the ego's formation to that fundamentally narcissistic experience which he calls the *mirror stage.*[16]

What Stephen sees in the mirror (the image which establishes the ego) is the image of a phallic body, which the narrator has taken pains to tell us was so from a very young age, a body Stephen's mother found "repulsive." This image which Stephen sees in the mirror does not accomplish "the amorous captivation of the subject" or offer her a "fundamentally narcissistic experience," but on the contrary inflicts a narcissistic wound, for that phallic body, and thus the ego, cannot be narcissistically loved.[17]

The fantasy of castration here, is explicitly associated with a failure of narcissism, the lack or threatened loss of a *female* body, from which would derive in consequence the defense of disavowal, the splitting of the ego, the ambiguous negation of the real. What is formed in the process of disavowal, then, is not a phallic symbol, a penis-substitute (indeed Stephen hates her masculine body), but a fetish—something that would cover over or disguise the narcissistic wound, and yet leave a scar, a trace of its enduring threat. Thus Stephen's fetish, the signifier of her desire, is the sign of both an absence and a presence: the denied and wished-for female body is both displaced and represented in the fetish, the visible signifiers and accoutrements of masculinity, or what Esther Newton has called "male body drag." That is the lure of the mannish lesbian—a lure for her and for her lover. The fetish of masculinity is what lures and signifies her desire, and what in her lures her lover, what her lover desires in her. Unlike the masculinity complex, the lesbian fetish of masculinity does not refuse castration but disavows it; the threat it holds at bay is not the loss of the penis in women but the loss of the female body itself, and the prohibition of access to it.

To conclude, in this lesbian text, the subject's body is inscribed in a fantasy of castration, which speaks a failure of narcissism. I cannot love myself, says the subject of the fantasy, I need another woman to love me (Anna Gordon was repulsed by her daughter) and to love me sexually, bodily (the sexual emphasis is remarked by the masturbation scene barely disguised in the passage). This lover must be a woman, not a man, and not a faulty woman, dispossessed of her body (such as I am) but a woman-woman, a woman embodied and self-possessed, as I would want to be and as I can only become by her love.

> But in fact we were always like this,
> rootless, dismembered: knowing it makes the difference.
> Birth stripped our birthright from us,
> tore us from a woman, from women, from ourselves
> so early on
> and the whole chorus throbbing at our ears
> like midges, told us nothing, nothing
> of origins, nothing we needed
> to know, nothing that could re-member us.

Only: that it is unnatural,
the homesickness for a woman, for ourselves,
for that acute joy at the shadow her head and arms
cast on a wall, her heavy or slender
thighs on which we lay, flesh against flesh,
eyes steady on the face of love; smell of her milk, her sweat,
terror of her disappearance, all fused in this hunger
for the element they have called most dangerous, to be
lifted breathtaken on her breast, to rock within her
—even if beaten back, stranded again, to apprehend
in a sudden brine-clear thought
trembling like the tiny, orbed, endangered
egg-sac of a new world:
This is what she was to me, and this
is how I can love myself—
as only a woman can love me.

  (Adrienne Rich, from "Transcendental Etude")[18]

Nevertheless, the fantasy of dispossession is so strong in the text that Stephen ends up still dispossessed, in spite of having had (and given up) a woman lover. If the sense of belonging to "one's own kind," the political presence of a community—the "thousands" and "millions" like her for whom Stephen writes and implores God at the close of the novel, mirroring the author's purpose in writing it and predicting its enormous success and impact on its readers—can soothe the pain and provide what Radclyffe Hall calls "that steel-bright courage . . . forged in the furnace of affliction," nevertheless the narcissistic wound remains, unhealed under the scar that both acknowledges and denies it. The wound and the scar, castration and the fetish, constitute an original fantasy that is repeated, reenacted in different scenarios, in lesbian writing and in lesbian eros.

Written as a short version of chapter 5 of *The Practice of Love* (in progress at that time) at the invitation of Susan Magarey, then editor of *Australian Feminist Studies,* and first published in *Australian Feminist Studies,* no. 13 (Autumn 1991), 15–26.

Chapter 5

Letter to an
Unknown Woman

Prologue

W hen I was invited to contribute to a volume on Freud's "Psychogenesis of a Case of Homosexuality in a Woman," I saw an opportunity for reconsidering what I had written on this singular case history a few years ago in *The Practice of Love*. In that book I revisited the classic texts of Freudian psychoanalysis on female homosexuality (Freud, Jones, Lampl-de Groot, Deutsch, and Lacan) as part of a larger project concerned with theorizing lesbian sexuality and desire. To that end, I reexamined Freud's theory of sexuality and what little he and others had said specifically on the topic of female homosexuality, in conjunction, in contrast, and in counterpoint with texts of lesbian self-representation—literary, filmic, and critical texts. My project was not clinically based but was conceptually framed in psychoanalytic terms and elaborated a model of desire that, while not disregarding the psychic structure of the Oedipus complex, did nevertheless exceed its terms. I called it *perverse desire.*

Shortly before and since my book was published, several essays devoted to Freud's "Psychogenesis" have appeared.[1] All of them contribute to the ongoing critical discourse on female (homo)sexuality, many referring to the Dora case history as well. They are insightful critiques of Freud's text, demonstrating the inadequacy of his conceptual framework and the blind spots of his analytical method, and raising issues of countertransference and personal or ideological bias. But, even as their authors prove as capable of astute textual analyses as Freud himself and often, as it were, beat him at his own game, they remain within the confines of a textual reading or an exegesis of the case history itself. None of them ventures beyond the master's narrative or seeks to theorize beyond the limitations they describe in it. My own reading of "Psychogenesis," coming as it did early on in the writing of the book, was also cast as a critique of Freud's text: It remarked its incoherence and distress in the face of a question, What does the homosexual woman want? and in the face of a girl who did not respond to treatment, to his theory of the Oedipus, or to him personally.

And yet the larger project of my book did intend to go beyond Freud, to elaborate a model of desire beyond the Oedipus, to understand lesbian sexuality beyond the commonplace of the masculinity complex and the pre-Oedipal fixation on the mother. Such a theory, I argued in *The Practice of Love*, Freud could not envision but in some way suggested in the *Three Essays on the Theory of Sexuality*. In the first essay, if only dimly, by negation, and clothed in ambiguity, he adumbrated a theory of sexuality as perversion, on which then, in the last two essays, he imposed the structuring narrative of the Oedipus complex. And it was finally Freud's later conception of disavowal [*Verleugnung*] and the psychic mechanism he named "splitting of the ego" [*Ichspaltung*] that allowed me to work out progressively, through several chapters of the book, a model of perverse or fetishistic desire that I saw reflected in the lesbian texts. But I never went back to reconsider Freud's singular "case of homosexuality in a woman" in light of that model.

My first thought, when I agreed to contribute to this volume, was to do just that, to reread the story of Freud's "girl" against my model of perverse desire. Soon, however, I realized that that could not be done because a case history belongs to its writer, not to its case: It is the history of a case, the reconstruction of a psychic trajectory, an interpretation, a representation, a text of fiction, and not a "true story." It is a text that bears the inscription of a subjectivity, a desire, that are much more its writer's, Freud's, than those of its central character, whether named or unnamed. As Madame Bovary "is" Flaubert, as Heathcliff "is" Emily Brontë, so is the girl a mirror reflecting Freud in his efforts to work out his theory of psychoanalysis, to refine his clinical technique, to further his understanding of homosexuality and/or bisexuality, and above all to confirm his belief in the Oedipus complex. What we know about the girl is what he tells us, what she says is in answer to his questions; even her indifference is a sign of *his* feeling rejected, unrecognized, irrelevant.

Thus, at the same time, I also realized why all the other commentators on this case history remained caught in the textual web of ambiguities, inconsistencies, contradictions, or evasions spun by Freud: If only exegetic one-upmanship or rhetorical escalation could provide an adequate reading, it was because Freud's text was the only game in town. Conversely, if I had been able to understand lesbian desire as structured by fetishism and disavowal rather than, as Freud does, by the (inverted) Oedipus complex, it was because the texts I was reading, unlike Freud's, inscribed a lesbian subjectivity and authorial desire. Were I now to undertake a second reading of "Psychogenesis," I could do no more than produce yet another exegesis of the case, perhaps another critique of Freud, but no advance would be made in illuminating "the mystery of [the girl's] homosexuality."[2]

For my contribution to this volume, then, I will extend my earlier reading of "Psychogenesis" (which will appear here in the section entitled "The Master's Narrative") to emphasize how Freud's understanding of the case was overdetermined by his own project—on the one hand, by his preoccupation with homosexuality and, on the other, by a passionate fiction, the Oedipus complex, which, after all, was the enabling fiction of his invention of psychoanalyis. For it is this Oedipal fantasy that structures the narrative of "Psychogenesis," although, as we shall see, Freud himself was dissatisfied with it. In the second part of this chapter, I will suggest that something else besides the Oedipus is going on in homosexual desire, and I will propose another, non-Oedipal model of sexual structuring that may account for the "psychogenesis" of lesbianism in some women.

I call this chapter "Letter to an Unknown Woman" in reference to a film by Max Ophuls [Oppenheimer], *Letter from an Unknown Woman* (United States, 1948), adapted from a 1924 novella by Stefan Zweig, the Viennese writer and friend of Freud's. The letter is written by Lisa (played by Joan Fontaine) just before dying to the man she has loved in silence all her life and by whom she conceived a child in the one night they spent together. The film is a single, uninterrupted flashback of scenes spread over a lifetime and joined together by Lisa's voiceover narration. Not unlike a psychoanalysis, the film represents a subject, Lisa, existing only through memory and desire; it reconstructs her from disconnected images and words by selecting events or scenes and giving them narrative continuity, as secondary elaboration does with the fragments of a dream.

"By the time you read this letter, I may be dead," Lisa's letter begins. Through the fiction of the letter addressed to Stefan (played by Louis Jourdan), the film recreates her now-ended existence and unending love for him, thus making Lisa and her desire known to the spectator as well. As my title suggests, I will be speaking of a woman who remains unknown, although Freud tells her story in "Psychogenesis." This is the only major case history of Freud's in which the patient is not given a (fictitious) name, and thus not given the status of fictional character; he simply calls her the girl, "*das Mädchen.*" But it is not only the girl's name that remains unknown to the reader; it is also the nature of her desire, which Freud attempts to analyze but is finally unable to explain to his satisfaction—or to mine. What I want to address here is the problem of representing (naming) the desire of a woman such as the girl in Freud's story and the conditions of its representability. My "letter," therefore, is addressed to whom it may concern.

The Master's Narrative

"A beautiful and clever girl of eighteen, belonging to a family of good standing, had aroused displeasure and concern in her parents by the devoted adoration with which she pursued a certain 'society lady' who was about ten years older than herself." Thus begins, in the best fashion of the genre, the master's narrative of "The Psychogenesis of a Case of Homosexuality in a Woman." Immediately before this sentence, in the first paragraph of the case history, Freud makes his customary invocation to the muse of method: Since female homosexuality has been heretofore neglected by psychoanalytic theory as it has been by the law, then even "the narration of a single case, not too pronounced in type, in which it was possible to trace its origin and development in the mind with complete certainty and almost without a gap may, therefore, have a certain claim to attention" (147). But the presumption of "complete certainty" that opens what promises to be a full account ("almost without a gap") of the heroine's homosexual development is cast in serious doubt several pages later:

> This amount of information about her seems meager enough, nor can I guarantee that it is complete. It may be that the history of her youth was much richer in experiences; I do not know. As I have already said, the analysis was broken off after a short time, and therefore yielded an anamnesis not much more reliable than the other anamneses of homosexuals, which there is good cause to question. Further, the girl had never been neurotic, and came to the analysis without even one hysterical symptom, so that opportunities for investigating the history of her childhood did not present themselves so readily as usual. (155)

This pattern of alternating assertion and disclaimer, certainty and doubt, presumption and condescension recurs in each of the four parts that make up the story and the analysis. Each part contains elements of both: a diegetic section about the girl's history is preceded or followed by an exegetic or interpretive section, often augmented by considerations of a theoretical nature in the form of digressions on analytic technique and dream interpretation, as well as digressions on bisexuality and homosexuality itself. For example, part II opens with these words: "After this highly discursive introduction I am only able to present a very concise summary of the sexual history of the case under consideration. In childhood the girl had passed through the normal attitude characteristic of the feminine Oedipus complex" (155); and the paragraph ends with the disclaimer about the unreliable anamnesis I cited earlier. Part IV also begins with the words, "I now come back, after this digression, to the consideration of my patient's case" (167).

While the pattern may recall the actual movement of the analysis, with its slow progress, setbacks, and occasional breakthroughs, it also underscores the contrast between Freud's confidence in his doctrinal premises and the need to have recourse to them in moments of uncertainty, as if to find reassurance and interpretive strength against the difficulties caused by the patient's unreliability, her unforthcoming or negative transference, and his own problematic (unavowed) countertransference.

The latter difficulties are not new to Freud, since he encountered them in the analysis of "Dora" and recorded them in *Fragment of an Analysis of a Case of Hysteria,* originally published in 1905.[3] There, too, the stumbling block was the patient's resistance to an interpretation in which the father "played the principal part" both in the diegesis (the girl's father or his substitutes) and in the exegesis (Freud, the analyst, with his undisguised wish to be loved): "In reality she transferred to me the sweeping repudiation of men which had dominated her ever since the disappointment she had suffered from her father. . . . But I still believe that, beside the intention to mislead me, the dreams partly expressed the wish to win my favor."[4] Like Dora, this patient resists Freud's attribution of her problems to her resistance against the Oedipal imperative and will not gratify him by assenting to what he can only see as "her keenest desire—namely, revenge" (160) against her father(s). Dora's "revenge" had been to break off the analysis, to give him a two-week notice as one would a paid employee, one socially inferior; and so does this girl, in effect, "by rendering futile all his endeavours and by clinging to the illness" (164); so much so that he is forced to break off treatment himself and recommend *a woman doctor* as someone better equipped to continue the treatment.

However, whereas Dora apparently had problems, manifested by her various hysterical symptoms, this girl clearly does not.[5] So Freud now must explain why her homosexuality is a problem. It would be simple enough to repeat that it is a problem only for her parents, who sought his advice because they were preoccupied with social conventions (although the father is more than just angry with her, as Freud perceptively notes: "There was something about his daughter's homosexuality that aroused the deepest bitterness in him" [149]). But Freud does not leave it at that. He has some stake in proving that it is a problem for the girl as well. For one might ask: So what, if "she changed into a man and took her mother [substitute] in place of her father as the object of her love" (158)—what's wrong with that? What's wrong with a woman's masculinity complex provided she is not in the least neurotic and has no symptoms? Why is this not simply one outcome of that "universal bisexuality of human beings" (157), which Freud has just defined, a moment ago, with Olympian serenity: "In all of us, throughout life, the libido *normally* oscillates between male and female objects" (158, emphasis added). Pressed closely by such feminist arguments, however, his answer is adamant: No, the problem is that in her the libido did not oscillate, and "[h]enceforth she *remained* homosexual out of defiance against her father" (159, emphasis added). Defiance and resistance, in other words, are the specific symptoms of female homosexuality; they are what makes it perverse and such that, unlike neurosis and hysteria, psychoanalysis is impotent to alter it.

From the start, it must be added in all fairness, Freud did caution us that this was not "the ideal situation for analysis." The girl was not ill, had no symptoms, no complaint of her condition, and no will to change: "She did not try to deceive me by saying that she felt any urgent need to be freed from her homosexuality. On the contrary, she said she could not conceive of any other way of being in love" (153). Thus his analytic task was most difficult, for it consisted not in resolving a neurotic conflict but in converting one variety of genital organization into the other. And "such an achievement," Freud pleads, if possible at all, is

> never an easy matter. On the contrary I have found success pos-
> sible only in specially favorable circumstances, and even then the
> success essentially consisted in making access to the opposite sex
> (which had hitherto been barred) possible to a person restricted to
> homosexuality, thus restoring his full bisexual functions. (151)

At this point in the text, the narrative has given way to a theoretical digression on the topic of homosexuality, where Freud discusses various cases in his experience, their causal factors, their prognoses, and their resolutions. If one has the definite impression that he is speaking of male patients here, it is less by dint of the masculine pronoun, or the familiarity one may have with his only other written case of (presumed) female homosexuality, "A Case of Paranoia," than because of Freud's dispassionate and almost benevolent tone, which is set early on by his equanimous admission of having a rather poor track record in successful treatments.[6] It is as if these failures, these patients' "abnormalities" and their bisexual or homosexual genital organizations, did not affect his professional self-esteem or make his analytic task particularly difficult, as does the case of the girl.

On the positive side, however, at least as far as the reader is concerned, the difficulties brought about by this case make Freud work harder, both as analyst and as theorist. Somehow he is impelled by this girl to come to terms with homosexuality in its female form, to try to figure out how it fits into his overall theory, to explain why "full bisexuality" is not really an option, or a cure, for this patient, and just what kind of perversion it is. For all his troubles, he scores one victory and one defeat. The victory is diegetic and analytic: The enigma of the story is solved by the birth of a brother, when the girl was sixteen, and the dénouement provides the explanation for her homosexuality as a rejection of the Oedipal imperative compounded by revenge against the father. The enigma, as the narrative presents it, is: Why did the girl become "a homosexual attracted to mature women, and remained so ever since" (156) when, in fact, her mother favored the girl's brothers, generally acted unkindly toward her, and vied with her for the father's love? Freud answers:

> The explanation is as follows. It was just when the girl was experiencing the revival of her infantile Oedipus complex at puberty that she suffered her great disappointment. She became keenly conscious of the wish to have a child, and a male one; that what she desired was her *father's* child and an image of *him,* her consciousness was not allowed to know. And what happened next? It was not *she* who bore the child, but her unconsciously hated rival, her mother. Furiously resentful and embittered, she turned away from her father and from men altogether. After this first great reverse she forswore her womanhood and sought another goal for her libido. In doing so she behaved just as many men do who after a first distressing experience turn their backs forever upon the faithless female sex and become woman-haters. (157)

There are as many holes in this explanation as there are turns in the narrative: The girl is conscious of wanting a child but unconscious of wanting the father's child (his image); she is unconscious of hating the mother/rival yet consciously rejects her and, with her, both femininity and motherhood; she consciously hates and defies the father but unconsciously (still loves and) identifies with him; she consciously falls in love with a woman and becomes a woman-hater. Because the toggle-switch term *conscious/unconscious*—which Freud here uses in the common, rather than technical or systemic sense—acts as a sort of joker in the exegetic game, the holes turn out to be, rather, loopholes, and make it as difficult to disprove or argue against each of these propositions as it would be to prove them. However, it is clear that the whole house of cards rests on the founding stone of the positive Oedipus complex (the wish for a child by the father). This is the first move of Freud's interpretive "journey" here as elsewhere with regard to female sexuality. He imagines it as the (asymmetrical) counterpart of the male's positive Oedipus complex, which leads him to the conclusive parallel with men and the last, paradoxical proposition: Women who love women hate women. (Freud's notorious disregard for a girl's erotic attachment to the mother—what he would later call the negative Oedipus complex—was subsequently redressed and amended by women analysts such as Lampl-de Groot and Deutsch but with no significant gain as regards changing the Oedipal paradigm.)

On the strength of this interpretation, finally, it would seem that the girl's masculinity complex, already "strongly marked" since childhood, was reinforced and perverted by the "occasion" of the mother's late pregnancy, which pushed it over the brink and made the girl "fall a victim to homosexuality" (168). Freud's hard-won interpretive victory, however, is a Pyrrhic victory in that it is accompanied by a defeat in the theoretical project of explaining homosexuality. For in part IV of the text, as he retraces forward the steps that the analysis had followed backward, he must admit that "we no longer get the impression of an inevitable sequence of events which could not have been otherwise determined. We notice at once that there might have been another result" (167). This statement all but unravels the complicated exegetic skein: The causes of the girl's homosexuality, which the analytic narration reconstructed "with complete certainty and almost without a gap" into a seamless narrative, where every "external factor" could be accounted for, are now said to be by no means a necessary or sufficient condition of her homosexual disposition, a disposition that may or may not have been acquired but, at any rate, at least in part, "has to be ascribed to inborn constitution" (169). And if we search the text for signs of what that inborn constitution might be, we can only find that "strongly marked 'masculinity complex,'" which the girl "had brought along with her from her childhood":

A spirited girl, always ready for romping and fighting, she was not at all prepared to be second to her slightly older brother; after inspecting his genital organs [. . .] she had developed a pronounced envy for the penis, and the thoughts derived from this envy still continued to fill her mind. She was in fact a feminist; she felt it to be unjust that girls should not enjoy the same freedom as boys, and rebelled against the lot of woman in general. (155, 169)

Freud's concern with theorizing homosexuality beyond the context of this particular case—and hence what I have called his theoretical defeat—is evident in the digressions on the topic that appear in parts I and IV, where he makes reference to the sexological arguments he had addressed in the *Three Essays* fifteen years earlier, and which, by 1920, had already become known or popularized outside the domain of medical knowledge. Thus, in part I, Freud entertains the queries he expects from the lay reader: "Readers unversed in psychoanalysis will long have been awaiting an answer to two other questions. Did this homosexual girl show physical characteristics plainly belonging to the opposite sex, and did the case prove to be one of congenital or acquired (later-developed) homosexuality?" (153). He answers no to the first question and offers the case history itself as his answer to the second: "[W]hether this was a case of congenital or acquired homosexuality, will be answered by the whole history of the patient's abnormality and its development. The study of this will show how far this question is a fruitless and inapposite one" (154).

But lo and behold, the fruitless question reappears in part IV, where Freud unabashedly contradicts himself by reproposing its terms as still viable instead of displacing or replacing them with something more apposite. He states that, if at first the analysis indicated that this might be "a case of late-acquired homosexuality," a fuller "consideration of the material impels us to conclude that it is rather a case of congenital homosexuality" (169). The subsequent cautionary remark, that "it would be best not to attach too much value to this way of stating the problem" (170), does not sufficiently undercut the previous statement to dispel the reader's sense of having just read a diagnosis of congenital homosexuality. In a similar way, in the third of the *Three Essays*, he had reintroduced and continued to use as valid the notions of perversion and genital primacy that, in the first essay, he had criticized and effectively shown to be theoretically untenable.[7]

In "Psychogenesis," the final appeal to an inborn constitution that might have affected what appeared to be an "acquired disposition (if it *was* really acquired)," as Freud perversely insinuates (169), leaves the reader with no clearer view of homosexuality—or, for that matter, bisexuality—than could be gleaned from the *Three Essays* and, if anything, with greater uncertainty. It leaves Freud's position on homosexuality enmeshed in that same structural ambiguity or inconsistency that is so conspicuous in the *Three Essays*. Once again, the pivot on which the inconsistency turns is the imposition of a structuring narrative, or a structuring fantasy, onto the "material" of the case history. In other words, again the theory strains against the structure but is finally contained, as perhaps all theories must be, by a passionate fiction. In this case, the fiction is the fantasy of the "positive" Oedipus complex—the fantasy that a girl must desire the father and wish to bear a child in his image.

The Mystery of Homosexuality

Other critics have noted the inconsistencies, reversals, or exegetic somersaults in Freud's account of female homosexuality in this case history, which in some respects resembles that of Dora written twenty years earlier, although here homosexuality, and not hysteria, is the explicit problem to be addressed.[8] But if both times Freud failed to cure or resolve the patients' problems, here he takes on directly the issue of female homosexuality, which he had relegated to the footnotes, almost an afterthought, in Dora's case;[9] and if the unconscious "homosexual current of feeling" he surmised in Dora could be ignored in the analysis of hysteria, even as he remarked on the evidence of a "fairly strong homosexual predisposition" in neurotics,[10] here he can no longer evade the issue because "the mystery of homosexuality" (170) stares him in the face.

Although Freud was to articulate the complete Oedipus complex, in its positive and negative form—positive, when the object of the erotic cathexis is the parent of the other sex, negative when it is the parent of the same sex—only a few years later in *The Ego and the Id*[11]—the conception of a fourfold structure is already present in the interpretation of "Psychogenesis":

> From very early years [the girl's] libido had flowed in two currents, the one on the surface being one that we may unhesitatingly designate as homosexual. This latter was probably a *direct and unchanged continuation of an infantile fixation on her mother*. Probably the analysis described here actually revealed nothing more than the process by which, on an appropriate occasion, the deeper heterosexual current of libido, too, was deflected into the manifest homosexual one. (168–69, emphasis added)

Here the Oedipus complex is mentioned explicitly only in relation to the girl's father, that is, as positive; however, the "fixation" on the mother is precisely what Freud will later imagine as the girl's negative Oedipus complex. In short, he argues that the two currents of the libido are present in the girl: The homosexual is manifest and conscious (perversion), while the heterosexual, arising from the positive Oedipus complex, is deeper and unconscious.[12] And in light of the observation that "homosexual men have [also] experienced a specially strong fixation on their mother," Freud then concludes that "a very considerable measure of latent or unconscious homosexuality can be detected in all normal people" (171).

Given these "fundamental facts" devolving from the Oedipus complex, however, it would seem that homosexuality should hardly be a "mystery," for it is fundamentally a manifestation of what Freud calls the "universal bisexuality of human beings." The libido or instinctual disposition is bisexual, he asserts, and can flow both ways; which direction will prevail is a matter of the contingencies and vagaries of individual life. And yet Freud continues to perceive it as a problem. Why? Through the years he will reiterate that homosexuality is not a psychic illness, and such that psychoanalysis cannot cure it.[13] And yet he ends "Psychogenesis" with an admission of defeat, analogous to the sense of failure that haunts his papers on female sexuality in the 1930s; just as, there, in the matter of the riddle of femininity, psychoanalysis must turn to the poets, so here, in the matter of homosexuality, it must yield to biological science.

I think Freud is aware that something else is going on in homosexuality, although he cannot quite grasp it. I propose that the reason why he cannot grasp it lies at the very foundation of his theory, in the founding fiction of the Oedipus complex. However, the unresolved contradictions in his thinking about "the mystery" of homosexuality are, to my mind, related to a contradiction in his thinking about sexuality which is equally founding, in the sense that it dates back to the *Three Essays*—a contradiction I discussed at length in chapter 1 of *Practice of Love*. To summarize it briefly, in the first essay Freud argued that the sexual drive does not have a preassigned or natural object and that its aim is solely pleasure. But he also held another, contradictory belief, which is apparent in the second and third essays: the belief that something in human sexuality obeys the biological command to reproduce the species, as manifested in the sexual drive and in those psychic structures he calls phylogenetic, such as the primal scene and the Oedipus complex. I am not interested in discussing this point now, but I say this because it was that inconsistency in Freud that prompted my project.

Perverse Desire

In *Practice of Love* I wanted to understand conceptually a form of desire that I saw represented in many texts written by lesbians and that I have experienced in my own life: the sexual desire for another woman. I wanted to understand how it could occur or come about. The contradiction in Freud prompted me to leave aside the normative Oedipal narrative to follow instead the path traced by the perversions (in particular, fetishism). That enabled me to articulate a model of perverse desire, that is to say, to imagine how a desire that is non-Oedipal and nonreproductive may be constituted and structured. I call such a desire *perverse* in the etymological sense of perversion as deviation from a given path.

The "normal" path of sexual desire is the reproductive one, Freud wrote in the *Three Essays:*

> The normal sexual aim is regarded as being the union of the genitals in the act known as copulation.[14]

> Perversions are sexual activities which either (a) extend, in an anatomical sense, beyond the regions of the body that are designed for sexual union, or (b) linger over the intermediate relations to the sexual object which should normally be traversed rapidly on the path toward the final sexual aim.[15]

In this view, *perversion* means deviation from the path leading to the "final" or "normal" sexual aim of copulation, a deviation from the path linking the drive to the reproductive object (i.e., a person of the other sex). But if we follow up Freud's other argument, that the sexual drive does not have a natural or pre-assigned object and that its aim is not reproduction but pleasure, then *perversion* describes the very nature of the sexual drive, its mobility with regard to objects and its not being determined by a reproductive aim.

Let me say it another way: If the sexual drive is independent of its object, and the object is variable and chosen for its ability to satisfy, as Freud maintains, then the concept of perversion loses its meaning of deviation from nature (and hence loses the common connotation of pathology) and takes on the meaning of deviation from a socially constituted norm. This norm is precisely "normal" sexuality, which psychoanalysis itself, ironically, proves to be nothing more than a projection, a presumed default, an imaginary mode of being of sexuality that is in fact contradicted by psychoanalysis's own clinical evidence.

Perversion, on the other hand, is the very mode of being of *sexuality* as such, while the projected norm, in so-called normal sexuality, is a requirement of social *reproduction*, both reproduction of the species and reproduction of the social system. Now, the conflation, the imbrication, of sexuality with reproduction in Western history has been shown by Foucault to come about through what he called "the technology of sex" and has been analyzed by feminist theory in the concept of compulsory heterosexuality.[16] And it is, obviously, still a widely held or hegemonic notion. But my point is that the specific character of *sexuality* (as distinct from *reproduction*) and the empirically manifested form of sexuality, *as far as psychoanalysis knows it,* is indeed perversion, with its negative or repressed form, neurosis.

This second view of perversion suggests to me another model of sexual structuring, one based on perverse desire, that stands in contrast to the model of sexual structuring implied by the first definition of perversion, namely, the model based on Oedipal desire.[17] Freud himself contributed further to the articulation of what I call perverse desire with his analysis of the psychic mechanism of disavowal (*Verleugnung*) in "Fetishism" and "Splitting of the Ego in the Process of Defense," although he restricted fetishistic desire to men.[18] Disavowal is a psychic process that, at the same time, recognizes *and* refuses to recognize a traumatic perception. What the male fetishist disavows is the perception of a body without a penis (the mother's body), for such perception threatens the body-ego, or the subject's bodily integrity and pleasure.

The body is the starting point of Freud's reflection, and this is indeed one of the main attractions that his psychoanalysis has for me and may have had for many other women since the time of Freud. But precisely because the body was so central to his theory, the theory had to be constructed from his own experience of the body; that is, the body as experienced and understood by a man of his culture and of his socio-historical and personal situation. In such a body, he tells us (and I can do nothing else but take him at his word), the penis is the foremost organ of pleasure. Therefore, the threat of castration for a male child is as strong as the threat of loss of life; it is a threat to his body-image and body-ego, a threat of nonbeing (Lacan's *manque à être*).

A female body, however, usually has no such organ, and since the penis is not part of her body-ego, a female child has no perceptions or pleasure from it or fear of losing it (here you can do nothing else but take me at my word). To the boy, a body without penis may appear damaged, wounded, imperfect, inadequate to give pleasure or to be loved, inferior; the absence of the penis is like a wound to the integrity of his body-ego, and thus a narcissistic wound. What can cause a narcissistic wound and the threat of nonbeing to a girl? They cannot depend on losing or not having a body part of which she has no perception; for this reason, the often literal understanding of the castration complex in women has been justly contested. I think, however, that the narcissistic wound and the threat of castration also depend, as they do for the boy, on a damaged body-image, the fantasy of having a body that is imperfect, faulty, or inadequate to give pleasure and to be loved. And since the body-image constitutes the first matrix of the ego, an inadequate or unlovable body is a threat to the body-ego, a threat of nonbeing. This narcissistic wound, for the girl, is equivalent to the boy's fear of castration, but it is not due to the loss or lack of a penis, and it is not perceived as such, at least initially.

Here, then, is how I would revise Freud's story of femininity. As the girl child grows up, her sense of having a body that is inadequate, imperfect, or inferior finds confirmation and an explanation in the family practices, the social arrangements, and the cultural forms that privilege men both socially and sexually—in short, the whole choreography of gender. Since the penis is a relatively small bodily difference, but one that is taken as the symbol of male privilege, she herself may (or may not) come to accept the explanation and attribute her sense of being imperfect to the fact that she does not have a penis (whence Freud's impression of women's penis envy). Indeed, as she grows older, all those around her direct her to expect pleasure from the penis in a man's body and to look forward to the attainment of a perfect female body through motherhood; everything in her culture tells her that she can regain her narcissistic pride in becoming a mother. (In this sense Freud says that the baby she can have is the compensation and the equivalent of the penis she does not have. For this reason maternity is an extremely important fantasy for all women, as evidenced by the many lesbians who seek insemination, a technology that has been developed to favor the reproduction of "normal" middle-class and upper-class white families.)

In Freud's theory of the Oedipus complex, the boy can heal his narcissistic wound and restore the narcissistic ego-instincts [*Ichtriebe*] or self-love necessary for psychic survival by identifying with his father or a father-figure who represents the phallus he can aspire to have when he grows up (the phallus is the penis endowed with *social and sexual* power). The girl's wound can be healed or repaired, and her narcissistic ego-instincts restored, by identifying with her mother or a mother-figure and wanting to be loved as a mother. In a way, this is to say that the threat of castration, the narcissistic wound, in both the boy and the girl, is healed or repaired by identification with a figure of power; the phallus and the mother are both figures of power, more or less power depending on the particular culture.[19]

The male fetishist described by Freud sees that a female body (the mother's) has no penis but refuses to believe in that perception, which threatens him with his own possible castration. His erotic investment in the mother's body and his own body is then displaced onto something else, a fetish, which temporarily repairs the narcissistic wound and suspends the threat to his body-ego and his pleasure. As is well known, Freud says that women cannot be fetishists because they are already castrated; that is, they have no penis to lose. But if the female equivalent of castration, her narcissistic wound, is understood as the perception of an inadequate or unlovable body-image, then she, too, can disavow that perception (i.e., recognize it *and* not recognize it) and thus displace her erotic investment from the mother's and her own body onto something else. For the female, as for the male fetishist, the something else (the fetish) is an object or sign that signifies not only the lost object of desire—the beloved, lovable body—but also the subject's capacity to desire. It takes the place of the phallus as signifier of desire.

Thus the phantasmatic "lost object" of female perverse desire is neither the mother's body nor the paternal phallus; it is the subject's own lost body, which can be recovered in fantasy, in sexual practice, *in and with* another woman. This perverse desire is not based on the masculinity complex (the denial of sexual difference), nor is it based on a regressive attachment to the mother (a regression to the pre-Oedipal or the phallic phase). It is based on the post-Oedipal disavowal of that loss—the loss of one's body-ego, the loss of being. By "post-Oedipal disavowal" I mean that the desiring subject has gone through the Oedipus complex, but the form of desiring is not dependent on its binary terms; as a result of disavowal, it attaches itself to other objects, fetish-objects, which sustain and represent her *being-in-desire;* in Freud's terms, these would engage at once both object-libido and ego-libido.

The model of perverse desire that I have sketched here and articulated more elaborately in *Practice of Love* is different from the Oedipal model of normal or inverted desire (positive or negative Oedipus complex). As a *conceptual* model of sexual structuring, perverse desire places sexuality beyond the terms of the family schema—mother, father, child—and its reproductive teleology. But one model does not merely replace or exclude the other. Perverse desire may coexist with some of the effects of the Oedipus complex, and the latter indeed may play an important role in the subject's identifications, notably in gender identity and possibly in racial or ethnic identity as well.

The psyche is a complex and dynamic phenomenon, subject to historical and personal vicissitudes, shaped and reshaped by fantasies public and private. The Oedipal narrative, which framed Freud's understanding of human life and enabled his invention of psychoanalysis (and still dominates the practice and most of the theory of psychoanalysis), is a passionate fiction, a fantasmatic scenario that informs the social imaginary and incites subjective desires. Now, at a time when the institution of the family and the reproduction of the white middle class seem endangered, the Oedipal narrative is being emphatically reproposed in Hollywood movies and the popular media in the most benign and sentimental forms. But at the same time, concurrently with the Oedipal fantasy, it is quite possible to imagine other scenarios of desire.

I have no doubt that other cultural narratives can produce other fantasies and other desires. In non-Western cultures there may be no Oedipal narrative, or it may have no effect in structuring sexuality, as Frantz Fanon asserts in *Black Skin, White Masks*.[20] In Western cultures, too, the Oedipus fantasy may be eventually superseded in the wake of technological and social change. My own attempt to theorize, to articulate conceptually, the ways and "psychogenesis" of a desire that exceeds and eludes the confines of the Oedipal script is the construction of another passionate fiction, one that now represents my life and my desire much better than the Oedipal fantasy does. But I would not say that Freud was "wrong," since I myself experienced the positive Oedipus complex through adolescence, and I completely identified with Oedipus when I first read Freud at age thirty. In some perverse way, I still do.

Written as a contribution to the volume of essays devoted to Freud's only case history of female homosexuality, *That Obscure Subject of Desire: Freud's Female Homosexual Revisited,* ed. Ronnie C. Lesser and Erica Schoenberg (New York: Routledge, 1999), 37–53. This reprinting of my essay offers the occasion to gloss the statement that the woman who was Freud's patient "remains unknown." A comprehensive biography of her long life (1900–1999), spanning two world wars and three passionate love relationships with women may be found in Ines Rieder and Diana Voigt, *Sidonie Csillag: Homosexuelle chez Freud, lesbienne dans le siècle,* Paris: Epel, 2003 (translated by Thomas Gindele from the original German *Heimliches Begehren: Die Geschichte der Sidonie C.,* Vienna: Deuticke, 2000). The authors were able to meet her as an old woman and, by using a pseudonym, enrich their extensive research with personal details and photographs. I thank Pascale Molinier for bringing the book to my attention.

Chapter 6

Public and Private Fantasies in David Cronenberg's
M. Butterfly

> To many common people the baroque and the operatic
> appear as an extraordinarily fascinating way of feeling and
> acting, a means of escaping what they consider low, mean and
> contemptible in their lives and education in order to enter a
> more select sphere of great feelings and noble passions. . . . But
> opera is the most pestiferous because words set to music are
> more easily recalled, and they become matrices in which thought
> takes shape out of flux.
> —Antonio Gramsci[1]

> There is no politics without human desire and madness.
> —David Cronenberg[2]

> Listening to Puccini's *Madama Butterfly* (1904), I unwittingly
> participate in a history of racist imperialism. And yet at
> moments the opera works against its pernicious frame. . . .
> When Butterfly enters, I drift away from fixed vantage-point; the
> noose of gender loosens, and I begin to breathe.
> —Wayne Koestenbaum[3]

One of the first thinkers in the twentieth century to reflect on popular culture as a political force was Antonio Gramsci. In his prison notebooks, Gramsci traces a connection between politics and particular expressive forms that, in each country, inscribe its dominant cultural narratives. For example, he remarks that the rise and fortunes of opera in Italy and of the popular novel in France and England in the eighteenth and nineteenth centuries coincided with the "appearance and expansion of national-popular democratic forces throughout Europe."[4] Considered as a whole, as a genre, rather than as the expression of individual artists, the blossoming of opera was a "historico-cultural" event on a par with that of the novel, and both were forms of "popular epic" (378). We can certainly say the same of cinema in our century.

Those expressive forms, Gramsci observes, were clearly marked as fictional and served the purpose of entertainment or escape from the reality of daily life; but their effects had the power of "something deeply felt and experienced" (378). While they allowed the common people to escape from "what they considered low, mean and contemptible in their lives" and enter into an exalted "sphere of great feelings and noble passions," thus producing an artificial, cliché, deluded view of social relations, these popular forms also provided structures of cognition as well as feeling, "matrices in which thought takes shape out of flux" (378). Opera, Gramsci scornfully remarks, was "the most pestiferous" because it instigated in the Italian people what he calls "the operatic conception of life" (*la concezione melodrammatica della vita*) (377); but he immediately takes back the sarcastic emphasis to remark on the significance of the effect: for its viewers/listeners, who were uneducated, common people but not "superficial snobs," opera had the effect of "something *deeply felt and experienced*" (378, emphasis added).

Popular culture forms have the effect of something *deeply felt and experienced,* and yet they are *fictional* representations. I want to suggest that they perform, at the societal level and in the public sphere, a function similar to that of the private fantasies, daydreams, and reveries by which individual subjects imagine or give images to their erotic, ambitious, or destructive aspirations. In "Creative Writers and Day-Dreaming," Freud put it in a nutshell: "His Majesty the Ego [is] the hero alike of every day-dream and every story."[5] In this sense, the narratives inscribed in popular culture forms and their scenarios or mise-en-scène, complete with characters, passions, conflicts, and resolutions, may be considered *public fantasies.*

Gramsci further speculates that, if in Italy opera alone attained the popularity that the novel had elsewhere in Europe, this was because "its language was not national but cosmopolitan, as music is," and did not necessitate the presence of a national-popular culture, which Italy lacked, or the "strict nationalization of indigenous intellectuals" that occurred in other countries of Europe at that time (378–79). To support his view of the cosmopolitan character of Italian opera, he observes that

> the plot of the libretti is never "national," but European, in two senses. Either because the "intrigue" of the drama takes place in all the countries of Europe, and more rarely in Italy, using popular legends or popular novels. Or because the feelings and passions of the drama reflect the particular sensibility of eighteenth-century and Romantic Europe. This European sensibility nevertheless coincides with prominent elements of the popular sensibility of all countries, from which it had in any case drawn its Romantic current. (This fact should be connected to the popularity of Shakespeare and the Greek tragic dramatists, whose characters, overcome by elementary passions, jealousy, paternal love and revenge, are essentially popular in every country.) (379)

Do Gramsci's speculations in the first decades of the twentieth century retain some value into its closing years and beyond? As we move from the nineteenth-century forms of popular epic to those produced in the twentieth by the historico-cultural events of cinema, television, and the internet, the notion of a national-popular culture yields to that of a multinational, mass media culture with global reach. Perhaps we can no longer hypothesize a particular sensibility common to all Western countries, and surely the meaning of *cosmopolitan* has expanded beyond the European continent to, at least, the planet. Moreover, the former distinction between high and low cultures, between an elite culture of the educated classes and a popular culture of the "common people," is no longer tenable, owing in part to the social technologies of cinema, television, and the paperback industry. And yet, precisely

through these technologies, the passions and dramas of popular mythologies—jealousy, revenge, violence, and indeed paternal love (now
seeking to supplant maternal love)—continue to replay in the contemporary imagination, repackaged in the popular epic forms of our time,
commercially successful films, television serials, and supermarket fiction.
(Think of the film industry's standard practice of making famous novels
and plays into films, and then making successful films into, precisely,
remakes.)

As for a romantic sensibility in today's popular culture, is the romance
of the child in Steven Spielberg's films, from *Close Encounters of the
Third Kind* (1977) and *E.T.* (1982) to *Jurassic Park* (1993) and *A.I.*
(2001), anything other than the sentimental reduction or, as Gramsci
put it, the "politico-commercial degeneration" (379) of Wordsworth's
vision of the child as father to man? Conversely, however, can one
speak of degeneration for films like James Cameron's *Terminator* (1984)
or *Terminator 2: Judgment Day* (1991), where the romantic elements
of Christian epic, Genesis, and the Oedipus myth are re-imaged with
the most spectacular special effects in a science fiction film? Perhaps
the legend of King Oedipus no longer has the "universal" power to
move it had for Freud; and yet it did have it for Pier Paolo Pasolini,
who re-imaged himself as Oedipus in his film *Edipo Re* (Italy, 1967);
for Matsumoto Toshio, who recast Oedipus as a young homosexual
transvestite in *Funeral Parade of Roses* (*Bara no soretsu*, Japan, 1969);
for Joy Chamberlain, who rescripted the story with an all-female cast
in the British Broadcasting Corporation production *Nocturne* (United
Kingdom, 1991); even, apparently, for the Hollywood audiences of
Robert Zemeckis's *Back to the Future* (United States, 1985) and the
two sequels it has spawned to date (1989, 1990).

And again, although Greek tragedy may no longer have the emotional
impact attributed to it by Gramsci and Marx, think how many films in
recent years have restaged Shakespeare's plays and how many of Jane
Austen's eighteenth-century novels have been made and remade into
films. Can we read such trends as symptoms of a national-popular drive
resurfacing perversely in these times of global politics? Or is it rather
the symptom of a dearth of new narratives in Western postmodernity?
In any case, my purpose is not to reiterate a worn distinction between
an authentic national-popular culture and its politico-commercial de-

generation but to reflect on the re-use and mixing of popular forms and narratives in the cinematic construction of public fantasies.

Public and Private Fantasies

Fantasy is a fundamental human activity based on the capacity for imagining and imaging; for making images in one's mind (imagining) and making images in material expressions (imaging) by various technical means that include, say, drawing and photography but also language and even one's own body, for example, in performance. Psychoanalytic theory understands fantasy as a primary psychic activity, a creative activity that animates the imagination and produces imaginary scenes or scenarios in which the subject is protagonist or in some other way present. With the term "fantasy" Freud designates both these imaginary scenes and the activity of fantasizing, the psychic mechanism that produces the imaginary scenes. These, he notes in *The Interpretation of Dreams,* are in some cases conscious (e.g., daydreams, reveries, or "daytime fantasies") but often "remain unconscious on account of their content and of their origin from repressed material."[6] Freud insists that both types of fantasies share many of the properties of dreams, and thus point to a common psychic activity or structure:

> Like dreams, [fantasies] are wish-fulfillments; like dreams, they are based to a great extent on impressions of infantile experiences; like dreams, they benefit by a certain degree of relaxation of censorship. If we examine their structure, we shall perceive the way in which the wishful purpose that is at work in their production has mixed up the material of which they are built, has rearranged it and has formed it into a new whole. They stand in much the same relation to the childhood memories from which they are derived as do some of the Baroque palaces of Rome to the ancient ruins whose pavements and columns have provided the material for the more recent structures.[7]

One of the great contributions of Freud's work to twentieth-century conceptions of the subject in culture is to have dissolved the qualitative distinction between fantasy as mere illusion and reality as something that really is. For Freud, psychic reality is everything that in our minds takes on the force of reality, has all the consistency of the real, and on the basis of which we live our lives, understand the world, and act in it. Fantasy is the psychic mechanism that structures subjectivity by reworking or translating social representations into subjective representations and self-representations.

Film theory has analyzed the ways in which our capacity to fantasize is intensely stimulated in watching a fiction film. By engaging the spectator's desire and identification in the scenarios and the movement of its narrative, the film *moves* us (in both senses of the word) along with it, binding fantasy to images; placing, shifting, and re-positioning the spectator as a figure in that imaginary, imaged world, as one present or emotionally participating in it. That is to say, the film constructs a narrative space and makes a place in it for those who watch it.[8] The film's construction of a field of vision and meaning that are perceived to originate in those who watch it produces the spectator as the point of its coherence; it thus contributes to the production of subject positions and the construction—more rarely, the deconstruction—of social, gendered identities for its viewers in the very process of viewing (a process that film theory calls spectatorship). This is another way of saying that the construction of a popular imaginary by means of cinematic representations, cinema's public fantasies, produces in the spectators structures of cognition as well as feeling, what Gramsci calls "matrices in which thought takes shape out of flux," and these interface and resonate with the subjective fantasy structures of individual spectators.

What I mean by public fantasies, then, are dominant cultural narratives and scenarios of the popular imagination that have been expressed in myths, medieval sagas, sacred texts, epics, and other forms of oral, written, or visual narrative that tell the story of a people, a nation, or a representative individual (Everyman) and reconstruct their origin, their struggles, and their achievements. We are all familiar with some of these narratives in Western cultures, from Homer and the Bible to the *Niebelungenlied* and *Kalevala,* from Dante's *Divina Commedia* to Milton's *Paradise Lost,* and their modern counterparts in cinema: *The Birth of a Nation* (1915), *Battleship Potemkin* (1925), *Triumph of the Will* (1935), *Paisan* (1946), *Ben-Hur* (1959), *Gone with the Wind* (1939), *Apocalypse Now* (1975), *Terminator,* and many more. All of them represent, through various types of conflicts and moral choices, the construction of Nation, of a new society, and the place of the individual as agent and subject in that new world.

Some public fantasies narrow their focus to the individual character's story or to one aspect of the individual's development in a struggle between good and evil, from Goethe's *Faust* to *Raging Bull* (1980), from Flaubert's *Madame Bovary* to *Now, Voyager* (1942), from *The Wizard of Oz* (1939) to the hologram of Leonardo da Vinci in *Star Trek: Voyager* (1997). Other times the focus is set on a particular locale or narrative topos in which are played out the conflicts and moral choices of the members of a specific group, for example, a family, a school, a prison camp, or the United States–Mexico border—from Orson Welles's classic *Touch of Evil* (1958) to John Sayles's *Lone Star* (1996).[9] A comparison of the last two films would serve quite well to illustrate beyond a doubt how the construction of a popular imaginary—what I call public fantasies—by means of cinematic representations does not merely take up but significantly rearticulates existing cultural narratives. That is to say, it reuses their structures and thematic concerns, but brings in new material, new contents, new characters or cultural agents, new issues and themes drawn from the contemporary world and its social arrangements.

Here, however, I will take as my case study a film which, in addition, explicitly thematizes the effects of public fantasies on individual lives. David Cronenberg's *M. Butterfly* (United States, 1993) takes up and makes use of a dominant cultural narrative, although one not epic but sentimental and yet equally concerned with a "universal" problem: the questions of desire, of the cultural and racial other, and the so-called difference between the sexes. As its title suggests, the film re-proposes a stereotyped image of femininity, made popular by the heroine of Giacomo Puccini's opera *Madama Butterfly;* but it does so in light of contemporary discourses on gender, sexuality, and racial-cultural difference from the vantage point of postcoloniality. In re-presenting it with another cast of characters, the film at once deconstructs and reappropriates the narrative of feminine love and honor as eternal and selfless devotion to her husband and young son, built around the exemplary figure of Butterfly. It deconstructs it by showing it to be a Western patriarchal construct and an orientalist fantasy based on hierarchies of gender, race, and colonial and political domination. It reappropriates it by showing the narrative's enduring power to affect and even shape individual lives precisely because it works in the cultural imaginary as a fantasy, as "something deeply felt and experienced."

M. Butterfly is about that fantasy and is itself, in turn, a fantasy that links three continents and two centuries, that connects North America and Europe via Asia and reconnects the popular epic form of our century, cinema, with its nineteenth-century equivalent, opera. But the Butterfly fantasy did not originate with the opera that has made it famous worldwide.[10] It already had a cosmopolitan history of its own when Puccini set it to music.

Birth of a Fantasy

Its history begins in yet another genre of popular culture, travel literature, and from there the fantasy is reinscribed, translated, and transformed in other popular genres—the short story, personal diary, drama, opera, and film. In the process, the heroine's name changes from Chrysanthème (O-kiku-san) to Butterfly (Cho-cho-san) to Song Liling. To give just a very brief summary of her incarnations, she first appeared in 1887, when a French naval officer, Julien Viaud, published an account of his sojourn in Japan and his temporary marriage to a young woman of Nagasaki named O-kiku-san (Chrysanthemum). The book was titled *Madame Chrysanthème* (1887) and its author's name (a pseudonym) was Pierre Loti (1850–1923).[11] More a travel book than a love story, *Madame Chrysanthème* was very successful; it fit into the vogue for the exotic, the Oriental, and in particular the fascination that the West—Europe and the United States—had for Japanese culture, art, and design in the second half of the nineteenth century, no doubt encouraged by Japan's opening of its ports to Western trade and travel around 1860. The story Loti told was not new, as Western sailors frequently engaged in temporary unions with Japanese women. But the success of *Madame Chrysanthème* owed more to Western fascination with the Orient and Loti's descriptions of life in Japan than to its heroine, whom her husband depicted as rather surly, dull, and unresponsive; so much so that when he left her, declaring the marriage failed, she practically rejoiced in the end of an advantageous economic transaction.

This businesslike character of Loti's Chrysanthème, her lack of shame over selling her body to a Westerner, and her emotional independence from her "husband," were not acceptable to the authors of her next two incarnations: in 1893 she reappeared as the lead role in an opera by André Messager (libretto by Georges Hartmann and André Alexandre),

Madame Chrysanthème, that was popular until the beginning of the twentieth century; and in 1894, as the author of a "diary," *Le Cahier rose de Mme Chrysanthème,* actually written by the French illustrator and Japanologist Félix Régamey, which retells the story of Loti's marriage to Chrysanthème from her point of view and as if written by her. Already by this (her third) reincarnation, in only seven years, Chrysanthème has become the tragic heroine that will be Butterfly: she's been seduced and abandoned; she's love-stricken and contemplating suicide.

She next appears in the United States, four years later, in a short story by John Luther Long published in *The Century Magazine.* Although Long acknowledges Loti's book as his source, her name is now Madame Butterfly (Cho-cho-san) and the cynical "husband" is an American navy officer named Pinkerton. The fantasy is here approaching its final form of melodrama, as we know it from Puccini's opera, but it still has something of a happy ending in that now Butterfly gives birth to a son and, when Pinkerton returns accompanied by his legal, American wife, Butterfly runs away to live together with her child. However, her suicide is fated to come with the next incarnation in David Belasco's one-act play, written in collaboration with Long and also titled *Madame Butterfly,* which opened in 1900 and which the Italian composer Giacomo Puccini happened to see at its London premiere.

On Belasco's play, as well as all the previous ones, is based the classic version of the fantasy, Puccini's opera *Madama Butterfly.* Here Cho-cho-san, cast out by her family for marrying the Westerner, cursed by the high priest, abandoned by Pinkerton, also loses her child, whom she gives up so he can live the good life in America, and kills herself with the dagger of her father. The ritual suicide (*seppuku*) restores her honor.

Those being the early, heady days of cinema, it is not surprising that Butterfly found its way into three silent films as well. In the United States, it served as a Mary Pickford vehicle, a *Madame Butterfly* directed by Sidney Olcott in 1915 and based on Long's story. In Germany, in 1919, Fritz Lang directed a film known as *Hara Kiri* but whose only surviving copy, found in the Nederlands Filmmuseum, bears the title *Madame Butterfly* and the subtitle *Naar de Wereldberoemde Opera in zes acten* (after the world-renowned opera in six acts).[12] Again in the United States, in 1922, Chester Franklin directed *The Toll of the Sea,* with Anna May Wong as Lotus Flower rescuing a Pinkerton character (named Allen Carver) washed ashore and nearly drowned. Although set in China—like Cronenberg's film—the screenplay by Frances Marion follows Long's *Madame Butterfly* to the point of giving exact quotations from it in the intertitles.[13]

By the mid-1920s the vogue of japonisme, chinoiseries, and so forth, was over, but the sentimental tale of Chrysanthème/Butterfly had taken root in the Western cultural imaginary and could live on by any other name: Japan and China were interchangeable loci, stage sets, or intimations of an orientalist fantasy that, in Cronenberg's words, has now become "a cultural truism." It is not a coincidence that the best known version of her story, and the one the film utilizes, is, in fact, the opera *Madama Butterfly*, composed by Puccini, which was first performed at La Scala in Milan in 1904 and has been on every opera company repertoire ever since.[14] (As Gramsci said, opera is "the most pestiferous.")

At the end of the twentieth century, in times of multinational finances and information superhighways, Cronenberg's film *M. Butterfly* refigured in contemporary terms the cosmopolitanism and romantic sensibility that belonged to opera in eighteenth- and nineteenth-century Europe. The film displays the features of popular epic noted by Gramsci—cosmopolitan setting and plot, romantic sensibility—but reframes the narrative in the ironic mode of postmodernist aesthetics, articulating it to the cultural issues of gender, race, and sexuality in a postcolonial West.

M. for Trouble

M. Butterfly is a film made by a Canadian director, produced in the United States, and in part financed by Japan's Sony Corporation.[15] The film is based on the Tony Award-winning play by Chinese-American playwright, David Henry Hwang, which is in turn based on a *New York Times Magazine* story about the treason trial of a French embassy attaché and a Beijing opera singer.[16] The title and the storyline refer to an Italian opera about a Japanese geisha and an American navy officer. The setting of the film—China during the 1960s Cultural Revolution and Paris during the student uprising of May 1968—is as exotically distant from Toronto, Canada (Cronenberg's hometown and the setting of many of his films) as the Japanese port of Nagasaki, home of the fictional Butterfly, was from the European audiences of Puccini's opera. Most of the scenes set in Paris were actually filmed in Budapest, except for the brief shot of Jeremy Irons (playing René Gallimard) on a motorcycle riding past Notre Dame. The Red Guard parade in Beijing that culminates in the burning of Peking opera costumes was filmed with five hundred extras from Toronto's Chinese community dressed in Red Guard uniforms made in France.

So the cosmopolitanism of opera is inscribed in the very production of the film, as well as, of course, its international distribution. But what of the romantic sensibility today, in a world where issues are less international than global, where the relations among peoples and countries are defined by postcoloniality, and aesthetic representation is under the aegis of postmodernism? The title of the film provides the first indication of this different cultural climate: *M. Butterfly,* where the M. cannot possibly mean Madame or Miss or Mrs.—or even Ms. Even for those who do not know that M. stands for *Monsieur* in French, there is already something troubling, something off-key in the title. That something, which the film will reveal to be a trouble with gender, is the first of several ways in which the film's recasting of the Butterfly story will trouble, ironize, deconstruct, and ultimately reappropriate the dominant narrative.

First, "Butterfly" reincarnated in Song Liling (played by John Lone) turns out to have a male body, to be a spy for the People's Republic, and to be familiar with the opera plot to the point of pretending to have given birth to a child: "I need a baby, a Chinese baby with blond hair," he sarcastically demands of comrade Chin, the utterly unfeminine woman who is his Party contact. I say "he" because it is precisely in this scene that the spectators are informed, just in case we missed it before, that Song is a man.[17] But the problem of how to refer to Song Liling remains, as we shall see, a constant reminder of the constructedness of gender and its overdetermination by language.

A second troubling of the popular narrative is that Song is perfectly aware that the Butterfly story comes from a Western fantasy of the Orient that is Orientalist, in the sense specified by Edward Said's book *Orientalism;*[18] that is to say, a fantasy of the Orient that is inflected by the political and economic interests of Western imperialism and by its ideology of racial supremacy. Song is quite scornful of it, and so informs Gallimard in their first conversation: "It's your fantasy, isn't it? The submissive Oriental woman and the cruel white man."

And yet—here is a third, more troublesome twist—Song willingly plays the role of Butterfly and risks the labor camp for the sake of his desire and his forbidden homosexual relationship with René. His Butterfly is not a victim of the colonial master, the "white devil," or a passive object of his desire; Song Liling's Butterfly is not guileless and not passive, not an object but indeed the subject—the conscious and willful subject—of a fantasy that sustains the agency of his own desire ("I invented myself just for him," Song says at the trial). In Hwang's play, Song is already a spy before meeting Gallimard; in Cronenberg's film, he becomes one in order to continue their relationship. The four shots of the servant Shu Fang watching their first sexual encounter through the window do not simply signify voyeurism, as we may at first assume, but have a narrative function: they tell us why Song must "spy." For Shu Fang will inform the Party cadre, Comrade Chin, that Song is carrying on a (homo)sexual affair, and Comrade Chin will then pay her visit to Song. Thus, when Song says, "As we embark on the most forbidden of loves, I'm afraid of my destiny," he knows that his destiny is not only that of Butterfly, abandonment and death; in the historical context of the film's setting, China during the Cultural Revolution, embarking on *the most forbidden* of loves, that is, homosexuality, is most likely to earn him imprisonment in a labor camp. While both the film and the play contain an explicit political critique of the Western orientalist fantasy, for Cronenberg, in particular, "there is no politics without human desire and madness," and that is to say, there is no politics without fantasy.[19] Fantasy and desire are what move human beings and cannot be separated off from any form of human agency, whether it is expressed in art, in daily living, or in political action.

A further, ironic troubling of the popular narrative is that the role or, I should rather say, the soul of Butterfly transmigrates from one character, Song Liling, to the other, crossing gender, cultures, and bodies. In the end, it is Gallimard, formerly the Pinkerton character, whose self-inflicted death we watch as a cheap tape recorder blares the famous aria of Puccini's opera. He, too, becomes Butterfly in an elaborate tragic performance in which we see him putting on costume and makeup as he speaks: he literally becomes Butterfly under our eyes. As we watch his transformation on the prison stage, our look is multiplied by those of the prison inmates who are Gallimard's diegetic audience.

M. for Mirror

The film presents the figure Butterfly as a narrative image, an image that sums up and evokes the cultural narrative popularized by Puccini's opera. But *M. Butterfly* re-presents *Madama Butterfly* as a mirror construction, a mise-en-abîme: it reframes the opera as a mirror for the film's two male protagonists.[20] The story of Butterfly is encased and relayed to the spectator by the story of Song and René, who mediate the spectator's access to the Butterfly fantasy—for thus the film represents the story: as a public fantasy that has acquired a life of its own beyond the opera, but whose power to incite desire is most effective through its formal configuration in the opera. In turn, Song and René mirror the spectator's relation to the film, demonstrating the ways in which a public fantasy (an opera, a film) may elicit spectatorial, subjective desire.

The mirroring is achieved by formal means. For example, the awareness on the part of the characters that Butterfly is a fantasy is relayed back to the spectators by a particular articulation of looks: looking at the screen, we see René looking at Song during the recital, and later as he performs at the Beijing opera; we see René looking and listening to the opera, and jumping in, as it were, to assume a place in it. The repeated framing of René as spectator of a performance (even as he listens to the French consul, the seating arrangement is formal, theatrical; and even during the brief sequence of the trial, in which we see only Song testify, René appears as the spectator of yet another performance, Song's performance as a male spy) is so insistent throughout the film that we must come to see *ourselves,* in turn, *as spectators* of a performance, of a fantasy, and of the film, whether or not we are caught up in its fantasy.

Song Liling as well, after their first encounter, assumes a place in what he knows to be a fantasy, and begins playing the role of Butterfly. His performance is doubly coded as such because he already plays a similar role in his daily work as an actor of the Beijing opera; and in traditional Chinese opera, much as on the Elizabethan stage, only men were allowed to act, some of them trained from childhood to play exclusively female roles. (That a role similar to Butterfly's was a staple of Chinese opera may be known from another film released coincidentally the same year, *Farewell My Concubine,* by the Chinese director Chen Kaige [1993].)[21] The framing of Song as Butterfly, as well, constructs a vision of femininity for the spectator that is not the femininity of Puccini's Butterfly but that of the film's fantasy: either he's framed by a door or a curtain, usually at center screen, as if making the diva's grand entrance (after the recital, emerging from the building and descending the stairs; in the Beijing opera dressing room his face is framed by a white curtain; at the trial the heavy doors swing open as he enters flanked by two guards) or he's framed in a corner, barely visible, huddled on the stairs with the baby like a mannerist madonna, or hiding on the staircase outside René's apartment. He's both a glamorous diva and a demure, self-effacing little woman, the two extremes of the feminine.[22] Many of these shots are *not* subjective or strictly from the point of view of René, who is often included in the frame, as a spectator as we are. The last shots of the film are only for us: Song sits in the airplane about to fly back to China, dressed as a man, and no longer a prisoner of the French government (his handcuffs are removed). But even here we are addressed as spectators of a performance: when the airplane door is shut, in the very last image of the film, it has the effect of a curtain falling.

With the significant individual contributions of actors, their performances and/or star personas, of camera operators, image and sound editors, and so forth, cinema constructs its own scenario of desire in the film. Consider, for example, the soundtrack. The operatic arias and orchestral movements, the Schubert quartet, and the Chinese music associated with Song Liling work as an apparatus of spectatorial interpellation: they call to us, draw us into the passion, the longing, the sadness of Song and René, pulling us into the aural space of a fantasy which is not that of the opera but the film's own operatic fantasy.

And so, watching the film, anyone must realize that Madama Butterfly is not merely an opera, which one may or may not have seen or heard: it is a Western cultural fantasy based on a stereotype of femininity, a femininity that can be put on as a costume, can be performed as an effective masquerade by anyone, woman or man, who has compelling reasons to do so.

David Henry Hwang notes that, when he got the idea for the play from the *New York Times* news story, he had never seen the opera:

I didn't even know the plot of the opera! I knew Butterfly only as a cultural stereotype; speaking of an Asian woman, we would sometimes say, "She's pulling a Butterfly," which meant playing the submissive Oriental number. Yet, I felt convinced that the libretto would include yet another lotus blossom pining away for a cruel Caucasian man, and dying for her love. Such a story has become too much of a cliché not to be included in the archetypal East-West romance. . . . Sure enough, when I purchased the record, I discovered it contained a wealth of sexist and racist clichés.[23]

Cronenberg, in discussing with Hwang the screenplay he (Hwang) was adapting from his own stage play, insisted that Gallimard need not have ever heard of the opera; for the figure of Butterfly, the cliché of the submissive oriental woman, is "a cultural truism": "technically you could take any man off the street in Western culture and he would believe all of these things. He doesn't have to ever have seen Madame Butterfly."[24]

The film explicitly evokes the figure of Butterfly as a cliché, a stereotype set in a threadbare orientalist narrative, which, nevertheless, like many other public fantasies, still has the power of "something deeply felt and experienced." The work of the film is to analyze that power, to show how the public fantasy translates into a subjective fantasy and is experienced as an erotic fantasy by both René and Song, informing the scenario or mise-en-scène of their desire; in other words, to show how the stereotype becomes a fetish.[25] For in the figure of Butterfly the performance of femininity actually comes to embody it, for both men, regardless of anatomy; and in this sense Butterfly is a fetish or fantasy object that sustains their different desires.

The power of fantasy to elicit desire is represented cinematically—visually and aurally, by the specific codes of narrative cinema—in a scene, near the beginning, when Gallimard first sees Song Liling on stage during the recital at the embassy. René is sitting next to Frau Baden, the German woman with whom he will have his first extramarital affair, and she's telling him the bare bones of the opera plot. Song enters singing and René is transfixed.

Song's entrance is filmed in a very long shot, with the camera positioned behind the seated audience; the music on the soundtrack is from Butterfly's entrance in act I of the opera. Then the camera cuts to a medium shot of Gallimard and Frau Baden seated among the audience

and talking. Then cut again to the stage with Song in long shot singing, while the camera pans slowly left to right. This shot/reverse-shot
pattern is repeated twice, and each time the camera cuts to the stage,
a new aria is being sung ("Vogliatemi bene" on the wedding night in
act I and "Un bel dí" from act II), condensing real time to film time
and suggesting the elliptic temporality of fantasy. In the third reverse
shot of Gallimard, the camera zooms slowly from a medium distance
to a close-up of his face. Then again cut to Song, still in long shot; that
is, the focal distance has not changed, the camera is still at the same
distance from the stage, giving us the point of view of Gallimard, whose
distance from the stage is, of course, fixed. Then, in the next shot of
Gallimard, he sits up, moves his body forward as if to see better, and
moves into a (profilmic) light that illuminates the upper half of his face;
this creates the impression that he is transfixed, for the light that shines
on his eyes seems to come from inside him, as if he were suddenly lit up
by an internal source—desire. (Note how this formal, rigorous framing
of Song in long shot during the entire scene is more effective to convey
René's fascination than a zoom-in on Song would have been.)[26]

What this sequence of shots suggests is that the fantasy is being born
before his eyes, reborn in his imagination, even without costumes, sets,
or orchestra: something in the story, the music, the white-clad Oriental
woman on stage resonates with something in René, like an unconscious
fantasy suddenly breaking through into preconscious thought. He will
fill out the details of plot and mise-en-scène later on, buying the record,
going to the opera, and so on, throughout his life; but the desire is born
with the slightest sketch of the narrative figure of Butterfly and the
epiphanic sight of her embodied in Song Liling on the stage. Thus the
public fantasy expressed in the opera becomes René's private, subjective fantasy; at first inchoate, merely the intimation of another scene,
then actively, consciously reconstructed as the compelling and exclusive
scene of his desire. For the rest of the film, René and Song will work
at restaging the complete scenario of the fantasy in ever fuller, more
elaborate details, following the script provided by the opera unto its
bitter end. And switching places against their will. Song's participation
in the intersubjective construction of the fantasy that sustains their different desires is as crucial as the opera that gives it formal expression.

Direct references to opera in various forms of cultural circulation are
interspersed throughout the film: after the recital at the Swedish embassy

where they meet, René looks at the album in his office; his wife hums a few notes of *Madama Butterfly*'s most popular aria. René first visits the Beijing opera in its traditional form, where Song performs "Drunken Beauty"; on his second visit, he finds a cheery, Cultural Revolution version of Chinese opera. Song at the labor camp turns when the Butterfly aria suddenly plays on the soundtrack, as if beckoning him—bridging spatial and temporal discontinuity in the manner of the dreamwork; the next shot takes us (with him) to the Paris opera house where Rene sits watching/listening to Puccini's opera, crying. At home in his Paris apartment René plays a recorded version of the opera just before Song calls his name and then appears, as if conjured up by the music (which is, in fact, the humming chorus preceding the entrance of Butterfly). Last comes René's performance of Butterfly in prison.[27]

These recurrent references to the opera in its ability to cross cultures and to appeal to multiple sensory registers (visual, aural, and tactile) emphasize the perceptual quality of fantasy as origin and support, prop and mise-en-scène of the subject's desire. They not only have the function of referring the characters, and the spectator, back to the cultural narrative that shapes the fantasy of René and Song and may fulfill itself in them but further, in three of the sequences mentioned, the operatic music produces for the spectator a special effect of perceptual presence. We know, of course, that when Song at the labor camp turns screen-right, he does not actually hear the aria that we hear recorded on the soundtrack; and that his materializing outside René's apartment is not an effect of the Dolby sound system. We may also know that it is the narrativity of the operatic music, its linking of musical phrases and motifs to characters and events in the drama, that produces the spectatorial expectation of Song's appearance while the record plays the humming chorus (just as Butterfly appears in the opera) and joins China to Paris as Butterfly sings her fantasized reunion with Pinkerton. We may know. But we suspend our disbelief because the music's narrative charge, redoubled by the cinematic narrative construction and conveyed by the "imaginary signifier" of cinema, confers to what we see and hear the perceptual dimension of the real, as in a dream or a hallucination.[28] This effect is also mirrored for us in the final prison scene, when René looks at himself made up as Butterfly in the mirror with which he cuts his throat; he actually sees the Butterfly that his words and the music have conjured up, and he thus experiences *her* death with all *his* senses.

In other words, the recurrent references to the opera contribute to re-present or make present the fantasy as something perceptually experienced, drawing us into its visual and aural space, and punctuating it with the rhythm of an obsession. They are insistent, even didactic indications of how a public fantasy may take hold in a particular subjectivity or, rather, in two quite distinct subjectivities, and work for them as a private fantasy and all-consuming passion. For if Song is willing to risk the labor camp or worse for the sake of his desire, René jeopardizes his career and eventually loses his job as the fantasy becomes his psychic reality, impinging on his judgment and inflecting his reading of political events in the outside world. René misreads China's attitude toward the United States during the Vietnam War because he projects his own Butterfly fantasy onto the two countries, China being, of course, identified with Song, and the United States with himself. The imbrication of the personal in the political and the projection of private fantasies into the public sphere are the flip side of the effects of public fantasy in subjectivity.

M. for Masquerade

The film re-presents the Butterfly fantasy inscribed in Puccini's opera (the diegetic fantasy) as pursued and reenacted by Song and René, and at the same time deconstructs it, showing the ideological presumption of hierarchy implicit in the opposite pairs East and West, woman and man, female and male, self and other. In so doing, however, the film stages its own fantasy of Butterfly as an Orientalist fantasy that is shared and consciously orchestrated by two men—one Asian and one European, one homosexual and one heterosexual—a fantasy that, for one of them, will mean psychic disintegration, loss of self, and death. But it will be René, the white man, the Pinkerton character, who dies Butterfly's death in the film. How can we read this reversal?

In narratological terms, the narrative that forms the setting of the fantasy must be played out to its ending, for all stories must end happily or tragically, an ending is necessary to a story. But the tragic ending of the nineteenth-century Butterfly story need not be repeated in its postmodern replay. Indeed, if we saw the film as Song Liling's story, its ending would not be tragic, merely unhappy. *M. Butterfly*, however, tells René's story. In the director's stated intention, the film is about the inner transformation of a man; and Cronenberg will tell the story of the Western heterosexual man, although he means to cast doubts as to who or what that man really is by looking into the murky areas of his psyche.[29]

The transformation of René into Butterfly, in which the difference of the film's fantasy from the diegetic fantasy is most apparent, occurs after the trial and the revelation that Song is a man. When, on their way to prison, in the paddy wagon scene, Song, naked at his feet, tries to convince René to accept the Butterfly fantasy as a gay fantasy ("under the robes, beneath everything, it was always me. . . . I am your Butterfly"), René rejects him, saying: "I'm a man who loved a woman created by a man. Anything else simply falls short."[30] He cannot accept Song's transvestite fantasy of Butterfly, ostensibly because his fantasy is heterosexual; one could say, heterosexist.[31] But what is *a woman created by a man* if not the masquerade of femininity? Then it is not the revelation of Song's maleness—which René has obviously disavowed, known and not known, all along—that causes him to lose his love object, but the end of the masquerade. With it comes the realization that what he loved was not Song but Butterfly, the masquerade of femininity; that the object of his desire is a fantasy object, Butterfly, and that object alone can sustain his desire.

Butterfly, then, is a fetish in the classical, psychic sense defined by Freud: it is an object which wards off the threat of castration always looming above the male subject and allays his fear of homosexuality.[32] It is quite literally an object, the sum of the accoutrements that make up the masquerade of femininity: the Oriental woman costume, the long black hair, the face paint and rouge, the long red fingernails—all the props that René will barter from the prison guard for his final performance. But the fetish is a particular object, set in a mise-en-scène and a scenario, a narrative, from which it acquires its psychic value as object and signifier of desire. This is Butterfly, a fantasy object which enables René's desire and the very possibility of existing as a desiring subject, for desire is the condition of psychic existence. From the moment of this realization, having lost Butterfly in Song, René can only become the object of his desire, or lose it altogether. And he does both.

His erotic and narcissistic investment in Butterfly is vital: he cannot let it go. So, first, he introjects the lost object, takes it into himself, identifies with it, and becomes Butterfly. Then, the fantasy fulfills itself in him, for, paradoxically, only her immolation to him will prove that he is the powerful/potent man who can be loved forever by the perfect woman.

Another reading is possible in metapsychological terms. With his last words, he identifies himself as "René Gallimard, also known as Madame Butterfly." The transformation could be seen as the result of the psychic process that Freud names melancholia, a pathological condition of narcissism in which the ego identifies with the lost object. With the loss of the loved object, Freud writes in "Mourning and Melancholia," the ego becomes completely impoverished, incapable of love or achievement; it regresses from narcissistic object choice (a love object chosen for its similarity with the subject) to narcissistic identification with the lost object. "The ego can kill itself only if, owing to the return of the object-cathexis, it can treat itself as an object—if it is able to direct against itself the hostility which relates to an object and which represents the ego's original reaction to objects in the external world. . . . In the two opposed situations of being most intensely in love and of suicide the ego is overwhelmed by the object, though in totally different ways."[33]

The way of suicide, Freud clarifies, can occur when the love for the lost object was ambivalent; that is to say, mixed with resentment or hatred toward the one who has abandoned or betrayed us. It is the hatred toward the object, now introjected into the ego, that overwhelms the melancholic subject and produces the tendency to suicide. In *Beyond the Pleasure Principle,* he speculates that "the riddle of life" consists in the co-presence of two opposing forces, the life instincts (Eros) and the death instincts, which "were struggling with each other from the very first."[34] In this perspective, René's suicide is both the ultimate realization/consummation of the cultural fantasy (the death of Butterfly) and the representation of death at work in the cinema—the imbrication of the erotic drive in the death drive.

In all of Cronenberg's films, the death drive is consistently represented in conjunction with the sexual drive, nowhere more explicitly—and indeed literally—than in *Crash* (1996), where the compulsion to repeat violent and traumatic experiences is intertwined with the sexual drive in the erotization of traffic accidents. Speaking of his films, Cronenberg insists that death is only a transformation (compare the scene of the dragonfly in *M. Butterfly*, which was not in the script but was added by the director, on impulse, during the shooting in Beijing). Here René's death is figured as a transformation that is more properly a transfiguration: what he sees in the mirror is both a death mask and a living legend, the fantasy of Butterfly come alive once more.

Thus the reading of René's suicide as an effect of melancholia does not contradict but rather complicates the interpretation of Gallimard/Butterfly's death scene as a supreme expression of fetishistic desire. For the latter is supported by several considerations. First, he ends his life with an elaborate, well-planned, public performance not suggestive of a melancholic subject but rather of a willful if deluded one. Second, with this performance he reaffirms his narcissism, his existence as subject of desire, his masculine potency: he has been loved by the perfect woman (the fetishist's phallic mother), and he is still loved by her since she is now about to die for him. Third, his restaging of the fetish—Butterfly in all the spectacular accoutrements of the masquerade, complete with the "immortal" music of Puccini's opera, bears witness to the rigid, formal, and compelling nature of the fetishistic fantasy. Finally, in Puccini's *Madama Butterfly* the turn to the tragic ending also occurs with a revelation. When Cho-cho-san sees Pinkerton's American wife, who has come with him to take away her child, she realizes that she has been repudiated as wife: she has lost not only the objects of her love, Pinkerton and the child, but also her honor and, thus, the possibility of existence as social subject, which is defined, for a woman, by being a wife and a mother. When Song's maleness is revealed, René loses the possibility of existence as a desiring subject. Hence Cronenberg's brilliant idea to replace the *seppuku* dagger (symbol of social honor), not with its modern Western equivalent but with the mirror (symbol of narcissistic self-love), supports the interpretation of fetishism.

But René's death is not the apotheosis of a hero, does not result in the attainment of a higher order of knowledge, as does the death of Oedipus at Colonus, or in the creation of a new heroic legend of the birth of a nation in the way the legacy of Oedipus is the creation of the Athenian democratic state. René's death is the do-it-yourself replica of a worn cultural cliché on a makeshift institutional stage. In this regard, the manner of death is significant. The shard of mirror with which René kills himself is a densely polyvalent visual signifier, a poetic metaphor by which the film-text knots together multiple associative threads.[35] Death by mirror on a prison stage cannot but suggest the function of the psychoanalytic mirror stage defined by Lacan as the first matrix of the ego, an ego constituted by narcissistic, self-aggrandizing impulses and in the misrecognition of its mortality, its division, its death drive.

Western man looks into the mirror and sees the face of his other(s), an Orientalist pastiche of Chinese and Japanese costume and makeup. This is the stereotype of the racial, cultural, and gendered other that he himself has constructed for his civilization, his history, his desire; and he is finally consumed like Dr. Frankenstein by his own creation, his own will to domination. In René Gallimard's end—his name is the epitome of Western philosophy and French high culture: René for Descartes and Gallimard for the French publishing company—the discontents of Western civilization have come full circle, and the aggression that it had displaced onto its colonized others now turns around upon itself, upon the colonizer. The once mighty Western man is reduced to a pathetic figure in drag slumped on the prison floor in a heap of colored rags, without even the homage of a majestic panorama paid by Visconti to the protagonist of his *Death in Venice* (Italy, 1971).

And yet . . . what lives on through the repeat performance of Butterfly in Cronenberg's film is the staging of the fantasy, the mise-en-scène of love and death in which the masquerade of femininity, the colonial fetish, Butterfly, sustains Western man's desire, his capacity to disavow, his narcissistic self-absorption: "I'm a man who loved a woman created by a man. *Anything else simply falls short.*" Paradoxically, René must die Butterfly's death so that his desire may live in the consummation of the fantasy, as eros, the vital principle, only ever delays the inexorable movement toward death. Just as Butterfly, time and again reborn with each performance, is the fetish that sustains René's desire, cinema is a fetish that sustains our belief in the Western subject's desire in postcolonial times.

The ability to hold two contrary beliefs, which Freud named disavowal (*Verleugnung*), is the psychic mechanism that sustains fetishistic desire. Cinema, with its lush scenarios, the privileged vision afforded by its close-ups, the mobility of its cameras, its image and sound editing techniques, the ever-renewed wonder of its special effects, endlessly rearticulates popular culture narratives, Shakespeare and the novel, opera and Oedipus, public and private fantasies, engaging the spectator's identification and desire in what Coleridge, before Freud, named the "willing suspension of disbelief." Christian Metz observes that the technical, material apparatus of cinema itself works as a fetish for the spectator. As the masquerade of femininity in *M. Butterfly* is the fetish object that constitutes Butterfly as the body of desire, so is

> the technical equipment of the cinema with respect to the cinema as a whole. A fetish, the cinema as a technical performance, as prowess, as an *exploit,* an exploit that underlines and denounces the lack on which the whole arrangement is based (the absence of the object, replaced by its reflection), an exploit which consists at the same time of making this absence forgotten. The cinema fetishist is the person who is enchanted at what the machine is capable of, at the *theater of shadows* as such.[36]

In this sense Cronenberg's film is also a metacinematic meditation on cinematic fetishism, on cinema itself as fetish, fantasy object, spectacular performance, and artifice. *M. Butterfly's* masquerade of femininity mirrors the masquerade that is cinema, relaying its effect as a fantasy object that sustains the illusion of desire. Perhaps this is what underlies the popularity of cinema and its capacity to entertain (etymologically, hold between), to capture the look and solicit identifications, to position and *hold* the spectator between its shots, its images and sounds. In the particular fetish objects of cinema's fantasy scenarios, as in the very essence of cinema as fetish, one can find and live the fantasy of existing as a desiring subject.

Cinema's Fantasies

With the term fantasy I have designated both the activity of fantasizing, whether individual or collective, and its products—an imaginary scene, an imagined scenario, a mise-en-scène, a fictional world. These may be represented mentally, as in subjective fantasies (imagining), expressed in private or semiprivate situations, or may be constructed materially (imaging) in cinema, opera, and other public contexts of performance. Cronenberg's film is at once the public representation of a fantasy and an exploration of the effects of public fantasies on the private fantasies of individuals; it thus lends itself particularly well to an analysis of the different aspects and levels of fantasy in the cinema.

M. Butterfly is an ironic re-presentation—a deconstruction and a reappropriation—of the popular, public fantasy inscribed in Puccini's opera. The film ironizes and deconstructs the cultural narrative of femininity contained in the opera libretto by showing that it is an orientalist fantasy based on hierarchies of gender, race, and political domination;[37] but it also reappropriates that fantasy to its own ends. The film poses the questions of fantasy and desire very directly and explicitly in relation to gender, sexuality, and racial-cultural difference in postcoloniality; these issues are completely imbricated in one another both in the relationship of Song and René and in their respective relations to the Butterfly fantasy. And just as they are caught up in the operatic scenario that sustains their respective desires, so is the spectator moved by the film's narrative and its scenario of desire. As the opera mediates the relation of Song and René to the fantasy they share, articulating its desiring positions, they in turn mediate the spectator's relation to the film's fantasy and the desiring positions it inscribes.

Thus, in *M. Butterfly,* fantasy is not only a thematics but a mise-en-abîme, the structuring device of the film's mirror construction. There are three levels of fantasy at work in the film:

1. *The diegetic fantasy.* This is the fantasy portrayed in the world of the film, the fantasy of Butterfly as inscribed in Puccini's opera and pursued, reenacted by the two characters.

2. *The film's fantasy.* Even as it deconstructs the diegetic fantasy as an orientalist fantasy, the film restages its own fantasy of Butterfly as an orientalist fantasy that is, nevertheless, shared by two men, one Asian and one European, one homosexual and one heterosexual, and sustains their sexual relationship and respective desires; a fantasy into which the film invites the spectator as a participant voyeur.

3. *The spectator's fantasy.* And then there is the fantasizing that the film elicits in its spectator. This is, of course, mental and subjective; moreover, a good deal of our fantasies remain unconscious. Thus spectatorial fantasies can only be glimpsed in the ways spectators respond to the film, in the effects of identification, pleasure and displeasure that the film produces in each viewer, traces of which

may be found, for instance, in the reviews or critical readings of the film, including the one I've been sketching here.

Critics (who, of course, are first of all spectators) have tended to direct their attention to one or two of these issues in particular, seldom to all three, and have based their interpretations of the characters on the issue(s) emphasized. Thus they may have seen the same film and yet they have not seen the same film, for each reading or review suggests a subjective viewing, a particular take or entry into the film from a certain point of spectatorial identification. But, one may well ask, what does "seeing a film" mean? Insofar as the film is a text, there can be no one meaning, no definitive vision, no single, comprehensive or total view. Moreover, any object seen, be it represented or perceptual, be it image or object of the "real world," is an object of vision; that is to say, it is seen by a viewing subject through a purposeful attending and a selective gathering of clues which may cohere into meaningful percepts.[38] While all seeing is selective and dependent on contextual expectations, seeing a film entails particular effects of *identification with,* as well as *identification of,* the objects seen.[39] The "willing suspension of disbelief" that marks our complicity in cinema's fantasies also stimulates and elicits the activity of fantasizing in the spectator. In this sense, viewers may see the same film but produce different fantasies in relation to it.

When Cronenberg, speaking about his casting of Song Liling, says, "I wanted a man. When Gallimard and Song are kissing I wanted it to be two men. I wanted the audience to feel that," he may be playing his own role of Hollywood's *enfant terrible,* shocking the conservatives in the audience. For, when he discusses the film in interviews and states his ideas about characters' motivations and his directorial choices, he expresses a view of sexuality that is quite conservatively framed by the traditional gender polarity of maleness and femaleness: "Sexuality has become detached from the physiology of reproduction and so it now is almost an abstract force," a bisexual potential for self-creation and transformation, "an agreed-upon fantasy" between any two lovers, who play out "all the maleness and femaleness" between them.[40] For Cronenberg, then, sexuality is propped on gender performance—the qualities, gestures, behavior, masquerade of gender, rather than the bodies of the lovers. As in the science-fiction fantasy of Ursula K. Le Guin's *The Left Hand of Darkness,*[41] any two lovers in Cronenberg's fantasy will always agree upon a fantasy in which one is the man and the other the girl: someone must be "the girl on the set," and it will not be Gallimard, with whom Cronenberg identifies as indicated by the pronoun "she" that he most often uses in reference to Song/Lone. "The way I talked to John Lone about [the character] was that Song meets Gallimard, does her routine almost tongue in cheek, sees that he's actually falling for it, gets him isolated from his embassy staff in case somebody tells him that she's not a woman and sees how far she can go. She's flattered, excited and aroused to have him start to fall in love with her and be seduced by her. And then she is caught with him."[42]

The equivocation between gender and sexuality is apparent in the next sentence, which identifies Song as homosexual (as a man) and the director's wish to shock his audience: "I added a shot—Song's housemaid Shu Fang peeking through the window at them—on the day of shooting. I wanted to suggest that she blows the whistle on Song, who is then forced to spy, or it's a serious labor camp for being a homosexual."[43]

And yet, in spite of the fact that he takes pains to make Song's desire explicit in the film, in the climactic scene in the paddy wagon Song is no longer a homosexual but only the foil of Gallimard's disenchantment: "Song is this creature: male, female, east, west, invented. Song is no longer this thing they created. . . . It's really very applicable to a lot of normal relationships. A lot of marriages fall apart when that willed suspension of disbelief collapses and suddenly the thing that you've created together is not there any more. *You see each other plain and you don't like what you see because it's not enough.*"[44]

I emphasized the last sentence to point out that while "you see each other" ostensibly refers to both members of the couple, in fact it only refers to one: Song has always seen Gallimard "plain" but that, for him, is "enough." For the director, then, the emotional point of view, his point of identification in the film's fantasy, is Gallimard. While he casts two men in the film, still his fantasy is heterosexual: the scenario demands a girl ("the girl on the set") to cajole and play to the man's desire—just as in marriage (John Lone "really was the girl on the set and that was great. If you needed femaleness, he was it").

Similarly, if with contrary emphasis, Richard Corliss, reviewing the film in *Time* magazine, decries Lone's "five-o'clock shadow [which] gives him away to everyone but the diplomat." The critic's displeasure in the failed womanliness of Lone's Butterfly is the flip side of the director's pleasure in her "femaleness": "If you needed femaleness, he was it." And they do need it, they both see or need to see Song from the point of view of Gallimard as a woman. Corliss's fantasy of Butterfly, however, is perfectly embodied in another Chinese actor, "Leslie Cheung, the beautifully androgynous star of *Farewell My Concubine*. . . . He is enough woman for any man to fall for."[45] Which is another way of saying, as Gallimard says: "I am a man who loves a woman created by a man. Anything else simply falls short." In other words, the Butterfly fantasy also works for Corliss; it's simply the "five-o'clock shadow" that doesn't—that falls short, as it were.

Further extolling the charms of Leslie Cheung, Corliss describes the actor's characterization of "a homosexual star of the Peking opera" in *Farewell My Concubine* as "both steely and vulnerable, with a sexuality that transcends gender—a Mandarin Michael Jackson."[46] One wonders what sort of sexuality the critic imagines such a character to have (Does one have a sexuality as one has sex, or as one has, say, black hair?); moreover, what is a sexuality that transcends gender, although it evidently does not transcend racialization?[47] Whatever it may be, clearly there is no possibility for the *Time* reviewer to own or identify with it: such a sexuality pertains to the other, Butterfly or Concubine, the Chinese actor(s), the homosexuals, the Michael Jacksons of various colors, who are "enough woman" for *any man* to fall for.

Many people, nowadays, use the word gender to speak of sexuality. The rhetorical confusion, when it is not equivocation, between two terms or discursive entities that, albeit mutually implicated, have very different histories and cultural locations, is rendered more acute by the media-generated public awareness of practices of transvestism, the choreography of transsexualism, and the growing currency of the term "transgender," all of which are independent of sexual object-choice (i.e., their subjects or practitioners may desire or engage in heterosexual, same-sex, self-sex, heterogeneous-sex, even no-sex practices). The rhetorical assimilation of gender and sexuality serves many purposes, from euphemism in polite conversation to disrupting the moral status quo, all the way to the conceptual evacuation of the very terms "sexuality" and "gender"; and who stands to gain or to lose from rendering them indistinct is an interesting question that I must leave for another discussion. For the purposes of this discussion of the film *M. Butterfly*, I use the terms in the old-fashioned sense: gender for masculine or feminine identification; sexuality for heterosexual or same-sex desire. I noted earlier that the problem of how to refer to Song Liling by personal pronouns is a constant reminder of the discursive constructedness of gender. Now I will add that it is also a sign of spectatorial identification. For example, Cronenberg's referring to Song as "she," which signals his identification *of* Song as a woman ("Butterfly"), suggests his identification *with* Gallimard. Another spectator/critic refers to Song Liling as "she" but with a different set of identifications.

Rey Chow's "The Dream of a Butterfly" is, to my knowledge, the most theoretically rich and historically contextualized critical reading of the film published to date.[48] In many ways, my reading is in solidarity with hers. I concur with her assessment of the central role of fantasy in the film and with her argument against a simply "political," didactic reading of the Orientalist *content* of the fantasy. I admire her lucid discussion of Lacan's concept of the gaze in relation to the film. Moreover, Chow's reading of Song's masquerade of femininity is also similar to mine here, with one distinction. Whereas I call the femininity represented in M. *Butterfly* a *fetish*, Chow calls it the phallus: "Song exists for Gallimard as the phallus in Lacan's sense of the term" (74); thus, in the paddy wagon scene, when he undresses before Gallimard, "Song fails to see that what Gallimard 'wants' is not him, Song, be he in the definitive form of a woman or a man, but, as Gallimard says, 'Butterfly.' Because Gallimard's desire hinges on neither a female nor a male body, but rather on the phallus, the veiled thing that is the 'Oriental woman,' Song's candid disclosure of his physical body . . . serves not to arouse but extinguish desire" (77).

The distinction between our two conceptualizations of the Butterfly trope in the film is the distinction between fetish and phallus. By saying that Song's Butterfly is the phallus, which must remain veiled, masqueraded ("the veiled thing that is the 'Oriental woman'"), Chow adheres to the Lacanian definition of woman's position in desire: she wants to be the phallus, the signifier of the desire of the Other. But what about Song's desire? Since the Butterfly fantasy is also the scenario of Song's desire, to equate "Butterfly" with the phallus is to assume that Song's homosexual desire is from the position of a woman (woman as phallus). Which is to see homosexuality as sexual and gender inversion, in the old sexological formula that Lacan's theory raises to a higher level of abstraction.[49] Here is where my reading and Chow's part ways or diverge—on the issue of the nature of desire and the conditions of spectatorial identification. Not surprisingly, the film elicits in me a very different fantasy.

Chow uses the feminine personal pronoun "she" to identify the character Song Liling by gender or self-presentation rather than by anatomical sex. While this may indicate respect for one's choice of gender identity, it ignores Song's homosexual desire. In this Chow follows Cronenberg and Hwang,[50] both of whom deny or minimize the significance of Song's homosexual desire for René, although her identification, unlike theirs, is not with Gallimard but with Song; in other words, Chow's referring to Song as "she" signals her identification *of* Song as a woman, but also her identification *with* Song as a woman. However, if one defines Song as a woman solely on account of gender, without consideration of sexuality and desire, the motivation for his actions and his sexual relationship with René can only be a political one: Song is a spy, does what he does for the love of his country, not of René—a characterization the film ironizes (most evidently in the two scenes between Song and Comrade Chin) and openly disallows.[51] Alternatively, Song's motivation is one of anticolonial resistance and revenge: he just plays the role of Butterfly to turn the Orientalist fantasy against its colonial, imperialist creator. In my view, the film also belies this reading, especially (but not only) in the paddy wagon scene after the trial, when Song tries in vain to convince René to accept his transvestite fantasy of Butterfly as a gay fantasy. There, when the spying game is all played out, it seems to me beyond doubt that, whatever else he may be, Song is a man who loves a man.

And yet, if one identifies Song as a woman, and *with* Song as a woman, one sees a different film. Chow, for example, writes: "At no moment in the film M. *Butterfly* does Song's subjectivity and desire become lucid to us . . . until in the 'showdown' scene in the police van. In that scene, we see for the first time that what she 'wants' is a complete overturning of the laws of desire that have structured her relationship with Gallimard. In other words, in spite of her love for the Frenchman, what the 'Oriental woman' wants is nothing less than the liquidation of his entire sexual ontological being—his death" (87).

After the paddy wagon scene, in which Song's homosexual desire can no longer be in doubt, Chow's interpretation moves to the allegorical level, and Song is read as a figure for the avenging "Oriental woman" who, in the end, goes off in her airplane like Pinkerton on his ship, leaving the Western man to his demise, humbled as he had humbled Butterfly, the tables turned. Such an interpretation could be given of the text of the stage play and is, in fact, the interpretation favored by the playwright: "The Frenchman fantasizes that he is Pinkerton and his lover is Butterfly. By the end of the piece, he realizes that it is he who has been Butterfly, in that the Frenchman has been duped by love; the Chinese spy, who exploited that love, is therefore the real Pinkerton."[52] However, this reversal of the roles of the dominant narrative, by ignoring Song's desire, denies his subjectivity and turns him into a trope for political liberation, an allegorical figure, a counter-Butterfly, no less ideological than Puccini's Cho-cho-san who wanted so much to be Mrs. Pinkerton, an American. But this is precisely the didactic interpretation that Chow herself wants to discredit.

The contradiction in Chow's reading of the film suggests to me the active presence of a spectatorial fantasy: the spectator projects her own wish into the film's scenario and narrative resolution, sees herself in—identifies with—the character of Song, and invests it with the role that she herself would play in the fantasy scenario; that is, the role of the woman who will not die for love of the imperialist, Western "devil" but wants his death instead, "the liquidation of his entire sexual ontological being." This, however, is not a fantasy of vengeance or simple role reversal. In the brief coda that includes the last long passage quoted, Chow extends her reading of the film to pose anew the question of cultural and gender difference, making explicit the critical and political nature, as well as the subjective grounds, of her identification *with* and *of* Song as a woman: "By definition, the death of the white man signals the dawn of a fundamentally different way of coming to terms with the East. The film closes with 'Butterfly' flying back to China. This 'Oriental woman' who existed as the white man's symptom—what will happen to her now that the white man is dead? That is the ultimate question with which we are left" (87).

It seems to me that John Lone's performance of the character, in keeping with Cronenberg's (re)vision, does not sustain such a reading and that Chow's concluding question can only emerge as an effect of a compelling, political and personal, spectatorial fantasy. His expression as he sits on the plane, in male clothes, is not one of victory or revenge but one of sadness and loss. Closing as it does on this image of Song, the film reaffirms his presence as the man whom neither Gallimard nor the director (nor some spectators) can or wish to see. Or so it seems to me. For my spectatorial identification is also with Song although, from the beginning of the film, I identified him as a man, and hence have been referring to him by the masculine pronoun throughout this reading.

Concomitant with the necessary, narrative identification with Gallimard as the "hero" of the film, my fantasmatic identification is with Song. As far as I can know (or think I know), my spectatorial fantasy is based on his politically incorrect desire, which exists in spite of his awareness of its Orientalist, colonialist nature and indeed in spite of its impossibility. I identify with the predicament that Song not only exemplifies but also lives with conscious determination, for his desire *is* the predicament: he can be loved only as a woman created by a man and *for* a man—the predicament of femininity; he can be loved by a man only as a woman—the predicament of a homosexual in a heteronormative world. In other words, the predicament of desire: to be loved in a scenario in which your part is scripted by the other, and to be loved as a woman when one is not one.

First published with the title "Public and Private Fantasies: Femininity and Fetishism in David Cronenberg's *M. Butterfly*" in *Signs: Journal of Women in Culture and Society* 24. 2 (Winter 1999): 303–34.

III

Epistemologies

© 1993 ZOE LEONARD, "ANATOMICAL MODEL OF A WOMAN'S
HEAD CRYING" (1993). GELATIN SILVER PRINT.
COURTESY OF THE ARTIST.

Chapter 7

Eccentric Subjects

onsciousness, as a term of feminist thought, is poised on the divide that joins and distinguishes the opposing terms in a series of conceptual sets central to contemporary theories of culture: subject and object, self and other, private and public, oppression and resistance, domination and agency, hegemony and marginality, sameness and difference, and so on. In the early 1970s, in its first attempt at self-definition, feminism posed the question, Who or what is a woman? Who or what am I? And, as it posed those questions, feminism—a social movement of and for women—discovered the nonbeing of *woman:* the paradox of a being that is at once captive and absent in discourse, constantly spoken of but of itself inaudible or inexpressible, displayed as spectacle and still unrepresented or unrepresentable, invisible yet constituted as the object and the guarantee of vision; a being whose existence and specificity are simultaneously asserted and denied, negated and controlled.[1]

In a second moment of self-conscious reflection, then, addressing the question to itself, feminism would realize that a feminist theory must

start from and centrally engage that very paradox. For if the constitution of the social subject depends on the nexus language/subjectivity/
consciousness—if, in other words, the personal is political because the
political becomes personal by way of its subjective effects through the
subject's experience—then the theoretical object or field of knowledge
of feminism and the modes of knowing we want to claim as feminist
(method, knowledges, or consciousness) are themselves caught in the
paradox of woman. They are excluded from the established discourse
of theory and yet imprisoned within it or else assigned a corner of their
own but denied a specificity.

That, I will argue, is precisely where the particular discursive and
epistemological character of feminist theory resides: its being at once
inside its own social and discursive determinations and yet also outside
and excessive to them. This recognition marks a further, or third, moment in feminist theory, which is its current stage of reconceptualization
and elaboration of new terms: (1) a reconceptualization of the subject
as shifting and multiply organized across variable axes of difference; (2)
a rethinking of the relations between forms of oppression and modes
of formal understanding—of doing theory; (3) an emerging redefinition
of marginality as location, of identity as dis-identification; and (4) the
hypothesis of self-displacement as the term of a movement that is concurrently social and subjective, internal and external, indeed political
and personal.

These notions all but dispel the view of a feminism singular or unified
either in its rhetorical and political strategies or in its terms of conceptual analysis. That view of feminism is prevalent in academic discourse
in spite of the current emphasis on the cultural, racial, and political
differences that inform an indefinite number of variously hyphenated
or modified feminisms (white, black, Third World, Jewish, socialist,
Marxist, liberal, cultural, structural, psychoanalytic, and so forth).
Here, however, I will use the term "feminist theory," like the terms
"consciousness" or "subject," in the singular, to mean not a single,
unified perspective, but a process of understanding that is premised
on historical specificity and on the simultaneous, if often contradictory, presence of those differences in each of its instances and practices, a process that, furthermore, seeks to account for their ideological
inscriptions.

The Paradox of Woman

"Humanity is male," wrote Simone de Beauvoir in 1949, "and man defines woman not in herself but as relative to him; she is not regarded as an autonomous being. . . . He is the Subject, he is the Absolute—she is the Other." And to stretch the point further, she quoted Emmanuel Lévinas: "Otherness reaches its full flowering in the feminine, a term of the same rank as consciousness but of opposite meaning. . . . Is there not a case in which otherness, alterity (*altérité*) unquestionably marks the nature of a being, as its essence, an instance of otherness not consisting purely and simply in the opposition of two species of the same genus? I think that the feminine represents the contrary in its absolute sense."[2] How does it come to pass that woman, who is defined on the one hand in relation to man, although as lesser than man or an "imperfect man," is simultaneously made to represent otherness in its absolute sense?

For de Beauvoir "the category of *Other* is as primordial as consciousness itself" or, put another way, "Otherness is a fundamental category of human thought." She finds in Hegel the sense of a "hostility" of consciousness to the other: "the subject can be posed only in being opposed—he sets himself up as the essential, as opposed to the other, the inessential, the object" (xx). Thus, she suggests, by attempting to deny any reciprocity between subject and object, the (male) subject of consciousness casts woman as object in a realm of radical alterity; but because he continues to need her as "the sex," the source of sexual desire as well as offspring, he remains related (or kin) to her, and she to him, by a reciprocal need not unlike that of the master to the slave. Hence, the paradoxical definition of woman as a human being fundamentally essential to man and at the same time an inessential object, radically other.[3]

The question arises for de Beauvoir, Why does woman acquiesce to the status of object? Whence comes the submission or complicity that makes her "fail to lay claim to the status of subject"and forsake the aspiration to consciousness? For if the reciprocal need of man and woman is "equally urgent for both," as de Beauvoir says of the need of master and slave, "it always works in favor of the oppressor and against the oppressed" (xxiii). Her answer is that the bond which unites woman to her oppressor is not comparable to any other (such as the proletariat's to the bourgeoisie or the American Negro's to the white master) in that it can never be broken, since "the division of the sexes is a biological fact, not an event in human history . . . the cleavage of society along the line of sex is impossible" (xxiii). Herein lies, for de Beauvoir, "the drama of woman, [the] conflict between the fundamental aspiration of every subject (ego)—who always regards the self as the essential—and the compulsion of a situation in which she is the inessential" (xxxiv).

Several questions arise for a contemporary reader of this text: Who grants de Beauvoir the status of subject of her discourse on woman? What consciousness can she lay claim to, in the perspective of existentialist humanism, if not the very same consciousness that opposes subject and object, except that perhaps woman may be recovered for the side of the Subject and granted "full membership in the human race" (xxxiv), while radical alterity is relocated elsewhere? Is it enough that she and a few more women, "fortunate in the restoration of all the privileges pertaining to the estate of the human being, can afford the luxury of impartiality" and so be "qualified to elucidate the situation of woman" with an "objective" attitude of "detachment" (xxxi–xxxii)? In a contemporary feminist perspective, these questions are both moot and still very much at issue. In the first instance, they are moot because history has answered them, not in her favor. The history of feminism—with its compromises, its racial arrogance, its conceptual and ideological blind spots—has made the answers painfully explicit. In the second instance, however, a self-conscious and historically conscious feminist theory cannot dispense with the paradox, the inconsistency or internal contradiction which those questions reveal in what has become one of the classic texts of feminism.

The reason we cannot dispense with it is that, for women, the paradox of woman is not an illusion or a seeming contradiction but a real one. As Catharine A. MacKinnon argues, in what appears to be a direct response to de Beauvoir, feminism is a critique of male dominance and of the male point of view which "has forced itself upon the world, and does force itself upon the world as its way of knowing." Gender itself, she continues, is less a matter of (sexual) difference than an instance of that dominance; and the appeal to biology as determining the "fact" of women's sexual specificity is an ideological by-product of the male way of knowing, whose epistemological stance of objectivity reflects not only the Western subject's habit of control through objectification (de Beauvoir's "hostility" of consciousness) but also its eroticization of the act of control itself. In this sense, "the eroticization of dominance and submission creates gender. . . . The erotic is what defines sex as inequality, hence as a meaningful difference. . . . Sexualized objectification is what defines women as sexual *and as women* under male supremacy."[4]

To remark this point, elsewhere MacKinnon quotes John Berger's compelling account of sexual objectification in *Ways of Seeing* and significantly extends the analysis into the domain of the visual:

> A woman must continually watch herself. She is almost continually accompanied by her own image of herself. . . . She comes to consider the surveyor and the surveyed within her as the two constituent yet always distinct elements of her identity as a woman. . . . Men look at women. Women watch themselves being looked at. This determines not only most relations between men and women but also the relation of women to themselves. The surveyor of woman in herself is male: the surveyed, female. Thus she turns herself into an object—and most particularly an object of vision: a sight.[5]

Thus, it is objectification that constitutes woman as sexual, instating sexuality at the core of the material reality of women's lives, rather than the other way around, as notions of biological determinism would have it in claiming that sexual difference defines woman and causes her objectification, or as the process appears (reversed) in the "culturalist" ideology of gender. For even if "one is not born, but rather becomes, a woman," making herself into an erotic object for man, as de Beauvoir put it (301), the manner of that becoming may still be explained in a similar way by arguing that it is the cultural apprehension of woman's innate sexual specificity ("difference") which causes her to be objectified in male-directed culture.

MacKinnon's point is that that sexual specificity itself is constructed at once as "difference" and as erotic by the eroticization of dominance and submission. In other words, objectification, or the act of control, defines woman's difference (woman as object/other), and the eroticization of the act of control defines woman's difference as sexual (erotic), thus, at one and the same time, defining "women as sexual and as women." And, MacKinnon suggests, this constitutive, material presence of sexuality as objectification and self-objectification ("she turns herself into an object—and most particularly an object of vision") is where the specificity of female subjectivity and consciousness may be located (26). I would further suggest that precisely that constant turn of subject into object into subject is what grounds a different relation, for women, to the erotic, to consciousness, and to knowing.

The relations between domination, sexuality, and objectification in the male "way of knowing" and the possible configuration of a female epistemological and ontological point of view are posed by Nancy Hartsock in terms at once similar and quite divergent from MacKinnon's "agenda for theory." Both writers start out from Marx, taking the Marxian concepts of work and labor, class oppression, and class (proletarian) standpoint as directly pertinent to feminist theory. In one case, "just as Marx's understanding of the world from the standpoint of the proletariat enabled him to go beneath bourgeois ideology, so a feminist standpoint can allow us to understand patriarchal institutions and ideologies as perverse inversions of more humane social relations."[6] In the other case, as MacKinnon writes: "Marxism and feminism are theories of power and its distribution: inequality. They provide accounts of how social arrangements of patterned disparity can be internally rational yet unjust."[7] However, while Hartsock assumes Marx's meta-theoretical stance (that only the point of view of the oppressed class can reveal the real social relations and so lead to change them) and seeks to convert the notion of proletarian standpoint to a feminist standpoint based on "the sexual division of labor," MacKinnon sets up a metatheoretical parallelism between the two theories based on two terms that inscribe the relations of the subject to power and to consciousness: "Sexuality is to feminism what work is to Marxism: that which is most one's own, yet most taken away" (1). The resulting trajectories diverge.

Hartsock's analysis of the sexual division of labor, where "women as a sex are institutionally responsible for producing both goods and human beings,"[8] is coupled with an account of human psychological development loosely derived from object relations theory. Together, they lead her to argue that women are like workers but better, or rather, more so: "Women and workers inhabit a world in which the emphasis is on change rather than stasis, a world characterized by interaction with natural substances rather than separation from nature, a world in which quality is more important than quantity, a world in which the unification of mind and body is inherent in the activities performed" (290). However, as women also (re)produce human beings, this activity affords them a heightened, specifically female "experience of continuity and relation—with others, with the natural world, of mind and body" which in turn "provides an ontological base for developing a non-problematic [non-contradictory?] social synthesis" (303). Hartsock's scenario suggests a happy ending, although the trajectory runs through a path uncharted toward a structurally wobbly utopia: "Generalizing the activity of women to the social system as a whole would raise, for the first time in human history, the possibility of a fully human community, a community structured by connection rather than separation and opposition" (305). She concludes her essay by quoting Marx, amended by writing women in, in lieu of men.

MacKinnon's trajectory, on the other hand, ends up in post-Marxism, doubling the Marxist critique back upon itself in a scenario of continuing struggle by what could be called a subject-in-process, in the here and now.

> Feminism stands in relation to marxism as marxism does to classical political economy: its final conclusion and ultimate critique. Compared with marxism, the place of thought and things in method and reality are reversed in a seizure of power that penetrates subject with object and theory with practice. In a dual motion, feminism turns marxism inside out and on its head.[9]

The point of divergence of the two trajectories is the notion of sexuality and its relation to consciousness. Although Hartsock does not use the word "sexuality" in her essay, women's specificity as social beings is said to consist in their reproductive labor, mothering, which constructs "female experience" as sensuous, relational, in contact with the concreteness of use values and material necessity, in continuity and connectedness with other people and with the natural world, and thus in direct opposition to "male experience" as "abstract masculinity."[10] The "profound unity of mental and manual labor, social and natural worlds" that characterizes women's work and the "female construction of self in relation to others" (and hence the feminist standpoint derived from them) "grows from the fact that women's bodies, unlike men's, can be themselves instruments of production."[11] What affords women a true, nonperverse viewpoint and the potential for fully human community in a world of perverse sociosexual relations is their cultural construction as mothers (or mothering), based on the specific productivity of their bodies, their biological sexuality. Similarly, although the word "consciousness" does not appear in the essay, it is implicit in the notion of standpoint as an "engaged" vision, one which is available to the oppressed group but must be achieved or struggled for: "I use the term 'feminist' rather than 'female' here to indicate both the achieved character of a standpoint and that a standpoint by definition carries a liberatory potential" (289). Thus, in Hartsock's view, women's sexuality and consciousness of self stand in a direct, noncontradictory relation of near-synonymity. Both are subsumed in the activity of mothering, and both are exploited thereby. What may transform female experience into feminist consciousness, what produces consciousness, is left unexplained.

MacKinnon, on the contrary, focuses on consciousness as product and the form of feminist practice, the ground of a feminist standpoint or method, and of feminism's divergence from Marxism. "Consciousness raising is the major technique of analysis, structure of organization, method of practice, and theory of social change of the women's movement."[12] Through consciousness raising, that is to say, through "the collective critical reconstitution of the meaning of women's social experience, as women live through it" (29), feminism has allowed women to see their social and sexual identity as both externally constructed and internalized. MacKinnon writes:

> In order to account for women's consciousness (much less propagate it) feminism must grasp that male power produces the world before it distorts it. . . . To raise consciousness is to confront male power in this duality: as total on one side and a delusion on the other. In consciousness raising, women learn they have *learned* that men are everything, women their negation, but that the sexes are equal. The content of the message is revealed true and false at the same time. . . . Their chains become visible, their inferiority—their inequality—a product of subjection and a mode of its enforcement. (28)

If consciousness raising is seen as feminist method, its difference from the method of dialectical materialism will be a crucial area of discrepancy between the two theories because "method shapes each theory's vision of social reality" (13). Unlike dialectical materialism, which "posits and refers to a reality outside thought" and requires the separation of theory as "pure" science from situated thought, for the latter is never immune from ideology, feminist consciousness posits and refers to a reality, women's sociosexual existence, that is a "mixture of thought and materiality" and seeks to know it "through a process that shares its determination: women's consciousness, not as individual or subjective ideas, but as collective social being." Put another way, feminist "method stands inside its own determinations in order to uncover them, just as it criticizes them in order to value them on its own terms—in order to *have* its own terms at all." Consequently, feminist theory is not directed outward, toward (the analysis of) an object-reality, but turns inward, toward the "pursuit of consciousness" and so "becomes a form of political practice." Finally, MacKinnon writes, if "consciousness raising has revealed gender relations to be a collective fact, no more simply personal than class relations," it can also reveal that "class relations may also be personal, no less so for being at the same time collective" (29).

This last point is particularly significant in view of the attempts, in recent Marxist theory, to establish the link between ideology and consciousness in the realm of subjectivity. Louis Althusser's own effort to define the construction of the subject in ideology by the state ideological apparatuses made him step into the area of theoretical overlap between Marxism and psychoanalysis,[13] opening up not merely the long-standing question of their possible integration but a speculative terrain in which the social relations of class may be addressed in conjunction with gender and race relations.[14] Yet, Althusser's opening of Marxist theory to the question of the subject, defined in Lacanian terms, resulted in the reaffirmation of a scientific knowledge (theory) unaffected by ideology or practices, with the consequent expulsion of subjectivity from knowledge, the containment of the subject in ideology, and of consciousness in false consciousness. MacKinnon's suggestion that feminist consciousness can grasp the personal, subjective effects of class or race relations, as it knows the personal yet collective effects of gender relations, is one I find more hopeful as well as more accurate and consonant with my own view of the position of the feminist subject vis-à-vis the ideology of gender.[15]

MacKinnon purports to steer clear of psychoanalysis, while Hartsock completely relies on the works of Nancy Chodorow and Dorothy Dinnerstein for her central argument that "as a result [of the developmental account provided by object relations theory] women define and experience themselves relationally and men do not."[16] Yet, it is MacKinnon whose notion of sexuality engages, or at least raises, questions of identity and identification, the relations of subjectivity to subjection and of objectification to internalized self-image, the conflict of representation with self-representation, the contradictions between consciousness and ideological (unconscious) complicity.

Asking questions such as these, which have been the focus of the feminist critique of representation in film and literature, the media and the arts (of which the Berger passage quoted earlier sketches one of the main areas of inquiry), has contributed to feminist theory much of its present depth, especially in the understanding of the central role of sexuality in the processes of female subjectivity and women's social identity. For example, it has contributed to dislodging female sexuality (to say nothing of pleasure) from the Procrustean bed of reproduction where patriarchal ends confine it, whether in the name of motherhood or by the name of labor. Asking the question of female sexuality and women's psycho-socio-sexual identity has meant asking it, at least initially, of psychoanalytic theory (particularly neo-Freudian psychoanalysis), because no other theory availed to articulate the terms of a female sexuality autonomous from reproduction or biological destiny. That psychoanalytic theory, in and of itself, remains inadequate to imaging—let alone accounting for—the modes and processes of a female sexuality autonomous from male sexuality, is made clear in feminist neo-Freudian or Lacanian works,[17] as well as in those based on object relations theory.[18] Nevertheless, if Hartsock's proposal of a feminist standpoint collapses on the fragility and reductionism of the latter's account of sexuality and subjectivity, MacKinnon's argument for the determining role of sexuality in women's material existence and (self)definition would only stand to gain in strength and articulation from the feminist psychoanalytic project of understanding the internalization, persistence, and reproduction of oppressive social norms within female subjectivity.

The specific contribution of neo-Freudian psychoanalysis to this understanding lies, as Juliet Mitchell emphasizes, in the notion of the unconscious: "The way we live as 'ideas' the necessary laws of human society is not so much conscious as *unconscious*—the particular task of psychoanalysis is to decipher how we acquire our heritage of the ideas and laws of human society within the unconscious mind, or, to put it another way, the unconscious mind is the way we acquire these laws."[19] Commenting on this passage, in the context of the conflictual history of feminism, psychoanalysis, Marxism, and Marxist feminism, Jacqueline Rose argues that if psychoanalysis can be seen "as the only means of explaining the exact mechanisms whereby ideological processes are transformed, via individual subjects, into human actions and beliefs," it is because psychoanalysis, like Marxism, sees those mechanisms "as determinant, but also leaving something in excess."

> The political case for psychoanalysis rests on these two insights together—otherwise it would be indistinguishable from a function- alist account of the internalisation of norms. . . . The difficulty is to pull psychoanalysis in the direction of both these insights—to- wards a recognition of the fully social constitution of identity and norms, and then back again to that point of tension between ego and unconscious where they are endlessly remodelled and endlessly break. (7)

When feminists and Marxists insist that any concept of psychic dy- namic or internal conflict is detrimental to politics, because the attention thereby accorded to fantasy denies "an unequivocal accusation of the real" (12), Rose states, they rely on a misconceived dichotomy between external events (oppression), which are seen as real, and internal events (the psychic manifestations of internalized oppressive norms, such as fantasy or the compulsion to repeat), which are seen as unreal.

> I would argue that the importance of psychoanalysis is precisely the way that it throws into crisis the dichotomy on which the appeal to the reality of the event . . . clearly rests. Perhaps for women it is of particular importance that we find a language which allows us to recognise our part in intolerable structures—but in a way which renders us neither the pure victims nor the sole agents of our distress. (14)

MacKinnon does recognize women's part in these "intolerable struc- tures" and their internal and conflictual character.

> I think that sexual desire in women, at least in this culture, is socially constructed as that by which we come to want our own

self-annihilation. That is, our subordination is eroticized in and as female. . . . This is our stake in this system that is not in our interest, our stake in this system that is killing us. I'm saying that femininity as we know it is how we come to want male dominance, which most emphatically is not in our interest.[20]

But her analytical framework, with its emphasis on the reality of the event—the reality of oppression as event—deflects or deemphasizes the understanding of resistance in psychic terms (through processes of identification or fantasy, for instance) and thus pushes the notion of agency in the direction of what Rose calls "a politics of sexuality based on assertion and will."[21]

On the other hand, to understand the unconscious "as a point of resistance" and to take into account its specific ability to exceed the mechanisms of social determination can lead to the realization of another crucial aspect of agency and its potential for feminist politics. This is, I would agree, an issue of particular relevance to feminist theory and one that cannot be addressed in the terms of MacKinnon's method of consciousness raising, which ignores the theory of the unconscious elaborated by neo-Freudian psychoanalysis, and whose notion of consciousness derives rather from ego psychology, although reclaimed and filtered through Georg Lukács's class consciousness. MacKinnon's dismissal of the American Freud limits her theory of feminist consciousness to a functionalist view of internalization by disallowing an account of the psychic mechanisms by which objectification is not only internalized but also resisted in female subjectivity. However, Rose's argument for the French Freud also cannot suggest a way to go beyond the institutional description of those mechanisms. "If psychoanalysis can give an account of how women experience the path to femininity, it also insists, through the concept of the unconscious, that femininity is neither simply achieved nor is it ever complete" (7), Rose states. And that is so, of course. But let me suggest that, in order for that resistance of the unconscious to be more than pure negativity, for it to be effectively agency rather than simply unachieved or incomplete femininity, one must be able to think beyond the conceptual constraint imposed by the term "femininity" and its binary opposite—its significant other—"masculinity."

That is precisely where, in my opinion, the notion of the unconscious as excess(ive) may be most productive. Could one think, for instance, of excess as a *resistance to* identification rather than unachieved identification? Or of a *dis-identification* with femininity that does not necessarily revert to or result in an identification with masculinity but, say, transfers to a form of female subjectivity that exceeds the phallic definition? These are questions that have not been posed by any denomination of psychoanalytic feminism but are nonetheless compatible with a theory of the unconscious as excess. Here I can do no more than suggest them as a crucial area of work in feminist theory.

Short of that, both Rose's and MacKinnon's views of female sexuality have a common limit in their equation of woman with femininity and in the pressure that the latter term exerts to close the critical distance between woman and women. As it stands, on the ground of that equation, Rose's eloquent case for the relevance of psychoanalysis to feminist theory goes no further than restating "the concept of a subjectivity at odds with itself" (15), which is only the starting point, the premise to be found in Freud's own writings on female sexuality, rather than the development of a feminist psychoanalytic theory. On her own terms, MacKinnon's absolutist emphasis on the (hetero)sexual monopoly of "male power" ("heterosexuality is the structure of the oppression of women"),[22] unmitigated by any possibility of resistance or agency through non-normative or autonomous forms of female sexuality (excessive, subversive, perverse, invert, or lesbian sexual practices), unintentionally works to recontain both feminist consciousness and female sexuality within the vicious circle of the paradox of woman. I propose that a point of view, or an eccentric discursive position outside the male (hetero)sexual monopoly of power/knowledge—which is to say, a point of view excessive to, or not contained by, the sociocultural institution of heterosexuality—is necessary to feminism at this point in history; that such a position exists in feminist consciousness as personal-political practice and can be found in certain feminist critical texts; and that position has, in effect, provided impulse, context, and direction to feminist theoretical work, including MacKinnon's, all along.

» » »

Except for its emphasis on sexuality, a concept much more encompassing and complexly articulated in contemporary thought, feminist and otherwise, than de Beauvoir's "sexual desire and the desire for offspring,"[23] MacKinnon's analysis of women's condition is still surprisingly similar to *The Second Sex,* of which it could be read as a historical reappraisal as well as critique. "Feminism has not changed the status of women" (2), MacKinnon writes in the introduction to her *Feminism Unmodified: Discourses on Life and Law,* forty years and a second wave of feminism since de Beauvoir's more optimistic introduction to *The Second Sex.* And if we ask "why feminist insights are often criticized for replicating male ideology [as de Beauvoir was], why feminists are called 'condescending to women' [as *The Second Sex* may certainly be called], when what we are doing is expressing and exposing how women are condescended to," her answer is, "Because male power has created in reality the world to which feminist insights, when they are accurate, refer" (59). That is, in de Beauvoir's words, "humanity is male" (xviii).

Several things have changed, however, forty years and several social movements later, and with them, the conceptual analysis of the social relations by which that humanity is comprised. Something of that change is adumbrated in the parallel structure of the two footnotes whereby de Beauvoir and MacKinnon support and extend their respective arguments, first citing the male writers' statements for their exemplary clarity, then criticizing their limitations due to their male-focused and self-serving point of view. De Beauvoir's criticism of Lévinas is that his description of the "mystery" of woman, "which is intended to be objective, is in fact an assertion of masculine privilege" (44), and MacKinnon criticizes Berger for failing to recognize that women's sexual (self)objectification "expresses an inequality in social power"; and further, in support of that statement, she refers to an essay entitled "The Normative Status of Heterosexuality."[24]

In the intervening years, the critique of scientific objectivity and the understanding of the situatedness of thought itself as cultural-historical production (and hence Michel Foucault's notion of "subjugated knowledges," for example) have been developed in the context of an analysis of power, not only in economic relations but in all social relations as they are produced, articulated, and regulated by the discourses and institutions of knowledge.[25] The hegemony of objectivity as epistemological stance in all domains of knowledge, characteristic of modern Western thought, has been shaken by a reappraisal of the situatedness or "tendentiousness" of all discourses and practices—a tendentiousness that is not only class based, as in the Marxist analysis, but that is also based in any major division of power, any axis along which power differentials are organized and distributed, such as race and gender. Whence the revaluation of minority discourses and the affirmation of subjugated knowledges in the critique of colonial discourse, as well as in the feminist critique of Western culture and of Western (white) feminism itself.

From this perspective, what de Beauvoir saw as a philosopher's masculine privilege now appears as a differential rate in social power maintained and legitimated by the ideological apparatuses that construct the social subject, not as transcendental Subject but as subject of material social relations.[26] If, as feminist theory argues, gender is one such apparatus, with sexuality as its material ground and the body as its support or "prop,"[27] then what (re)produces and regulates a specific power differential between women and men through gender—whatever other power differentials may exist concurrently for those same women and men—is not "biological fact" but rather the institution of heterosexuality. Masculine privilege, in this light, is not something that could be given up by an act of goodwill or a more humane ethics, for it is constitutive of the social subject engendered by a heterosexual social contract.[28]

The understanding of heterosexuality as an institution is a relatively recent development in feminist theory and not a widely accepted one among feminists.[29] The common usage of the term "heterosexuality" to denote sexual practices between a female and a male, as distinct from homosexual or same-sex practices (more modestly, the *American Heritage Dictionary of the English Language* defines the adjective "heterosexual" as "characterized by *attraction* to the opposite sex" [emphasis added]), presents the former as "natural" in opposition to the latter, "deviant" or "unnatural" acts. Thus, the very term tends to obscure the unnaturalness of heterosexuality itself—that is to say, its socially constructed nature, its dependence on the semiotic construction of gender rather than on the physical (natural) existence of two sexes. Moreover, the tenacious mental habit of associating sexuality (as sexual *acts* between people) with the private sphere or individual privacy, even as one is constantly surrounded by representations of sexuality (visual and verbal *images* of sexual acts, or images allusive to sexual acts between people), tends to deny the obvious—the very public nature of the discourses on sexuality and what Foucault has called "the technology of sex," the social mechanisms (from the educational system to jurisprudence, from medicine to the media, and so forth) that regulate sexuality and effectively enforce it—and that regulate and enforce it *as heterosexuality*.

The deep-seated and enduring meaning effects of such ideological reversals extend, beyond common usage and understanding, to cultural critics and theorists, feminists included, and militate against the full comprehension of the implications of otherwise accepted notions: not only the fundamental feminist concept that the personal is political but also Foucault's highly influential reconceptualization of sex as a social technology or the Lacanian view that language, or the (eminently social) Symbolic order of culture, is the "cause" of the subject, the structuring order of both subjectivity and the unconscious. The inescapable corollary of the latter view is that sexuality is located, indeed constituted, at the join of subjectivity and sociality, in the name of the Father (which, rephrased in feminist terms, is to say that sexuality is exactly "that which is most one's own, yet most taken away").[30] An example of how the common usage sense of "custom," as local and private practice, steers the comprehension of the term "heterosexuality" away from the abstract sense of institution, "something apparently objective and systematic," deflecting it toward the restricted sense of personal relationship or "action" between individuals, is Ann Ferguson's objection to Adrienne Rich's essay on "Compulsory Heterosexuality and Lesbian Existence," that it does not account for "some heterosexual couples in which women who are feminists maintain an equal relationship with men."

> The notion that heterosexuality is central to women's oppression is plausible only if one assumes that it is women's emotional dependence on men as lovers in conjunction with other mechanisms of male dominance (e.g., marriage, motherhood, women's economic dependence on men) which allow men to control women's bodies as instruments for their own purposes. But single mothers, black women, and economically independent women, for example, may in their heterosexual relations with men escape or avoid these other mechanisms. . . . If feminism as a movement is truly revolutionary, it cannot give priority to one form of male domination (heterosexism) to the exclusion of others.[31]

The point missed here is that those heterosexual women who individually manage to avoid sexual or financial domination at home by individual men are still subjected, in the public sphere, to the objective and systematic effects of the institution that defines them, for all men and even for themselves, as women—and, in fact, as heterosexual women (for example, in issues of employment discrimination, sexual harassment, rape, incest, etc.); the institution of heterosexuality is intimately imbricated in all the "other mechanisms of male dominance" and indeed coextensive with social structure and cultural norms.

The very fact that, in most theoretical and epistemological frameworks, gender or sexual division is either not visible, in the manner of a blind spot, or taken for granted, in the manner of an a priori, reflects a heterosexual presumption—that the sociosexual opposition of "woman" and "man" is the necessary and founding moment of culture, as Monique Wittig remarks:

> Although it has been accepted in recent years that there is no such thing as nature, that everything is culture, there remains within that culture a core of nature which resists examination, a relationship excluded from the social in the analysis—a relationship whose characteristic is ineluctability in culture, as well as in nature, and which is the heterosexual relationship.[32]

Thus, it is not a question of *giving* priority to heterosexism over other systems of oppression, such as capitalism, racism, or colonialism, but of understanding the institutional character and the specificity of each and *then* of analyzing their mutual complicities or reciprocal contradictions.

The Eccentric Subject

I now want to suggest that feminist theory came into its own, or became possible as such—that is, became identifiable as feminist theory rather than a feminist critique of some other theory or object-theory—in a postcolonial mode. By this I mean it came into its own with the understanding of the interrelatedness of discourses and social practices, and of the multiplicity of positionalities concurrently available in the social field seen as a field of forces: not a single system of power dominating the powerless but a tangle of distinct and variable relations of power and points of resistance.[33] With regard to feminism, this understanding of the social as a diversified field of power relations was brought home at the turn of the 1980s, when certain writings by women of color and lesbians explicitly constituted themselves as a feminist critique of feminism, an intervention in feminist theory as a form of political practice in "pursuit of consciousness." They intervened in and interrupted a feminist discourse that was anchored to the single axis of gender as sexual difference (or rather, heterosexual difference, however minutely articulated in its many instances) and that was finding itself stalemated once again in the paradox of woman.

On the notion of sexual difference as an opposition of female to male, Woman to Man, or women to men, an opposition along the axis of gender, earlier feminism built its understanding of power relations as a direct, one-way relation of oppressor to oppressed, colonizer to colonized subject. We spoke of ourselves as a colonized population and conceived of the female body as mapped by phallic desire or territorialized by Oedipal discourse. We imagined ourselves looking only through male eyes. We thought of our speech as symptomatic or unauthorized and took our writing, at its best, to express the silence of women in the language of men. Strategies of resistance and struggle derived from such understanding developed in two principal directions. One aimed toward equal status: it accepted the definition of woman as biologically, emotionally, and socially different but complementary to man and demanded the same rights—without considering how "the rights of man" vary with the social relations of race and class that determine the existence of actual men. That project meant, then, seeking assimilation and a place for women within a hegemonic discourse, within "the ideology of the same," as Luce Irigaray phrased it in her critique of "femininity."[34] Alternatively, the direction of radical separatism took a polarized, oppositional stance to "men" and pressed either to construct a counterhegemonic discourse, as in the anglophone notions of "women's language" and "women's culture," or to reclaim a symptomatic language of the body, as in the francophone *écriture féminine*, presumed to be subversive of the "phallogocentric" order of culture.

Both of these distinct, if intersecting, strategies were and continue to be important in particular or local contexts, but as theories they were both recontained within the boundaries of hegemonic cultural discourses. Cast as they were in the terms of liberal pluralism, socialist humanism, and aesthetic modernism, they remained unselfconsciously complicit in their racism, colonialism, and heterosexism. For even in the second strategy, although the issue of separatism itself is much more complex that its use as a label lets on, and the case can certainly be made for separatism as unavoidable, desirable, or even constitutive of feminism,[35] much early radical separatism was predicated entirely on a sense of moral outrage. Having no specific theory or conceptual analysis outside of its ethical condemnation of "patriarchy," this abso-lute opposition assumed the enemy's definition of the world by either adopting or reversing its terms, which were readily available at the institutional level, and thus set out to seek a territory for feminism to occupy, a wilderness to colonize, a nature in the image of woman, a "gyn/ecology" or an ethics of "pure lust."[36] How this radical feminist metaethics colluded with the ideology of the same is remarked by Audre Lorde in her "Open Letter to Mary Daly."

> I ask that you be aware of how this serves the destructive forces of racism and separation between women—the assumption that the herstory and myth of white women is the legitimate and sole herstory and myth of all women to call upon for power and back-ground, and that nonwhite women and our herstories are note-worthy only as decorations, or examples of female victimization. I ask that you be aware of the effect that this dismissal has upon the community of Black women and other women of Color, and how it devalues your own words. . . . When patriarchy dismisses us, it encourages our murderers. When radical lesbian feminist theory dismisses us, it encourages its own demise.[37]

The intervention or speaking out *within and against* feminism by women of color on racism, Jewish women on anti-Semitism, and les-bians of any color on heterosexism has forced feminism to confront, both emotionally and conceptually, the presence of power relations that just could not be analyzed, altered, or even addressed by the concepts of gender and sexual difference. Moreover, it showed that not only the latter, with its overt or latent stake in heterosexuality, but also a parallel notion of homosexual difference (i.e., personal and/or politi-cal lesbianism as the single requirement for membership in a utopian women's collectivity) were inadequate to account for social and power relations that were and are being (re)produced between and within women—relations causing oppression between women or groups of women and relations enforcing the repression of differences within a single group of women or within oneself.

Now, those charges of racism, heterosexism, and social privilege that were brought to feminism have been in the main accepted as well founded (although one may distinguish omission from commission, unconscious repression from hypocrisy), but perhaps they have been accepted too readily. That is to say, the claims of other stakes, other axes along which "difference," and consequently oppression, identity, and subjectivity are organized and hierarchized—the claims of race or color, ethnic, and sexual identification—have been accepted and given, as it were, equal status with the axis of gender in feminist discourse. These various axes are usually seen as parallel or coequal, although with varying "priorities" for particular women. For some women, the racial may have priority over the sexual in defining subjectivity and grounding identity; for other women the sexual may have priority; for others still it may be the ethnic/cultural that has priority at a given moment—hence the phrase one hears so often now in feminist contexts: "gender, race, and class," or its local variant, "gender, race, and class, and sexual preference." But what this string of seemingly coequal terms, conveying the notion of layers of oppression along parallel axes of "difference," does not grasp is their constant intersection and mutual implication or how each one may affect the others—for example, how gender affects racial oppression in its subjective effects.

In her essay "Toward a Black Feminist Criticism," written in 1977 and many times reprinted, Barbara Smith wrote that black male critics "are, of course, hampered by an inability to comprehend Black women's experience *in sexual as well as racial terms.*"[38] Experience is articulated, she argues, not only in sexual terms, which to a feminist seems easily understood, but also in racial terms, so that, for instance, black men, not comprehending black women's experience in sexual terms, do not comprehend it in racial terms either; that is, they do not comprehend black women's experience of racism. This is not so easy a concept for a white woman to grasp, because, from a position that is presumed to be racially unmarked, one might assume simply that all black people experience the same racism and black women also experience sexism, in addition. But what Smith is saying—and it seems plain enough a statement, almost a tautology, yet how elusive it has proved to be—is that black women experience racism not as "blacks" but as black women.

It was spelled out in the ironic title of the first black women's studies anthology, *All the Women Are White, All the Blacks Are Men, but Some of Us Are Brave*. The term "blacks" does not include (comprehend) black women any more than the term "man" (white men) includes or comprehends (white) women. The black feminist concept of a simultaneity of oppressions[39] means that the layers are not parallel but imbricated into one another; the systems of oppression are interlocking and mutually determining. Smith's point, then, on the one hand, confirms that gender is a fundamental ground of subjectivity—not coincidentally she speaks as a black feminist, a black woman, and a black lesbian. But, on the other hand, it implies that, if the experience of racism shapes the experience of gender and sexuality, any white woman would be no closer than a black man to "comprehending" a black woman's experience in sexual terms, her experience of sexism, her experience of gender, and hence her sense of self as social subject. If equality by gender is no less a myth than equality by other means, then the experience of gender is itself shaped by race relations, and that must be the case, however different the outcome, for all women.

One particular account of how racial determinations are inscribed in a white woman's identity, and can be analyzed and deconstructed through the writing of "personal history," is given in Minnie Bruce Pratt's politico-biographical essay "Identity: Skin Blood Heart."[40] Its implications for feminist theory are illuminated by Biddy Martin and Chandra Mohanty in their insightful reading of the essay as a feminist critical text and an enactment of the process of consciousness itself. From the purely personal, visceral sense of identity conveyed in the title, they argue, the essay moves toward "a complicated working out of the relationship between home, identity and community that calls into question the notion of a coherent, historically continuous, stable identity"[41] and works to expose "the exclusions and repressions which support the seeming homogeneity, stability, and self-evidence of 'white identity'" (193). Thus, they remark, the latter appears to be constituted on the marginalization of differences that exist inside as well as outside the boundaries drawn around any unitary notion of self, home, race, or community.

Pratt's autobiographical narrative is constructed as a nonlinear passage through the writer's several identities (white, middle-class, Christian-raised, southern, lesbian) and the communities that were her homes at various times of her life. Because the writing of this "personal" history is undertaken as one with the questioning of the specific geographic, demographic, architectural, and social histories of those communities—a questioning that brings to light local histories of exploitation and struggle, "histories of people unlike her," which had never been mentioned in the history told by her family—a tension between "being home" and "not being home" becomes apparent in each geographical location. Each station of the narrative becomes a site at once of personal and of historical struggles, yielding the realization that "home was an illusion of coherence and safety based on the exclusion of specific histories of oppression and resistance [and on] the repression of differences even within oneself" (196). Thus, while the historical narrative form makes for a "reanchoring" of the self in each of the concrete historical situations and discursive positions in which Pratt locates herself as writer and subject, nevertheless the contradictory existence of that self in each location, its "not being home," and the continual dislocation of consciousness from each form of identity to the repressed differences that support it, undercut any notion of identity as singular, coherent, unitary, or totally determined.

Yet again, as the return to the past provides the critical knowledge that "stable notions of self and identity are based on exclusion and secured by terror," so there is no simple escape to liberation, "no shedding the literal fear and figurative law of the father, and no reaching a final realm of freedom." To Martin and Mohanty, Pratt's personal history is a series of successive displacements from which each configuration of identity is examined in its contradiction and deconstructed but not simply discarded; instead, it is consciously assumed in a transformative "rewriting of herself in relation to shifting interpersonal and political contexts" (197). If there is a privileged point of identification, lesbianism, which gives impetus to the work of self-(de)construction, that is not, however, a truer or essential or unifying identity, but precisely the critical vantage point, the crucial stake, "that which makes 'home' impossible, which makes her self non-identical" (201).

> Her lesbianism is what she experiences most immediately as the limitation imposed on her by the family, culture, race, and class that afforded her both privilege and comfort, at a price. Learning at what price privilege, comfort, home, and secure notions of self

are purchased, the price to herself and ultimately to others is what makes lesbianism a political motivation as well as a personal experience. . . . In Pratt's narrative, lesbianism is that which exposes the extreme limits of what passes itself off as simply human, as universal, as unconstrained by identity, namely, the position of the white middle class. (210)

Finally, then, the concept of home itself is given up, not only the home of her childhood and the family, but any other "home," such as a women's community that would replicate the conditions of home, that is to say "the suppression of positive differences [that] underwrites familial identity" (203). And it is replaced by a notion of community as inherently unstable and contextual, not based on sameness or essential connections, but offering agency instead of passivity; a community that is "the product of work, of struggle . . . of interpretation" (210).

The stake of Martin and Mohanty's own interpretation, which is itself a critical intervention in the contested terrain of feminist theory, is stated earlier on in their essay:

What we have tried to draw out of this text is the way in which it unsettles not only any notion of feminism as an all-encompassing home but also the assumption that there are discrete, coherent, and absolutely separate identities—homes within feminism, so to speak—based on absolute divisions between various sexual, racial, or ethnic identities. (192)

The critical and self-critical questioning of conventional notions of experience and identity in feminist writings such as this disallows the view of a single, totalizing, "Western" feminism that would necessarily be oppressive or at best irrelevant to women of color in the world. That view, they claim, is inadequate to the situation of white women in the West; moreover, it perpetuates the opposition of West to East and white to nonwhite, leaving intact the ideological construct of their respective "unity" and so contributes to the image of a (false) homogeneity of "the West."

The understanding of feminism as a community whose boundaries shift and whose differences can be expressed and renegotiated through connections both interpersonal and political goes hand in hand with a particular understanding of individual experience as the result of a complex bundle of determinations and struggles, a process of continuing renegotiation of external pressures and internal resistances. Similarly, identity is a locus of multiple and variable positions, which are made available in the social field by historical process and which one may come to assume subjectively and discursively in the form of political consciousness.[42] The subject of this feminist consciousness is unlike the one that was initially defined by the opposition of woman to man on the axis of gender and purely constituted by the oppression, repression, or negation of its sexual difference. For one thing, it is much less pure. Indeed, it is most likely ideologically complicit with "the oppressor" whose position it may occupy in certain sociosexual relations (if not in others). Second, it is neither unified nor singly divided between positions of masculinity and femininity but multiply organized across positions on several axes of difference and across discourses and practices that may be, and often are, mutually contradictory; or, like the postmodern, marginal subject envisioned by Samuel Delany, made up of "fragments whose constitutive aspects always include other objects, other subjects, other sediments (in all of which, the notion of 'other' splits under the very pressure of analysis the split 'self' applies to locate it)."[43] Finally, and most significantly, it has agency (rather than "choice"), the capacity for movement or self-determined (dis)location, and hence social accountability.

» » »

I suggested earlier that feminist theory came into its own in a postcolonial mode. I will now restate that as follows: if a history of feminism may be said to begin "when feminist texts written by women and a feminist movement conscious of itself came together,"[44] a feminist critical theory as such begins when the feminist critique of sociocultural formations (discourses, forms of representation, ideologies) becomes conscious of itself and turns inward, as MacKinnon suggests, in pursuit of consciousness—to question its own relation to or possible complicity with those ideologies, its own heterogeneous body of writing and interpretations, their basic assumptions and terms, and the practices which they enable and from which they emerge. It starts by "recognizing our location, having to name the ground we're coming from, the conditions we have taken for granted," as Rich writes in her "Notes toward a Politics of Location."[45] It then proceeds to articulate the situatedness, political-historical (now) as well as personal-political, of its own thought. But then, or again, in order to go on with the work of social and subjective transformation, in order to sustain the movement, it has to dislocate itself, to dis-identify from those assumptions and conditions taken for granted. This feminist theory, which is only just beginning, does not merely expand or reconfigure previous discursive boundaries by the inclusion of new categories, but it also represents and enacts a shift in historical consciousness.

The shift entails, in my opinion, a dis-placement and a self-displacement: leaving or giving up a place that is safe, that is "home"—physically, emotionally, linguistically, epistemologically—for another place that is unknown and risky, that is not only emotionally but conceptually other; a place of discourse from which speaking and thinking are at best tentative, uncertain, unguaranteed. But the leaving is not a choice: one could not live there in the first place. Thus, both aspects of the displacement, the personal and the conceptual, are painful: they are either, and often both, the cause and/or the result of pain, risk, and a real stake with a high price. For this is "theory in the flesh," as Cherríe Moraga has called it,[46] a constant crossing of the border (*Borderlines/"La Frontera"* is the title of Gloria Anzaldúa's book about "the new *mestiza*"), a remapping of boundaries between bodies and discourses, identities and communities—which may be a reason why it is primarily feminists of color and lesbian feminists who have taken the risk.

That displacement—that dis-identification with a group, a family, a self, a "home," even a feminism, held together by the exclusions and repression that enable any ideology of the same—is concurrently a displacement of one's point of understanding and conceptual articulation. Thus, it affords a redefinition of the terms of both feminist theory and social reality from a standpoint at once inside and outside their determinations. I believe that such an eccentric point of view or discursive position is necessary for feminist theory at this time, in order to sustain the subject's capacity for movement and displacement, to sustain the feminist movement itself. It is a position of resistance and agency, conceptually and experientially apprehended outside or in excess of the sociocultural apparatuses of heterosexuality, through a process of "unusual knowing"[47] or a "cognitive practice"[48] that is not only personal and political but also textual, a practice of language in the larger sense.

Something of that displacement is inscribed in the very title of Wittig's

1981 essay, "One Is Not Born a Woman," a phrase from de Beauvoir's *The Second Sex* rewritten by the writer of *The Lesbian Body.* The repetition invokes, ironically, the heterosexual definition of woman as "the second sex" and displaces it by shifting the emphasis from the word *born* to the word *woman* (a displacement that is doubled by Wittig's geographical and cultural dislocation from France to the United States, where she lived and worked for many years). In the following pages, I will use this extraordinarily rich and suggestive text to gather the threads of the argument I've been pursuing in my intertextual meanderings across a discursive space of writings by women as far (or as little) apart historically as 1949 France and the U.S. *frontera* in 1987.

Like de Beauvoir, Hartsock, and MacKinnon, Wittig starts from the premise that women are not a "natural group" with common biological features, whose oppression would be a consequence of that "nature," but a social category, the product of an economic relation of exploitation, and an ideological construct. Therefore (and here she leaves de Beauvoir, taking instead the materialist feminist analysis of Christine Delphy), women are a social class with shared interests based on their specific condition of exploitation and domination, gender oppression, which affords them a standpoint, a position of knowledge and struggle, that is (as Hartsock argues, but in quite another direction) analogous to the standpoint of the proletariat. Women can thus attain consciousness of themselves as a class, and this coming to consciousness in a political movement is what feminism represents. "The condition of women," writes Delphy, "became 'political' once it gave rise to a struggle, and when at the same time this condition was thought of as oppression."[49] As the oppression of the proletariat was the necessary premise for Marx's theory of capital, and the conceptualization of that oppression was only possible from the precise location of the oppressed, similarly, "it is only from the point of view and life experience of women that their condition can be seen as oppression" (218). The women's movement and the simultaneous feminist conceptualization of women's experience as a specific oppression in and through sexuality make sexuality a major site of class struggle. This adds a new domain of experience to historical materialist analysis and brings about a new understanding of the political domain that "may overturn it from top to bottom. The same thing could be expressed by saying that women's consciousness of being oppressed changes the definition of oppression itself" (218).

This redefinition of *oppression* as a political and subjective category that is arrived at from the specific standpoint of the oppressed, in their struggle, and as a form of consciousness—and thus distinct from the economic, objective category of exploitation—rejoins the original formulation of oppression and identity politics given in the mid-1970s by the U.S. black feminist group, the Combahee River Collective.

> Black feminists and many more Black women who do not define themselves as feminists have all experienced sexual oppression as a constant factor in our day-to-day existence . . . However, we had no way of conceptualizing what was so apparent to us, what we *knew* was really happening . . . before becoming conscious of the concepts of sexual politics, patriarchal rule, and most importantly, feminism, the political analysis and practice that we women use to struggle against our oppression. . . .
>
> This focusing upon our own oppression is embodied in the concept of identity politics. We believe that the most profound and potentially most radical politics come directly out of our own identity. . . . Although we are feminists and Lesbians, we feel solidarity with progressive Black men and do not advocate the fractionalization that white women who are separatists demand. . . . We struggle together with Black men against racism, while we also struggle with Black men about sexism. . . . We need to articulate the real class situation of persons who are not merely raceless, sexless workers, but for whom racial and sexual oppression are significant determinants in their working/economic lives. Although we are in essential agreement with Marx's theory as it applied to the very specific economic relationships he analyzed, we know that his analysis must be extended further in order for us to understand our specific economic situation as Black women.[50]

This fundamental redefinition of social and economic oppression in relation to subjectivity and identity, on the one hand, and to the subject's capacity of resistance and agency, on the other, hinges on the notion of consciousness that I have been trying to delineate as historically specific to contemporary feminism and the basis of feminist theory as such. Not coincidentally, therefore, Delphy's analysis has also several points of contact with MacKinnon's, and her critique of hyphenated Marxist-feminism suggests a post-Marxist stance.

In "A Materialist Feminism *Is* Possible" (1980), a lengthy response to a review by Michèle Barrett and Mary McIntosh (1979), Delphy argues that "if the left refuses a materialist analysis [only in relation to women's oppression] it is because this risks leading to the conclusion that it is men who benefit from patriarchal exploitation, and not capital . . . men are the class which oppresses and exploits women."[51] If socialist feminists persist in seeing the oppression of women as a "secondary consequence of class antagonism *between men*" (180), and if they so desire to exempt men from responsibility for the oppression of women, it can only be in consequence of the belief "that there must necessarily be close and permanent relations between most females and most males at all times" (180), a belief that has its basis in the ideology of heterosexuality (and was adamantly stated by de Beauvoir in the passage quoted above). Delphy concludes with what seems to be a prophecy but is actually an understatement: "I think that this will be the next debate in the movement . . . the breaking of the last ideological barrier *and* the way out of the tunnel on the question of the relationship between lesbianism and feminism" (180). For in the essay here under discussion, written at approximately the same time and in the same context—the work of the French journal, *Questions féministes*—Wittig has already crossed that barrier and taken Delphy's analysis very far from home.

Indeed, the way out of the tunnel leads to what I see as a crossroads for feminist theory at this moment: one road (if women are not a class for themselves) leads back to the paradox of woman, the maze of sexual difference, the axial oppositions of gender, race, and class, the debate on priorities, and so on; the other road (if women are an oppressed class, that is, involved in the struggle for the disappearance of all classes) leads toward the disappearance of women. The divergence of this road, the one taken by Wittig, from the previously outlined scenarios of a feminist future appears most drastic when she imagines what female people would be like in such a classless society. It is suggested to her by the very existence of a "lesbian society" which, however marginal, does function in a certain way autonomously from heterosexual institutions. For, she claims, lesbians are not women: "the refusal to become [or to remain] heterosexual always meant to refuse to become a man or a woman, consciously or not. For a lesbian this goes further than the refusal of the *role* 'woman.' It is the refusal of the economic, ideological, and political power of a man."[52] I will return to this after summarizing her argument.

Also situating herself in the materialist feminist perspective that here I have been calling post-Marxist, in the sense indicated by MacKinnon, Wittig mobilizes the discourses of historical materialism and liberal feminism in an interesting strategy, one against the other and each against itself, proving them both inadequate to defining the subject in materialist terms. First, she deploys the Marxist concepts of ideology, social relations, and class to critique mainstream feminism, arguing that to accept the terms of gender as sexual difference, which construct woman as an "imaginary formation" on the basis of women's biological-erotic value to men, makes it impossible to understand that the very terms "woman" and "man" "are political categories and not natural givens" and thus to question the real socioeconomic relations of gender (50). Second, however, claiming the feminist notion of self, a subjectivity that, although socially produced, is apprehended in its concrete—personal—singularity, Wittig holds *that* notion against Marxism, which, on its part, denies an individual subjectivity to the members of the oppressed classes. Although "materialism and subjectivity have always been mutually exclusive," she insists on both class consciousness and individual subjectivity at once: without the latter "there can be no real fight or transformation. But the opposite is also true; without class and class consciousness there are no real subjects, only alienated individuals" (53).

What joins the two, and what permits the redefinition of both class consciousness and individual subjectivity as "personal history," is the concept of oppression I discussed earlier and its relation to feminist consciousness.

> When we discover that women are the objects of oppression and appropriation, at the very moment that we become able to perceive this, we become subjects in the sense of cognitive subjects, through an operation of abstraction. Consciousness of oppression is not only a reaction to (fight against) oppression. It is also the whole conceptual reevaluation of the social world, its whole reorganization with new concepts, from the point of view of oppression . . . call it a subjective, cognitive practice. The movement back and forth between the levels of reality (the conceptual reality and the material reality of oppression, which are both social realities) is accomplished through language. (52)

Wittig's "subjective, cognitive practice" is a reconceptualization of the subject, of the relation of subjectivity to sociality, and of knowledge itself from a position that is experientially autonomous from institutional heterosexuality and therefore exceeds the terms of its discursive-conceptual horizon.

> Lesbian is the only concept I know of which is beyond the categories of sex (woman and man), because the designated subject (lesbian) is *not* a woman, either economically, or politically, or ideologically. For what makes a woman is a specific social relation to a man, a relation that we have previously called servitude, a relation which implies personal and physical obligation as well as economic obligation ("forced residence," domestic corvée, conjugal duties, unlimited production of children, etc.), a relation which lesbians escape by refusing to become or to stay heterosexual. (53)

Here, then, is the sense in which she proposes the disappearance of women as the goal of feminism. The struggle against the ideological apparatuses and socioeconomic institutions of women's oppression consists in refusing the terms of the heterosexual contract,[53] not only in one's practice of living but also in one's practice of knowing. It consists, as well, in concurrently conceiving of the social subject in terms that exceed, are other than, autonomous from, the categories of gender. The concept "lesbian" is one such term.

The difficulty in grasping or defining a term excluded from a given conceptual system, according to Marilyn Frye, is that "the standard vocabulary of those whose scheme it is will not be adequate to the defining of a term which denotes it."[54] If the term "lesbian" proves to be "extraordinarily resistant to standard procedures of semantic analysis" (153)—and Frye proves that it is—it is because lesbians are "not countenanced by the dominant conceptual scheme" (154), as well as being absent "in the lexicon of the King's English" (155); so much so that even the attempt to come to a definition of the term "lesbian" by cross-references through several dictionaries is "a sort of flirtation with meaninglessness—dancing about a region of cognitive gaps and negative semantic spaces" (154). Why is it, she asks to begin with, "that when I try to name myself and explain myself, my native tongue provides me with a word . . . which means one of *the people from Lesbos?*" (160). And she goes on to demonstrate how the foreclosure of lesbianism from conceptual reality is systematically overdetermined with such "metaphysical overkill" (162) that its motivation becomes apparent as the design to keep "women generally in their metaphysical place" (173). However, Frye also claims that being outside a conceptual system puts one "in a position to see things that cannot be seen from within" (173); to assume that position, to displace oneself from the system, to dis-locate, dis-affiliate, or disengage one's attention from it, is to experience "a reorientation of attention . . . a feeling of disengagement and re-engagement of one's power as a perceiver" (171–72).

Like Rich's white woman "disloyal to civilization,"[55] like Anzaldúa's "new *mestiza*" and Smith's "home girls," Frye's lesbian "disloyal to phallocratic reality" (171) is the subject of an "unusual knowing," a cognitive practice, a form of consciousness that is not primordial, universal, or coextensive with human thought, as de Beauvoir believed, but historically determined and yet subjectively and politically assumed. Like them, Wittig's lesbian is not simply an individual with a personal "sexual preference" or a social subject with a simply "political" priority, but an eccentric subject constituted in a process of struggle and interpretation, a rewriting of self—as Martin and Mohanty say—in relation to a new understanding of community, of history, of culture. And this is what I take Wittig's "lesbian society" to be: not a descriptive term for a type of (nontraditional) social organization, nor a blueprint for a futuristic, utopian, or dystopian society—like the ones imagined in Joanna Russ's *The Female Man* or even like the amazon community of Wittig's own *Les guérillères*—but rather the term for a conceptual and experiential space carved out of the social field, a space of contradictions, in the here and now, that need to be affirmed but not resolved; a space in which the "Inappropriate/d Other," as Trinh T. Minh-ha imagines her, "moves about with always at least two/four gestures: that of affirming 'I am like you' while pointing insistently to the difference; and that of reminding 'I am different' while unsettling every definition of otherness arrived at."[56]

Wittig's terms "lesbian" and "lesbian society" sustain the tension of that multiple and contradictory gesture. Even as she asserts that lesbians are not women, she cautions against the writings of "lesbian-feminists in America and elsewhere" that would have us again entrapped in the myth of woman. Yet, refusing to be a woman does not make one become a man. Finally, therefore, "a lesbian *has to* be something else, a not-woman, a not-man."[57] Thus, when she concludes "It is *we* who historically must undertake the task of defining the individual subject in materialist terms," that *we* is the dis-placed point of articulation from which to rewrite both Marxism and feminism, rejoining the critique of the sex-gender system with the "political economy of sex,"[58] as Gayle Rubin once called it. But Wittig's "we" is not the privileged women of de Beauvoir, "qualified to elucidate the situation of woman"; nor does her "lesbian society" refer to some collectivity of gay women, any more than "lesbian" refers to an individual woman with a particular "sexual preference." They are, rather, the theoretical terms of a form of feminist consciousness that can only exist historically, in the here and now, as the consciousness of a "something else."

We, lesbian, *mestiza*, and inappropriate/d other are all terms for that excessive critical position which I have attempted to tease out and re-articulate from various texts of contemporary feminism: a position attained through practices of political and personal displacement across boundaries between sociosexual identities and communities, between bodies and discourses, by what I like to call the eccentric subject.

———————

Written in 1987 as a contribution to a projected volume on the history of consciousness to be edited by Hayden White, which never came to fruition. First published with the title "Eccentric Subjects: Feminist Theory and Historical Consciousness" in *Feminist Studies*, vol. 16, no. 1 (Spring 1990): 115–50.

Chapter 8

Upping the Anti [*sic*] in Feminist Theory

Essentialism and Anti-Essentialism

Nowadays, the term *essentialism* covers a range of metacritical meanings and strategic uses that go the very short distance from convenient label to buzzword. Many who, like myself, have been involved with feminist critical theory for some time and who did use the term, initially, as a serious critical concept, have grown impatient with this word—essentialism—time and again repeated with its reductive ring, its self-righteous tone of superiority, its contempt for "them"—those guilty of it. Yet, few would deny that feminist theory is all about an essential difference, an irreducible difference, though not a difference between woman and man, nor a difference inherent in "woman's nature" (in woman as nature), but a difference in the feminist conception of woman, women, and the world.

Let us say, then, that there is an essential difference between a feminist and a non-feminist understanding of the subject and its relation to institutions; between feminist and non-feminist knowledges, discourses, and practices of cultural forms, social relations, and subjective processes; between a feminist and a non-feminist historical consciousness. That difference is essential in that it is constitutive of feminist thinking and thus of feminism: it is what makes the thinking feminist, and what constitutes certain ways of thinking, certain practices of writing, reading, imaging, relating, acting, etc., into the historically diverse and culturally heterogeneous social movement which, qualifiers and distinctions notwithstanding, we continue with good reasons to call feminism.[1] Another way to say this is that the essential difference of feminism lies in its historical specificity—the particular conditions of its emergence and development, which have shaped its object and field of analysis, its assumptions and forms of address; the constraints that have attended its conceptual and methodological struggles; the erotic component of its political self-awareness; the absolute novelty of its radical challenge to social life itself.

But even as the specific, essential difference of feminism may not be disputed, the question of the nature of its specificity or what is of the essence in feminist thought and self-representation has been an object of contention, an issue over which divisions, debates, and polarizations have occurred consistently, and without resolution, since the beginning of that self-conscious critical reflection that constitutes the theory of feminism. The currency of the term "essentialism" may be based on nothing more than its capacity to circumvent this very question—the nature of the specific difference of feminism—and thus to polarize feminist thought on what amounts to a red herring. I suggest that the current enterprise of "anti-essentialist" theorists engaged in typologizing, defining and branding various "feminisms" along an ascending scale of theoretico-political sophistication, where "essentialism" weighs heavy at the lower end, may be seen in this perspective.[2]

Which is not to say that there should be no critique of feminist positions or no contest for the practical as well as the theoretical meanings of feminism, or even no appeal for hegemony by participants in a social movement which, after all, potentially involves all women. My polemical point here is that either too much or too little is made of the "essentialism" imputed to most feminist positions (notably those labeled cultural, separatist or radical, but others as well, whether labeled or not), so that the term serves less the purposes of effective criticism in the ongoing elaboration of feminist theory than those of convenience, conceptual simplification or academic legitimation. Taking a more discerning look at the *essence* that is in question in both *essentialism* and *essential difference,* therefore, seems like a very good idea.

Among the several acceptations of "essence" (from which "essentialism" is apparently derived) in the *Oxford English Dictionary,* the most pertinent to the context of use that is in question here are the following:

1. Absolute being, substance in the metaphysical sense; the reality underlying phenomena.
2. That which constitutes the being of a thing; that "by which it is what it is." In two different applications (distinguished by Locke as *nominal essence* and *real essence* respectively):
   a. of a conceptual entity: The totality of the properties, constituent elements, etc., without which it would cease to be the same thing; the indispensable and necessary attributes of a thing as opposed to those which it may have or not. . . .
   b. of a real entity: Objective character, intrinsic nature as a "thing-in-itself;" "that internal constitution, on which all the sensible properties depend."

Examples of (a), dated from 1600 to 1870, include Locke's statement in the *Essay on Human Understanding:* "The Essence of a Triangle, lies in a very little compass . . . three Lines meeting at three Angles, make up that Essence"; and all the examples given for (b), from 1667 to 1856, are to the effect that the essence of a real entity, the "thing-in-itself," is either unknown or unknowable.

Which of these "essences" are imputed to feminist "essentialists" by their critics? If most feminists, however one may classify trends and positions—cultural, radical, liberal, socialist, poststructuralist, and so forth—agree that women are made, not born, that gender is not an innate feature (as sex may be) but a sociocultural construction (and precisely for that reason it is oppressive to women), that patriarchy is historical (especially so when it is believed to have superseded a previous matriarchal realm), then the "essence" of woman that is described in the writings of many so-called essentialists is not the *real essence,* in Locke's terms, but more likely a *nominal* one. It is a totality of qualities, properties, and attributes that such feminists define, envisage, or enact for themselves (and some in fact attempt to live out in "separatist" communities), and possibly also wish for other women. This is more a project, then, than a description of existent reality; it is an admittedly feminist project of "re-vision," where the specifications *feminist* and *re*-vision already signal its historical location, even as the (re)vision projects itself outward geographically and temporally (universally) to recover the past and to claim the future. This may be utopian, idealist, perhaps misguided or wishful thinking, it may be a project one does not want to be a part of, but it is not essentialist as is the belief in a God-given or otherwise immutable nature of woman.

In other words, barring the case in which woman's "essence" is taken as absolute being or substance in the traditional metaphysical sense (and this may actually be the case for a few, truly fundamentalist thinkers to whom the term essentialist would properly apply), for the great majority of feminists the "essence" of woman is more like the essence of the triangle than the essence of the thing-in-itself: it is the specific properties (e.g., a female-sexed body), qualities (a disposition to nurturance, a certain relation to the body, etc.), or necessary attributes (e.g., the experience of femaleness, of living in the world as female) that women have developed or have been bound to historically, in their differently patriarchal sociocultural contexts, which make them women, and not men. One may prefer one triangle, one definition of women and/or feminism, to another and, within her particular conditions and possibilities of existence, struggle to define the triangle she wants or wants to be—feminists do want differently. And in these very struggles, I suggest, consist the historical development and the specific difference of feminist theory, the essence of the triangle.

It would be difficult to explain, otherwise, why thinkers or writers with political and personal histories, projects, needs, and desires as different as those of white women and women of color, of lesbians and heterosexuals, of differently abled women, and of successive generations of women, would all claim feminism as a major—if not the only—ground of difference; why they would address both their critiques or accusations and their demands for recognition to other women, feminists in particular; why the emotional and political stakes in feminist theorizing should be so high, dialogue so charged, and confrontation so impassioned; why, indeed, the proliferation of typologies and the wide currency of "essentialism" on one hand, countered by the equally wide currency of the term "male theory" on the other.[3] It is one of the projects of this paper to up the *anti* in feminist theoretical debates, to shift the focus of the controversy from "feminist essentialism," as a category by which to classify feminists or feminisms, to the historical specificity, the essential difference of feminist theory itself. To this end I first turn to two essays which prompted my reflection on the uses of "essentialism" in current Anglo-American feminist critical writing, Chris Weedon's *Feminist Practice and Poststructuralist Theory,* published in London in 1987, and Linda Alcoff's "Cultural Feminism versus Post-Structuralism: The Identity Crisis in Feminist Theory," published in the spring 1988 issue of *Signs.* Then I will go on to argue that the essential difference of feminist theory must be looked for in the form as well as the contents of its political, personal, critical, and textual practices, in the diverse oppositional stances feminism has taken vis-à-vis social and cultural formations, and in the resulting divisions, self-conscious reflection, and conceptual elaboration that constitute the effective history of feminism. And thus a division such as the one over the issue of "essentialism" only *seems* to be a purely "internal," intra-feminist one, a conflict within feminism. In fact, it is not.

The notion of an "essential womanhood, common to all women, suppressed or repressed by patriarchy" recurs in Weedon's book as the mark of "radical-feminist theory," whose cited representatives are Mary Daly, Susan Griffin, and Adrienne Rich. "Radical-feminist theory" is initially listed together with "socialist-feminist and psychoanalytic-feminist theories" as "various attempts to systematize individual insights about the oppression of women into relatively coherent theories of patriarchy," in spite of the author's statement, on the same page, that radical-feminist writers are hostile to theory because they see it as a form of male dominance which co-opts women and suppresses the feminine (6). As one reads on, however, socialist feminism drops out altogether while psychoanalytic feminism is integrated into a new and more "politically" sophisticated discourse called "feminist poststructuralism." Thus, three-fourths of the way through the book, one finds this summary statement:

> For poststructuralist feminism, neither the liberal-feminist attempt to redefine the truth of women's nature within the terms of existing social relations and to establish women's full equality with men, nor the radical-feminist emphasis on fixed difference, realized in

a separatist context, is politically adequate. Poststructuralist feminism requires attention to historical specificity in the production,
for women, of subject positions and modes of femininity and their
place in the overall network of social power relations. In this the
meaning of biological sexual difference is never finally fixed. . . .
An understanding of how discourses of biological sexual difference
are mobilized, in a particular society, at a particular moment, is the
first stage in intervening in order to initiate change. (135)

There is more than simple irony in the claim that this late-comer, poststructuralist feminism, dark horse and winner of the feminist theory
contest, is the "first stage" of feminist intervention. How can Weedon,
at one and the same time, so strongly insist on attention to historical
specificity and social—not merely individual—change, and yet disregard
the actual historical changes in Western culture brought about in part,
at least, by the women's movement and at least in some measure by
feminist critical writing over the past twenty years?

One could surmise that Weedon does not like the changes that have
taken place (even as they allow the very writing and publication of her
book), or does not consider them sufficient, though that would hardly
be reason enough to disregard them so blatantly. A more subtle answer
may lie in the apologetic and militant project of her book, a defense
of poststructuralism vis-à-vis both the academic establishment and the
general educated reader, but with an eye to the women's studies corner
of the publishing market; whence, one must infer, the lead position in
the title of the other term of the couple, feminist practice. For, as the
Preface states, "the aim of this book is to make poststructuralist theory
accessible to readers to whom it is unfamiliar, to argue its political
usefulness to feminism and to consider its implications for feminist
critical practice" (vii). Somehow, however, in the course of the book,
the preface's modest claim "to point to a possible direction for future
feminist cultural criticism" (vii) is escalated into a peroration for the
new and much improved feminist theory called feminist poststructuralism or, indifferently, poststructural feminism.

In the concluding chapter on "Feminist Critical Practice" (strangely
in the singular, as if among so many feminisms and feminist theories,
only one practice could properly be called both feminist and critical), the
academic contenders are narrowed down to two. The first is the poststructural criticism produced by British feminists (two are mentioned,

E. Ann Kaplan and Rosalind Coward) looking "at the mechanisms through which meaning is constructed" mainly in popular culture and visual representation; the second is "the other influential branch of feminist criticism [that] looks to fiction as an expression of an already constituted gendered experience" (152). Reappearing here, the word "experience," identified earlier on as the basis for radical-feminist politics ("many feminists assume that women's experience, unmediated by further theory, is the source of true knowledge" [8]), links this second branch of feminist (literary) criticism to radical-feminist ideology. Its standard-bearers are Americans, Showalter's gynocriticism and the "woman-centered criticism" of Gilbert and Gubar, whose reliance on the concept of authorship as a key to meaning and truth also links them with "liberal-humanist criticism" (154–55).

A particular subset of this—by now radical-liberal—feminist criticism "dedicated to constructing traditions" (156) is the one concerned with "black and lesbian female experience"; here the problems and ideological traps appear most clearly, in Weedon's eyes, and are "most extreme in the case of lesbian writing and the construction of a lesbian aesthetic" (158). The reference works for her analysis, rather surprisingly in view of the abundance of Black and lesbian feminist writings in the 1980s, are a couple of rather dated essays by Barbara Smith and Bonnie Zimmerman reprinted in a collection edited by Elaine Showalter and, in fact, misnamed *The New Feminist Criticism*.[4] But even more surprising—or not at all so, depending on one's degree of optimism—it is again poststructuralist criticism that, with the help of Derridean deconstruction, can set all of these writers straight, as it were, as to the real, socially constructed and discursively produced nature of gender, race, class, and sexuality—as well as authorship and experience! Too bad for us that no exemplary poststructuralist feminist works or critics are discussed in this context (Cixous, Kristeva, and Irigaray figure prominently, but as psychoanalytic feminists earlier in the book).

Now, I should like to make it clear that I have no quarrel with poststructuralism as such, or with the fundamental importance for all critical thinking, feminist theory included, of many of the concepts admirably summarized by Weedon in passages such as the following:

> For a theoretical perspective to be politically useful to feminists, it should be able to recognize the importance of the *subjective* in

constituting the meaning of women's lived reality. It should not deny subjective experience, since the ways in which people make sense of their lives is a necessary starting point for understanding how power relations structure society. Theory must be able to address women's experience by showing where it comes from and how it relates to material social practices and the power relations which structure them. . . . In this process subjectivity becomes available, offering the individual both a perspective and a choice, and opening up the possibility of political change. (8–9)

But while I am in complete agreement that experience is a difficult, ambiguous, and often oversimplified term, and that feminist theory needs to elaborate further "the relationship between experience, social power and resistance" (8), I would insist that the notion of experience in relation both to social-material practices and to the formation and processes of subjectivity is a feminist concept, not a poststructuralist one (this is an instance of that essential difference of feminism which I want to reclaim from Weedon's all-encompassing "poststructuralism"), and would be still unthinkable were it not for specifically feminist practices, political, critical, and textual: consciousness raising, the rereading and revision of the canon, the critique of scientific discourses, and the imaging of new social spaces and forms of community. In short, the very practices of those feminist critics Weedon allocates to the "essentialist" camp. I would also add that "a theory of the relationship between experience, social power and resistance" is precisely one possible definition of feminist, not of poststructuralist, theory, as Weedon would have it, since the latter does not countenance the notion of experience within its conceptual horizon or philosophical presuppositions; and that, moreover, these issues have been posed and argued by several non-denominational feminist theories in the United States for quite some time: for example, in the works of Biddy Martin, Nancy K. Miller, Tania Modleski, Mary Russo, Kaja Silverman, as well as myself, and even more forcefully in the works of feminist theorists and writers of color such as Gloria Anzaldúa, Audre Lorde, Chandra Mohanty, Cherríe Moraga, and Barbara Smith.

So my quarrel with Weedon's book is about its reductive opposition—all the more remarkable, coming from a proponent of deconstruction—of a *lumpen* feminist essentialism (radical-liberal-separatist and American) to a phantom feminist poststructuralism (critical-socialist-psychoanalytic and Franco-British), and with the by-products of such a *parti-pris:* the canonization of a few, (in)famous feminists as signposts of the convenient categories set up by the typology, the agonistic narrative structure of its account of "feminist theories," and finally its failure to contribute to the elaboration of feminist critical thought, however useful the book may be to its other intended readers, who can thus rest easy in the fantasy that poststructuralism is the theory and feminism is just a practice.

» » »

The title of Alcoff's essay, "Cultural Feminism versus Post-Structuralism: The Identity Crisis in Feminist Theory," bespeaks some of the same problems: a manner of thinking by mutually oppositional categories, an agonistic frame of argumentation, and a focus on division, a "crisis in feminist theory" that may be read not only as a crisis *over* identity, a metacritical doubt and a dispute among feminists as to the notion of identity, but also as a crisis *of* identity, of self-definition, implying a theoretical impasse for feminism as a whole. The essay, however, is more discerning, goes much further than its title suggests, and even contradicts it in the end, as the notion of identity, far from fixing the point of an impasse, becomes an active shifter in the feminist discourse of woman.[5]

Taking as its starting point "the concept of woman," or rather, its redefinition in feminist theory ("the dilemma facing feminist theorists today is that our very self-definition is grounded in a concept that we must deconstruct and de-essentialize in all of its aspects"), Alcoff finds two major categories of responses to the dilemma, or what I would call the paradox of woman (406). Cultural feminists, she claims, "have not challenged the defining of woman but only that definition given by men" (407), and have replaced it with what they believe a more accurate description and appraisal, "the concept of the essential female" (408). On the other hand, the poststructuralist response has been to reject the possibility of defining woman altogether and to replace "the politics of gender or sexual difference . . . with a plurality of difference where gender loses its position of significance" (407). A third category is suggested, but only indirectly, in Alcoff's unwillingness to include among cultural feminists certain writers of color such as Moraga and Lorde in spite of their emphasis on cultural identity, for in her view "their work has consistently rejected essentialist conceptions of gender" (412).

Why an emphasis on racial, ethnic, and/or sexual identity need not be seen as essentialist is discussed more fully later in the essay with regard to identity politics and in conjunction with a third trend in feminist theory which Alcoff sees as a new course for feminism, "a theory of the gendered subject that does not slide into essentialism" (422).

Whereas the narrative structure underlying Weedon's account of feminist theories is that of a contest where one actor successively engages and defeats or conquers several rivals, Alcoff's develops as a dialectics. Both the culturalist and the poststructuralist positions display internal contradictions: for example, not all cultural feminists "give explicitly essentialist formulations of what it means to be a woman" (411), and their emphasis on the affirmation of women's strength and positive cultural roles and attributes has done much to counter images of woman as victim or of woman as male when in a business suit; but insofar as it reinforces the essentialist explanations of those attributes that are part and parcel of the traditional notion of womanhood, cultural feminism may, and for some women does, foster another form of sexist oppression. Conversely, if the poststructuralist critique of the unified, authentic subject of humanism is more than compatible with the feminist project to "deconstruct and de-essentialize" woman (as Alcoff puts it, in clearly poststructuralist terms), its absolute rejection of gender and its negation of biological determinism in favor of a cultural-discursive determinism result, as concerns women, in a form of nominalism. If "woman" is a fiction, a locus of pure difference and resistance to logocentric power, and if there are no women as such, then the very issue of women's oppression would appear to be obsolete and feminism itself would have no reason to exist (which, it may be noted, is a corollary of poststructuralism and the stated position of those who call themselves "post-feminists"). "What can we demand in the name of women," Alcoff asks, "if 'women' do not exist and demands in their name simply reinforce the myth that they do?" (420).

The way out—let me say, the sublation—of the contradictions in which are caught these two mainstream feminist views lies in "a theory of the subject that avoids both essentialism and nominalism" (421), and Alcoff points to it in the work of a few theorists, "a few brave souls," whom she rejoins in developing her notion of "woman as positionality": "woman is a position from which a feminist politics can emerge rather than a set of attributes that are 'objectively identifiable," (434–35). In becoming feminist, for instance, women take up a position, a point of perspective, from which to interpret or (re)construct values and meanings. That position is also a politically assumed identity, and one relative to their sociohistorical location, whereas essentialist defini- tions would have woman's identity or attributes be independent of her external situation; however, the positions available to women in any sociohistorical location are neither arbitrary nor undecidable. Thus, Alcoff concludes,

> If we combine the concept of identity politics with a conception of the subject as positionality, we can conceive of the subject as nonessentialized and emergent from a historical experience and yet retain our political ability to take gender as an important point of departure. Thus we can say at one and the same time that gender is not natural, biological, universal, ahistorical, or essential and yet still claim that gender is relevant because we are taking gender as a position from which to act politically. (433)

I am, of course, in agreement with her emphases on issues and arguments that have been central in my work, such as the necessity to theorize expe- rience in relation to practices, the understanding of gendered subjectivity as "an emergent property of a historicized experience" (431), and the notion that identity is an active construction and a discursively mediated political interpretation of one's history. What I must ask, and less as a criticism of Alcoff's essay than for the purposes of my argument here, is: Why is it still necessary to set up two opposing categories, cultural feminism and poststructuralism, or essentialism and anti-essentialism, thesis and antithesis, when one has already achieved the vantage point of a theoretical position that overtakes them or sublates them?

Doesn't the insistence on the "essentialism" of cultural feminists re- produce and keep in the foreground an image of "dominant" feminism that is at least reductive, at best tautological or superseded, and at worst not in our interests? Doesn't it feed the pernicious opposition of low versus high theory, a low-grade type of critical thinking (feminism) that is contrasted with the high-test theoretical grade of a poststructuralism from which some feminists would have been smart enough to learn? As one feminist theorist who's been concurrently involved with feminism, women's studies, psychoanalytic theory, structuralism, and film theory from the beginning of my critical activity, I know that learning to be a feminist has grounded, or embodied, all of my learning and so en-gen-dered thinking and knowing itself. That engendered thinking and that embodied, situated knowledge (in Donna Haraway's phrase)[6] are the stuff of feminist theory, whether by "feminist theory" is meant one of a growing number of feminist critical discourses—on culture, science, subjectivity, writing, visual representation, social institutions, etc.—or, more particularly, the critical elaboration of feminist thought itself and the ongoing (re)definition of its specific difference. In either case, feminist theory is not of a lower grade than that which some call "male theory," but different in kind; and it is its essential difference, the essence of that triangle, that concerns me here as a theorist of feminism.

Why then, I ask again, continue to constrain it in the terms of essentialism and anti-essentialism even as they no longer serve (but did they ever?) to formulate our questions? For example, in her discussion of cultural feminism, Alcoff accepts another critic's characterization despite some doubt that the latter "makes it appear too homogeneous and . . . the charge of essentialism is on shaky ground" (411). Then she adds:

> In the absence of a clearly stated position on the ultimate source of gender difference, Echols *infers* from their emphasis on building a feminist free-space and woman-centered culture that cultural feminists hold some version of essentialism. I share Echols's *suspicion.* Certainly, *it is difficult to render the views of Rich and Daly into a coherent whole without supplying a missing premise* that there is an innate female essence. (412; emphasis added)

But why do it at all? What is the purpose, or the gain, of supplying a missing premise (innate female essence) in order to construct a coherent image of feminism which thus becomes available to charges (essentialism) based on the very premise that had to be supplied? What motivates such a project, the suspicion, and the inferences?

Theorizing beyond Reconciliation

For a theorist of feminism, the answer to these questions should be looked for in the particular history of feminism, the debates, internal divisions, and polarizations that have resulted from its engagement with the various institutions, discourses, and practices that constitute the social, and from its self-conscious reflection on that engagement;

that is to say, the divisions that have marked feminism as a result of the divisions (of gender, sex, race, class, ethnicity, sexuality, etc.) in the social itself, and the discursive boundaries and subjective limits that feminism has defined and redefined for itself contingently, historically, in the process of its engagement with social and cultural formations. The answer should be looked for, in other words, in the form as well as the contents that are specific to feminist political practices and conceptual elaboration, in the paradoxes and contradictions that constitute the effective history, the essential difference, of feminist thought.

In one account that can be given of that history, feminist theory has developed a series of oppositional stances not only vis-à-vis the wider, "external" context (the social constraints, legislation, ideological apparati, dominant discourses and representations against which feminism has pitched its critique and its political strategies in particular historical locations), but also, concurrently and interrelatedly, in its own "internal," self-critical processes.[7] For instance, in the 1970s, the debates on academic feminism vs. activism in the United States defined an opposition between theory and practice which led, on the one hand, to a polarization of positions either *for* theory or *against* theory in nearly all cultural practices and, on the other, to a consistent, if never fully successful, effort to overcome the opposition itself.[8] Subsequently, the internal division of the movement over the issue of separatism or "mainstreaming," both in the academy and in other institutional contexts, recast the practice/theory opposition in terms of lesbian vs. heterosexual identification, and of women's studies vs. feminist cultural theory, among others. Here, too, the opposition led to both polarization (e.g., feminist criticism vs. feminist theory in literary studies) and efforts to overcome it by an expanded, extremely flexible, and ultimately unsatisfactory redefinition of the notion of "feminist theory" itself.

Another major division and the resulting crucial shift in feminist thought were prompted, at the turn of the decade into the 1980s, by the wider dissemination of the writings of women of color and their critique of racism in the women's movement. The division over the issue of race vs. gender, and of the relative importance of each in defining the modes of women's oppression, resistance, and agency, also produced an opposition between a "white" or "Western feminism" and a "U.S. Third World feminism" articulated in several racial and ethnic hyphenations, or called by an altogether different name (e.g., black "womanism").[9]

Because the oppositional stance of women of color was markedly, if not exclusively, addressed to white women in the context of feminism—that is to say, their critique addressed more directly white feminists than it did (white) patriarchal power structures, men of color, or even white women in general—once again that division on the issue of race vs. gender led to polarization as well as to concerted efforts to overcome it, at least internally to feminist theoretical and cultural practices. And once again those efforts met with mostly unsatisfactory or inadequate results, so that no actual resolution, no dialectic sublation has been achieved in this opposition either, as in the others. For even as the polarization may be muted or displaced by other issues that come to the fore, each of those oppositions remains present and active in feminist consciousness and, I want to argue, must so remain in a feminist theory of the female-sexed or female-embodied social subject that is based on its specific and emergent history.

In the mid-1980s, the so-called feminist sex wars (Ruby Rich) pitched "pro-sex" feminists vs. the anti-pornography movement in a conflict over representation that recast the sex/gender distinction into the form of a paradoxical opposition: in these writings sex and gender are either collapsed together, and rendered both analytically and politically indistinguishable (MacKinnon, Hartsock) or they are severed from each other and seen as endlessly recombinable in such figures of boundary crossing as transsexualism, transvestism, bisexualism, drag and impersonation (Butler), cyborgs (Haraway), etc. This last issue is especially central to the lesbian debate on sadomasochism (*Coming to Power, Against Sadomasochism*), which recasts the earlier division of lesbians between the women's liberation movement, with its more or less overt homophobia (Bearchell, Clark), and the gay liberation movement, with its more or less overt sexism (Frye), into the current opposition of radical S/M lesbianism to mainstream–cultural lesbian feminism (Rubin, Califia), an opposition whose mechanical binarism is tersely expressed by the magazine *On Our Backs* punning on the long-established feminist periodical *off our backs*. And here may be also mentioned the opposition pro and against psychoanalysis (e.g., Rose and Wilson) which, ironically, was almost completely disregarded in these sexuality debates, even as it determined the conceptual elaboration of sexual difference in the seventies and has since been fundamental to the feminist critique of representation in the media and the arts.[10]

This account of the history of feminism in relation to both "external" and "internal" events, discourses, and practices suggests that two concurrent drives, impulses or mechanisms, are at work in the production of its self-representation: *an erotic, narcissistic drive* that enhances images of feminism as difference, rebellion, daring, excess, subversion, disloyalty, agency, empowerment, pleasure and danger, and rejects all images of powerlessness, victimization, subjection, acquiescence, passivity, conformism, femininity; and *an ethical drive* that works toward community, accountability, entrustment, sisterhood, bonding, belonging to a common world of women or sharing what Adrienne Rich has poignantly called "the dream of a common language." Together, often in mutual contradiction, the erotic and ethical drives have fueled not only the various polarizations and the construction of oppositions but also the invention or conceptual imaging of a "continuum" of experience, a global feminism, a "house of difference," or a separate space where "safe words" can be trusted and "consent" be given uncoerced. And, as I suggest in my discussion of an Italian feminist text by the Milan Women's Bookstore collective, an erotic and an ethical drive may be seen to underlie and sustain at once the possibility of, and the difficulties involved in, the project of articulating a female symbolic.[11] Are these two drives together, most often in mutual contradiction, what particularly distinguishes lesbian feminism, where the erotic is as necessary a condition as the ethical, if not more?

That the two drives often clash or bring about political stalemates and conceptual impasses is not surprising, for they have contradictory objects and aims, and are forced into open conflict in a culture where women are not supposed to be, know, or see themselves as subjects. And for this very reason perhaps, the two drives characterize the movement of feminism, and more emphatically lesbian feminism, its historically intrinsic, essential condition of contradiction, and the processes constitutive of feminist thought in its specificity. As I have written elsewhere, "the tension of a twofold pull in contrary directions—the critical negativity of its theory, and the affirmative positivity of its politics—is both the historical condition of existence of feminism and its theoretical condition of possibility."[12] That tension, as the condition of possibility and effective elaboration of feminist theory, is most productive in the kind of critical thinking that refuses to be pulled to either side of an opposition and seeks instead to deconstruct it, or better, to disengage it from the fixity of polarization in an "internal" feminist debate and to reconnect it to the "external" discursive and social context from which it finally cannot be severed except at the cost of repeatedly reducing a historical process, a movement, to an ideological stalemate. This may be the approach of those writers whom Alcoff would call "brave souls . . . attempting to map out a new course" (407). But that course, I would argue, does not proceed in the manner of a dialectic, by resolving or reconciling the given terms of an opposition—say, essentialism/anti-essentialism or pro-sex/anti-pornography—whether the resolution is achieved discursively (for example, alleging a larger, tactical or political perspective on the issue) or by pointing to their actual sublation in existing material conditions (for example, adducing sociological data or statistical arguments). It proceeds, in my view, by what I call upping the "anti": by analyzing the undecidability, conceptual as well as pragmatic, of the alternative *as given,* such critical works release its terms from the fixity of meaning into which polarization has locked them, and reintroduce them into a larger contextual and conceptual frame of reference; the tension of positivity and negativity that marks feminist discourse in its engagement with the social can then displace the impasse of mere "internal" opposition to a more complex level of analysis.[13]

Seen in this larger, historical frame of reference, feminist theory is not merely a theory of gender oppression in culture, as both MacKinnon and Rubin maintain, from the respective poles of the sex/gender and pro-sex/anti-pornography debates, and as is too often reiterated in women's studies textbooks;[14] nor is it the essentialist theory of women's nature which Weedon opposes to an anti-essentialist, poststructuralist theory of culture. It is instead a developing theory of the female-sexed or female-embodied social subject, whose constitution and whose modes of social and subjective existence include most obviously sex and gender, but also race, class, and any other significant sociocultural divisions and representations; a developing theory of the female-embodied social subject that is based on its specific, emergent, and conflictual history.

First published in *Conflicts in Feminism,* eds. Marianne Hirsch and Evelyn Fox Keller (New York: Routledge, 1990), 255–70.

Chapter 9

Habit Changes

> It is true that, so far as we know, no psychical apparatus exists
> which possesses a primary process only and that such an
> apparatus is to that extent a theoretical fiction. But this much is
> a fact: the primary processes are present in the mental apparatus
> from the first, while it is only during the course of life that the
> secondary processes unfold, and come to inhibit and overlay the
> primary ones.[1]

It is not the purpose of this article to engage with the terms of debate set forth in the title of this special issue. I have indeed written on all three—gender, feminism, and queer theory—in the pages of this journal and elsewhere, but the theory I want to meet here is (forgive the presumption) my own: a theory of sexuality, and in particular lesbian sexuality and desire, as outlined in my recent book *The Practice of Love.*[2] The occasion for this article and the reason for its appearance in this issue of *differences* are Elizabeth Grosz's review essay, also published here, and the opportunity it offered me for reflection, retrospection, and reconsideration of the ideas I developed in the book. What *is* the book about? What did I want to accomplish in it? What are its presumptions and conceptual limits, its unresolved or enabling questions, its contribution to a contemporary understanding of sexuality and desire?

Unlike some of my other works, *The Practice of Love* is not concerned with feminist theory, except insofar as feminist theory has concerned itself with lesbian sexuality. I say this not in order to distance myself from feminist theory, but rather to distance myself from the marketing trend that labels "feminist theory" any speculative work authored by a woman, whatever its critical approach, disciplinary framework, and political commitment. As for "queer theory," my insistent specification *lesbian* may well be taken as a taking of distance from what, since I proposed it as a working hypothesis for lesbian and gay studies in this very journal (*differences* 3.2), has quickly become a conceptually vacuous creature of the publishing industry.[3] I will add, therefore, that *The Practice of Love* is not about feminist theory or queer theory; it is a study of sexuality or, if you will (though it does sound pretentious), a theory of sexuality. But if it can be considered a work of feminist theory it is because my practice of critical writing, the form of address and the rhetorical strategies I chose, including what I call the politics of reference, are consistent with the practice of feminist theory as I see it.

For example, while I read Freud's theory as the elaboration of a passionate fiction, I do not claim otherwise of my own writing: I acknowledge that the impulse for this work comes from my own fantasies and experiential history, and I locate it in my particular socio-geographical and intellectual formation. Even more important, perhaps, I build my argumentation with reference to and in dialogue with works by other lesbians and feminists which I engage directly, sometimes critically, often painstakingly, and always explicitly because I want to acknowledge that the writings of these women—be they theorists or poets, novelists or critics—constitute the epistemological terrain of my own thinking no less than do the more prestigious writings of Freud, Lacan, or Foucault.

My practice of grounding arguments in particular texts, whether literary, filmic, or critical, is a deliberate and at times risky intellectual practice, a resistance to the institutional demands that would have me, the "author," be the sole and unique point of origin of my discourse. In other words, it is a manner of practicing what one preaches, so to speak, an effort to convey at once an intellectual attitude and a set of theoretical assumptions in the very *form* of one's writing, to instantiate or inscribe in that form the theoretical assumption that discourse—and thus, too, anyone's discourse, speech, writing, and thought itself—is constructed from other discourses; which does not mean that discourse is merely repetitious, mimetic, univocally predetermined or finally contained in an unchanging Symbolic order. On the contrary, it is the very constructedness of discourse, its overdetermination, and its slipperiness that allow for what Judith Butler calls "a reiterative or rearticulatory practice."[4] Put another way: it is precisely the intrinsically dialogic and situated character of discourse that makes it possible to intervene in the symbolic order through practices of reappropriation or resignification which affect and to some extent alter the symbolic and which, I argue, affect and alter the imaginary as well.

In this context, the project of *The Practice of Love* is a rereading of Freudian psychoanalysis in order to rethink lesbian sexuality both within and against its epistemological and conceptual framework. But this *thinking within and against* should not be equated with some simple, voluntaristic notion of subversive or transgressive theoretical practice (the recent history of the world should have cured us of the illusions of the 1960s and 1970s). *Thinking within and against* is the condition of all critical thinking. Mine is no exception.

There are two main theoretical objectives or critical directions in the book. One is the reevaluation of the concept of perversion in Freud, as distinct from the pathological, and its resignification in what I call perverse desire, a type of desire fetishistic in a general sense and specifically homosexual or lesbian. The other is the effort to theorize what Foucault calls the "implantation of perversion" in the subject, to analyze the mechanisms social and psychic by which the subject is produced at once as a social and a sexual subject through her solicitation by and active participation in various discourses, representations, and practices of sex. These sexual-representational practices, I argue, both overdetermine and continually inflect sexual structuring. I will come back to this term, this awkward gerund-phrase, and why I use it. But first let me give you, briefly, a sense of my argument.

The constitutive ambiguity of Freud's discourse on sexuality from the *Three Essays on the Theory of Sexuality* of 1905 to the posthumous works on fetishism makes it possible to read two theories of sexuality in his work: one is explicit and affirmative, a positive theory of "normal" sexuality that goes from the infantile stage of polymorphous perversity to a successfully Oedipalized, normal, heterosexual adulthood. The other, I contend, is implicit and negative, appearing as the nether side or clinical underground of the first: it consists of two modalities, perversion and neurosis, depending on the presence and degree of repression (there can of course be repression or neurosis with/in perversion—the two are not mutually exclusive). In this theory, what is called "normal" sexuality is not an innate disposition or configuration of the sexual instinct, but rather the result of particular negotiations that a subject manages to achieve between the internal pressures of the drives, the various component instincts or partial drives, and the external, parental and societal pressures.

This latter theory follows from Freud's radical insight that the relation between an instinct or drive [*Trieb*] and its object [*Objekt*] is not natural, preordained by "biology," fixed, or even stable. The sexual instinct, he wrote, is "in the first instance independent of its object,"[5] and later added:

> The object of an instinct is the thing in regard to which or through which the instinct is able to achieve its aim. It is what is most variable about an instinct and is not originally connected with it, but becomes assigned to it only in consequence of being peculiarly fitted to make satisfaction possible.[6]

In this sense, perversion is not a distortion of "nature," a deviation from a biologically determined law that assigns one and only one type of object to the sexual drive, but is rather an inherent way of being of the drive itself, which continuously seeks out the objects best fitted to its aim of pleasure and satisfaction. Thus, if the drive is independent of its object, and the object is variable and chosen for its ability to satisfy, then the concept of perversion loses its meaning of deviation from nature (and hence loses the common connotation of pathology) and takes on the meaning of deviation from a socially constituted norm. This norm is precisely "normal" sexuality, which psychoanalysis itself, ironically, proves to be nothing more than a projection, a presumed default, an imaginary mode of being of sexuality that is in fact contradicted by psychoanalysis's own clinical evidence. Perversion, in this sense, is virtually the opposite of pathology, as it is formally the opposite (the positive, Freud said) of neurosis: perversion is the very mode of being of *sexuality* as such, while the projected norm, in so-called normal sexuality, is a requirement of social *reproduction,* both reproduction of the species and reproduction of the social system. Now, the conflation, the imbrication, of sexuality with reproduction in Western history has been shown by Foucault to come about through what he called "the technology of sex" and has been analyzed by feminist theory in the concept of compulsory heterosexuality. And it is, obviously, still central to hegemonic discourses. But my point is that the specific character of *sexuality* (as distinct from *reproduction*), the empirically manifested form of sexuality, as far as psychoanalysis knows it, is perversion, with its negative or repressed form, neurosis.

Following up in this perspective, the second part of my study undertakes the elaboration of what I call perverse desire. Rereading the classic studies on female homosexuality, the case histories written in the 1920s and 1930s by Freud himself, Jeanne Lampl-de Groot, Helene Deutsch, and Ernest Jones, in conjunction with the classic novel of female inversion, Radclyffe Hall's *The Well of Loneliness* (1928), and with contemporary lesbian literary and filmic texts of the 1980s by Cherríe Moraga, Adrienne Rich, and Sheila McLaughlin, among others, I delineate a type of desire whose signifier is not the phallus but something (object or sign) more akin to a fetish; that is to say, in the texts I analyze, the object-choices of a lesbian subject appear to be ruled, as in fetishism, by the psychic mechanism of disavowal [*Verleugnung*], which is at once the denial and the acceptance of castration.[7] All my texts exhibit an unmistakable fantasy of castration or dispossession.

To articulate such a desire into a formal model (a model with general validity), I undertake a reconsideration of the fantasy of castration in relation to a female body. The reconsideration is necessary because the threat of castration can only work in relation to what Freud calls a bodily ego or body-ego;[8] in other words, in order to be effective, the threat of castration must mean the possible loss of something on which the subject has bodily aims, something which is a source of sensations, pain and pleasure. I argue, therefore, that the threat that confronts the female subject (and that is disavowed by the formation of a fetish) is not the lack or loss of a penis but the lack or loss of a libidinally invested body-image, a body that can be narcissistically loved, and that loss of a bodily ego is tantamount to a loss of being, or a loss *in* being. Thus the fantasmatic "lost object" of perverse desire is neither the mother's body nor the paternal phallus; it is the subject's own lost body, which can be recovered in fantasy, in sexual practice, only in *and with* another woman. This perverse desire is not based on the masculinity complex (the denial of sexual difference), nor is it based on a regressive attachment to the mother (a regression to the pre-Oedipal or the phallic phase). It is based on the post-Oedipal disavowal of that loss—the loss of one's body-ego, the loss of being.

Finally, then, what I call perverse desire is a form of female (lesbian) desire that *passes through* the Oedipus complex but, contrary to all psychoanalytic accounts, including feminist ones, does not remain caught in its binary terms and moves on to other objects. These fetish-objects sustain and represent the subject's desire, her possibility of *being-in-desire;* in Freud's terms, they would engage at once both object-libido and ego-libido. But how do particular objects or signs become cathected or invested by the drives?

Perhaps the most ambitious part of my project is the effort to delineate the paths by which the drives select and invest their objects, and thus the paths through which psychic reality interacts with external reality. The drives, for Freud, are innate, but sexuality is not. As we understand it since and from Freud, sexuality is neither innate nor *simply* acquired, but is constructed or dynamically structured by psychic processes and forms of fantasy—conscious and unconscious; subjective, parental, and social; private and public—which are culturally available and historically specific. Fantasies, in Laplanche and Pontalis's famous phrase, are the scenarios (scripts or stage settings) of the subject's desire, and sexuality itself is constituted in the field of fantasy.[9] It seems to me that if desire is dependent on the fantasy scenario that the object evokes and helps to restage, then it is in that restaging that an object—any object—acquires the fantasmatic value of object of desire. So now the question to ask is, how do objects become attached to a desiring fantasy?

Reading Freud with Peirce, I speculate that sexuality is a particular instance of semiosis, the general process of sign and meaning formation, a process which articulates and enjoins subjectivity to social signification and material reality. How objects become assigned to instincts, in Freud's words, can be conceptualized through Peirce as a semiosic process in which objects and bodies are displaced from external to internal or psychic reality (from dynamic object to immediate object in Peirce, from real body to fantasmatic body in Freud) through a chain of significate effects or interpretants, habits, and habit-changes. With the concept of habit, in particular, I emphasize the material, embodied component of desire as a psychic activity whose effects in the subject constitute a sort of knowledge of the body, what the body "knows" or comes to know about its instinctual aims. The somatic, material, and historical dimensions that the Peircian notions of *habit* and *habit-change* inscribe in the subject reconfigure sexuality as a *sexual structuring,* a process overdetermined by both internal and external forces and constraints.

I use this awkward gerund-phrase, *sexual structuring,* instead of more familiar ones like sexuality or sexual identity, because the gerund form conveys, both etymologically and performatively, the sense of an activity, a dynamic and interactive process: *gerund* comes from the Latin *gerere,* to carry, and the gerund form carries the meaning of the verb, makes the verb work in its meaning, its signifying, or makes that meaning a working, an activity. This is not conveyed in the term *identity,* or *sexuality,* nor is it clearly conveyed in the term *sexuation,* used in Romance languages, the noun form of which also suggests something solid, definitive, the outcome of a process but still an outcome, a result, something achieved, done with, or final. By *sexual structuring* I want to designate the constructedness of sex, as well as of the sexual subject, its being a process, an accumulation of effects that do not rest on an originary materiality of the body, that do not modify or attach to an essence, matter or form—whether corporeal or existential—prior to the process itself. In other words, neither the body nor the subject is prior to the process of sexuation; both come into being in that continuous and life-long process in which the subject is, as it were, permanently under construction.[10]

Several years ago I argued the same apropos of gender; I wrote that the subject is effectively en-gendered in an interactive subjection to what I called the technology of gender. I wrote *en-gendered* with a hyphen (it was in the mid-1980s, a time when word punning by diacritical marks like hyphens, parentheses, slashes, etc., was becoming very popular). The subject is *en-gendered,* I wrote—that is, produced or constructed, and constructed-as-gendered—in the process of assuming, taking on, identifying with the positionalities and meaning effects specified by a particular society's gender system.[11] Recently, Judith Butler has elaborated on the concepts of assumption and identification in her book *Bodies That Matter;* she argues that the assumption of or identification with the norms of sex (or of gender) on the part of a subject is a reiteration of the symbolic law, a kind of "citationality," a citing of the law, and thus a performativity (12–14), which does not preclude agency in subjectivation (what a few lines above I called *interactive subjection,* borrowing the term from video games, one of the latest social technologies). Butler also argues, however, paradoxically, that agency or subjectivation "in no way presupposes a choosing subject" and must be seen rather as "a reiterative or rearticulatory practice, immanent to power" (15), without an agent or a subject who acts. "There is not power that acts," she states, "but only a reiterated acting that is power in its persistence and instability" (9). Power has no subject, Butler insists; and if we think of power as having a subject, it is purely an effect of grammar and of the humanist discourse that places the human subject or, in his stead, power, at the origin of activity and agency.

To be sure, this early-Foucaultian argument is still a powerful critique of the Cartesian subject, who appears to be alive and thriving in some circles, in spite of Freud, Nietzsche, Foucault himself, deconstruction, postmodernism, and so on. But in Butler's book, the radical delegitimation of the subject lives uncomfortably with a "progressive," or redemptive, political project: namely, the reinscription of excluded, abjected, queer bodies into the body politic by a "resignification of the symbolic domain" (22) and thus their revaluation, inclusion, or legitimation as bodies that matter. For me, Butler's argument and her project live uncomfortably together because it is difficult to imagine how symbolic resignification is to occur, and to result in such revaluation and legitimation of the abjected bodies, without agents or subjects of those practices of reiteration, citation, and reappropriation that Butler identifies in, for example, drag, passing, and renaming.

For the purposes of my study of sexuality, it is not only bodies that matter; the subjects, each of them constructed and constrained through a bodily boundary, must also matter; for me they are indispensable in a theory of sexuality, queer theory, or any other. For, if sexual structuring, sexuation or subjectivation, is an accumulation of effects that does not accrue to a preexisting subjectivity or to a primal, original materiality of the body, nevertheless the process takes place in and for a bodily ego; and moreover, a body-ego that is constituted, literally comes into being, through what Freud calls *Urphantasien,* primal or original fantasies, which are also fantasies of origin.[12]

What is this subject, then? In my reading of Freud, the subject is a body-ego, a projected perceptual boundary that does not merely delimit or contain the imaginary morphology of an individual self but actually enables the access to the symbolic: in my reading of Freud, the body-ego is a permeable boundary—an open border, so to speak—a site of incessant material negotiations between the external world, the domain of the real, comprising other people, social institutions, etc., and, on the other side, the internal world of the psyche with its instinctual drives and mechanisms of defense—disavowal, repression, and so forth. To map those negotiations, which is one of the objectives of *The Practice of Love* and of my practice of theory, I try to bring together three unwonted bedfellows: Freud, Peirce, and Foucault—not only the Foucault of the technology of sex but also and especially the Foucault of the practices of the self.

For my study of perverse desire, although more concerned with intrapsychic than with institutional mechanisms, is premised on a conception of the sexual that is actually closer to Foucault than to Freud, namely that individual sexual structuring is both an effect and a condition of the social construction of sexuality. While Foucault's first volume of the *History of Sexuality* describes the discursive practices and institutional mechanisms that implant sexuality in the social subject, Freudian psychoanalytic theory describes the subjective or psychic mechanisms through which the implantation takes, as it were, producing the subject as a sexual subject.

I suggest that Peirce's notions of interpretant and habit-change may serve as the juncture or point of theoretical articulation of Freud's psychosexual view of the internal world with Foucault's sociosexual view: the chain of interpretants and its resulting habit may serve as a model of the semiosic process in which objects and bodies are displaced from external to psychic reality—from dynamic object to immediate object in Peirce, and from real body to fantasmatic body in Freud. In each set, the objects and the bodies are contiguous but displaced in relation to the real; and the displacement occurs through a series of significate effects, habits or habit-changes. The site of this displacement is what I call the subject: that is to say, the subject is the place in which, the body in whom, the significate effects of signs take hold and are contingently and continuously realized.

When, reading one of Foucault's last published works which outlines his projected study of the "Technologies of the Self," I encountered the term self-analysis in relation to the introspective exercises and the writing of self that, according to him, defined a new experience of the self in Greco-Roman thought of the first two centuries AD, the coincidence of that term, *self-analysis*, with Peirce's "self-analyzing habit" could hardly fail to strike me. Could Foucault be reconciled with Peirce? I propose that, yes, this may be more than a coincidence. You may be skeptical, but hear me out.

In volumes 2 and 3 of his *History,* as Foucault's research shifts from the macro-history of modern sexuality in the West to the micro-history of localized practices and discourses on one type of sexuality (that between men and boys), his focus, too, shifts from the social to the subjective, from the technology of sex to the "technologies of the self," the discursive practices and techniques of the individual's construction of self. As he describes it retrospectively, his project was

> a history of the experience of sexuality, where experience is un-
> derstood as the correlation between fields of knowledge, types of
> normativity, and forms of subjectivity in a particular culture. . . .
> But when I came to study the modes according to which individuals
> are given to recognize themselves as sexual subjects, the problems
> were much greater . . . it seemed to me that one could not very
> well analyze the formation and development of the experience of
> sexuality from the eighteenth century onward, without doing a
> historical and critical study dealing with desire and the desiring
> subject. . . . Thus, in order to understand how the modern indi-
> vidual could experience himself as a subject of a "sexuality," it
> was essential first to determine how, for centuries, Western man
> had been brought to recognize himself as a subject of desire. . . .
> It seemed appropriate to look for the forms and modalities of the
> relation to self by which the individual constitutes and recognizes
> himself qua subject.[13]

In the introductory volume, Foucault had indicted psychoanalysis as complicit with the dominant power-knowledge apparati of the modern era. Here, even as he speaks of the subject of desire, he pointedly sidesteps the psychoanalytic knowledge on that subject, looking instead for another approach. The whole first part of volume 3, for example, is devoted to Artemidorus's *Interpretation of Dreams* without a single reference to Freud, whose homonymous text also marked the starting point and first elaboration of his theory of desire on the basis, as we know, of his self-analysis. (And indeed Freud refers to Artemidorus's *Oneirocritica* in his *Traumdeutung*).[14]

Now, it is impossible to imagine that Foucault missed these obvious analogies; on the contrary, he must have purposely implied them to emphasize the distance between Freud's scientific project, if based on his personal, Oedipal fantasy, and Foucault's own critical genealogy of desire. But neither his pointed taking of distance from psychoanalysis nor his much greater historical distance from his materials and sources can altogether erase the effective presence of an enabling fantasy, though not an Oedipal one, in Foucault's authorial subject of desire. The care with which the erotic relations between men and boys are examined, described, and pursued from Greece to Rome, through modifications in sexual ethics, to the development of "an art of existence" and the constitution of the self "as the ethical subject of one's sexual behavior",[15] more than suggests the presence of both a *self-analysis* and an enabling fantasy in Foucault's theory. While the enabling fantasy of Freud's theory is admittedly Oedipal, Foucault's is the fantasy of a non-Oedipal world, beyond the Fall, perversion, repression, or Judeo-Christian self-renunciation, a world sustained instead by a productively austere, openly homoerotic, virile ethics and practice of existence.

It is in the context of this genealogical project, effectively a genealogy of man-desiring man, that Foucault speaks of self-analysis. In describing the "new experience of self" derived from introspection, from taking care of oneself, and from the practice of writing about oneself that was prominent in the second century AD, he highlights Marcus Aurelius's "meticulous concern with daily life, with the movements of the spirit, with self-analysis."[16] This latter term, *self-analysis*, together with *self-exercise* (27) and other techniques "which permit individuals to effect by their own means or with the help of others a certain number of operations on their own bodies and souls, thoughts, conduct, and way of being" (18), seems to me altogether convergent with Peirce's notion of habit as final interpretant: the *"deliberately formed, self-analyzing* habit—self-analyzing because formed by the aid of analysis of the *exercises* that nourished it."[17] This, for Peirce, is the "living" effect of semiosis. In short, the new *experience* of self that Foucault describes is, in effect, a habit-change.

I don't know yet what significance to find in the fact that the works of Freud's and of Foucault's I drew on in this last section of the book are works they wrote as they were approaching death. Perhaps the conceptual limits of my project—the wild attempt to map a space between heterogeneous theoretical domains by means of analogies, tropes, word associations; and the presumption to account for a kind of desire that I have lived in the terms of a conceptual universe, that of Freud's psychoanalysis, in which it is not understood or contemplated but through which I nevertheless do think—perhaps these limits have something to do with the limit that is imposed by a growing awareness of death. As I get older, time gets shorter every day, one needs to hurry.

Questions have been raised in several quarters regarding my working through psychoanalysis (which I think of rather as a working-through of psychoanalysis). The most frequent is, why look to psychoanalysis for an account of female—let alone lesbian—desire, when Freud himself finally gave up, saying it could only be asked of poets? Or, why buy into a conceptual system that altogether precludes the possibility of a female desire, as Elizabeth Grosz rephrases that question in her thoughtful "interrogation" of *The Practice of Love* in this issue? Moreover, Grosz states, psychoanalysis is "a discourse whose time has come," a "dying discourse," and would best be buried. Yet she proceeds to take issue with my improper or unorthodox use of psychoanalytic concepts: if one insists in seeking understanding through psychoanalysis, then one should accept its founding assumptions and rigorously employ its concepts—e.g., castration—and not willfully stretch them to the point of theoretical incoherence. Can the fetish, for example, ever be anything but a morphological inflection of the phallus? Further, Grosz suspects that my attempt to take psychoanalytic theory where none of its adepts has gone before implies a revisionist project; in other words, my book is not the funeral ode to psychoanalysis that she would auspicate, but an implicit (surreptitious) attempt to prop it up or resuscitate it by the infusion of a seemingly progressive problematic, the lesbian question. It thus appears to her as a recuperative project aimed at insulating psychoanalysis from the criticisms of those social subjects whom psychoanalysis does not contemplate and therefore, it is alleged, excludes. Conversely (perversely), however, Grosz also argues that my elaboration of a model that distinguishes between lesbian and heterosexual female desire can be seen as an *anti*-psychoanalytic move, a covert attempt to create a lesbian *psychology*, leading to a particular, unchanging, fixed, or reified configuration of (lesbian) subjectivity. And finally, she asks, why would one want to "know" lesbian desire—to make lesbian desire the object of "intellectual, scientific or discursive investigation," to subject it to the will to know? Isn't a formal model of lesbian desire tantamount to normalizing lesbianism and taming desire? These are harsh questions, coming from one who is supposed to know.

Other readers have given me the benefit of the doubt, suggesting that it is as a feminist scholar of literature and film that I can inhabit "the radical edge of psychoanalytic thinking" in a country where psychoanalysts still secretly believe that homosexuality is an illness;[18] or that my reading of "a subversive Freud" succeeds in moving lesbian sexuality "out of its ghetto within the academy and into the spotlight of twentieth-century Euro-Western discourses," and seeks to settle the score for "decades of, at the very least, mental abuse that we lesbians have suffered from psychoanalytic and feminist theorists."[19] Needless to say, I tend to agree with them.

With regard to the second critical direction of my project, the reading of Freud with Peirce to find a linkage between Freud's privatized view of the sexual subject and Foucault's eminently social view of sexuality—a reading which I consider just as theoretically risk-taking as the theorizing of a perverse desire—no one has yet, to my knowledge, commented or questioned it.[20] And the silence may be more ominous than the harsh criticisms. But because the notion of a perverse lesbian desire and what in the book I call the seductions of lesbianism to a feminist imaginary appear to be more immediately catching, I will now take up some of the issues that have been raised concerning that part of my project.

In fact, I have posed some of those questions myself, in the book. It is possible, I suggested, that what I call perverse desire can account for other forms of sexuality than those represented in the texts I analyze, that my work can enable thinking about other so-called "perversions" or other forms of female sexuality that are ostensibly heterosexual. It is even possible that my notion of perverse desire may be productive toward a theorizing of male homosexuality, and all these possibilities are most welcome to me. But that was not the project of this book: masochism, female heterosexuality, bisexuality, and male homosexuality are not within my competence and not my fantasy. Or they are not at this moment.

I did, however, spend some time addressing the question, why psychoanalysis, why Freud, what can they contribute to an understanding of lesbian desire? For one thing, since sexuality is "the essential contribution of psychoanalysis to contemporary thought," as Laplanche put it,[21] we cannot think the sexual outside of psychoanalytic categories or, much more often, outside of psychoanalytic myths and reductive vulgarizations of those categories. Second, it is true that psychoanalysis was developed within the apparati of power-knowledge that one class, the bourgeoisie, deployed in the nineteenth century to ensure its own reproduction and survival as a class, as Foucault argues, but he also adds:

> [I]n the great family of technologies of sex, which goes so far back into the history of the Christian West, of all those institutions that set out in the nineteenth century to medicalize sex, [psychoanalysis] was the one that, up to the decade of the [nineteen] forties, rigorously opposed the political and institutional effects of the perversion-heredity-degenerescence system.[22]

This is an important factor in one's choice of understanding lesbian sexuality through psychoanalysis, and as distinct from heterosexual female sexuality, precisely because the perversion-degeneracy system (and some version of heredity, now possibly heredity-as-nurture) is still operative, if not explicitly invoked, in mainstream views of lesbianism as contrasted to a healthy, maternally inclined, female *hetero*sexuality; and that psychoanalytic tradition—just now one hundred years old—of political opposition to the medicalization of perversion, homosexuality in particular, can be reactivated and rearticulated, if need be, against the psychoanalytic clinical establishment.

There is still, however, the issue of theoretical coherence. How far can a notion like castration be stretched or resignified before it loses its structural value and epistemological effectivity? I have suggested that the texts I analyze are thematically centered on a fantasy of dispossession, which can be read as a fantasy of castration *because* of its structural role in the formation of a fetish. That fetish, which in some (but only some) of my texts appears as variously coded signs of masculinity,[23] is not the *paternal* phallus, although it retains its structural function of signifier of desire. In Freud's account, the fetish is a substitute for the maternal penis that the male child expects to see in the mother's body but finds missing; his apperception of a body without penis produces castration anxiety, which is relieved by the fetish. By the same account, no fetishism is possible for women since the castration complex is produced quite otherwise in the female, namely, by her seeing a body with penis, a male body, and not the mother's body, which is said to be "like" her own. But is it *like* her own?

I proposed that, for the female subjects of my texts, the castration complex rewrites in the symbolic—and therefore in the terms of (hetero)sexual difference, penis, no-penis—a prior or concurrent perception: the perception, or rather the non-perception, of no-body; that is to say, the perception that her own body is precisely *not like* the mother's, and hence not desirable, not lovable, a no-body. This threat of castration as non-being is based on a non-perception (a fantasy), just as the threat of castration for the male fetishist is based on the non-perception of the (missing) maternal penis. In other words, there is a clear homology, at least in this theoretical speculation, between the male's fetish in the classic theory of fetishism and the female's fetish in my formulation, although they are based on two distinct corporeal morphologies, both of which are of course fantasmatic. In the two cases, the fetish stands to disavow the lack or loss, to represent the object that is missing but narcissistically wished for: the penis/phallus in one case, the female body in the other. In both instances, the fetish, in its various and contingent forms, is nothing but the signifier of desire.

It seems to me that this formulation of female fetishistic or perverse desire is, if anything, too structurally coherent with the psychoanalytic model (one might say that it is truly a case of fearful symmetry), and may be too coherent for our own good. Thus, if incoherence is charged, may it not be out of adherence to the *letter* of the law, and a wish to uphold the *paternal* phallus above all? For what I have suggested is that the fetish in perverse desire takes on the function of the phallus as signifier of desire, but leaves behind the paternal function of the phallus, its role in physical and sociosymbolic reproduction. In other words, the fetish releases sexuality from its embeddedness in *reproduction,* and thus demonstrates that reproduction is not a feature of sexuality as such, but rather an effect of the construction of sexuality in modern Western cultures.

Now, I do not think that such a project is revisionist in the sense of a conservative move to restore psychoanalysis as good object and protect it from the criticisms of those for whom it is or has become a bad one.

It is, I think, a critical reading, an effort to work through critically—to work with and against—the concepts and the rhetorical and conceptual ambiguities of Freud, in order to remobilize their potential for resistance. It is true that Freudian psychoanalysis cannot envisage female homosexuality—not even as a perversion—and can only assimilate it to either female heterosexuality or male homosexuality. And yet Freud's own project, as Sander Gilman argues in *The Case of Sigmund Freud,* was not only marked but also enabled by his "racial difference," his "racial" inscription as a Jew, and the struggle with scientific paradigms which cast him, a doctor, as primitive, degenerate, and diseased.[24] For, in an actual instance of poetic justice, the theory of psychoanalysis enabled Freud to resignify those categories as the very stuff civilization is made of, and thus to transform the conditions of representability and the paradigms of knowledge of his time. That is one of the lessons I would draw from Freud: that no science and no theory is an immutable decalogue written in stone, and, therefore, if he could not imagine such a thing as lesbian desire, while others can, then it is for those others to attempt to resignify the categories of his theory from the location of their own difference and for their own time.

To conclude, I would like to say something about one of the questions that remains unresolved in the book, and unresolved for me, namely, the relation of fetishism to narcissism in perverse desire; that is to say, whether the particular form of primary narcissism that is involved in perverse desire can be related to the secondary narcissism that Freud said to be specifically feminine. The narcissistic dimension in perverse desire, I argue, is related to primary narcissism and infantile autoeroticism because it is the loss of a narcissistically invested body-image that threatens the ego with a loss of being and prompts the defense process of disavowal. For this reason, I propose, that threat is equivalent to the threat of castration in the male subject: both are narcissistic wounds that threaten the ego—the respective body-egos—with a loss of being. However, secondary narcissism, too, is an effect of the castration complex in women, according to Freud. He describes it as a sort of reimbursement that femininity demands for the loss of the penis, and says that it can stand in the way of object-cathexes, as in the case of "narcissistic women," who love only themselves "with an intensity comparable to that of the man's love for them."[25]

In my notion of perverse desire, primary and secondary narcissism cannot be distinguished as clearly as in Freud's metapsychological essay. However, as I pointed out, Freud is characteristically ambiguous in his theory of narcissism, which he bases on a distinction between ego-libido and object-libido (or ego-instincts and sexual instincts): at times the distinction is given as an opposition, while at other times they are said to coexist side by side. Taking the latter hypothesis—let us give Freud the benefit of his own uncertainties—it may be the case that so-called feminine narcissism is in fact coextensive or homologous to the ego-enhancing, autoerotic primary narcissism. This was the view held by Lou Andreas-Salomé, one of Freud's closest interlocutors. As Biddy Martin remarks in *Woman and Modernity*, Salomé challenged "the privilege Freud seem[ed] to accord to object-libido over narcissism"[26] and argued for primary narcissism as an indeed primal, original "connection with All," which she associated explicitly with femininity and with an autotelic development of the feminine psyche (205). According to Martin, Salomé believed that this original, innate narcissism was particularly strong in women, as well as creative artists and (male) homosexuals, and hence her notion of "a fundamental bisexuality" of women (211).

But this notion, now popular among feminist theorists, much like Freud's postulate of a latent or potential homosexuality in all human beings, cannot finally account for why or how particular object-choices are made by each individual. It seems to me that the distinction—not an opposition, but a distinction between two psychic forces that can coexist with one another—between ego-libido or narcissistic disposition and the object-choice component of sexual desire is usefully maintained when one is concerned to articulate the sexual difference between lesbian and heterosexual female desire. The question of bisexuality, if it is a question, should be addressed not before but after the modalities of such sexual dispositions have been understood. To posit an a priori, potential or latent bisexuality, as Freud and Salomé did, goes a very short way toward illuminating the psychic forms and socio-sexual practices of homosexuality, heterosexuality, or even actual bisexuality itself.[27]

Distinguishing between these socio-sexual practices and supposing that they entail and produce distinct socio-symbolic forms of subjectivity are not at all the same as saying that one and only one structure of desire can exist for any one subject, are not the same as saying that subjectivity is necessarily fixed, stable, or unchanging over the course of an individual's life. I coined the awkward term *sexual structuring* precisely to designate the permanently-under-construction character of socio-sexual subjectivity in its ongoing, overdetermined relation to fantasies and representations that are both intra- and inter-subjective. It is only by disregarding this part of my project that one can see in it a reification of lesbian sexuality or the creation of a lesbian "psychology" as the product of a will to knowledge that would spell out and normalize the makeup of a lesbian identity. Especially since the question of *identity* is not one of the questions asked in *The Practice of Love*.

I will end by saying that my book is not intended to revise or improve psychoanalysis but to displace the limits of the conceptual categories through which I, and not I alone, can think the sexual. So I would like my readers to think of this work as a series of hypotheses, speculations, contentions, dialogues, and reflections for the staging of a theoretical fiction that addresses itself not to psychoanalysis but *through* psychoanalysis . . . to whom it may concern.

Written as a response to Elizabeth Grosz's review of *The Practice of Love* and first published, together with the review, in *differences: A Journal of Feminist Cultural Studies* 6.2–3 (Summer–Fall 1994): 296–313. The entire issue was later reprinted as *Feminism Meets Queer Theory*, eds. Elizabeth Weed and Naomi Schor (Bloomington: Indiana University Press, 1997).

Chapter 10

The Intractability
of Desire

M
y work on female subjectivity—interdisciplinary research that
has unfolded over a period of about twenty years, mainly
in the United States—is rooted in the practices of North
American feminism, but makes use of theoretical contributions and
epistemological perspectives originating in Europe.

I would like now to take up again and reflect upon certain concepts
or terms that, to my way of thinking, constitute the key problems, the
points of articulation of lesbian and feminist thought on subjectivity. I
will try to compare these to current Italian thought.

The terms I have chosen, in the order of a personal chronology of my
own, are: *gender* and *sexual difference, identity* and *politics, sexuality*
and *desire.* My argument may seem somewhat schematic in its translation or transportation of these terms into the Italian context, but at
times translation (which, as we know, is always also a betrayal) can
produce a shift, a conceptual leap, an additional meaning that pushes
thought ahead and detaches it from reified concepts and clichés.

Gender and Sexual Difference

The concept of gender as such has only recently been acquired in Italian and generally European critical thought, while in the United States and in other Anglophone countries it was born with the women's movement in the 1970s, and was elaborated by feminist criticism in the context of women's studies. This being the case, current gender studies in North America emerged much later and precisely in opposition to radical feminism and the kind of research that privileges female cultural production and women's studies.

In the 1970s, then, *gender, sexual difference,* and *sexuality* were practically synonyms in feminist discourse. They then split—more or less in the 1980s—into two antithetical categories. On the one side were sexuality and sex, thought of as natural, biological facts, even if not in a heteronormative sense. On the other was gender or sexual difference, seen as patriarchal social and ideological constructs that worked entirely to the disadvantage of women (and of certain men). The ethical principle of integrity or coherence between life and political thought ("the personal is political") that still constitutes a founding premise of feminism remained firm, however. This brought with it the idea of a natural female sexuality onto which patriarchal society imposed gender as an institutional structure of the oppression of women.[1]

In this context, my work on "technologies of gender" (one chapter of which is translated into Italian in my book *Sui generiS*) analyzed the social construction of gender and its introjection or assumption on the part of individuals as an effect of discourses and representations that, as Foucault teaches us, are anchored to mechanisms of power. That is, they are tied to social institutions such as the family, school, medicine, law, language, the mass media, but also to cultural practices (literature, art, cinema) and to disciplinary—disciplined—knowledges such as philosophy or theory.[2] The social subject, I maintained, is not endowed with a natural, innate or original, sexuality, but is constituted—and is constituted as sexed—as an effect of representations of gender, in identifying itself in these, in making them its own. The subject is therefore constructed, or better, engendered in a continuous interaction—in an interactive subjection, we might say today, in the language of video games—with the technologies of gender. The awareness deriving from

these analyses, and from the analysis of the macroinstitution that subtends all technologies of gender, that is, the institution of heterosexuality,
places the subject of feminism—and I don't mean the female subject—in
a critical, distanced, and eccentric position in relation to the ideology
of gender. This is the reason I have called it an *eccentric subject,* that
is to say, not immune or external to gender, but self-critical, distanced,
ironic, exceeding—eccentric.[3]

In light of the current resumption of the Italian debate on the question
of compulsory heterosexuality, of which I will speak in a moment, one
must remember that without an analysis of this macroinstitution of male
power over women, feminism cannot go beyond emancipationist strategies and limits itself to the utopic or visionary moment which is always
necessary but never sufficient. Without such an analysis, in my view,
we lose track of those possibilities of negotiation that women actually
have within the structures of power when these powers are conceived
of, as in Foucault, as a force field in which powers and resistances are
exercised from mobile and variable points. There is no need to use the
example of Lysistrata, it is enough to think of the changes and shifts
that have occurred in late capitalist Western societies in the last twenty
to thirty years, in the period that corresponds to second-wave feminism.
I say shifts in a force field, rather than victories, because such changes
have not marked a simple progression in the women's struggle against
patriarchy, but have reconfigured the respective positions and modalities of both resistance and power.

At the present time in North America, sex, sexuality, and gender have
gone back to being almost synonyms, for example in so-called post-gen-
der discourse, in whose postmodern, functionalist, and voluntarist view
both sex/sexuality and gender are seen as discursive constructs which
consequently can be re-signified through practices of performance or
even remade surgically. Currently, the term *sexual difference,* conceived
of exclusively as the difference between man and woman (or rather, as
difference that groups human subjects in two antithetical categories each
excluding the other—all men in one, all women in the other—despite
the many other factors that take part in the constitution of the subject,
such as culture, class, race, sexual disposition or choice, religion, and
so on), has fallen into disuse even in the theory and practices of radical
feminism. It has instead been substituted by the plural, *sexual differences,* or rather, differences between various types of sexual disposition

that may be deviant or not with respect to heteronormative sexuality, and that contribute to the (trans)formation of subjectivity, but are not the sole determinant of it.

By *subjectivity,* I mean the ways and modalities of my being a subject that in *Sui generiS* I articulated in the concept of *experience* but which in my work in progress I am rethinking as *self-translation.* I mean *subject* in the double sense of 1) being, individual, person subjected to rules, constraints, more or less rigid social norms (e.g., the very rigid rules of the kinship system; the slightly less rigid constrictions that define social classes; the norms that regulate the behaviors and expectations of gender; the pseudo-scientific as well as ideological discourses on race, ethnicity, etc.); but also 2) subject in the sense of grammatical subject: one who exists, acts, carries out the actions described by the predicate, a subject or "I" endowed with existence, capacity to act, to want, and so on.

The term subjectivity, then, has two valences. One is that of subjection to determined social (but not only social) constraints. The other is that of the capacity for self-determination, self-defense, resistance to oppression and to the forces of the external world, but also resistance to and self-defense from forces that act in the internal world, what Freud calls the id and the superego. We need only think of the psychic mechanisms of ego defense—repression, disavowal, projection, and so forth. Just above I said "but not only social" because the social subject is always also a psychic subject, and thus traversed by conscious and unconscious desires, drives, fantasies or phantasms which constitute another modality of constraint. And often these two modalities contradict each other. For example: "there are certain nuances of my sensibility that don't coincide with my will to be feminist and with the practice I've made in feminism," says Adriana Cavarero during a dialogue with Rosi Braidotti held at the Filo di Arianna in Verona and published with the title "The Decline of the Subject and the Dawn of Female Subjectivity."[4]

Unlike Cavarero's affirmation of ambivalence, which regards the contradiction within the subject in its singularity, the title makes explicit a contradiction on the discursive-theoretical level, inasmuch as it seems to want to uncouple female subjectivity from the (presumably Cartesian) subject which is by now on the wane, to then reconstitute it ex novo, in the new light of that which Braidotti calls "this post-woman period" (73). But the question of what female subjectivity may be reconstituted in this way remains ambiguous and contradictory. The organizers explain, in fact, citing Braidotti, that "the 'I' is only a grammatical necessity," but then add: "we are feminists because we want it strongly, with all the energy and passion that a subject is able to express" (71). This "I" who *wants* strongly, therefore, cannot be only a grammatical necessity. Instead, it still expresses a positive subjectivity, a subject without divisions or ambivalences, enriched by a technologically empowered corporeality and acted upon—it would seem—only by will.

This recent example, taken from the Italian context, reconfirms a contradiction that I had identified as a characteristic of North American feminism back in the 1980s: "a double tension in opposite directions—the critical negativity of its theory, and the affirmative positivity of its politics—is at the same time feminism's historical condition of existence and its theoretical condition of possibility."[5]

The contradiction that arises from this double tension cannot therefore be resolved, but should be highlighted and analyzed since, if to live the contradiction is the condition of existence of a feminist subjectivity, to analyze it is the condition of a feminist politics.

Let me explain: we can all agree with Braidotti that the "I"—like gender, like the body—is a social and linguistic construct, an effect of discourse, and not a natural given, a priori, predating the social or the semiotic. And yet the "I" is also a political necessity, a necessity of survival both physical and psychic, and therefore also epistemological. It is a corporeal "I," a bodily ego, as Freud says, perhaps imaginary (says Lacan), but such that however much it is extended by operating on the physical facts of the body, reconstructing its parts, organs, genitals, strengthening or modifying it with prostheses, in short, however much it is made into a cyborg, so much the more must this body make reference to an "I," a desiring and political subject. It is a subject caught in a double tension, erotic and ethical, which at times immobilizes it and at other times opens the doors and windows of the unthinkable.

In certain cases the subject poses resistance to the optimism of the will: "What I was trying to say about singular corporeality is, from the political perspective, a point of resistance. It is what I want to oppose to the technological invasion . . . it is also necessary to face the negations and the limitations of one's own body" ("Cavarero," 83). In other cases, the subject advances claims, aspirations and rights, and first among all these, the right to social recognition. For example, in the early 1980s Donna Haraway's "Cyborg Manifesto" reclaims social recognition for a female subject then rising up in the United States, the woman of color. In the 1990s an analogous manifesto by Sandy Stone asks for social recognition of the transsexual subject.[6] Again in the 1990s, the affirmation of a lesbian identity in Italy is an example of a feminist political subjectivity that, turning to other women, asks—rather, demands—the recognition of its own existence and of its own specific difference with the aim of articulating a common political project.

Identity and Politics

But why is it at times so difficult to understand one another about what might constitute a common political project? Is it inevitable that the aspiration to recognition expressed in terms of identity should lead to an identity politics? What relation is there between subjectivity and politics? The discussion between the Milanese editors of the *Violet Notebooks* [*I quaderni viola*] and the Bologna-based "Laboratory of Lesbian Criticism" [Laboratoria di critica lesbica] is based on material furnished by the Laboratory and carried out during three meetings (the last of which is reported in the text). The text, which the editors describe as a "several-month journey into lesbian politics,"[7] seems to me to be exemplary in this regard. The text of the *Violet Notebooks* was motivated by an "obstinate desire to understand one another, beyond languages and different approaches" (18). It was meant as the beginning of a dialogue between the feminist and lesbian movements which had not yet taken place in Italy—in part, paradoxically, impeded by specific political categories of Italian feminism, such as the so-called "practice of relations between women."[8] As such, it is exemplary insofar as it emphasizes both the political motivations of the two groups in their attempt to converge toward a common project (a strong feminism in the fight against patriarchy for the transformation of the structures of power) and, on the other hand, a fundamental incomprehension around the meaning and affective valence of certain terms.

Moving from a comparison of the terms *identity and difference* and *identity and politics,* on which there do not seem to be irreconcilable differences, the discussion goes on to focus on and get bogged down in the question of *compulsory heterosexuality.* On the one side, they recognize the political value of lesbianism for all women and the vital importance of a lesbian identity for lesbian women:

> Lesbianism is rendered invisible because it expresses female free-dom and female independence, which are intolerable in that net of relations that relegates women to the role of "reproducers." This ought to be the obvious link between lesbians and feminists. That's why I don't conceive of a feminism that doesn't see the political value of lesbianism; it seems to be a weak feminism that doesn't really know what it's talking about when it talks about patriarchy (and just for that reason can permit itself to call it finished and not talk about it any more!). . . . Lesbian visibility is fundamental because it creates an imaginary for all women, not just for lesbians. (Giulia, *Violet Notebooks,* 27)

> The question of identity has been important for oppressed or segregated or discriminated-against subjects, who have had to reconstruct their own image first of all for themselves, because they had often internalized the invalidation and the contempt of others. In the case of lesbians, identity can coincide with the very possibility of existence: we can not know we exist because the ab-solute silence that has traditionally surrounded lesbianism deprives us of the very possibility of recognizing ourselves, transforming existence into an indefinite discontent. . . . I interpret needs-iden-tity-project as articulations of political subjectivity. (Lidia, *Violet Notebooks,* 20)

On the other side, they ask that sexuality's capacity to structure not only subjectivity, but also social relations, be recognized, and thus also that the concept of compulsory heterosexuality be accepted as a politi-cal category of feminism. Antonia, of the Laboratory, asks:

> What does it mean . . . mediation between lesbians and hetero-sexual women? Finding some points in common? What are the objectives that we might share? Certainly recognizing in the dy-namics of the world the rules of negation and social and symbolic overpowering that function in relation to women and lesbians can be considered a point of departure for both subjects. That is not enough, it is only the beginning from which a radical plan for transforming the structures of power must be developed. One of these structures is . . . compulsory heterosexuality. (*Violet Note-books,* 26)

And Cristina, also of the Laboratory, writes:

> When we come to ask you to verify an evident obligation to heterosexuality, that is entirely to the advantage of the male human gender, we are not proposing that you become lesbians, but that you admit compulsory heterosexuality as a criterion of political intelligibility, useful for a better definition of the problems. We are asking you to note that the obligation to heterosexuality is constantly erased from political reflection, despite being so important that it interferes with our happiness and freedom. (*Violet Notebooks*, 31)

And here begin the misunderstandings. The editors of the *Violet Notebooks* admit that "lesbian criticism of heterosexuality also broadens my heterosexual horizons" (Rosa, 24), that "if one can choose, it changes the meaning itself of the heterosexual choice" (Nadia, 25), and that "to put into question the obviousness of heterosexuality can have a political significance" in that the patriarchy uses it to perpetuate itself (Francesca, 29). However, they also claim not to understand: "I don't understand from the point of view of political method; I don't understand the essence [of the argument] and I don't understand what practical implications the critique of compulsory heterosexuality might have" (Lidia, 31).

What is not understood, it seems to me, is the double register in which this term operates, sliding imperceptibly from one semantic field to another. In one heterosexuality stands for "choice" or sexual behavior, in the other heterosexuality is equivalent to a social institution.[9] The very fact that the term *heterosexual institution* or *institution of heterosexuality*, now commonly used in Anglo-American feminist discourse, never appears in this text, where instead what is spoken of is "the lesbian critique of heterosexuality" or a "fierce *lesbian attack* on compulsory heterosexuality" (28), is a clue to the shift in emphasis from the political category of institution to the private one of sexual behavior.

Something similar happened in the United States at the beginning of the 1980s. At this time, it was objected that compulsory heterosexuality was a category relevant to the oppression of women only in the case of women tied to men by chains of economic, social, or affective dependence which give men control over the female body, such as work, marriage, or maternity. It was said, for example, that economically independent women, unwed mothers, or black women (assigned economic and affective role as head of the family on account of the frequent absence of the father and of other particulars of African-American culture) could avoid such chains even though they had sexual relations with men. But it has become evident that even those women who individually manage to avoid economic or affective dependence on their own partners in their own homes are, in the public sphere, equally subject to the systematic effects of a symbolic and social imaginary which define them as women in the eyes of all men and in their own eyes, as well. More precisely, they define them, as they define all women, as *heterosexual*: at work, for example, or as concerns the possibilities of sexual harassment, rape, incest, and so on.

This shows that the presumption of heterosexuality is in any case implicit not only in civil institutions—family, work, maternity—but also in all the other mechanisms of male domination. It is a pillar of the social structure and an ideological a priori, unsaid, hidden or unconscious, of all the dominant cultural formations. It is in this sense that heterosexuality is compulsory: it is institutionalized, it has assumed the normative, systematic, and abstract (abstractable from the actions of single individuals) character proper to institutions. It can therefore be analyzed as an institution, or even as a macroinstitution that subtends and on which are founded other institutions and social technologies.[10]

If, in the discussions published in the *Violet Notebooks,* the critique of heterosexuality was received in the end as a criticism of heterosexual feminists by lesbian women, as sectarian claim or as *ressentiment* (21), it is in part because the sliding of the term from one register to another takes place in the discourse of both groups. In one of the materials proposed by the Laboratory we read:

> One part of the women's political movement has made us discover figures of female freedom whose distinctive trait is the subtraction of the self from the sexual pact with men. Female saints, nuns, female so-called heretics are the examples of freedom. Why? These women chose for themselves the only possibility that a woman has to be truly free: shifting her own sexual desire away from men. Removing herself from the materiality of the relation with men is the primordial form, the primary condition of a project of freedom. It is necessary to assume sexuality not as mere behavior, even less as a choice that can distinguish our sexual preferences, but as a code that signifies in an originary way the subjects and the order of discourses and meanings.[11]

Even if the meaning of the last proposition is clear and perfectly summarizes the theoretical concept on which the Laboratory turns, the rhetorical construction and the argumentation of the passage I have cited tend to muddy the waters. It is not only the magisterial tone or the axiomatic nature of these affirmations that provokes the impression of sectarianism, but also the conceptual slippage of the discourse from the particular to the general. This slippage moves from single individuals (female saints, nuns, female heretics—who are presumed to have made a choice which to me seems based above all on the mythology of a certain feminism) to their status as exempla (*"figures* of female freedom"). It moves from concrete subjects (women who have chosen to "shift their own sexual desire away from men") to the abstraction of a primordial form ("To subtract oneself from the materiality of relations with men is the primary condition of a project of liberation"). Finally, it moves from heterosexuality as sexual behavior to heterosexuality as semiotic macrocode, that is to say, as institution ("It is necessary to assume . . .").

A possible explanation of the theoretical ambiguity of this passage, and perhaps also of the incomprehension on the part of its interlocutors, can be found in the texts proposed by the Laboratory as the basis for the discussion and reprinted in the "Documents" section of the fourth *Violet Notebook*. Among these, beside recent things, there are two essays of the late 1970s, "The Straight Mind" by Monique Wittig and "Some Reflections on Separatism and Power" by Marilyn Frye.[12] These represent two theoretical and political positions historically very important for the development of radical lesbian and feminist thought in North America, but dated to the debates of those years. In these, just as in the famous essay by Adrienne Rich of the same period (compare note 10), sexuality is conceived of principally as the terrain, the place and the means of gender oppression, and the discourse on desire is totally absent. It is my impression that those ideas on sexuality contained in the texts that the Laboratory reproposes in the contemporary Italian context, together with the themes of the *pensiero della differenza* (e.g., female freedom), produce the conceptual slippage by which we pass from the critique of the heterosexual institution to the prescription of removing oneself from heterosexual relations.

Lidia's response is therefore to the point, focussing on the fundamental problem:

I know perfectly well that sexual desire can change for ideological, cultural and social reasons. But I also know that this doesn't happen on command or because of a coherent and intransigent development of the critique of patriarchal society. . . . Certainly, a heterosexual feminist lives contradictions and torments that can be serious, but where is it written that a lesbian is so serene and reconciled with herself, or that, if she has contradictions, they are all linked to the social taboo? It seems to me that lesbian literature tells quite another story. (21)

Sexual desire, which was expelled from the formulation of political subjectivity ("needs-identity-project"), repressed or set aside by the need for ideological coherence, now returns unexpectedly, or rather erupts symptomatically as the discussion heats up. And it makes us think about Silvia's observation, unfortunately ignored by the other women: "if social imposition works, it means that it encounters a phantasm in the individual which gives in to it. Heterosexual culture has so much power because it encounters within us our destiny as daughters and sons, the phantasm of filiation. . . . Man is a formidable narcissistic temptation for women" (28).

If, then, it is so difficult to understand one another about the critique of compulsory heterosexuality as a founding category of a common political project for the future, this is not so much because the political validity of its radical critique of patriarchy isn't recognized by both sides, as much as because, as Lidia says (and let's all say it once and for good), we can't control desire. It is this irreducibility or intractability of desire which makes the term *compulsory heterosexuality* slide from a category of political intelligibility to a phantasmatic scenario—and this is true, with a different valence, for both lesbians and heterosexual women. Another dimension of subjectivity thus appears: no longer simply political but precisely subjective, singular, tied to desire, to phantasms, to a body's experience and knowledge, to libidinal and narcissistic investments that can oppose political will and resist conceptual comprehension. And this dimension of subjectivity brings with it not identity but division.

Sexuality and Desire

In a series of articles on female writings—memories, reflections, thoughts and fantasies of women—which came out in the magazine *Noi Donne*

[*We Women*] between 1989 and 1992, Lea Melandri collected enlightening accounts of the fantasy of filiation and the narcissistic temptation of the love relationship. In these fragments of private writing, Melandri reads the heterosexual love relationship as a phantasm of corporeal plenitude, the illusion of finding again a unity or completeness lost at birth and with the separation from the maternal body. For one of the writers, the phantasm manifests itself when she becomes pregnant, since only in becoming a mother does she feel once more "worthy of my mother's body . . . worthy of my female body. . . . I was 'full of grace'" (62–63). For another, it manifests itself in the desire to hold "within herself, on her skin, within her sex . . . the memory of the man who had possessed, desired, raped her" (60). Melandri comments:

> Solitude, which re-emerges every time to gather up the cry of a little girl or of a woman, shows itself then in its double function: testimony of an irreparable loss and obstinate reaffirmation of the desire for absolute possession, like a return to the warm encasement of a mother or the clutching to oneself of the man son, lest its separate and extraneous rising signal the beginning of history, of every story.[13]

Solitude, the sense of separateness and division that constitutes the corporeal I and marks the beginning of every story and the very possibility of history—personal history, collective history, history in the sense of story, writing, narration—is configured in various forms in twentieth-century thought. It takes the names of separation from the maternal body, division of the subject in language, *différence*, alienation, alterity, and so forth. Here are born desire and the illusions that sustain it, as are the phantasms by which sexuality is shaped and, with it, the corporeal and psychic dimension of subjectivity. But here are also born political projects, the need for identity and recognition, for individuality and collectivity, for singularity and belonging.

The experience of separation, lived simultaneously in the subjective and social senses, and in the political sense that some still call separatism, can provide the stimulus to imagine, construct, theorize, and live a subjectivity both political and sexed, an erotic body that represents itself—instead of eliding itself—in a social body, a subject which reinterprets and redefines itself in a history *in fieri*, that is, under construction. As Liana Borghi writes:

It is by now a commonplace among us that sexuality is the heart of lesbian identity; that the lesbian is by antonomasia the lover . . . that lesbian identity depends very much on the crossing of the lover's body and thus on the recognition, which follows from this, of a change in perception with regard to heterosexual schemata. . . . If the relation lover-beloved has as its aim the re-appropriation of the erotic body, the relation lesbian-community is configured as the place of the re-appropriation of the social body, as the space of will and of political project-making, as the terrain where the construction of a common language actualizes the new self. It is also the place where the subject represents itself as historical subject interpreting an individual and collective past as tradition, as history.[14]

But in the dimension of subjectivity that I have called corporeal and psychic, which is crisscrossed by life and death drives, by repressions, ambivalences and compromises, desire is configured in phantasms of unity *and* of division: it is articulated in the word that creates symbolic space, self-representation, projects, theory, politics, but it is also manifested in symptomatic gestures, in the repetition of affective patterns and phantasmatic scenarios that impede the affirmative word, hinder projects, interpose negativity, and resist the steady progression of history.

It is useful to reread some texts that take into account, analyze, or at least thematize this negativity or intractability of desire. Such texts are in a certain sense "originary" in Italian feminist thought because they are linked to one of its first practices, "the practice of the unconscious." It is useful, I would even say necessary, as Ida Dominijanni does in her introduction to *La politica del desiderio* [*The Politics of Desire*] by Lia Cigarini, to re-introduce the figures of extraneousness, of the "mute woman," of the "unpolitical."

> The return of the repressed threatens all of my projects for work, for research, for politics. Does it threaten, or is it the really political thing about me, to which I should give relief, space? . . . There has been a change, I have seized the right to speak, but in this period I have understood that the affirmative part of me was again taking up all the space. I am convinced that the mute woman is the objection that is most fertile for our politics. The "unpolitical" excavates caverns that we must not seal off.[15]

More than an introduction, Dominijanni's essay is a reasoned re-reading, attentive to Cigarini's voice and to her particular contribution to collective writings. It is accompanied by references to other women authors and more recent writings, related or not to the women's movement, in a critical dialogue that gives a concrete measure of that relationship of exchange, negotiation and female mediation on which Cigarini insists. It is a re-reading, necessarily partial and properly subjective, which traces a journey of its own, a trajectory of thought indicated by Dominijanni's very title, *Il desiderio di politica* [*The Desire of/for Politics*], which reverses Cigarini's, *La politica del desiderio* [*The Politics of Desire*]. To me Cigarini's beautiful metaphor, "the 'non-political' excavates caverns that we must not seal off," suggests a profound awareness of the importance of negativity in theorizing the (also political) subjectivity of women. In Dominijanni's reversed perspective, however, it indicates an absolute positivity: "the figure of the mute woman opens the door to a subjectivity freed from the master-slave dialectic and to a politics moved no longer by reactive victimism but by active desire" (12).

Rereading the 1976 *Sottosopra* along with the red *Sottosopra* of 1996, it is clear that the trajectory indicated by Dominijanni is parallel to that followed by the Women's Bookstore of Milan in the past twenty years. The red *Sottosopra* speaks of an active female desire, designed "to conquer the world," which is carried out through the performative word that asserts it, names it, and thus creates it, or "gives birth to it" [lo mette al mondo].[16] Counterposed to this quick and victorious desire, which invests, earns and is traded on the market (3, 6), is a "pathology of female desire unable to speak," whose figures still belong to the classical, pre-Freudian pathology of sexuality: the hysteric, the melancholic, the depressed woman, and why not—if we continue to go down the typology—why not the lesbian? But the numerous authors of this *Sottosopra* do not speak of her, for they are convinced that sexual difference is always only that biological difference between men and women. It is "irreducible, because it is of the body in its insurmountable opacity" (4). So much so that, having made the "discovery" that there is also a "male difference," they must conclude for the sake of coherence that both differences and both sexualities, male and female, are categories in themselves unitary, compact, and each rigorously determined by a state of nature, which precedes any symbolic order: the respective opaque body that founds the difference between the two differences.

This conception of sexuality and of the relation body-subjectivity, however, is no longer compatible with a practice of the unconscious because it is not compatible with the Freudian theory of the unconscious, of the body-ego or of the hysteric who, in somatizing, demonstrates precisely the non-opaqueness of the body, its continued permeability by the symbolic. Missing, therefore, are the necessary theoretical premises for the "material" politics that Dominijanni—and I with her—wishes for, a politics that can put back into circulation "the repressed of the social relation[:] body, desire, sexuality, fantasies, fears, unconscious processes" (10). Moreover, if the hysteric of the 1970s was an emblematic figure to which was assigned the crucial task of permitting access to the symbolic mother and to female freedom, as described by Dominijanni (but I do not agree with this interpretation of the hysteric), in the 1990s "the figure of the hysteric has been replaced by . . . the figure of the depressed woman" (*Sottosopra* 3). And the depressed woman of today is not at all the hysteric of yesterday.

The depressed woman of the red *Sottosopra* is no longer the mute woman, she makes no objection, she brings nothing to the politics of women; she is a loser and that's all. Do not care about her, but look and move on. Only in this way is it possible to bet on the end of the patriarchy, declare finished its "control of the fertile female body and its fruits" (1) and a few pages later make a reference en passant to the "'strange war' that has infested the former Yugoslavia" and to the "concomitance of female silence with a fierce and notably stupid male war-mongering" (4). From 1976 to 1996, in the political topography of the two *Sottosopras,* in which the depressed woman corresponds to the hysteric and the losing silence of the Bosnian woman corresponds to the fertile objection of the mute woman, a reversal of perspective has occurred, an inversion of values. Not by chance, then, desire, defined as "preceding every history and every sense of belonging, even that of gender" (3) becomes once more neutral, asexual.

In such a "political" vision of desire and of female subjectivity the cognition of the non-political, that is to say, the limits of politics, has been lost. The same is true of the psychoanalytic understanding of desire as the internal limit of the I, that is to say, the sense in which desire is negativity, dis-identification, disgregation, dispersion of the coherence (not to say of the will) of the I. It is an ecstatic moment of explosion/implosion, in which the I comes apart, crumbles, no longer holds together.

Even this ecstatic moment of eclipse, risk, or loss of self in the desire of the other, male or female, is part of subjectivity, the part that most pertains to sexuality. And it is the latter that disturbs the positivity, the functionality, the performativity of a politics of triumphant desire.

Is it because of the problems it creates that sexuality is not easily come by in the discourses on female subjectivity, to the point that desire itself, in order to be always victorious, must be de-sexualized and purified of its negativity? I insist on the intractability and stubbornness of desire, and on the negativity quotient that remains active in the experience of every sexed subject. This does not mean that I want to oppose or simply substitute the negativity of desire for the positivity of politics. Rather to the double valence of the female subject in feminist philosophical political discourse—negativity of theory, positivity of politics—I see a corresponding double valence of subjectivity as regards desire and sexuality. These are both bearers of activity and passivity, word and silence, phantasms of unity and division, union and aggression. Even this double valence, or more precisely, ambivalence, must not be re-solved ideologically in one direction or another, nor must it be negated or minimized, but must be taken into account, faced up to each time, and, if possible, negotiated.

To those who are interested in articulating a common political project of women through our many and multiple differences, I therefore pro-pose rethinking subjectivity in a material dimension, broadly speaking, of which sexuality is the central nexus, the place in which the instances of the corporeal, of the psychic and of the social interweave to constitute subjectivity and the limits of the I. Said another way, in the words of Simonetta Spinelli, I propose rethinking female subjectivity taking ac-count of what practices it involves and what *necessity* may lie beneath the desire acted out by a woman's *body*.

> From a material relation is born the sign of an understanding that is reflected in our relational practices and therefore in our social practices. . . . Understanding surfaced for me when I had a mate-rial encounter with another woman. Then I repressed it because it bothered me. When my awareness was awakened together with other women in feminism, the base was this repressed that I had left behind. I say that knowledge and understanding for a lesbian woman surface when there is this first material encounter with another [woman].[17]

If the theory of subjectivity that I am delineating here is reflected in the words of a lesbian, it is not only through the felicitous intellectual practice of "starting from oneself," but also because, as other women quoted above confirm, sexuality is the "common-place" of lesbian existence. It is the place in which an erotic "crossing of the body" of the other [woman] and of one's own takes place, with a consequent, and often surprising, "change in perception with regard to heterosexual schemata" (see Borghi, note 14). This is the case as much with regard to the schemata of the female and male bodies produced by the social imaginary as with regard to the image of the body-ego that each subject constructs for itself and (re)elaborates in relation to those schemata. It is the place, therefore, of a practice of love from which "surfaces an understanding," a corporeal knowledge and a knowing of oneself and the world—in short, a subjectivity—that leads to another production of meaning, another cognition of the social relation, other modalities of acting in the world.[18] They are other, that is, in respect of those of a subjectivity that constitutes itself in relation to heterosexuality.

For every woman, every female subjectivity, sexuality is the place from which the subject (re)elaborates the image of the self and of the erotic body in the encounter with the male or female other, and (re)elaborates its own corporeal knowledge, its own understanding, its ways of relating and acting in the world. This means that sexuality is the "common-place" of every subjectivity, but is a place not usually marked in the topographies of the places and means of women's politics. There are certainly many reasons for this elision. Some of them have already been suggested: the difficulty of living contradictions and ruptures between will and affect; the resistance to coming to terms with the limitations of one's own body; the awareness of the risk that sexuality always involves for anyone defined as a woman in a social system held up by the heterosexual institution; the relegation to a devalued social space identified as female and thus identified with the narrow ambit of the body, in opposition to the unlimited space of the mind or of thought which is attributed to the male; the need, which is vital as well as political, to belong to a gender and to be recognized by other women.

These and others are reasons, ambivalences, that we all know personally but about which we rarely talk to one another in the political confrontation between us. And the non-political no longer has a place in the presumption of a universal positivity of women's politics. Avoiding looking into that place of solitude and desire, of phantasms, ambivalences and necessity in which sexuality is shaped, the very reasons for such a politics, or rather the women who are its concrete subjects, are lost from sight. It seems to me that, today, a feminist theory of political agency must take into account, not only the differences among women, but also the constraints, both external and internal to the subject, the limits of the ego and the necessity which sustain it, the productivity of desire but also its intractability.

Written in Italian as an intervention in the turn that occurred in Italian feminist theory in the 1990s, and published as "Irriducibilità del desiderio e cognizione del limite" in Teresa de Lauretis, *Soggetti eccentrici* (Milan: Feltrinelli, 1999). First published in this English translation by Sarah Patricia Hill with the title "Subjectivity, Feminist Politics, and the Intractability of Desire" in *Italian Feminist Theory and Practice: Equality and Sexual Difference*, eds. Graziella Parati and Rebecca West (London: Associate University Press and Teaneck, N.J.: Fairleigh Dickinson University Press, 2002), 117–35.

Chapter 11

Figures of
Resistance

I.

In spring 2004, I was invited to lecture at Trinity College, Dublin, on the occasion of the centenary of women's entrance into the academy in Ireland.[1] The event, intended to honor women's contributions to knowledge, was something of a personal celebration as well, for although that was only my second time in Dublin, it was for me the occasion of many returns. I had first visited Trinity College during my college years in Italy. My thesis director and professor of British and American literatures, Charles Haines, was an American expatriate who had received his degree from Trinity College and spoke of the school with reverence and awe—or perhaps the awe was mine, as I listened to him in an auditorium filled with over three hundred students in Milan. Being in Dublin again marked a return to that time of my life, so long ago, in which I began the critical study of literature written in English.

The event itself also brought back the memory of two other such occasions. The first was the tercentenary celebration of the first doctorate ever conferred upon a woman, to which I was invited to speak by the young and very militant Women's Studies Department at the University of Wisconsin in 1978.[2] The event commemorated there concerned a Venetian noblewoman named Elena Lucrezia Cornaro Piscopia, who received her doctorate in philosophy from the University of Padua in 1678. She was the daughter of the procurator of San Marco, who traced his lineage back to the Roman family of the Cornelii, whence the name Cornaro, the very family that gave four doges to the Venetian Republic, three popes and eight cardinals to the Catholic Church, and one queen to the Island of Cyprus: Caterina Cornaro, less famous for her political rule than for having been portrayed by Titian, Tintoretto, and Veronese.

The second event that came to mind was the inaugural address I delivered in November 1991 as Belle van Zuylen Visiting Professor under the auspices of the Women's Studies Department at the University of Utrecht.[3] In those august surroundings, the figure of Elena Lucrezia was conjured up by the symbolic presence of two women under whose aegis and in whose name, literally, I owed my presence in the Aula Magna. One was Anna Maria van Schuurman, the first woman who was allowed to study at the University of Utrecht, provided she remained hidden in "a wooden room inside the lecture hall, screened off by a board with holes in it." So states a brochure of the Center for Advanced Research in Women's Studies that the University of Utrecht named after her, the Anna Maria van Schuurman Center, where I was doing research in 1991. She was a contemporary of Elena Lucrezia and their stories are rather similar, though Anna Maria died in 1678, the year Elena Lucrezia received her doctorate.

The other woman was Belle van Zuylen, or Isabelle de Charrière, who lived in the eighteenth century and after whom was named the chair I occupied; Belle van Zuylen who, from her castle overlooking the lovely Utrecht countryside, wrote in French, not in her native language, just as I wrote and spoke my lecture neither in Dutch nor in my native language, Italian, which was also Elena Lucrezia's native language, although she had to prove her knowledge in Latin. My feminist genealogy began, then, with these women whose especial talent for languages went hand in hand with a difficult and complicated relationship to language, with the necessity of silence or linguistic exile.

THE NUNNERY

As a further token of her exile, Elena Lucrezia's story was first told in English by the American scholar and bibliophile Monsignor Nicola Fusco, pastor of St. Peter's Church in New Kensington, Pennsylvania. Since her childhood, Elena Lucrezia's prodigious scholastic achievements were encouraged by her father. She was tutored in grammar, languages, mathematics, and music. By the time she was twenty-six, she sang, played and composed music, spoke or translated from four modern languages and five classical languages including Hebrew, Arabic, and Chaldean, and participated in academic *disputationes* which gathered scholars and men of science from many countries to the Cornaro Palace in Venice. By the time she was twenty-six, then, her father consented to let her move to Padua (where he owned another Cornaro Palace) so that she could continue her study of philosophy, theology, dialectics, and astronomy near the university, for of course women were not allowed *in* the university at that time. Or if exceptionally one was, precautions had to be taken, as they were with Anna Maria van Schuurman.

At that time, the University of Padua, which had been founded in 1222, was among the most famous in Europe: Galileo Galilei had taught there, and Cardinal Bembo, Sperone Speroni, Scaliger, and Torquato Tasso all had deserved statues, among which Elena Lucrezia's own statue still stands.[4] Wanting public recognition of her learning, her father petitioned the rector that she be allowed to defend a thesis for the doctorate in theology. The reply of the Ecclesiastical Authority, in the person of Cardinal Barbarigo, Bishop of Padua and Chancellor of the Theological Faculty of the University (now Saint Gregorio Barbarigo), was a flat NO, at first. "What? A female doctor and teacher of Theology? Never! . . . Woman is made for motherhood, not for learning."[5]

However, academic policy being as it was (way back then) tied to realpolitik, Saint Barbarigo saw the advantages of complying with what today would be called affirmative action and allowed the procurator's daughter to try for a doctorate in philosophy. She did, and received her degree on June 25, 1678. She was thirty-two years old. Here is an account of the event, written by her biographer:

> Anticipation of the forthcoming convocation filled Elena Lucrezia with dread. She abhorred the whole idea. Her native mod-

esty shrank from so public a display of her amazing learning and cultural understanding. In preparation for the ordeal she prayed incessantly, and received the sacraments as if she were preparing for death.

A half hour before the solemn program began, it was necessary for her confessor to appeal to her humility and urge her to submit. Finally she obeyed. . . . At the last moment, the multitude of guests and spectators was so large that the convocation was transferred from Padua University Hall to the Cathedral of the Blessed Virgin. The most distinguished personalities of Italy together with a great number of scholars from various European universities filled the vast auditorium beyond capacity—all eager to see and hear this first female aspirant to the highest academic honor.

The examiners showed no leniency because of the applicant's age, sex, or family standing. They allowed no superficial inquiry. The powerful prestige of the University was to be augmented here, not diminished. As question after question of the most difficult nature was answered by Elena Lucrezia, with a simple ease and dignity which won all hearts, cheer and applause burst forth repeatedly from the great audience gathered to hear her.

The examination being satisfactorily concluded, Elena Lucrezia Cornaro Piscopia was invested with the *Teacher's Ermine Cape,* received the *Doctor's Ring* on her finger, was crowned with the *Poet's Laurel Crown,* and was elevated to the high dignity of *Magistra et Doctrix Philosophiae*—Master and Doctor of Philosophy. The whole assembly then stood and chanted a glorious *Te Deum.* (Fusco, 37–38)

One may remark, parenthetically, that the entire event as described bears a uncanny resemblance to the accounts of heretics' and "witches'" trials that were also taking place during that period, at the peak of the Counterreformation, throughout the Catholic world. At any rate, after such an "ordeal," it is not surprising to read that Elena Lucrezia died six years later, at age 38. But, her biographer assures us, she died in sanctity, while everywhere in Padua and Venice the people cried "The Saint is dead! The Saint is dead!" "Under her usual clothes, she wore the long scapular of the oblates [of the Benedictine order]. . . . She had refused three or four advantageous marriages and secretly observed the monastic rule in all its austerity" (Fusco, 34).

REFLECTIONS

This secret link to monastic life was no longer surprising. Feminist research on women writers in the Renaissance indicates that, at least in Italy, the great majority were either courtesans or nuns, of noble birth and highly educated families. But the question elicited by Elena Lucrezia's both typical and atypical story was, Why? Why this recurrent connection between intellectual activity and the nunnery (in its Elizabethan double meaning of cloister and brothel, the utterly spiritual and the basely sexual), between writing and silence, knowledge and confinement? What "madness most discreet" did Elena Lucrezia cultivate in the sheltered garden of her nunnery?[6] Could it have been simply the love of writing or, in the words of the postmodern literary critic Ihab Hassan, "the pleasure of intellectual order and beauty, the surprise of mind in struggle with itself, the delight in language as it breaks and plays continuously on the edge of silence"? Yet, muses the same critic, woman is "hostile to the imagination."[7] Indeed, even as late as the 1970s, as Sandra Gilbert and Susan Gubar note, readers of Emily Dickinson were brooding upon the incompatibility of poetry and femininity. If there was a connection between them, and one was certainly there in Dickinson, it had to be somewhere in her "inner life," her biographer John Cody surmises:

> Had Mrs. Dickinson been warm and affectionate, more intelligent, effective and admirable, Emily Dickinson early in life would probably have identified with her, become domestic, and adopted the conventional woman's role. She would then have become a church member, been active in community affairs, married, and had children. The creative potentiality would of course still have been there, but would she have discovered it?[8]

While her biographer thus discusses the tormenting absence of romance in Dickinson's life, another critic, John Crowe Ransom, speaks of its presence and the fulfillment it "finally" afforded her: "Most probably [Dickinson's] poems would not have amounted to much if the author had not finally had her own romance, enabling her to fulfill herself like any other woman." Neither critic, remark Gilbert and Gubar, "imagines that poetry itself could possibly constitute a woman's fulfillment."[9]

But why, then, did so many women, like Elena Lucrezia, nurture their love of writing "under their usual clothes?" What kept Anna Maria's attention riveted inside her wooden box? How did they live out the "madness" of their imagination "between the boudoir and the altar"? Were they, too, like the "Saints" of Jean Toomer described by Alice Walker—"black women whose spirituality was so intense . . . that they stumbled blindly through their lives . . . creatures so abused and mutilated in body [that they] stared out at the world, wildly, like lunatics . . . or quietly, like suicides," women who entered loveless marriages without joy, who became prostitutes without resistance, who became mothers of children without fulfillment—were they, too, "driven to a numb and bleeding madness by the springs of creativity in them for which there was no release"? Or were they, as Walker suggests, "moving to music not yet written," dreaming "dreams that no one knew—not even themselves, in any coherent fashion"?[10]

That women did not have other career opportunities may be a "fact" of history or sociology, but it does not explain the desire for intellectual creation. What prompted and sustained, under adverse and self-restricting conditions, such women's desire for formal or abstract knowledge, for poetry, or theory? What explains the desire for a knowledge not useful, not exchangeable on the market, not even admitted? If Elena Lucrezia's and Anna Maria's stories were atypical, their very names exemplify how the silence of women has been culturally constructed and written into gender identity. Anna Maria was named so she would cast her life as imitation of silent, self-sacrificing, Christian motherhood: St. Anne and Mary. And the two pagan namesakes of Elena Lucrezia—Helen the beautiful, "the face that launched a thousand ships / and burnt the topless towers of Ilium" (Marlowe), and Lucrezia [Lucrece], the advocate of man's honor, on whose violated body was built the republican state of Rome—inscribe between them, as an absence, the woman who would be scholar and strive, like Dr. Faust, after knowledge.

In searching the archive of my educated-woman's memory, I found many images of women in whom language was joined to silence, and knowledge to madness, beginning with the Sphinx, whose liminal position between human and non-human, between language and silence, is the source of a knowledge and a power that man must seek to overcome. Her enigma is reinscribed in the sibylline words of Cassandra and in the speechless smile of Mona Lisa, in Ophelia's song and in the "nothing" of Cordelia; frozen in the quiet stare of Toomer's "saints" or in the silent gestures of Charcot's hysteric patients photographed at La Salpêtrière and again signalled by the "no" of Dora to Freud's therapeutic explanation.

These are representations, to be sure, images fashioned or constructed by men. They are nevertheless powerful images that focalize desire and identification for women as well as men. Like the femmes fatales, doomed heroines of film noir, they are figures of power; a power we have come to associate with sexuality as uncontrollable, defiant of the Law and the social institutions that seek to bind it, such as the family; a power that exceeds even the textual strategies intended to contain it. But those representations also inscribe another, more subtly seductive figuration: the possibility of a desire, a vision that is conveyed in a gaze "mute as a great stone," a knowledge that shrouds itself in silence or, which is the same, in a private and self-directed language, in neurosis, madness, narcissism, symptomatic behavior. And are these not contemporary places of confinement, analogues of the nunnery?

MADNESS

The association of women with madness and silence, the identification of femininity with a power that culture has been at pains to exorcise or neutralize, and language to elide, has been a recurrent topos in feminist criticism. Whether it writes of woman and her representations in the literary writings of men, or whether it writes as woman, reclaiming "sexual difference" as women's radical otherness, much feminist writing, too, has seen femininity as the repressed of masculinity, as the unrepresentable excess whose exclusion shores up the stability and order of a logical, rational world. Given the persistent association between women and silence, the question then arises: what is the relation of women to language and writing, including the writing of feminist theory?

The network of semantic complicities and conceptual incompatibilities in which the terms woman and madness both attract and repel one another in a tangle of metaphor and paradox is outlined by Shoshana Felman in a review of two texts of the 1970s that are paradigmatic, and in a way exemplary, of a discourse of women spanning the Atlantic Ocean in those years: feminist sociological research in the United States, represented by Phyllis Chesler's *Women and Madness* (1972), and the feminist philosophical critique in Europe represented by Luce Irigaray's *Speculum of the Other Woman* (1976). In response to Chesler, who argues that "madness" is imposed on women by an all-powerful so-cial conditioning which makes them culturally dependent and helpless, and hence that women's "mental illness is a request for help," Felman replies with a question both necessary and uncompromising: to whom is this request addressed if not to men? And, were it heeded, wouldn't the very "cure" reinforce the symptom, the dependency it signifies? As for Irigaray, Felman argues, if woman is barred access to the theoreti-cal locus of speech, from where can the statement of her otherness be uttered? "Who is speaking here, and who is asserting the otherness of woman?" Felman asks. "Is [Irigaray] speaking the language of men, or the silence of women?"[11]

This strikes me as a most appropriate way to put the question of women's writing in feminist theory: Is it speaking the language of men or the silence of women? And I would answer, both. For the contradic-tion specific to, and even constitutive of, feminist theory is precisely one that elementary logic would identify as internal contradiction. Felman is not quite so bold and in conclusion chooses to avoid confronting the contradiction that she so lucidly points out in the feminist texts.

> If, in our culture, the woman is by definition associated with mad-ness, her problem is how to break out of this (cultural) imposition of madness without taking up the critical and therapeutic positions of reason: how to avoid speaking both as mad and as not mad. The challenge facing the woman today is nothing less than to "re-invent" language, to re-learn how to speak: to speak not only against, but outside the specular phallogocentric structure.[12]

Re-inventing language was indeed the often-stated goal of many women writing in those years. But how could it be achieved? Felman's suggestion was not viable. For how can one speak "outside" of lan-guage—neither as "mad" nor as "not mad," neither as woman nor as man—if language itself is what constitutes those very terms, as well as the ground and the play of difference between them? Precisely this paradox is at the heart of what Felman calls "the phallacy of masculine meaning" and what defines the status of discourses. Women, like men, are defined by discourse and yet are speaking subjects. The phallacy cannot be challenged without confronting or engaging the paradox.

For women to avoid it, to avoid speaking as both mad and not mad, is to avoid speaking at all, and so to fall back into a silence which is not merely *the unspoken,* that is to say, the historical silence of women, but also *the unspeakable,* that is to say, the theoretical silence of "woman," the negation of women as subjects of discourse. Another way, however, is possible: it is to speak at once "the language of men" and "the silence of women," or better, to pursue strategies of discourse that will speak the silence of women in, through, against, over, under, and across the language of men. And hence, too, the necessity to pursue, develop or invent practices of language where gender is neither elided nor abstracted into pure discursivity, but at the same time claimed and refused, posed and displaced, asserted and negated.

But let us ask further, Is that silence of women nothing more than the effect of a single cause or intentionality? Whether we think of it as historical, theoretical, or both—as the repressive devaluation of women's speech imposed by a history of cultural domination, or as the impossibility for women to speak as subjects of a discourse founded on the a priori exclusion of women from the polis and its communal language (koiné)—is the silence of women nothing more than the effect of logos, the patriarchal symbolic order, the language and the culture of "Man"? And again, is the contradiction inscribed in that silence to be thought of solely as the result of cultural marginality, a by-product of oppression and domination, or can that silence be thought of in terms of a specificity of women's historical, material, and semiotic existence? To answer these questions, let us consider a text written by a woman, a text of fiction that is not a hagiography in the manner of Elena Lucrezia's story but a sort of critical fiction, another name for what I will also call theory.

II.

LANGUAGE AND SILENCE

Nearly a century ago, invited to speak on women and fiction to an audience of college women, Virginia Woolf "sat down on the banks of a river and began to wonder what the words meant."[13] Not herself a university woman, but one of the greatest writers of English prose, Woolf knew the difficult relation of women to language, the burden of silence that accompanies all efforts of expression. The text in which she recreated her 1928 lectures, *A Room of One's Own,* came inevitably into my thoughts as I prepared my Trinity College lecture. For me, as well, to speak on women's contributions to formal (academic) knowledge could not but begin with a reflection on language.

A Room of One's Own, Woolf's fictional lecture to the women of "Oxbridge," addresses the paradox of women in discourse not by stating it but by performing it. The text also opens with a direct address: "But, you may say, we asked you to speak about women and fiction—what has that got to do with a room of one's own? I will try to explain" (3). The words "women and fiction" might mean, she speculates, simply a few remarks about Jane Austen, Fanny Burney, the Brontës, Mrs. Gaskell (the few female English novelists then accepted in the canon); or they might mean "women and what they are like," or "women and the fiction they write," or "women and the fiction that is written about them"; or all of these together. This last possibility is of course the most interesting, the speaking "I" concedes, but has "a fatal drawback," for in that case,

> I should never be able to come to a conclusion. I should never be able to fulfill what is, I understand, the first duty of a lecturer—to hand you after an hour's discourse a nugget of pure truth to wrap up between the pages of your notebooks and keep on the mantelpiece for ever. All I could do was to offer an opinion upon one minor point—a woman must have money and a room of her own if she is to write fiction; and that, as you will see, leaves the great problem of the true nature of woman and the true nature of fiction unsolved. (3–4)

Woolf's irony was not lost on the feminists of my generation, for the point, of course, is not minor, nor is the argument simply an economic one. The point is, women's material and semiotic existence is marked by a specificity at once sexual and social—we used to call it gender—that simply cannot be understood by recourse to categories such as poverty or fiction, which are not gender-specific.[14] The originality of Woolf's insight comes from her posing the economic question not in terms of class but more specifically of class and gender. It is not my purpose here to repropose Woolf's argument that a room of one's own and five hundred pounds a year would enable women's writing, although I certainly agree with it, mutatis mutandis. The value of this text is in the answer it provides, as a text, to the question of women and language, which I believe is still the same today as it was in the 1970s, when it was taken up by feminist scholars such as Felman, Chesler, Irigaray, and Spender, among others.[15] Woolf's text, I suggest, performs another practice of language: it speaks both the language of men and the silence of women; or better, it speaks the silence of women in, through, and against the language of men.

Woolf's subtle irony and rampant understatement underscore both the theme and the strategic gesture of her title and, like an echo chamber, cause them to resonate and to expand. It thus becomes quite clear that the self-effacement and denegation conveyed by such disclaimers as "I should never be able to . . ." or "all I could do was . . . offer an opinion upon one minor point," are not mere formulas of scholarly propriety or womanly modesty. Less obviously but more adroitly than Elena Lucrezia's "shrinking," they serve to redefine the space of Woolf's inquiry, to mark a boundary within which she can focus on what she wants and likes to write and speak about (being paid for it!); a boundary which at the same time keeps out the things she does not want to deal with, the questions defined for her by others, in their terms, questions that might be inappropriate or simply uninteresting to her (such as the literary canon and the "true nature" of women or fiction).

Those disclaimers are obviously a strategy of discourse. Like the four walls of a room, like the convent and the brothel, they allow the speaker/writer to be with and for herself; they demarcate a space of unhampered movement of thought, of fantasy, perhaps desire, that may be nothing more and nothing less than the freedom to pose a question in her own terms. A freedom that paradoxically is paid for by surrendering the very thing one needs it for: by surrendering one's body to the cloister in order for it not to be owned by others, surrendering one's body to all men so as not to belong to one, surrendering one's intelligence to matters of no interest in order to pursue one's interests. In other words, give up part of oneself, even the greatest part—the house for a room, the world for a cell, the vast public domain for a small private enclosure; give up the forest for an oak tree, as Woolf's Orlando does, or, like Alice Walker's Meridian, give up sexual pleasure for "sanctuary" in sex.[16] Often, however, even this does not work, and a woman ends up not writing at all. She is then, Woolf imagines, Shakespeare's sister, who "found herself with child . . . and so—who shall measure the heat and violence of the poet's heart when caught and tangled in a woman's body?—killed herself" (50).

This other paradoxical connection, death and birth continually joined at the core of women's material existence, is explored by Woolf across the spectrum of British literary history and social landscape.

> What had our mothers been doing then that they had no wealth to leave us? Powdering their noses? . . . If only Mrs. Seton and her mother and her mother before her had learnt the great art of making money and had left their money, like their fathers and their grandfathers before them, to found fellowships and lectureships and prizes and scholarships appropriated to the use of their own sex . . . we might have been exploring or writing. . . . Only, if Mrs. Seton and her like had gone into business at the age of fifteen, there would have been—that is the snag in the argument—no Mary Seton. . . . Making a fortune and bearing thirteen children—no human being could stand it. (21)

The snag in the argument. Not only is giving birth the paradoxical nexus of a woman's physical existence or non-existence, but it defines her social and historical existence as well. The specificity of gender consists precisely in that "snag," that empty space of contradiction that inhabits women as both mothers and/or mother's daughters. In this sense, the death of the Judith Shakespeare Woolf imagines, who died with child and never wrote a word, and the birth of her utopian counterpart, who one day will "live and write her poetry" if we work to make it possible, as Woolf concludes her peroration (118), are not terminal points of a linear trajectory in an objective history; they exist concurrently in the here and now of historical process. Life and death, existence and nonexistence, are joined for women in a specific way, psychically as well as socially, and as paradoxically as are speaking and silence, knowledge and confinement.

The value of the organizing metaphor of Woolf's text, a room of one's own, consists in its representation of a textual space at once public and private—a public lecture hall which her ironic rhetorical strategy construes as a silent room and a space of writing; a published text in which the inscription of the subject's voice bears the trace of a silence at the core of its material existence, the silence of what did not happen because women were busy having children and otherwise reproducing human material existence. The text evokes the figure of an empty center, a space of contradiction where opposites converge and cancel each other out: birth and death, existence and nonexistence, like language and silence, occupy and preempt that space. Yet it is only from that space that women's speech can come. In other words, the text actually produces the representation of its contradiction, and it is the contradiction of a female-sexed subject: the inscription of writing in silence and the inscription of silence in one speaking and writing as a woman. For, on the one hand, the specificity of women's writing and their relation to language—which is the real issue of Woolf's lecture—cannot be approached frontally or directly ("women and fiction remain, so far as I am concerned, unsolved problems," she states). It can be approached only circuitously, or better, asymptotically, that is to say, not referentially but figurally, by means of images, metaphors, metonymies—figures of speech. On the other hand, the possibility, the very condition of speaking as a woman depends on the recognition of the contradiction that her speech must represent.

As Paul de Man observed in *Blindness and Insight,* "The ironic . . . writer or philosopher constitutes by his language [a two-fold self:] an empirical self that exists in a state of inauthenticity and a self that exists only in the form of a language that asserts the knowledge of this inauthenticity." Therefore, de Man argues in his reading of Baudelaire, "absolute irony is a consciousness of madness . . . a consciousness of a non-consciousness, a reflection on madness from the inside of madness itself."[17] Consider, in this regard, Woolf's initial disclaimers, the appeal to "all the liberties and licenses of a novelist," to fiction as poetic license, and the primary disclaimer:

> I need not say that what I am about to describe has no existence: Oxbridge is an invention; so is Fernham; "I" is only a convenient term for somebody who has no real being. . . . Call me Mary Beton, Mary Seton, Mary Carmichael or by any name you please—it is not a matter of any importance. (4–5)

The "I" of the speaker, a woman's speech itself, is possible only as fiction. Woolf's "I" repeatedly performs the trope of parabasis: the intrusion in the text of a narrating or speaking voice—a consciousness of a non-consciousness, as de Man puts it—that points to the nature of the text as fictional, not empirical, reality, thus disrupting the fictional illusion even as it creates it.

Nowhere in Woolf's text do the terms "woman" or "women" appear with an objective referent; instead, they are figures produced, held and shifted by the tension between enunciation and address. The text opens with an "I" addressing a "you" (in fact, we get a "you" first!), anticipating an objection and setting up a dialogue between "I" and "we," voices that are, for the moment, undefined. The "I" then proceeds to make a series of disclaimers ("I should never be able to come to a conclusion . . ., all I could do was to offer you an opinion upon one minor point. . . ."). The "I," a linguistic figure "with no real being" ("call me by any name you please") addresses a "you" as yet unspecified; a dialogue ensues; then the enunciation shifts to Mary Beton, one of various avatars of the "I," and subsequently to Woolf—or rather, to another "I" ("I will end now in my own person," [109]). This "I" now addresses "women":

> Young women, I would say, and please attend. . . . You are, in my opinion, disgracefully ignorant. You have never made a discovery of any sort of importance. You have never shaken an empire or led an army into battle. The plays of Shakespeare are not by you, and you have never introduced a barbarous race to the blessings of civilization. What is your excuse? It is all very well for you to say, pointing to the streets and squares and forests of the globe swarming with black and white and coffee-coloured inhabitants, all busily engaged in traffic and enterprise and love-making, we have had other work on our hands. Without our doing, those seas would be unsailed and those fertile lands a desert. We have born and bred and washed and taught, perhaps to the age of six or seven years, the one thousand six hundred and twenty-three million human beings who are, according to statistics, at present in existence, and that, allowing that some had help, takes time. (116)

Clearly, the audience so addressed is itself a figure of the text, a voice raising objections, asking questions, speaking back as "we." If the conversation among the different pronominal figures—I, you, and we—signals the convergence of enunciation and address in an actual process of communication, yet no referential relation can be established and no natural bond can be presumed between the (female) speaker/writer and the (female) audience, between woman and women. On the contrary, their relation is established by the rhetorical strategy of the text, which thus builds the sense of a common bond of women in their life's work, in the specificity of their material and affective existence, and in a shared purpose.

This process relies upon another trope, a personification, a fictional figure that conveys at once the passage from silence to language and the continuing presence of silence in language. It is the figure of the poet who was Shakespeare's sister; she was never sent to school and died in silence and in shame, one lonely winter's night. But "she lives," Woolf writes, "in you and in me, and in many other women who are not here tonight, for they are washing up the dishes and putting the children to bed" (117). This fictional figure, which links the "I," the "you" and the "they" in a "common life" predicament, is at once metonymy and metaphor: Judith Shakespeare is a part of every woman's history and an image of what does or can happen to any woman.

Resonating with others across centuries and cultures as diverse among themselves as Elena Lucrezia is from Meridian, this silent poet is the figure of an embodied life ("the common life which is the real life and not . . . the little separate lives which we live as individuals") that links women on either side of the Oxbridge gate and enjoins those inside ("with some time on your hands and with some book learning in your brains") to write "even in poverty and obscurity" and to work for her coming. But it is also a figure of the text's own figurality: it parallels the movement of the text from the silent room of one's own to the world citizenship afforded by access to language and education; and, at the same time, it figures the still, empty silence at the heart of language—death or nonexistence—which the text covers over, creating the illusion of that very movement. Only "great poets do not die," Woolf writes, and I would gloss: only great poets know that language *both* creates *and* dispels the illusion of consciousness, presence, and continuity of the self.

THEORY

Since Woolf delivered her lectures and wrote *A Room of One's Own,* many women have taken up the kind of questions she was asking. And while in 1929 the library shelves contained books written by men about women, today there are libraries filled with books by women who write about women. A very large body of work already exists, not only in fiction, poetry and the arts, in criticism, history and the human sciences, but in theory as well: literary theory, film theory, psychoanalytic theory, cultural theory. But, you may ask, why theory? Why that most abstract of discourses, direct descendant of philosophy, from which woman has always kept at a distance, as if to underscore the nonrelationship in language that suggested to Nietzsche the conceit of their identity? Philosophy has until recently been in the business of system building, subsuming the real in the symbolic, ordering it in conceptual categories, constructing walls of meaning, then cities and empires; making History with a capital H. If we only think of the great men in the University of Padua at the tail end of the Renaissance—Galileo writing his *Dialogo dei massimi sistemi,* Tasso composing the last heroic epic of Christian deliverance, Bembo shaping the Italian language for the centuries to come in *Prose della volgar lingua*—we cannot but wonder, What indeed was Elena Lucrezia doing there?

Well, of course, she was not there. Whether in her father's palace or in the nearby convent, she was outside the University, outside philosophy. What pleasure or power or knowledge she might have derived from her studies, what desire, what madness most discreet did keep her wandering near the gates, we can only speculate on the basis of our own desire, our knowingly ek-centric relation to language and history, and our effort nevertheless to question them, engage them, reexamine them. For our desire for writing, whether poetry, fiction, or theory, is not for the building of systems but, on the contrary, for the excavation or undermining of their foundations. As a feminist philosopher put it, such work responds "to an ethical and political drive which is constitutive of feminist thought and which characterizes it above and beyond any of its thematics."[18] Perhaps, I suggest, the fascination with language and theory, for feminist scholars, is but the counterpart of that silence that has long marked women's material and intellectual existence.

In its various genres and styles, feminist writing combines the desire for abstract and formal knowledge with the narcissistic drive to self-affirmation; it joins the possibility of political subjecthood to the creation of new figures of our destiny, figures of social subjects who are both female-sexed and desiring. Before a public reading of her poetry at Stanford University, addressing her audience in a manner both like and unlike Virginia Woolf's, Audre Lorde said "I am a Black feminist lesbian warrior poet mother doing my work," and then she asked, "Who are you and how are you doing yours?" My own itinerary as a scholar,

teaching and doing my work in the university, has been guided by the
words of such women as by Ariadne's thread; a scattered, fragmented
lineage of female thought and writing that is neither a tradition nor a
kinship of dispossessed mothers and daughters, but rather the trace of
a discontinuous, inconsistent, ever under-construction, feminist genealogy. Under these conditions, the journey has not been easy and its
destination not quite clear. There have been times, indeed, when the
past seemed more hospitable than the present, and old stories more
comforting than new ones.

When I first traced my feminist genealogy for the audience at the
University of Utrecht in 1991, I concluded it with the words of a woman
who was never granted a doctorate in philosophy because she was in
prison at the time when she would have completed her dissertation, but
whose work has inspired two generations of women and men the world
over and is now my colleague and friend at the University of California, Santa Cruz: "The most difficult challenge facing the activist is to
respond fully to the needs of the moment and to do so in such a way
that the light one attempts to shine on the present will simultaneously
illuminate the future."[19] Angela Davis wrote those words in 1990 but
the challenge is no less difficult in these early years of the new century,
even as more women speak on television in talk shows and from the
White House lawn, in various capacities and professions; and as more
women speak and write as college teachers and scholars, though most
of them do so in relative obscurity and with typically lower academic
salaries. In these postfeminist times, when genders are multiple and
multiplying, and many women's studies programs in the United States
have changed their name to "gender studies," some have argued that
there is no such thing as *women,* as each person is multiply modified
by her location in class, race, gender, sexual or other identities. Similarly, there is no longer feminism but an indefinite number of multiply
hyphenated feminisms.

Conducting a graduate seminar on feminist theory, as I have done
fairly regularly since the early 1980s, has given me a measure of the passage of time and the changing conceptions of feminism and of women
over two decades. To the extent that any feminism is claimed today, it is
global, ecumenical, ecological, transnational, transgender, and transpe-
cies in its concern with world events, peoples, and animals. Its practices—epistemic and activist—rely on the discourses of disciplines such

as anthropology, sociology, psychology, politics, and law, discourses in which women's relation to language is not questioned but taken for granted: access to speech is presumed as one among other civil rights, guaranteed by the U.S. constitution. In this brave new century, Woolf's *Room of One's Own* appears to paint a liberal utopia, Eurocentric, old-fashioned, and at best politically naïve. It is, in other words, *merely* a fiction.

III.

THE RESISTANCE TO THEORY

Teaching in this context is to encounter what Paul de Man called "the resistance to theory."[20] There is unintended irony in this situation in that "theory" has a prestigious and desirable status in the North American academy today. Theory, of any kind—from cultural theory to film or literary theory, from poststructuralist to postcolonial, from feminist to queer to critical race theory—is taken to be a sort of intellectual capital. The very word *theory* connotes something more elevated and exalting than your run-of-the-mill academic subject like history, biology, or literature. And herein lies the paradox: what de Man meant by "the resistance to theory" was in fact the resistance to language, and more exactly a resistance to the rhetorical or tropological dimension of language that is explicitly foregrounded in literature.

When I decided, in fall 2003, to conduct my feminist theory seminar with a reading list consisting mainly of novels, I knew it was a radical as well as risky shift in pedagogical practice. Not that the idea is new or that the practice is unprecedented. Indeed, reading fiction written by women, and writing about it, whether as literary criticism or history, was common practice in women's studies in the 1970s and early 1980s, but that was not part of feminist theory as such, if by feminist theory one means a controlled reflection and self-reflection, not on women in general but rather on feminism itself as a historico-political formation. There was, of course, theory—semiotics, poststructuralism, neo-Marxist critical theory, and neo-Freudian psychoanalytic theory; in literature studies, in particular, there was the literary theory associated with the name and the teaching of Paul de Man. But all of these were not in the main, so to speak, feminist-friendly.

Returning to that literary theory after two decades, with the advantage of the feminist theory that was subsequently developed, and in light of the legitimation and impasse it seemed to have reached, I saw in the literary fiction written by women the potential to reenergize feminist theory by the figures of resistance inscribed in certain texts. In 2003, after two decades of identity politics and in a world ever more divided, traumatic, and enigmatic, those texts of the 1970s appeared to take on an unexpected relevance to feminist studies: by reviving the attention to writing, to the figurality and otherness of language, literary theory offered a site of resistance to the new conformism—when it is not fundamentalism—that plagues most social movements and much academic work in the United States.

I tested in that seminar the wisdom of de Man's contention that the resistance to theory is a resistance to reading; not to reading for the plot, for "information," or for the "meaning" of a text, but rather a resistance to go with the figural movement of literary language, abandoning the stable, familiar ground of strictly referential meaning, and ultimately a resistance to the idea that language may refer primarily to itself. Before I say more about my experiment to reanimate feminist theory through literature and about the students' both expected and surprising responses, let me say something about how one might explain such a resistance to theory.

In the essay by that name, de Man accounts for the vicissitudes of literary theory, or what has come to be known as literary theory, in the United States since the mid-1960s, in the wake of imported critical trends such as structuralism and poststructuralism, semiotics, and post-Heideggerian hermeneutics. "The advent of theory," he states, "the break that . . . sets it aside from literary history and from literary criticism, occurs with the introduction of linguistic terminology" in speaking or writing about literature. By linguistic terminology he means "a terminology that designates reference prior to designating the referent" (8), so that the object of study of literary theory is not the aesthetic, moral or truth value of literature, but rather *literariness,* the particular aspect of language, its figurality or self-referentiality, that is foremost in literary works, or in the language of literature.

Literariness is not, of course, solely a property of literature; it is also present in various forms of writing and speech, most notably in advertising or political campaign slogans, whenever tropes such as paronomasia or other word play draw attention to the linguistic, not phenomenal nature of the utterance; that is to say, they draw attention to the reference, not the referent, to "the materiality of the signifier, not the materiality of what it signifies" (*Resistance*, 11). If literature, as de Man says, is "the place where this negative knowledge about the reliability of linguistic utterance is made available" (10) most consistently; or, said otherwise, if literature is the site in which the self-referentiality of language is made most visible, this does not mean that literature denies the referential function of language: if it did, no one would cry while reading a book, or feel moved or persuaded to action.

The rhetorical or figural specificity of literary language does not deny or refuse to acknowledge the "reality" of the material world but questions its own ability to know it; as de Man soberly puts it, literature "is not *a priori* certain" that language can represent, more or less accurately, the phenomenal world. To think of literature as language, therefore, is to doubt the "authority [of language] as a model for natural or phenomenal cognition." This, in turn, blurs "the borderlines between literary and non-literary discourse" (11), upsetting all criteria for what counts as literature, as well as the established canon of literary works. But further, once we consider literature, theory or science as discourses, or distinct modalities of language constituting what Foucault calls *discursive formations* (his examples are medicine, economics, and grammar),[21] then the opposition between fiction and reality breaks down. And this, as de Man writes, seriously disturbs "the stable cognitive field that extends from grammar to logic to a general science of man and of the phenomenal world" (17).

While grammar and logic refer to an extra-linguistic and generalizable set of phenomena, rhetoric refers only to language itself, creating a tension of ambiguity, an undecidability between the literal and the figural status of words and phrases. Thus, if grammar and logic, which are also necessary functions of language, confirm me as a subject of cognition, a *subject* for whom those phenomena are *objects* of inquiry, knowledge, or action (no coincidence in that the terms *subject* and *object*, used in scientific and critical discourses, are in the first place grammatical terms), the rhetorical function of language undercuts that certainty, instigates a doubt: in producing the possibility of misreading, it shakes up the ground in which I, reader or speaker, presume to be the subject, and the text or the other, my object.

"Did you say 'pig', or 'fig'?" flashed the grin of the Cheshire Cat. Alice, whose confidence in the stability of meaning in bourgeois Victorian England is unshakable, remains undaunted even in the catachrestic world of Wonderland. But for most of us, the ambiguity of figural language poses what de Man calls a "persistent threat of misreading." The resistance to theory, then, is a resistance to reading. For reading entails a confrontation with an otherness in the text that escapes my ability to grasp it, retain it, hold it in my head (as Roland Barthes said, "the work can be held in the hand, the text is held in language").[22] The failure of the interpretive moment shakes up the ground of my hermeneutic self-confidence and the certainty of my position as subject. In "open[ing] up vertiginous possibilities of referential aberration,"[23] figurality confronts us with the intimation of a chasm between language and the real that indeed, and not coincidentally, can only be represented figurally, as in de Man's metaphor of *vertigo* or in the metaphor I have just used, *chasm,* or in another that comes directly to mind, the graphic figure of a *chaos-cosmos* ("chaosmos") in Joyce's *Finnegans Wake.*

Another such figure, I have attempted to show, is the core of silence at the heart of language figured in Woolf's *A Room of One's Own,* the empty space of contradiction that, in the text, through the fictional figure of Judith Shakespeare, is indissociably linked to the nexus of life and death, existence and nonexistence, for women. As a final reflection on the work of figurality in Woolf's text, it is not insignificant that Freud's view of psychic processes dominated by two primary classes of drives, life drives and death drives, which coexist all along in conflict and mutual contradiction, was first proposed by a woman analyst, Sabina Spielrein, in 1911. In a paper much later acknowledged by Freud, she argued that the drive to the preservation of the species, the wish to procreate or give birth, contains a destructive impulse: "As certain biological facts show [she wrote], the reproductive instinct, from the psychological standpoint as well, is made up of two antagonistic components and is therefore equally an instinct of birth and one of destruction."[24]

Read in this light, Woolf's entwined figures of Judith Shakespeare and a room of one's own evoke many other such figures inscribed in women's writing across the historical and sociogeographical spectrum, from the "bell jar" that Sylvia Plath made into the objective correlative of her own "madness" to the inexpressible chasm in the self that Toni

Morrison named Beloved. Much like the eye of the tornado in Plath's novel, that still, empty place in which, for women, existence tropes into non-existence is an effect rather than an absence of movement: it is the meeting place of opposing drives, the site in which life and death cancel each other out. Its figure is silence.

FIGURES OF RESISTANCE

The convergence of de Man's literary theory with Woolf's fictional writing suggested to me how feminist theory might be displaced from its currently reified, if prestigious, status of academic object of study and revitalized as a living practice, imbricated in one's experience of self and the world. After all, Woolf's fictional address to the women of the British academy, ironically written by one who had had no access to it, was precisely about language and writing as a way to take part in "the common life which is the real life." Feminist theory, then, might be so revitalized by the process of reading intended as a practice of language, something like translation, a learning to confront the otherness of language—what one of my seminar students, Shannon Brownlee, was to call "the implacability of figuration"—in a text, and thus also confront otherness or alterity in oneself, and otherness or heterogeneity in the world.[25] So, in fall 2003, I designed my feminist theory seminar as a project of reading, with the goal of learning to stand on the shaky ground of an unstable cognitive field in which the "inhuman" element in language, as de Man puts it, resists the self-assurance of subjecthood, and thus of reading women writers who both create and dispel the illusion of full consciousness and self-presence in the subject of speech.

The literary texts I chose were written between the 1920s and the 1990s, spanning literary genres from the autobiographical and the pseudo-biographical to science-fiction and the prose poem; ranging from realist to experimental in style, and from modernist to postmodernist in terms of periodization. They were *Nightwood* by Djuna Barnes, *The Female Man* by Joanna Russ, Virginia Woolf's *Orlando,* Monique Wittig's *The Lesbian Body* (regrettably in English translation), *Written on the Body* by Jeannette Winterson, *The Well of Loneliness* by Radclyffe Hall, and Toni Morrison's *Beloved.* We also read de Man, of course, and Barthes and Felman, and Walter Benjamin on "The Task of the Translator," plus several examples of critical misreadings of those novels. I also included selected essays by the French psychoanalyst

Jean Laplanche, whose reading of Freud is exemplary of the relation of reading to psychoanalysis, and whose theory of primal seduction, in envisaging the psyche as a space of translation, transfers beyond the clinical situation to the site of culture.

I titled the seminar *Trans-figuration in Literature*. I wrote "Trans-figuration" with a hyphen, the better to convey its being itself a trope, a figure of transit or transformation, and meant it to refer to the conceptual aspect of the theory as well as to the thematic and properly figural aspects of the novels. I asked the students to reflect on their own reading process, and to beware the pull of narrative; to focus on phrases, fragments, figures, rather than on narrative emplotment or overall "meaning." In the end, I asked them to write a paper addressing the question, Can one "do" feminist theory through literary fiction? Their responses both confirmed my fears and surpassed my expectations.

A few, unable to let go of the foothold of character and story, wrote of their likes and dislikes, honestly stating their inability to "make sense" of the writerly, anti-narrative texts of Russ and Wittig, for example, and otherwise looked for something in the diegesis, character, or situation with which they could identify or in which they could find some "universal" predicament or human values. Reiterating received ideas about literature, gender, and women, their papers sketched bland, comforting notions of feminism. Others, however, and in greater number, surprised me. In some cases the surprise was their ability to read theory and literature together so that each one reverberated on the other, with no attempt to "apply" theory to literature with the cookie-cutter method, as the saying goes; that is, with no attempt to impose theory like a conceptual grid on the text and so produce an interpretation of the novel.

Commenting on Felman's view of literature as the place where madness can speak—madness as unreason, as resistance to rationality, subversive of the logic of constituted power, and hence madness as the place of otherness—Christina Stevenson asked the question I myself asked long ago, How can one speak from the place of the other? If Orlando, despite his pursuit of logic, "cannot escape the unreason of language," she noted, Felman's equation of madness with literature and of the feminine with madness locates resistance and subversion in the woman character's dying words, the moment when language turns into silence.[26] Thus, she concluded despondently, one is left like Orlando, with either "the renunciation of all linguistic endeavors" or "running face first into metaphors." How can one speak from the place of the other? I suggested above (but had not done so in the seminar), that it is precisely by running face first into metaphors that Woolf, in *A Room of One's Own*, succeeds in speaking the silence within language and within women. But that the question recurs with urgency in a young woman's mind nearly a century later, confirmed the timeliness of reproposing the reading of literature and the theory of reading for feminist epistemology.

A greater surprise was the students' intellectual excitement for the deconstructive negativity of de Man's theory as well as Laplanche's conception of the unconscious as an enigmatic, unknowable otherness in the self that we, Sisyphus-like, attempt nevertheless to (re)translate. De Man's contention that the figural dimension of writing makes every reading a misreading suggested to Brownlee that the feminist ethics of responsibility is not a natural consequence of feminist belief or political practice, as is too often assumed, but is the result of self-analysis, an awareness of the possibility of misreading not only texts or other people, but also the memory-text of one's experience. To take and claim responsibility for one's (mis)readings "brings interpretation into the political realm," putting experience face to face with ideology.

The resistance of language to univocal meaning was brought home perhaps most directly by the personal pronouns in the novels by Russ, Woolf, Winterson, and Wittig. The "she" in *The Female Man,* the he/she of *Orlando,* the "I" in *Written on the Body,* and the *j/e* in *The Lesbian Body* are tropes, figures that resist grammatical meaning even as they convey it, thus suspending the logic of conventional assumptions about gender identity and gender difference, or even, in the case of Wittig, altogether evacuating the word *gender* of its meaning. But if certain literary works "effect such a radical opening of language," Anita Starosta argued, it is not just because literary language has the possibility of rhetorical displacement built into it, but rather because these particular novels "insist on articulating something inconceivable," as Radclyffe Hall does in *The Well of Loneliness,* or provoke the reader with "figures of the unspeakable," as Morrison does in *Beloved.*

I was particularly pleased by the recognition that the novels I chose do not simply portray characters or *images* of women that do not accord to established conceptions of gender, sexuality, and race, but, while doing so, they also construct *figures,* at once rhetorical and narrative, that in resisting the logic of those conceptions, point to another cognition, a reading *other-wise* of gender, sexuality, and race. This is the sense in which these texts "do" feminist theory and are not simply feminist fiction. *Beloved, Nightwood, The Female Man, Orlando,* and *The Lesbian Body* are more than titles or narrative images. They are conceptual figures, figurations of social and psychic spaces, of interhuman and intrahuman relations—conflicts, passions, fantasy and desire, conscious emotions and unconscious drives.

Whether or not they bear a mimetic relation to referential reality (*Orlando* clearly does not, the worlds of Stephen Gordon and Winterson's narrator do, *Beloved* both does and does not), these texts perform a transformation, a transfiguration, of what we refer to as reality. What enables passage from referential reality to the conceptual spaces that can only be designated as "Nightwood," "Well of Loneliness," "Lesbian Body," or "Beloved" is not solely the figurality inherent in language as one of its inescapable dimensions. It is also, and constitutively, the *figuration,* that is to say, the writer's work of linguistic invention that draws on the figurality, the otherness, of language in order to design that other space as one that opens onto the otherness in the world. And what is theory if not the elaboration of conceptual figures in language?

Each in its own fashion, the novels I chose inscribe the trope of transfiguration (transformation and transit to another space) thematically and diegetically, in their characters or events. Moreover, they are themselves figures of translation: while inciting or provoking (mis)readings in different times and places, they bear witness at once to the obstinacy of language and to the creative potential of its figural dimension. If the first-person narrator of Winterson's postmodern novel, for instance, figures a speaking subject beyond gender, it is because the grammatical and morphological structure of the English language makes it possible, if only in writing. Such a figure of writing is nearly impossible in, say, romance languages, whose morphology is heavily inflected by linguistic gender.[27] On the other hand, while Radclyffe Hall's representation of the "invert" in *The Well of Loneliness* may seem to some dated, of purely historical interest, that text, as Timothy Koths remarked, has been read and reread since its publication in 1928 as the figuration of something otherwise unspeakable at quite different historical moments, such as the butch lesbian in the 1950s-1970s and the transsexual subject in the 1990s.[28]

In tracing my feminist genealogy in 1991, I had also relied on figures of resistance inscribed in fictional narratives, written or oral, newly encountered or remembered; figures evoked and animated by the occasion and circumstances of those years, the history of *that* present. The texts I chose for the feminist theory seminar in 2003, although I was not aware of this at the time, traced another genealogy, responsive to a different present. At a moment in which feminist epistemology seemed to me to presume the authority of referentiality, I reproposed for feminist theory texts that, in undermining the referential function of language, do not negate or disallow the reality of the phenomenal world but deny the absolute authority of language as the basis of cognition.[29] The figures of resistance of this genealogy are figures of writing that, by disarticulating logic and rhetoric, question the self-complacency of referential language and the logocentric entitlement of the subject of speech. Ironically, they do so entirely through language, or rather, by the hint of a silence at the heart of language.

"Did you say 'pig' or 'fig'?" flashed the grin of the Cheshire cat.

Written for and first published in this volume based on two lectures given in 1991 and 2004, as referenced in the text and accompanying notes.

Notes

INTRODUCTION

1. "Queer Theory: Lesbian and Gay Sexualities," special issue of *differences: A Journal of Feminist Cultural Studies* 3.2 (Summer 1991).

2. *American Heritage Dictionary of the English Language*, s.v. "theory," http:// www.bartleby.com/61/20/T0152000.html (accessed October 20, 2005).

3. The term is Leo Bersani and Ulysse Dutoit's. See *The Forms of Violence: Narrative in Assyrian Art and Modern Culture* (New York: Schocken Books, 1985), vii, quoted in Teresa de Lauretis, *The Practice of Love: Lesbian Sexuality and Perverse Desire* (Bloomington: Indiana University Press, 1994), 3.

4. Teresa de Lauretis, *Technologies of Gender: Essays on Theory, Film, and Fiction* (Bloomington: Indiana University Press, 1987), 9–10.

5. Ibid., 26.

6. Ibid., 10; emphasis in the original.

7. Ibid., 24.

8. See for example, Teresa de Lauretis, "Cavani's *Night Porter:* A Woman's Film?" *Film Quarterly* 30 (Winter 1977): 35–38. The University of Wisconsin-Milwaukee's Center for 20th Century Studies was the site of a series of significant film theory conferences, beginning in 1975 under the directorship of Michel Benamou, and continuing after his death with Kathleen Woodward as director. Publications from those conferences include *The Cinematic Apparatus*, eds. Teresa de Lauretis and Stephen Heath (New York: St. Martin's, 1980); *Cinema and Language,* eds. Stephen Heath and Patricia Mellencamp (Frederick, Md.: University Publications of America, 1983); and *Re-vision: Essays, in Feminist Film Criticism,* eds. Mary Ann Doane, Patricia Mellencamp, and Linda Williams (Frederick, Md.: University Publications of America, 1984). Mellencamp, Modleski, and Judith Mayne were among the members of the UW-Milwaukee

community who, at various junctures, contributed an important feminist voice to these proceedings.

9. Also significant in this respect is the series de Lauretis edited for Indiana University Press, Theories of Representation and Difference, which included *Technologies of Gender* as well as groundbreaking works by feminist film theorists Mary Ann Doane, Kaja Silverman, Judith Mayne, and Laura Mulvey, to name a few.

10. This is reproduced in Teresa de Lauretis, *Alice Doesn't: Feminism, Semiotics, Cinema* (Bloomington: Indiana University Press and London: Macmillan, 1984), vii.

11. de Lauretis, *Technologies of Gender*, 135.

12. Teresa de Lauretis, "Eccentric Subjects: Feminist Theory and Historical Consciousness," *Feminist Studies* 16.1 (Spring 1990): 115–50, and "Sexual Indifference and Lesbian Representation," *Theatre Journal* 40.2 (May 1988): 155–77, included as chapters 7 and 2 of this volume.

13. de Lauretis, *Technologies of Gender*, 132.

14. Eve Kosofsky Sedgwick, *Epistemology of the Closet* (Berkeley: University of California Press, 1990); Judith Butler, *Gender Trouble: Feminism and the Subversion of Identity* (New York: Routledge, 1990), and *Bodies That Matter: On the Discursive Limits of "Sex"* (New York: Routledge, 1993).

15. This work includes Teresa de Lauretis, "The Stubborn Drive," *Critical Inquiry* 24, no. 4 (Summer 1998): 851–77, and "Becoming Inorganic," *Critical Inquiry* 29.4 (Summer 2003): 547–70.

16. "Figures of Resistance," 252.

17. Catharine A. MacKinnon, "Feminism, Marxism, Method, and the State: An Agenda for Theory," in *Feminist Theory: A Critique of Ideology*, ed. Nannerl O. Keohane, Michelle Z. Rosaldo, and Barbara C. Gelpi (Chicago: University of Chicago Press, 1981), 1, quoted in "Eccentric Subjects," 156.

18. Gayle Rubin, "Traffic in Women: Notes Toward a Political Economy of Sex," in *Toward an Anthropology of Women*, ed., Rayna Reiter (New York: Monthly Review Press, 1975), 157–210.

19. "Eccentric Subjects," 171.

20. Monique Wittig, "The Straight Mind," *Feminist Issues* 1.1 (Summer 1980): 106–7, quoted in *Technologies of Gender*, 18.

21. de Lauretis, *Technologies of Gender*, 26.

22. de Lauretis, *Alice Doesn't*, 186.

23. de Lauretis, *Alice Doesn't*, 153.

24. For example: "I will then rewrite my third proposition: *The construction of gender goes on today through the various technologies of gender . . . with power to control the field of social meaning. . . . But the terms of a different construction of gender also exist . . . and their effects are rather at the 'local' level of resistances, in subjectivity and self-representation,*" *Technologies of Gender*, 18, italics in original.

25. "Figures of Resistance," 247.

26. Monique Wittig, "One Is Not Born a Woman," *Feminist Issues* 2 (Winter 1981): 52.

27. The term is from C. S. Peirce; de Lauretis first discusses habit in "Semiotics and Experience," *Alice Doesn't*, 159. See also "Habit Changes."

28. *American Heritage Dictionary of the English Language*, s.v. "deictic," http://www.bartleby.com/61/32/D0103200.html (accessed October 21, 2005).

29. de Lauretis, *Alice Doesn't*, 143.

30. Another significant work from this period is de Lauretis's edited collection, *Feminist Studies/Critical Studies* (Bloomington: Indiana University Press, 1986, and London: Macmillan, 1988). De Lauretis elaborates on questions of women's cinema in "Guerrilla in the Midst: Women's Cinema in the 80s." *Screen* 31.1 (1990): 6–25.

31. Henry Abelove, Michèle Aina Barale, David M. Halperin, eds., *The Lesbian and Gay Studies Reader* (New York: Routledge, 1993).

32. Wittig, "Straight Mind," 111.

33. "The Lure of the Mannish Lesbian,"85.

34. A number of leading queer theorists engage with psychoanalysis quite centrally in their work. See, for example, Leo Bersani, *Homos* (Cambridge, Mass.: Harvard University Press, 1995); Judith Butler, *Bodies That Matter: On the Discursive Limits of "Sex"* (New York: Routledge, 1993); Diana Fuss, *Identification Papers* (New York: Routledge, 1995); and Lee Edelman, *No Future: Queer Theory and the Death Drive* (Durham, N.C.: Duke University Press, 2004).

35. *The Practice of Love*, xiv.

36. Feminist psychoanalytic critics have followed Jacques Lacan in defining castration as lack, theoretically distinct from the anatomical difference between the sexes. Kaja Silverman's work offers perhaps the most persuasive account. See, for example, "Lost Objects and Mistaken Subjects: A Prologue," *The Acoustic Mirror: The Female Voice in Psychoanalysis and Cinema* (Bloomington: Indiana Univeristy Press, 1988), 1–41.

37. "The Lure of the Mannish Lesbian," 90.

38. Judith Halberstam, *Female Masculinity* (Durham, N.C.: Duke University Press, 1988).

39. De Lauretis is also interested more generally in Cronenberg's films—or in what Kaja Silverman in *The Acoustic Mirror* calls an "authorial fantasmatic" (218); see, for example, "Becoming Inorganic."

40. Antonio Gramsci, *Selections from Cultural Writings,* ed. David Forgacs and Geoffrey Nowell-Smith, trans. William Boelhower (Cambridge, Mass.: Harvard University Press, 1985) 378, quoted in "Public and Private Fantasies," 119.

41. The reader will encounter the term "eccentric subject" earlier in the volume, in, for example, "When Lesbians Were Not Women," 73.

42. "The Intractability of Desire," 219.

43. "The paradox of a being that is at once captive and absent in discourse, constantly spoken of but of itself inaudible or inexpressible . . . a being whose existence and specificity are simultaneously asserted and denied, negated and controlled," "Eccentric Subjects," 151.

44. "The Intractability of Desire," 219.

45. For a version of the essay using the example of Italian feminist theory, see "The Essence of the Triangle or, Taking the Risk of Essentialism Seriously: Feminist Theory in Italy, the U.S., and Britain," *differences: A Journal of Feminist Cultural Studies* 1.2 (Summer 1989): 3–37.

46. "Upping the Anti," 197.

47. Sigmund Freud, *The Ego and the Id* (1923), in *The Standard Edition of the Complete Psychological Works of Sigmund Freud*, trans. and ed. James Strachey, 24 vols. (London: Hogarth Press, 1953–1974), 19:27. De Lauretis introduces this concept in *The Practice of Love*, 20–23.

48. C. S. Peirce, *Collected Papers*, vols. 1–8 (Cambridge, Mass.: Harvard University Press, 1931–1958). This passage, from vol. 2, para. 228, is cited in de Lauretis, *Alice Doesn't*, 172. See Kaja Silverman, *The Subject of Semiotics* (New York: Oxford University Press, 1983).

49. See "Habit Changes," 208.

50. For an elaboration of these ideas, see Teresa de Lauretis, "Difference Embodied: Reflections on *Black Skin, White Masks*," in "Fanon and the Impasses of Modernity," ed. by Ewa Plonowska Ziarek, special issue, *parallax* 23 (April–June 2002): 54–68.

51. See, for example, "Becoming Inorganic," *Critical Inquiry* 29 (Summer 2003): 547–70.

52. Virginia Woolf, *A Room of One's Own* (1929) (New York: Harcourt, Brace, Jovanovich, 1981).

CHAPTER 1: RETHINKING WOMEN'S CINEMA

I am very grateful to Cheryl Kader for generously sharing with me her knowledge and insight from the conception through the writing of this essay, and to Mary Russo for her thoughtful critical suggestions.

1. Silvia Bovenschen, "Is There a Feminine Aesthetic?" trans. Beth Weckmueller, *New German Critique* 10 (Winter 1977): 136. Originally published in *Aesthetik and Kommunikation* 25 (September 1976).

2. Laura Mulvey, "Feminism, Film, and the Avant-Garde," *Framework* 10 (Spring 1979): 6. See also Christine Gledhill's account "Recent Developments in Feminist Film Criticism," *Quarterly Review of Film Studies* 3.4 (1978).

3. Laura Mulvey, "Visual Pleasure and Narrative Cinema," *Screen* 16.3 (Autumn 1975): 18.

4. B. Ruby Rich, in "Women and Film: A Discussion of Feminist Aesthetics," *New German Critique* 13 (Winter 1978): 87.

5. J. Laplanche and J.-B. Pontalis, *The Language of Psycho-Analysis,* trans. D. Nicholson-Smith (New York: W. W. Norton, 1973), 206.

6. Lea Melandri, *L'infamia originaria* (Milan: Edizioni L'Erba Voglio, 1977) 27; my translation. For a more fully developed discussion of semiotic theories of film and narrative, see Teresa de Lauretis, *Alice Doesn't: Feminism, Semiotics, Cinema* (Bloomington: Indiana University Press, 1984).

7. See Audre Lorde, "The Master's Tools Will Never Dismantle the Master's House," and "An Open Letter to Mary Daly," in *This Bridge Called My Back: Writings by Radical Women of Color,* ed. Cherríe Moraga and Gloria Anzaldúa (New York: Kitchen Table Press, 1983), 96. Both essays are reprinted in Audre Lorde, *Sister Outsider: Essays and Speeches* (Trumansburg, N.Y.: Crossing Press, 1984).

8. "Chantal Akerman on *Jeanne Dielman,*" *Camera Obscura* 2 (1977): 118-19.

9. In the same interview, Akerman said: "I didn't have any doubts about any of the shots. I was very sure of where to put the camera and when and why. . . . I *let* her [the character] live her life in the middle of the frame. I didn't go in too close, but I was not *very* far away. I let her be in her space. It's not un-controlled. But the camera was not voyeuristic in the commercial way because you always knew where I was. . . . It was the only way to shoot that film—to avoid cutting the woman into a hundred pieces, to avoid cutting the action in a hundred places, to look carefully and to be respectful. The framing was meant to respect the space, her, and her gestures within it" (ibid., 119).

10. Janet Bergstrom, "*Jeanne Dielman, 23 Quai du Commerce, 1080 Brux-elles* by Chantal Akerman," *Camera Obscura* 2 (1977): 117. On the rigorous formal consistency of the film, see also Mary Jo Lakeland, "The Color of Jeanne Dielman," *Camera Obscura* 3-4 (1979): 216-18.

11. Kaja Silverman, "Helke Sander and the Will to Change," *Discourse* 6 (Fall 1983): 10.

12. Gertrud Koch, "Ex-changing the Gaze: Re-visioning Feminist Film The-ory," *New German Critique* 34 (Winter 1985): 144.

13. Sheila Rowbotham, *Woman's Consciousness, Man's World* (Harmonds-worth: Penguin Books, 1973), 28.

14. Claire Johnston, "Women's Cinema as Counter-Cinema," in *Notes on Women's Cinema,* ed. Claire Johnston (London: SEFT, 1974), 31. See also Gertrud Koch, "Was ist und wozu brauchen wir eine feministische Filmkritik?" *frauen und film* 11 (1977).

15. Mary Ann Doane, Patricia Mellencamp, and Linda Williams, eds., *Re-vision: Essays in Feminist Film Criticism* (Frederick, Md.: University Publica-tions of America and the American Film Institute, 1984), 4.

16. Ibid., 6. The quotation from Adrienne Rich is in her *On Lies, Secrets, and Silence* (New York: W. W. Norton, 1979), 35.

17. See Barbara Smith, "Toward a Black Feminist Criticism," in *All the Women Are White, All the Blacks Are Men, but Some of Us Are Brave: Black Women's Studies,* ed. Gloria T. Hull, Patricia Bell Scott, and Barbara Smith (Old Westbury, N.Y.: Feminist Press, 1982).

18. Helen Fehervary, Claudia Lenssen, and Judith Mayne, "From Hitler to Hepburn: A Discussion of Women's Film Production and Reception," *New German Critique* 24−25 (Fall/Winter 1981−82): 176.

19. Toni Morrison, *Sula* (New York: Bantam Books, 1975), 44.

20. Kathleen Hulser, "Les Guérillères," *Afterimage* 11.6 (January 1984): 14.

21. Anne Friedberg, "An Interview with Filmmaker Lizzie Borden," *Women and Performance* 1.2 (Winter 1984): 43. On the effort to understand one's relation as a feminist to racial and cultural differences, see Elly Bulkin, Minnie Bruce Pratt, and Barbara Smith, *Yours in Struggle: Three Feminist Perspectives on Anti-Semitism and Racism* (Brooklyn, N.Y.: Long Haul Press, 1984).

22. Interview in *Women and Performance,* 38.

23. Craig Owens, "The Discourse of Others: Feminists and Postmodernism," in *The Anti-Aesthetic: Essays in Postmodern Culture,* ed. Hal Foster (Port Townsend, Wash.: Bay Press, 1983), 57−82. See also Andreas Huyssen, "Mapping the Postmodern," *New German Critique* 33 (Fall 1984): 5−52, now reprinted in Huyssen, *After the Great Divide: Modernism, Mass Culture, Postmodernism* (Bloomington: Indiana University Press, 1986).

24. Borden's nonprofessional actors, as well as her characters, are very much part of the film's intended audience: "I didn't want the film caught in the white film ghetto. I did mailings. We got women's lists, black women's lists, gay lists, lists that would bring different people to the Film Forum . . ." (Interview in *Women and Performance,* 43).

25. Betsy Sussler, "Interview," *Bomb* 7 (1983): 29.

26. Stephen Heath, *Questions of Cinema* (Bloomington: Indiana University Press, 1981), 167.

27. The script of *Born in Flames* is published in *Heresies* 16 (1983): 12−16. Borden discusses how the script was developed in conjunction with the actors and according to their particular abilities and backgrounds in the interview in *Bomb.*

28. Interview in *Bomb,* 29.

29. Interview in *Women and Performance,* 39.

30. Adrienne Rich, "Compulsory Heterosexuality and Lesbian Existence," *Signs* 5.4 (Summer 1980): 631−60; Monique Wittig, "The Straight Mind," *Feminist Issues* 1.1 (Summer 1980): 110.

31. Interview in *Women and Performance,* 38.

32. Ibid., 44.

33. See Mary Ann Doane, "Film and the Masquerade: Theorising the Female Spectator," *Screen* 23.3–4 (September/October 1982): 74–87.

34. Interview in *Women and Performance*, 44–45.

CHAPTER 2: SEXUAL INDIFFERENCE AND LESBIAN REPRESENTATION

For many of the ideas developed in this essay, I am indebted to the other participants of the student-directed seminar on Lesbian History and Theory sponsored by the Board in Studies in History of Consciousness at the University of California, Santa Cruz in fall 1987. For support of various kinds, personal and professional, I thank Kirstie McClure, Donna Haraway, and Michael Cowan, Dean of Humanities and Arts.

1. Luce Irigaray "*Cosí fan tutti,*" in *This Sex Which Is Not One,* trans. Catherine Porter (Ithaca, N. Y.: Cornell University Press, 1985), 86. The phrase "sexual indifference" actually appeared in Luce Irigaray, *Speculum of the Other Woman* [1974], trans. Gillian C. Gill (Ithaca, N. Y.: Cornell University Press, 1985), 28.

2. Irigaray, *Speculum*, 101–3.

3. See Petitioner's Brief in *Bowers v. Hardwick,* cited by Mary Dunlap, "Brief Amicus Curiae for the Lesbian Rights Project et al.," *Review of Law and Social Change* 14 (1986): 960.

4. David M. Halperin, "Why Is Diotima a Woman?" in *One Hundred Years of Homosexuality and Other Essays on Greek Love* (New York: Routledge, 1990), 113. See also Halperin, "Plato and Erotic Reciprocity," *Classical Antiquity* 5.1 (1986): 60–80.

5. I am thinking in particular of Julia Kristeva, "Stabat Mater" (originally published as "Héréthique de l'amour") in *Tales of Love,* trans. Leon Roudiez (New York: Columbia University Press, 1987), and Jacques Derrida, *Spurs: Nietzsche's Styles,* trans. Barbara Harlow (Chicago: University of Chicago Press, 1979).

6. For a related reading of Aristotle and theater, see Sue-Ellen Case, "Classic Drag: The Greek Creation of Female Parts," *Theatre Journal* 37.3 (1985): 317–27. I have developed the notion of heterosexual contract (originally suggested in Monique Wittig, "The Straight Mind," *Feminist Issues* 1.1 [1980]: 103–11) in my "The Female Body and Heterosexual Presumption," *Semiotica* 67.3–4 (1987): 259–79.

7. Monique Wittig and Sande Zeig, *Lesbian Peoples: Material for a Dictionary* (New York: Avon Books, 1979).

8. See Biddy Martin and Chandra Mohanty, "Feminist Politics: What's Home Got to Do with It?" in *Feminist Studies/Critical Studies,* ed. Teresa de Lauretis

(Bloomington: Indiana University Press, 1986), 191–212, and Teresa de Lauretis, "Eccentric Subjects," chapter 7 of this volume.

9. Catharine R. Stimpson, "The Somagrams of Gertrude Stein," in *The Female Body in Western Culture: Contemporary Perspectives*, ed. Susan Suleiman (Cambridge, Mass.: Harvard University Press, 1986), 34.

10. Catharine R. Stimpson, "Zero Degree Deviancy: The Lesbian Novel in English," *Critical Inquiry* 8.2 (1981): 369.

11. Carolyn Allen, "Writing Toward *Nightwood:* Djuna Barnes' Seduction Stories," *Silence and Power: A Reevaluation of Djuna Barnes,* ed. Mary Lynn Broe (Carbondale: Southern Illinois University Press, 1991), 54–66.

12. Carolyn Allen, "'Dressing the Unknowable in the Garments of the Known': The Style of Djuna Barnes' *Nightwood*," in *Women's Language and Style,* ed. Douglas Butturft and Edmund Epstein (Akron: L&S Books, 1978), 116.

13. Esther Newton, "The Mythic Mannish Lesbian: Radclyffe Hall and the New Woman," *Signs* 9.4 (1984): 557–75. See also Madeline Davis and Elizabeth Lapovsky Kennedy, "Oral History and the Study of Sexuality in the Lesbian Community: Buffalo, New York, 1940–1960," *Feminist Studies* 12.1 (1986): 7–26; and Joan Nestle, "Butch-Fem Relationships: Sexual Courage in the 1950s," *Heresies* 12 (1981): 21–24, reprinted in Joan Nestle, *A Restricted Country* (Ithaca, N.Y.: Firebrand Books, 1987), 100–109.

14. See the discussion of Krafft-Ebing, Ellis, and others in George Chauncey Jr., "From Sexual Inversion to Homosexuality: Medicine and the Changing Conceptualization of Female Deviance," *Salmagundi* 58–59 (1982–83): 114–46, and in Carroll Smith-Rosenberg, "The New Woman as Androgyne," in *Disorderly Conduct: Visions of Gender in Victorian America* (New York: Oxford University Press, 1985), 245–349.

15. Gayle Rubin, "Thinking Sex: Notes for a Radical Theory of the Politics of Sexuality," in *Pleasure and Danger: Exploring Female Sexuality,* ed. Carole S. Vance (Boston: Routledge & Kegan Paul, 1984), 309; "The Traffic in Women: Notes on the 'Political Economy' of Sex," in *Toward an Anthropology of Women,* ed. Rayna R. Reiter (New York: Monthly Review Press, 1975), 157–210. On the feminist "sex wars" of the 1970s and 1980s, see B. Ruby Rich, "Feminism and Sexuality in the 1980s," *Feminist Studies* 12.3 (1986): 525–61. On the relationship of feminism to lesbianism, see also Wendy Clark, "The Dyke, the Feminist and the Devil," in *Sexuality: A Reader,* ed. *Feminist Review* (London: Virago, 1987), 201–15.

16. Michel Foucault, *The History of Sexuality* (New York: Pantheon, 1978), 106, cited by Rubin, "Thinking Sex," 307. For a critical reading of the relevance and limitations of Foucault's views with regard to female sexuality, see Biddy Martin, "Feminism, Criticism, and Foucault," *New German Critique* 27 (1982): 3–30, and Teresa de Lauretis, *Technologies of Gender: Essays on Theory, Film, and Fiction* (Bloomington: Indiana University Press, 1987), chapters 1 and 2.

17. Catharine A. MacKinnon, *Feminism Unmodified: Discourses on Life and Law* (Cambridge: Harvard University Press, 1987), 60.

18. Combahee River Collective, "A Black Feminist Statement," in *This Bridge Called My Back: Writings by Radical Women of Color,* ed. Cherríe Moraga and Gloria Anzaldúa (New York: Kitchen Table: Women of Color Press, 1983), 210.

19. Audre Lorde, *Zami: A New Spelling of My Name* (Trumansburg, N.Y.: The Crossing Press, 1982), 203 and 224.

20. "Writing. It's work. Changing the relationship with language. . . . Women's fictions raise theoretical issues: women's theorizing appears as/in fiction. Women's writing disturbs our usual understanding of the terms fiction and theory which assign value to discourses. . . . Fiction/theory has been the dominant mode of feminist writing in Quebec for more than a decade," states Barbara Godard for the editorial collective of *Tessera* 3, a Canadian feminist, dual-language publication that has appeared annually as a special issue of an already established magazine ("Fiction/Theory: Editorial," *Canadian Fiction Magazine* 57 [1986]: 3–4). See Nicole Brossard, *L'Amèr ou Le Chapitre effrité* (Montreal: Quinze, 1977) and *These Our Mothers, or, The Disintegrating Chapter,* trans. Barbara Godard (Toronto: Coach House, 1983). On Brossard and other Canadian writers of fiction/theory, see Shirley Neuman, "Importing Difference," and other essays in *A Mazing Space: Writing Canadian Women Writing,* ed. Shirley Neuman and Smaro Kamboureli (Edmonton: Longspoon Press and NeWest Press, 1986).

21. Elaine Marks, "Lesbian Intertextuality," in *Homosexualities and French Literature,* ed. George Stambolian and Elaine Marks (Ithaca, N.Y.: Cornell University Press, 1979), 353–77.

22. Monique Wittig, *The Lesbian Body,* trans. David LeVay (New York: William Morrow, 1975), 9, cited by Marks, 373.

23. Monique Wittig, "The Point of View: Universal or Particular?" *Feminist Issues* 3.2 (1983): 64.

24. See Hélène Vivienne Wenzel, "The Text as Body/Politics: An Appreciation of Monique Wittig's Writings in Context," *Feminist Studies* 7.2 (1981): 264–87, and Namascar Shaktini, "Displacing the Phallic Subject: Wittig's Lesbian Writing," *Signs* 8.1 (1982): 29–44.

25. Monique Wittig, *Le corps lesbien* (Paris: Minuit, 1973), 7. I have revised the English translation that appears in *The Lesbian Body,* 15.

26. The concept of "subjective, cognitive practice" is elaborated in Wittig, "One Is Not Born a Woman," *Feminist Issues* 1.2 (1981): 47–54. I discuss it at some length in my "Eccentric Subjects" (note 8, above).

27. Monique Wittig, *Les Guérillères,* trans. David LeVay (Boston: Beacon Press, 1985), 114.

28. Joanna Russ, *The Female Man* (New York: Bantam, 1975). See also

Catherine L. McClenahan, "Textual Politics: The Uses of Imagination in Joanna Russ's *The Female Man,*" *Transactions of the Wisconsin Academy of Sciences, Arts and Letters* 70 (1982): 114–25.

29. "Monique Wittig, "The Mark of Gender," *Feminist Issues* 5.2 (1985): 71.

30. Sue-Ellen Case, "Towards a Butch-Femme Aesthetic," in *Discourse,* 11.1 (Fall-Winter 1998–89): 55–73. The butch-femme couple, like Wittig's *j/e-tu* and like the s/m lesbian couple—all of whom, in their respective self-definitions, are one the name and the love of the other—propose a dual subject that brings to mind again Irigaray's *This Sex Which Is Not One,* though they all would adamantly deny the latter's suggestion that a non-phallic eroticism may be traced to the preoedipal relation to the mother. One has to wonder, however, whether the denial has more to do with the committedly heterosexual bias of neo-Freudian psychoanalysis and object relations theory, with their inability to work through the paradox of sexual (in)difference on which they are founded but perhaps not destined to, or with our rejection of the maternal body which phallic representation has utterly alienated from women's love, from our desire for the self-same, by colonizing it as the "dark continent" and so rendering it at once powerless and inaccessible to us and to all "others."

31. See, for example, Judith Mayne, "The Woman at the Keyhole: Women's Cinema and Feminist Criticism," and B. Ruby Rich, "From Repressive Tolerance to Erotic Liberation: *Maedchen in Uniform,*" in *Re-vision: Essays in Feminist Film Criticism,* ed. Mary Ann Doane, Patricia Mellencamp, and Linda Williams (Frederick, Md.: University Publications of America and the American Film Institute, 1984), 49–66 and 100–130; and Teresa de Lauretis, "Rethinking Women's Cinema," chapter 1 of this volume.

32. Elizabeth Ellsworth, "Illicit Pleasures: Feminist Spectators and *Personal Best,*" *Wide Angle* 8.2 (1986): 54.

33. Kate Davy, "Constructing the Spectator: Reception, Context, and Address in Lesbian Performance," *Performing Arts Journal* 10.2 (1986): 49.

34. Jill Dolan, "The Dynamics of Desire: Sexuality and Gender in Pornography and Performance," *Theatre Journal* 39.2 (1987): 171.

35. "To Be and Be Seen," in Marilyn Frye, *The Politics of Reality: Essays in Feminist Theory* (Trumansburg, N.Y.: The Crossing Press, 1983), 166–73; Adrienne Rich, "Disloyal to Civilization: Feminism, Racism, Gynephobia," in *On Lies, Secrets, and Silence: Selected Prose 1966–1978* (New York: Norton, 1979), 275–310.

36. Patricia White, "Madame X of the China Seas," *Screen* 28.4 (1987): 82.

37. The two essays discussed are Mary Ann Doane, "Film and the Masquerade: Theorising the Female Spectator," *Screen* 23.3–4 (1982): 74–87, and Laura Mulvey, "Afterthoughts on 'Visual Pleasure and Narrative Cinema' Inspired

by *Duel in the Sun,*" *Framework* 15/16/17 (1981): 12–15. Another interesting discussion of the notion of masquerade in lesbian representation may be found in Sue-Ellen Case, "Toward a Butch-Femme Aesthetic."

38. Jewelle Gomez, "Repeat After Me: We Are Different. We Are the Same," *Review of Law and Social Change* 14.4 (1986): 939. Her vampire story is "No Day Too Long," in *Worlds Apart: An Anthology of Lesbian and Gay Science Fiction and Fantasy,* ed. Camilla Decarnin, Eric Garber, and Lyn Paleo (Boston: Alyson Publications, 1986), 215–23. See also, *The Gilda Stories: A Novel* (Ithaca, N.Y.: Firebrand, 1991).

39. Michelle Cliff, "Passing," in *The Land of Look Behind* (Ithaca, N.Y.: Firebrand Books, 1985), 22.

40. Michelle Cliff, "Notes on Speechlessness," *Sinister Wisdom* 5 (1978): 7.

41. Michelle Cliff, "A Journey into Speech" and "Claiming an Identity They Taught Me to Despise," both in *The Land of Look Behind,* 11–17 and 40–47; see also her novel *No Telephone to Heaven* (New York: E. P. Dutton, 1987).

42. Yvonne Yarbro-Bejarano, "Cherríe Moraga's *Giving up the Ghost*: The Representation of Female Desire," *Third Woman* 3.1–2 (1986): 118–19. See also Cherríe Moraga, *Giving Up the Ghost: Teatro in Two Acts* (Los Angeles: West End Press, 1986).

43. Havelock Ellis, "Sexual Inversion in Women," *Alienist and Neurologist* 16 (1895): 141–58, cited by Newton, "The Mythic Mannish Lesbian," 567.

44. Joan Nestle, "Butch-Fem Relationships" (see note 13 above) and Amber Hollibaugh and Cherríe Moraga, "What We're Rollin' Around in Bed With," both in *Heresies* 12 (1981): 21–24 and 58–62.

CHAPTER 3: WHEN LESBIANS WERE NOT WOMEN

1. Monique Wittig, "The Straight Mind" (1980) in *The Straight Mind and Other Essays* (Boston: Beacon Press, 1992), 32. Subsequent page citations will appear in the text.

2. Renée Vivien, *A Woman Appeared to Me* (1904). Renée Vivien, née Pauline Tarn, was an Anglo-American poet, lover of Natalie Clifford Barney, and friend of Colette, living in France.

3. Teresa de Lauretis, "Eccentric Subjects," *Feminist Studies* 16 (Spring 1990): 115–50; "Soggetti eccentrici" in de Lauretis, *Soggetti eccentrici* (Milan: Feltrinelli, 1999), 11–57 and "Sujetos excéntricos" in de Lauretis, *Diferencias: Etapas de un camino a través del feminismo.* (Madrid: Editorial Horas y HORAS, 2000), 111–52; reprinted in this volume, 151–82.

4. A similar point is made by Namascar Shaktini: "Wittig's reorganization of metaphor around the lesbian body represents an epistemological shift from what seemed until recently the absolute, central metaphor—the phallus." "Dis-

placing the Phallic Subject: Wittig Lesbian Writing," *Signs: Journal of Women in Culture and Society* 8.1 (1982): 29.

5. See Homi K. Bhabha, *The Location of Culture* (London: Routledge, 1994).

6. The text that circulated in the anglophone world was Christine Delphy, *Close to Home: A Materialist Analysis of Women's Oppression,* trans. and ed. Diana Leonard (Amherst: University of Massachusetts Press, 1984).

7. See "The Combahee River Collective Statement" in *Home Girls: A Black Feminist Anthology,* ed. Barbara Smith (New York: Kitchen Table: Women of Color Press, 1983), 272–82.

8. Monique Wittig, "One Is Not Born a Woman," in *The Straight Mind and Other Essays* (Boston: Beacon Press, 1992), 13.

9. First she deployed the Marxist concepts of ideology, class, and social relations against liberal feminism. She argued that to accept the terms of gender or sexual difference, which constructed woman as an "imaginary formation" on the basis of women's biological-erotic value to men, makes it impossible to understand that the terms *woman* and *man* "are political categories and not natural givens," and thus prevents one from questioning the real socioeconomic relations of gender. Second, however, Wittig claimed the feminist notion of self as a subject who, although socially produced, is apprehended and lived in its concrete, personal singularity, and this notion of self she held against Marxism, which denied an individual subjectivity to the members of the oppressed classes. Although "materialism and subjectivity have always been mutually exclusive," she insisted on both class consciousness and individual subjectivity at once. Without the latter, "there can be no real fight or transformation. But the opposite is also true; without class and class consciousness there are no real subjects, only alienated individuals" ("The Straight Mind," 19).

10. Simone de Beauvoir, *The Second Sex,* trans. H. M. Parshley (1949, repr. New York: Vintage, 1974).) xxxii.

11. "No one is unaware of what takes place here, it has no name as yet" (my translation). Monique Wittig, *Le corps lesbien* (Paris: Éditions Minuit, 1973), 7.

12. Teresa de Lauretis, *Alice Doesn't: Feminism, Semiotics, Cinema* (Bloomington: Indiana University Press, 1984).

13. Robyn Wiegman, "Object Lessons: Men, Masculinity, and the Sign Women," *Signs: Journal of Women in Culture and Society* 26.2 (2001): 355–88.

14. Joan W. Scott, "The Evidence of Experience," *Critical Inquiry* 17 (Summer 1991): 773–97. The notion of *expérience vécue* has now become central to postcolonial and critical race theory stemming from the rereading of Frantz Fanon, while the concept of experience is now being revaluated in the writing of Foucault, which was formerly read as the staunch basis of the social-con-

structionist position against the essentialist position allegedly represented by "the evidence of experience."

15. A move to replace academic programs in women's studies with gender studies has met with very few objections. Leora Auslander, "Do Women's + Feminist + Men's + Lesbian + Gay + Queer Studies = Gender Studies?" *differences* 9.3 (1997): 1–25. The author's answer to the question in her title is an enthusiastic yes.

16. Judith Butler, *Gender Trouble: Feminism and the Subversion of Identity* (New York: Routledge, 1990), 124.

17. Here are some typical passages from *Gender Trouble:*

> Wittig's radical feminist theory occupies an ambiguous position within the continuum of theories on the question of the subject. On the one hand, Wittig appears to dispute the metaphysics of substance, but on the other hand, she retains the human subject, the individual, as the metaphysical locus of agency. (25)

> In her defense of the "cognitive subject," Wittig appears to have no metaphysical quarrel with hegemonic modes of signification or representation; indeed, the subject, with its attribute of self-determination, appears to be the rehabilitation of the agent of existential choice under the name of the lesbian. (19)

> As a subject who can realize concrete universality through freedom, Wittig's lesbian confirms rather than contests the normative promise of humanist ideals premised on the metaphysics of substance. (20)

> Clearly her belief in a "cognitive subject" that exists prior to language facilitates her understanding of language as an instrument, rather than as a field of significations that preexist and structure subject-formation itself. (154n27)

> Wittig's radical disjunction between straight and gay replicates the kind of disjunctive binarism that she herself characterizes as the divisive philosophical gesture of the straight mind. (121)

> Lesbianism that defines itself in radical exclusion from heterosexuality deprives itself of the capacity to resignify the very heterosexual constructs by which it is partially and inevitably constituted. As a result, that lesbian strategy would consolidate compulsory heterosexuality in its oppressive [as opposed to "volitional or optional" (121)] forms. (128)

> Wittig's materialism . . . understands the institution of heterosexuality as the founding basis of the male-dominated social orders. "Nature" and the domain of materiality are ideas, ideological constructs, produced by these social institutions to support the political interests of

the heterosexual contract. In this sense, Wittig is a classic idealist for whom nature is understood as a mental representation. (125)

Very similar statements appear in Rosi Braidotti, *Metamorphoses: Towards a Materialist Theory of Becoming* (Oxford: Polity Press, 2002), which attributes to Wittig "a naïve social constructivism which paradoxically works with an idealist position on language and social changes" (35) and damns her as "a humanist who is still caught in the metaphysics of substance" (102). Remarkably, Braidotti follows almost verbatim Butler's assessment of Wittig in the context of a critique of Butler, for the project of *Metamorphoses* is to challenge U.S. poststructuralist feminist philosophy as represented by Butler with a French poststructuralist feminist philosophy based in Deleuze and Irigaray.

18. Monique Wittig, *Les Guérillères,* trans. David LeVay (Boston: Beacon Press, 1985), 114.

19. Elaine Marks, "Lesbian Intertextuality," in *Homosexualities and French Literature,* ed. George Stambolian and Elaine Marks (Ithaca, N.Y.: Cornell University Press, 1979), 375.

20. Jean Laplanche, *Life and Death in Psycho-Analysis,* trans. Jeffrey Mehlman (Baltimore, Md.: Johns Hopkins University Press, 1976), ch. 6; see also Laplanche, "La pulsion de mort dans la théorie de la pulsion sexuelle," in *La pulsion de mort* (Paris: PUF, 1986).

CHAPTER 4: THE LURE OF
THE MANNISH LESBIAN

1. A shorter version of this paper was presented at the 1990 MLA convention in Chicago.

2. Havelock Ellis, "Sexual Inversion in Women," *Alienist and Neurologist* 16 (1895): 141–58. A similar view of female homosexuality is expressed in Ernest Jones, "The Early Development of Female Sexuality," *International Journal of Psycho-Analysis* 8 (1927): 459–72, and later repeated by Jacques Lacan, "Guiding Remarks for a Congress on Feminine Sexuality," in *Feminine Sexuality,* ed. Juliet Mitchell and Jacqueline Rose, (New York: W. W. Norton, 1983), 96–97.

3. This reconceptualization of perversion is made possible by Freud's notion of the sexual drive as independent of its object. See Arnold Davidson, "How to Do the History of Psychoanalysis: A Reading of Freud's *Three Essays on the Theory of Sexuality,*" in *The Trials of Psychoanalysis,* ed. Françoise Meltzer (Chicago: University of Chicago Press, 1987–88), 39–64.

4. Diane Hamer, "Significant Others: Lesbianism and Psychoanalytic Theory." *Feminist Review* 34 (Spring 1990): 143–45.

5. Radclyffe Hall, *The Well of Loneliness* (New York: Avon Books, 1981). See Esther Newton, "The Mythic Mannish Lesbian: Radclyffe Hall and the New Woman," *Signs* 9.4 (Summer 1984): 557–75, and Catharine R. Stimpson, "Zero

Degree Deviancy: The Lesbian Novel in English," in *Writing and Sexual Difference*, ed. Elizabeth Abel (Chicago: University of Chicago Press, 1982), 243–60. Rebecca O'Rourke, *Reflecting on the Well of Loneliness* (London: Routledge, 1989) contains an interesting, if partial, study of the novel's reception.

6. The distinction between repression (*Verdrangung*) and repudiation or foreclosure (*Verwerfung*) is that, while the repressed contents are accessible to consciousness and to be worked over, for example in analysis, what is repudiated or foreclosed is permanently repressed, forever lost to memory.

7. J. Laplanche and J. B. Pontalis, "Fantasy and the Origins of Sexuality," in *Formations of Fantasy*, ed. Victor Burgin et al. (London: Methuen, 1986), 5–34.

8. See Luce Irigaray's critique in "Commodities among Themselves," in *This Sex Which Is Not One*, trans. Catherine Porter (Ithaca, N.Y.:Cornell University Press, 1985), 2.

9. Kaja Silverman, "Fassbinder and Lacan," *Camera Obscura* 19 (1989): 79.

10. Stephen Heath, "Joan Riviere and the Masquerade," in *Formations of Fantasy*, 55.

11. As Lacan himself puts it, "The phallus is the privileged signifier of that mark where the share of the logos is wedded to the advent of desire. One might say that this signifier is chosen as what stands out as most easily seized upon in the real of sexual copulation, and also as the most symbolic in the literal (typographical) sense of the term, since it is the equivalent in that relation of the (logical) copula. One might also say that by virtue of its turgidity, it is the image of the vital flow as it is transmitted in generation" (*Feminine Sexuality*, 82).

12. Sigmund Freud, "Fetishism," in *The Standard Edition of the Complete Psychological Works of Sigmund Freud*, trans. and ed. James Strachey (London: Hogarth Press, 1953–74), 21:155–56.

13. Leo Bersani and Ulysse Dutoit, *The Forms of Violence: Narrative in Assyrian Art and Modern Culture* (New York: Schocken Books, 1985), 68–69.

14. Juliet Mitchell also extrapolates from disavowal and fetishism a more general, formal model of the constitution of the subject in her "Introduction I" to Lacan, *Feminine Sexuality*, 25.

15. Joan Nestle, *A Restricted Country* (Ithaca, N. Y.: Firebrand Books, 1987), 104–5.

16. Laplanche and Pontalis, "Narcissism," in *The Language of Psycho-Analysis* (New York: W. W. Norton), 256.

17. "A second theoretical characteristic of the castration complex is its impact upon narcissism: the phallus is an essential component of the child's self-image, so any threat to the phallus is a radical danger to this image; this explains the efficacity of the threat, which derives from the conjunction of two factors, namely, the primacy of the phallus and the narcissistic wound" (Laplanche and Pontalis, *Language of Psycho-Analysis*, 57).

18. Adrienne Rich, *The Dream of a Common Language: Poems 1974–1977* (New York: W. W. Norton, 1978) 75–76.

CHAPTER 5: LETTER TO
AN UNKNOWN WOMAN

1. See Mandy Merck, "The Train of Thought in Freud's 'Case of Homosexuality in a Woman,'" *Perversions: Deviant Readings* (New York: Routledge, 1993), 13–32; Diana Fuss, "Freud's Fallen Women: Identification, Desire, and 'A Case of Homosexuality in a Woman,'" *Yale Journal of Criticism* 6.1 (1993): 1–23; Judith Roof, *A Lure of Knowledge: Lesbian Sexuality and Theory* (New York: Columbia University Press, 1991); Noreen O'Connor and Joanna Ryan, *Wild Desires and Mistaken Identities: Lesbianism and Psychoanalysis* (London: Virago, 1993); and Mary Jacobus, "Russian Tactics: Freud's 'Case of Homosexuality in a Woman,'" *GLQ. A Journal of Lesbian and Gay Studies* 2.1–2 (1995): 65–79.

2. Sigmund Freud, "The Psychogenesis of a Case of Homosexuality in a Woman" (1920), *The Standard Edition of the Complete Psychological Works of Sigmund Freud* [hereinafter *Standard Edition*], ed. and trans. James Strachey, 24 vols. (London: Hogarth, 1953–1974) 18:145–72, 170. Further references will be included in the text.

3. Sigmund Freud, "Fragment of an Analysis of a Case of Hysteria" (1905), *Standard Edition*, 8:1–222.

4. Ibid., 164–65.

5. Or rather, did not upon entering treatment, for in the course of the analysis she produces "a lying dream": "The intention to mislead me, just as she did her father, certainly emanated from the preconscious, and may indeed have been conscious; it could come to expression by entering into connection with the unconscious wishful impulse to please her father (or father-substitute), and in this way it created a lying dream. The two intentions, to betray and to please her father, originated in the same complex" (166). I suggest that the attempted suicide may be seen precisely in this light. Like the occasional "lying dreams," the attempted suicide lacked the repetitive and uncontrollable character of actual neurotic symptoms. The presence of neurotic behavior due to (the resistance to) the Oedipal imperative does not contradict the girl's homosexuality (perversion or inversion, in Freud's terms). On the coexistence of neurosis and perversion, see Hans Sachs, "On the Genesis of Perversion" (1923), *American Imago* 48 (1991): 283–93.

6. In "A Case of Paranoia Running Counter to the Psycho-Analytic Theory of the Disease" (1915), *Standard Edition*, 14:261–272, the woman's homosexuality is merely presumed by Freud and nowhere admitted or suggested by the subject in question, and the case for homosexuality is even less convincingly argued than in the feminist readings of Dora. As even the customarily sober, scholarly, and factual editors of the *Standard Edition* are impelled to introduce

it, this case history is "an object-lesson to practitioners on the danger of basing a hasty opinion of a case on a superficial knowledge of the facts" (262). It is less an analysis than a peroration *pro domo sua* on the part of Freud, who is seeking confirmation of his freshly formulated theory of paranoia in the case of Judge Schreber—the "theory that the delusion of persecution invariably depends on homosexuality" (266).

7. I discuss this at length in chapter 1 of *The Practice of Love: Lesbian Sexuality and Perverse Desire* (Bloomington: Indiana University Press, 1994).

8. The similarities, also noted by Merck and Roof, include the length of the analysis and its early termination, the patient's attempted suicide, her choice of an older female object, her resistance or failed transference, and Freud's unavowed countertransference. Unlike the girl of "Psychogenesis," Dora has become a feminist heroine. The symbol of feminine resistance to patriarchy, she has inspired a play, two films, a biographical memoir, and a mass of critical essays, some of them collected in Charles Bernheimer and Claire Kahane, eds., *In Dora's Case: Freud—Hysteria—Feminism* (New York: Columbia University Press, 1985). What is especially intriguing is that a major theme in many of these works is Dora's alleged homosexuality, whereas Freud's only case history of a female homosexual has received much less feminist attention and almost exclusively from lesbian critics. Why have feminists equated Dora's hysteria with homosexuality? Is it only because Lacan treated the two cases as virtually interchangeable, or are there other possible explanations? I discuss these questions in chapter 2 of *The Practice of Love* and offer an interpretation in chapter 4 under the heading of "The Seductions of Lesbianism."

9. "Fragment," 105, 120.

10. Ibid., 60.

11. Sigmund Freud, *The Ego and the Id* (1923), *Standard Edition*, 19:12–66, 31–34.

12. This, we note, is the exact reversal of the situation Freud had described in Dora's case, where the homosexual current was the unconscious one. But, *mutatis mutandis*, the Oedipal structure remains in place.

13. See also the letter Freud wrote to an American mother in 1935, cited in Henry Abelove, "Freud, Male Homosexuality, and the Americans," in *The Lesbian and Gay Studies Reader*, eds., Henry Abelove, Michele Barale, and David Halperin (New York: Routledge, 1993), 381–93.

14. Sigmund Freud, *Three Essays on the Theory of Sexuality* (1905), *Standard Edition*, 7:123–245, 149.

15. Ibid., 150.

16. The concept was first articulated in Adrienne Rich, "Compulsory Heterosexuality and Lesbian Existence" (1980), in *Blood, Bread, and Poetry: Selected Prose 1979–1985* (New York: Norton, 1986), 23–75. I discuss it and amplify it in my "Eccentric Subjects: Feminist Theory and Historical Consciousness." *Feminist Studies*, 16.1 (1990), 115–50; reprinted here (151–82).

17. I use this somewhat awkward phrase, *sexual structuring,* to emphasize the permanently under-construction character of sexuality in the sociosexual subject, its being a process and not a stable structure that is set in place once and for all in childhood or adolescence. I would not, however, use terms such as *sexual orientation* or *sexual identity* because these do not sufficiently convey the overdetermination of sexuality by psychic and fantasmatic structures.

18. Sigmund Freud, "Fetishism" (1927) and "Splitting of the Ego in the Process of Defense" (1940), *Standard Edition,* 21:152–57 and 23:275–78, respectively.

19. It should perhaps be added that, contrary to current views, femininity can also be a figure of power, when it is socially and culturally valorized; there are women in whose personal experience and family or social situation femininity is something of value. In heterosexual relations femininity confers power, specifically the power of seduction, and in some lesbian subcultures the femme is a figure of empowered femininity, as is the drag queen in contemporary U.S. gay subcultures.

20. Frantz Fanon, *Black Skin, White Masks,* trans. C. L. Markmann (New York: Grove, 1967).

CHAPTER 6: PUBLIC AND PRIVATE FANTASIES
IN DAVID CRONENBERG'S *M. BUTTERFLY*

1. Antonio Gramsci, *Selections from Cultural Writings,* ed. David Forgacs and Geoffrey Nowell-Smith, trans. William Boelhower (Cambridge, Mass.: Harvard University Press, 1985), 378.

2. Chris Rodley, ed. *Cronenberg on Cronenberg* (London: Faber & Faber, 1993), 184.

3. Wayne Koestenbaum, *The Queen's Throat: Opera, Homosexuality, and the Mystery of Desire* (New York: Vintage, 1993), 199.

4. Gramsci, *Selections,* 378.

5. Sigmund Freud, "Creative Writers and Day-Dreaming" (1908), *The Standard Edition of the Complete Psychological Works of Sigmund Freud* [hereinafter *Standard Edition*], trans. and ed. James Strachey, 24 vols. (London: Hogarth, 1953–74) 9:150.

6. Sigmund Freud, *The Interpretation of Dreams* (1900), *Standard Edition,* 5:492.

7. Ibid.

8. Stephen Heath, "Narrative Space," in *Questions of Cinema* (Bloomington: Indiana University Press, 1980), 19–75.

9. I am indebted to Luz Calvo, a doctoral candidate in History of Consciousness, University of California, Santa Cruz, for her comparative reading of the two films. "Mise-en-Scène of Desire: The Mexico-U.S. Border." Qualifying Essay, History of Consciousness, University of California, Santa Cruz, 1988.

10. When I presented a version of this essay at the Seventh Tampere Conference on North American Studies in Finland, a member of the audience, who was herself a speaker at the conference, Professor Chalermsri Chantasingh of Silpakorn University in Thailand, very kindly informed me that a play drawn from the Butterfly story is performed in her country, without music and with Thai setting and characters. In the Japanese city of Nagasaki, a statue of Madame Butterfly, one arm outstretched toward the bay and the other holding her young son, is a favorite tourist attraction. I was told that an aria from Puccini's opera was played at the opening ceremony of the 1988 Winter Olympics in Japan, while female athlete Midori Ito carried the torch, dressed in what Westerners saw as a Butterfly costume. (Thanks to Judith Howard and Amy Singer.)

11. For the genealogy of the Madame Butterfly character, I am indebted to Peter Delpeut, *Chrysanthème en Butterfly: De genealogic van een onmogelijke heldin* (Amsterdam: Stichting Nederlands Filmmuseum, 1994). Delpeut, however, reports Loti's real name as Theodore Viaud instead of Julien Viaud (compare *Grand Larousse encyclopédique*, 10 vols. [Paris: Larousse, 1962] 6:857). An Italian commentator of Loti's *Madame Chrysanthème* states that her real name, as reported by Loti in a letter to his mother, was Okané-san. See Michele C. Catalano, *La donna e l'amore in Estremo Oriente* (Turin: Edizione Chiantore, 1941), 78. I owe the latter information to Nerina Milletti.

12. The names are changed: Cho-cho-san becomes O-Take-san (played by Lil Dagover) and Pinkerton becomes Olaf J. Anderson. Interesting detail: he buys her freedom from a brothel, so the marriage is not a question of lust but a question of honor.

13. *The Toll of the Sea* was a promotion for Technicolor's new two-color filmstock, blue-green and dark red (Delpeut, *Chrysanthème en Butterfly*, 22). In a remarkable instance of intertextuality, whether intentional or not, the star of this film, Anna May Wong, appears in *M. Butterfly* on a magazine cover as one of the models of femininity that Song Liling follows in his construction of himself as a modern-day Chinese Butterfly.

14. The libretto by Luigi Illica and Giuseppe Giacosa reached its definitive version in 1907.

15. Some of the information given in this paragraph comes from *M. Butterfly's* press release. I am much indebted to Jim Schwenterley, owner of the Nickelodeon Theatre in Santa Cruz, for facilitating my research on this and many other films.

16. David Henry Hwang, *M. Butterfly* (New York: Dramatists Play Service, Inc., 1988). Joyce Wadler, "The Spy Who Fell in Love with a Shadow," *New York Times Magazine*, August 15, 1993, 30–54. Credits for the film of *M. Butterfly* (Geffen Pictures, USA, 1993) include: directed by David Cronenberg, with Jeremy Irons (René Gallimard), John Lone (Song Liling), Barbara Sukowa, and Ian Richardson; produced by Gabriella Martinelli; director of photography, Peter Suschitzky; screenplay by David Henry Hwang, based on his play; music

by Howard Shore; edited by Ronald Sanders; production designer, Carol Spier; costume designer, Denise Cronenberg.

17. Speaking of his film in relation to Neil Jordan's *The Crying Game* (1992), which was released when *M. Butterfly* was in production, Cronenberg states: "*The Crying Game* made that thing of two men having a love affair—where one didn't know that the other one was a man—kind of sweet and innocent and pure and, in a weird way, not threatening. . . . I think it's because she (Jaye Davidson) really is a woman, even though she's got a cock. . . . That's why I wanted John Lone, not the equivalent of Jaye Davidson. I didn't want an unknown who was incredibly female, who was like a wonderful drag queen and almost undetectable. I wanted a man. When Gallimard and Song are kissing I wanted it to be two men. I wanted the audience to feel that." Rodley, ed. *Cronenberg on Cronenberg,* 180.

18. Edward Said, *Orientalism,* (New York: Pantheon, 1978).

19. Rodley, ed. *Cronenberg on Cronenberg,* 184–85.

20. "*Mise-en-abîme* refers to the infinite regress of mirror reflections to denote the literary, painterly or filmic process by which a passage, a section or sequence plays out in miniature the processes of the text as a whole." Robert Stam, Robert Burgoyne, and Sandy Flitterman-Lewis, *New Vocabularies in Film Semiotics: Structuralism, Post-structuralism and Beyond,* (London: Routledge, 1992), 201.

21. Incidentally, John Lone was himself trained as an actor by the Beijing Opera in Hong Kong, a repertory company that had fled China during the Cultural Revolution. In the performance of Song Liling, the "concubine" role he plays is from a 500-year-old opera titled "Drunken Beauty," in which a woman is driven to drink after being rejected by her Emperor lover. John Lone himself sings the part that we watch, together with René, at the theater.

22. In addition to his training as an actor of the Beijing opera, which certainly contributes to the queenly elegance of his performance of an opera diva, as well as his rendition of the character of Butterfly, John Lone chose always to appear as a woman during the film's production, according to the director: "John Lone was a very strong presence on set. There was a lot of interesting stuff going on between John and Jeremy. . . . He was so scrupulous about being a woman on set. He wanted Jeremy to not ever see him as a man. He really was the girl on the set and that was great. If you needed femaleness, he was it," Rodley, ed., *Cronenberg on Cronenberg,* 177.

23. Hwang, *M. Butterfly,* 86.

24. Rodley, ed. *Cronenberg on Cronenberg,* 173. Cronenberg himself may have seen it, but he has the title wrong—Madam*e* instead of Madam*a*—which unwittingly proves his point: anyone knows what Butterfly stands for.

25. As Homi Bhabha has argued in another context, the stereotype works as a fetish that constructs the subject in colonial discourse by both recognizing

and disavowing cultural difference. Homi Bhabha, "The Other Question?" *The Location of Culture* (London: Routledge, 1994), 66–84.

26. A passage in Christian Metz's theory of cinema as "imaginary signifier" accounts for the effectiveness of such a technical choice. Cinema, he argues, in eliciting the spectator's desire to see, engages what psychoanalysis calls the scopic drive (scopophilia, pleasure in looking) and the invocatory drive (Lacan's *pulsion invocante*, pleasure in hearing). "The 'perceiving drive'—combining into one the scopic drive and the invocatory drive—concretely represents the absence of its object in the distance at which it maintains it and which is part of its very definition: distance of the look, distance of listening. . . . If it is true of all desire that it depends on the infinite pursuit of its absent object, voyeuristic desire . . . is the only desire whose principle of distance symbolically and spatially evokes this fundamental rent [the subject's separation from the desired object]." Christian Metz, *The Imaginary Signifier: Psychoanalysis and the Cinema*, trans. Celia Britton, Annwyl Williams, Ben Brewster, and Alfred Guzzetti (Bloomington: Indiana University Press, 1982), 59–60.

27. The aria played on the cassette tape is "Un bel dí," and not "Addio, piccolo iddio," which in the opera is the death scene of Butterfly, saying good-bye to her son. Here the substitution is motivated, as the child is irrelevant to Gallimard.

28. See Christian Metz: "What is characteristic of the cinema is not the imaginary that it may happen to represent, but the imaginary that it is from the start, the imaginary that constitutes it as a signifier. . . . The activity of perception which it involves is real (the cinema is not a fantasy), but the perceived is not really the object, it is its shade, its phantom, its double, its *replica* in a new kind of mirror" (*Imaginary Signifier*, 44–45); and Jean-Louis Baudry: "The cinematographic apparatus is unique in that it offers the subject perceptions 'of a reality' whose status seems similar to that of representations experienced as perception. [The wish for cinema] consists in obtaining from reality a position, a condition in which what is perceived would no longer be distinguished from representations" ("The Apparatus: Metapsychological Approaches to the Impression of Reality in the Cinema," trans. Jean Andrews and Bertrand Augst, *Camera Obscura: A Journal of Feminism and Film Theory* 1 (1976): 120–21).

29. See Rodley, ed., *Cronenberg on Cronenberg*. Most of Cronenberg's earlier films are about physical transformations, degeneration, decay, mutation, monstrous metamorphoses, from his first feature film, *Shivers* (1975), about people in a high-rise apartment building invaded by internal bodily parasites, to *Rabid* (1976), *The Brood* (1979), *Scanners* (1980), *Videodrome* (1982), and *The Fly* (1986). Since *Dead Ringers* (1988) and *Naked Lunch* (1991) the emphasis has been on psychic transformation and fantasy. The theme of fetishism, which emerged in *M. Butterfly*, is taken up explicitly and quite literally in Cronenberg's *Crash* (1996).

30. On the specific appeal of opera to gay spectators/listeners, their identification with operatic heroines, and the fascination exerted by the figure of the prima donna (Callas above all), see Koestenbaum, *Queen's Throat*; Corinne E. Blackmer and Patricia Juliana Smith, eds., *En Travesti: Women, Gender Subversion, Opera* (New York: Columbia University Press, 1995); and Sam Abel, *Opera in the Flesh: Sexuality in Operatic Performance* (Boulder, Colo.: Westview, 1996).

31. Indeed, the film's representation of *women* is downright misogynist. As if to set off the femininity of Song, all the female characters are constructed by similarity and high contrast to "Butterfly": Gallimard's wife is ludicrous when, sitting in bed with a cold and blowing her nose, she sings a few notes of "Un bel dí" out of tune (and probably because of this soon disappears altogether from the diegesis); Frau Baden's matter-of-fact attitude toward sex, no less than her naked female body, only serves to incite Gallimard's desire for the white-robed, reticent, prepubescent girl's body he imagines in Song; Comrade Chin, whom Gallimard never sees, epitomizes the unwomanly woman—the masculinized, militarized, "communist," policewoman or prison matron—purely for the spectator's edification; and the servant Shu Fang, unlike Suzuki, her feminine counterpart in Puccini's opera, is genderless and merely functional to the plot as "servant."

32. See Sigmund Freud, "Fetishism" (1927), *Standard Edition*, 21:152–57. I have attempted to define fetishism in relation to homosexual/lesbian desire in *The Practice of Love: Lesbian Sexuality and Perverse Desire* (Bloomington: Indiana University Press, 1994). However, the classic Freudian definition pertains to Gallimard's heterosexual fetishism, where the fetish is a substitute for the phallus.

33. See Sigmund Freud, "Mourning and Melancholia" (1917), *Standard Edition*, 13:252.

34. See Sigmund Freud, *Beyond the Pleasure Principle* (1920), *Standard Edition*, 18:61.

35. In metacinematic terms, the fact that we watch René seeing (himself as) Butterfly in the mirror not only brings home to the viewers the artificial, constructed nature of Butterfly as a figure of performance, a fantasy figure, but also represents in miniature, in an image, the film's construction of the fantasy as a mise-en-abîme, i.e., the fantasy of Butterfly within the fantasy that is the film. It is not coincidental, I think, that this technique of visual and narrative construction, which in French is called *mise-en-abîme*, in English is called *mirror construction*.

36. Metz, *The Imaginary Signifier*, 74 (emphasis in the original).

37. This is made explicit in Song's comment to Gallimard about the Japanese experiments on imprisoned Chinese women during the war.

38. I have discussed this in "Imaging," chap. 2 of Teresa de Lauretis, *Alice*

Doesn't: Feminism, Semiotics, Cinema (Bloomington: Indiana University Press, 1984), 53–69.

39. See Elizabeth Cowie, "Identifying in the Cinema?" in *Representing the Woman: Cinema and Psychoanalysis* (London: Macmillan, 1997), 72–122.

40. Rodley, ed., *Cronenberg on Cronenberg*, 180, 186, 184. To the extent that, in this interview, Cronenberg is stating his ideas, intentions, and opinions about the film, these may be considered part of the director's fantasy, not of the film's fantasy, which is the result of multiple agents with their own fantasies and desires.

41. Ursula K. Le Guin, *The Left Hand of Darkness* (New York: Ace Books, 1969).

42. Rodley, ed., *Cronenberg on Cronenberg*, 185.

43. Ibid.

44. Ibid., 183–84 (emphasis added).

45. Richard Corliss, review of *M. Butterfly* and *Farewell My Concubine*, *Time*, October 4, 1993, 85.

46. Ibid.

47. In light of this observation, that sexual fantasy is even more strictly bound to "racial" images than it is to gender, it may be pointed out that while *M. Butterfly* deconstructs the cultural narrative of "the oriental woman" Butterfly, it does nothing to deconstruct the equally orientalist stereotype of the feminized Asian man. See Richard Fung, "Looking for My Penis: The Eroticized Asian in Gay Video Porn," *How Do I Look? Queer Film and Video*, ed. Bad Object-Choices (Seattle: Bay Press, 1999), 145–68.

48. Rey Chow, "The Dream of a Butterfly," in *Human, All Too Human* (Papers from the English Institute), ed. Diana Fuss (New York: Routledge, 1995), 61–92. Further references appear in the text.

49. I have attempted to reformulate the fetish as the general term for the signifier of perverse desire, of which the phallus/penis may be a particular instance, in chaps. 5 and 6 of *The Practice of Love*. See also "The Lure of the Mannish Lesbian," chapter 4 of this volume.

50. "To me, this is not a 'gay' subject, because the very labels heterosexual or homosexual become meaningless in the context of this story. Yes, of course this was literally a homosexual affair. Yet because Gallimard perceived it or chose to perceive it as a heterosexual liaison, in his mind it was essentially so. Since I am telling the story from the Frenchman's point of view," Hwang, *M. Buttlerfly*, cited by Chow, "Dream of a Butterfly," 89–90n14.

51. In the first of these scenes, Comrade Chin's surprise visit finds Song reading glossy magazines ("decadent trash"). The one picked out by the camera features on its cover a color photo of the Chinese-American actress Anna May Wong (see note 13, above) who, the camera seems to comment ironically, was a star in decadent and trashy Hollywood movies. What the camera does not

suggest, but some spectators may recall, is that Wong was also known to appear in male drag.

52. Hwang, *M. Butterfly,* 86. Although Hwang is credited for the film's screenplay, he did extensive rewriting according to the director's suggestions. See Rodley, ed., *Cronenberg on Cronenberg,* 172–73.

CHAPTER 7: ECCENTRIC SUBJECTS

Much of the thinking that went into this essay took place in the context of my teaching at the University of California, Santa Cruz, over the past four years. An earlier and shorter version was presented at the conference on "Feminism and the Critique of Colonial Discourse" held at UCSC on April 25, 1987; other versions were presented at several universities in Europe, Canada, and the United States. I am indebted to my students and colleagues in the History of Consciousness Program for both formal and informal discussions of these issues and to the UCSC Academic Senate for a 1986–87 grant that partially supported this research. A special debt of joyful wisdom I owe Kirstie McClure for her lucid criticisms of the manuscript and her enlightening discussion of these and other issues of feminist theory.

1. On the distinction between the terms "woman" (or "Woman") and "women"—a distinction crucial to grasping and conveying the paradoxical status of women in the dominant discourses of Western culture—see my book, *Alice Doesn't: Feminism, Semiotics, Cinema* (Bloomington: Indiana University Press, 1984), 5–6. In chapter 6, I also introduced and discussed other terms of particular relevance to feminist theory and to this essay, such as "experience," "subjectivity," and "(self)consciousness." See especially 159 and 184–86.

2. Simone de Beauvoir, *The Second Sex,* trans. H. M. Parshley (1949; New York: Vintage, 1974), xviii–xix; Emmanuel Lévinas, quoted, xix.

3. A similarly paradoxical definition of woman as both human subject and object of exchange between men, as both speaker and sign of the language (kinship) by which men, in making culture, communicate with one another across generations, is given in Claude Lévi-Strauss, *Les Structures élémentaires de la parenté,* also published in 1949. In fact, de Beauvoir thanks him for allowing her to see this work in proofs and acknowledges using it "liberally" in *The Second Sex* (xx).

4. Catharine A. MacKinnon, *Feminism Unmodified: Discourses on Life and Law* (Cambridge: Harvard University Press, 1987), 50, emphasis added.

5. John Berger, quoted in Catharine A. MacKinnon, "Feminism, Marxism, Method, and the State: An Agenda for Theory," in *Feminist Theory: A Critique of Ideology,* ed. Nannerl O. Keohane, Michelle Z. Rosaldo, and Barbara C. Gelpi (Chicago: University of Chicago Press, 1981), 26.

6. Nancy C. M. Hartsock, "The Feminist Standpoint: Developing the Ground for a Specifically Feminist Historical Materialism," in *Discovering Reality:*

Feminist Perspectives on Epistemology, Metaphysics, Methodology, and Philosophy of Science, ed. Sandra Harding and Merrill B. Hintikka (Dordrecht, Neth.: Reidel, 1983), 284.

7. MacKinnon, "Feminism, Marxism, Method, and the State," 2.

8. Hartsock, "Feminist Standpoint," 291.

9. MacKinnon, "Feminism, Marxism, Method, and the State," 30.

10. A version of Hartsock's 1983 essay, "The Feminist Standpoint," appears as chapter 10 of her *Money, Sex, Power: Toward a Feminist Historical Materialism* (Boston: Northeastern University Press, 1985). Elsewhere in the book, Hartsock does address the issue of sexuality, defining it quite broadly as "a series of cultural and social practices and meanings that both structure and are in turn structured by social relations more generally." She cites Jeffrey Weeks and Robert Stoller and gives as further footnote references for her view the anthropologists Sherry B. Ortner and Harriet Whitehead, as well as Adrienne Rich and Ann Ferguson et al. Because these "theorists have argued for this position in several different contexts," Hartsock states, "it seems unnecessary to go into detail here, but to indicate that I subscribe in a general way to their arguments" (156). Surely, however, the only "position" on sexuality that can be gleaned from such heterogeneous sources—two of whom are explicitly engaged in open debate (Rich and Ferguson, as I will discuss later on)—is little more than their minimal common denominator, that is, the overgeneralized view, indeed the cliché, that sexuality is "cultural." Such a reductive, if not outright simplistic, notion of sexuality is doubtless accountable for Hartsock's displeasure with feminist (lesbian) authors who, while "they see sexuality as a cultural creation . . . often go on to argue in ways that suggest that changing sexuality is an impossibility" (179); but what "changing sexuality" might mean, in fact, Hartsock does not say. That the authors in question are writing about lesbian pornography and sadomasochism is not coincidental, for most of this chapter on sexuality, entitled "Gender and Power: Masculinity, Violence, and Domination," deals with pornography and perversion. Thus, the overall view conveyed in the book is that sexuality is something defined and imposed by the masculine, negative eros, which is shared by women and men alike in a "community grounded on a sexuality structured by violence, domination, and death" (178). To this, then, Hartsock opposes the potential for a "fully human community" that is inherent in women's "experience" of maternal sexuality (256), erotic fusion and empathy with the sexual partner (257), and in the "capacity for a variety of relations with others that grows from the experience of being mothered by a woman" (158). In short, masculinity is to mothering (women) as abstract is to concrete, separation to connection, violence to nurturance, death to life, in a series of binary oppositions which are built on the primary couple nonreproductive (masculine) vs. reproductive (female) sexuality.

11. Hartsock, "Feminist Standpoint," 299.

12. MacKinnon, "Feminism, Marxism, Method, and the State," 5.

13. Compare "Freud and Lacan" as well as "Ideology and the Ideological State Apparatuses" in Louis Althusser's *Lenin and Philosophy and Other Essays*, trans. Ben Brewster (New York: Monthly Review Press, 1971).

14. For example, see Julian Henriques et al., *Changing the Subject: Psychology, Social Regulation, and Subjectivity* (London: Methuen, 1984), in the context of post-Althusserian debates on discourse theory in Britain, and the related work of the Marxist journal, *Ideology and Consciousness*.

15. See Teresa de Lauretis, *Technologies of Gender: Essays in Theory, Film, and Fiction* (Bloomington: Indiana University Press, 1987), chap. 1.

16. Hartsock, "Feminist Standpoint," 295.

17. For example, see Luce Irigaray, *Speculum of the Other Woman*, trans. Gillian C. Gill (Ithaca, N.Y.: Cornell University Press, 1985); Juliet Mitchell, *Psychoanalysis and Feminism* (London: Penguin, 1974); Jacqueline Rose, *Sexuality in the Field of Vision* (London: Verso, 1986); Jane Gallop, *The Daughter's Seduction: Feminism and Psychoanalysis* (Ithaca, N.Y.: Cornell University Press, 1982); Kaja Silverman, *The Subject of Semiotics* (New York: Oxford University Press, 1983); and Mary Ann Doane, *The Desire to Desire: The Woman's Film of the 1940s* (Bloomington: Indiana University Press, 1987).

18. See Jane Flax, "Political Philosophy and the Patriarchal Unconscious: A Psychoanalytic Perspective on Epistemology and Metaphysics," in *Discovering Reality;* Jessica Benjamin, "A Desire of One's Own: Psychoanalytic Feminism and Intersubjective Space," in *Feminist Studies/Critical Studies,* ed. Teresa de Lauretis (Bloomington: Indiana University Press, 1986), 78–101; and Nancy Chodorow, *The Reproduction of Mothering: Psychoanalysis and the Sociology of Gender* (Berkeley: University of California Press, 1978).

19. Juliet Mitchell, cited in Rose, 6.

20. MacKinnon, *Feminism Unmodified,* 54.

21. Rose, *Sexuality in the Field of Vision,* 17.

22. MacKinnon, *Feminism Unmodified,* 60.

23. De Beauvoir, *The Second Sex,* xxiii.

24. Purple September Staff, "The Normative Status of Heterosexuality," in *Lesbianism and the Women's Movement,* ed. Charlotte Bunch and Nancy Myron (Baltimore: Diana Press, 1975), cited by MacKinnon, *Feminism Unmodified,* 26.

25. See Wini Breines and Linda Gordon, "The New Scholarship on Family Violence," *Signs* 8 (Spring 1983): 490–531; Sandra Harding, *The Science Question in Feminism* (Ithaca, N.Y.: Cornell University Press, 1986); Evelyn Fox Keller, *Reflections on Gender and Science* (New Haven: Yale University Press, 1984); Ruth Bleier, *Science and Gender: A Critique of Biology and Its Theories on Women* (New York: Pergamon Press, 1984); and Donna Haraway, "Teddy-Bear Patriarchy," *Social Text* 11 (1984–85): 20–64.

26. For a discussion of Althusser and Foucault in relation to the issue of gender, see de Lauretis, *Technologies of Gender,* chap. 1.

27. For example, see Silverman; and Mary Ann Doane, "Woman's Stake: Filming the Female Body," *October* 17 (1981): 23–36.

28. I have developed the notion of a heterosexual or Oedipal social contract, suggested in Monique Wittig, "The Straight Mind," *Feminist Issues* 1.1 (Summer 1980): 103–10, in Teresa de Lauretis, "The Female Body and Heterosexual Presumption," *Semiotics* 67, nos. 3–4 (1987): 259–79:

> In the term "oedipal contract" I want to bring together and into view the semiotic homology of several conceptual frameworks: Saussure's notion of language as social contract; Rousseau's "social contract" with its gender distinction: Freud's "Oedipus complex" as the structuring psychic mechanism responsible for the orientation of human desire and the psychosocial construction of gender: the "cinematic contract" that stipulates the conditions of vision by encoding the specific relations of image and sound to meaning and to subjectivity for the film's spectator . . and finally, Wittig's "heterosexual contract" as the agreement between modern theoretical systems and epistemologies not to question the a priori of gender, and hence to presume the sociosexual opposition of "man" and "woman" as the necessary and founding moment of culture.

29. See Catharine A. MacKinnon, *Sexual Harassment of Working Women: A Case of Sex Discrimination* (New Haven: Yale University Press, 1979); Adrienne Rich, "Compulsory Heterosexuality and Lesbian Existence," in her *Blood, Bread, and Poetry: Selected Prose, 1979–1985* (New York: W. W. Norton, 1986); and Monique Wittig, "The Straight Mind," and "One Is Not Born a Woman," *Feminist Issues* 1.2 (Winter 1981): 47–54. Also see Ann Ferguson, "Patriarchy, Sexual Identity, and Sexual Revolution," *Signs* 7 (Autumn 1981): 158–72.

30. MacKinnon, "Feminism, Marxism, Method, and the State," 1. An interesting parallel to the trajectory of feminist thinking about heterosexuality from private sexual practice to institution, and its continuing slippage between the personal and the political, is the historical trajectory of the English word "institution" according to Raymond Williams's *Keywords: A Vocabulary of Culture and Society* (New York: Oxford University Press, 1976).

> Institution is one of several examples [cf. CULTURE, SOCIETY, EDUCATION] of a noun of action or process which became, at a certain stage, a general and abstract noun describing something apparently objective and systematic; in fact, in the modern sense, an institution. It has been used in English since C14, from fw [immediate forerunner] *institution,* oF [old French], *institutionem,* L [Latin], from rw [root word] *statuere,* L—establish, found, appoint. In its earliest uses it had the strong sense of an act of origin—something instituted at a particular point in time—but by mC16 there was a developing general

sense of practices established in certain ways, and this can be read in a virtually modern sense. . . . But there was still, in context, a strong sense of custom, as in the surviving sense of "one of the institutions of the place." It is not easy to date the emergence of a fully abstract sense; it appears linked, throughout, with the related abstraction of SOCIETY (q.v.). By mC18 an abstract sense is quite evident, and examples multiply in C19. . . . In C20 institution has become the normal term for any organized element of a society. (139–40).

It might be interesting to speculate whether, just as *institution* became affirmed as an abstract term concurrently with *society*, of which it is a primary condition of existence, the abstract sense of *heterosexuality* as institution came to feminism with the affirmation of *feminist theory* as a form of knowledge, a critical theory whose critical existence is conditioned by that institution. I note apropos that Williams's *Keywords* has no entry for Gender, Feminism, Sexuality (of any kind) or Consciousness (although the latter appears under class as class consciousness and under ideology as false consciousness).

31. Ferguson, 170, 171.

32. Wittig, "The Straight Mind," 107.

33. Michel Foucault, *The History of Sexuality,* vol. 1, *An Introduction,* trans. Robert Hurley. (New York: Vintage, 1980), 92–96.

34. Irigaray, 11–129.

35. See, for example, Marilyn Frye, *The Politics of Reality: Essays in Feminist Theory* (Trumansburg, N.Y.: Crossing Press, 1983), 95–109.

36. See Elaine Showalter, "Feminist Criticism in the Wilderness," in *Writing and Sexual Difference,* ed. Elizabeth Abel (Chicago: University of Chicago Press, 1982), 9–35; Susan Griffin, *Woman and Nature: The Roaring Inside Her* (New York: Harper & Row, 1978); Mary Daly, *Gyn/Ecology: The Metaethics of Radical Feminism* (Boston: Beacon Press, 1978), and *Pure Lust: Elemental Feminist Philosophy* (Boston: Beacon Press, 1984).

37. Audre Lorde, "Open Letter to Mary Daly," in her *Sister Outsider: Essays and Speeches* (Trumansburg, N.Y.: Crossing Press. 1984), 69.

38. See Barbara Smith, "Toward a Black Feminist Criticism," in *All the Women Are White, All the Blacks Are Men, but Some of Us Are Brave: Black Women's Studies,* ed. Gloria T. Hull, Patricia Bell Scott, and Barbara Smith (Old Westbury, N.Y.: The Feminist Press, 1982), 162, emphasis added.

39. Barbara Smith, ed., *Home Girls: A Black Feminist Anthology* (New York: Kitchen Table/Women of Color Press, 1983), 272–82.

40. See Minnie Bruce Pratt's "Identity: Skin Blood Heart," in Elly Bulkin, Minnie Bruce Pratt, and Barbara Smith, *Yours in Struggle: Three Feminist Perspectives on Anti-Semitism and Racism* (Brooklyn, N.Y.: Long Haul Press, 1984), 11–63.

41. Biddy Martin and Chandra Talpade Mohanty, "Feminist Politics: What's

Home Got to Do with It?" in de Lauretis, *Feminist Studies/Critical Studies,* 195.

42. The assumption of an identity as "women of color" in the United States (and similarly of a "black" identity in Britain) on the part of women from highly diversified cultural and ethnic backgrounds—Asian, Native American, black American and Caribbean women, Chicanas, Latinas, and so forth—is an example of personal-political consciousness that is not simply based on ethnic and cultural *differences* vis-à-vis the dominant white culture, and that is not at all the opposition of one set of cultural values, stable in a given ethnic minority, to the equally stable values of the dominant majority. The identity as a woman of color is one developed out of the specific historical experience of racism in the contemporary Anglo-American culture and the white- and male-dominated society of the United States today; it is developed out of an understanding of the personal-political need for building community across, in spite of, in tension, even in contradiction with the cultural values of one's ethnic background, one's family, one's "home." See Cherríe Moraga, *Loving in the War Years* (Boston: South End Press, 1984); Mirtha Quintanales, "I Paid Very Hard for My Immigrant Ignorance," in *This Bridge Called My Back: Writings by Radical Women of Color,* ed. Cherríe Moraga and Gloria Anzaldúa (New York: Kitchen Table/Women of Color Press, 1983), 150–56; Melanie Kaye/Kantrowitz, "Some Notes on Jewish Lesbian Identity," in *Nice Jewish Girls: A Lesbian Anthology* (Trumansburg, N.Y.: Crossing Press, 1982), 28–44; Cheryl Clarke, "Lesbianism: An Act of Resistance," in *This Bridge Called My Back,* 128–37; and Merle Woo, "Letter to Ma," in *This Bridge Called My Back,* 140–47.

43. Samuel R. Delany, "Interview" with Takayuki Tatsumi, *Diacritics* 16 (Fall 1986): 27–43.

44. Elaine Marks and Isabelle de Courtivron, eds. *New French Feminisms: An Anthology* (Amherst: University of Massachusetts Press, 1980), 3.

45. Rich would not call it theory, however, for theory, she believes, "isn't good for the earth," is too white-centered. It has not yet sufficiently engaged the political theory of black U.S. feminism and the texts of other women of color (see Rich, *Blood, Bread, and Poetry,* 210–31). And in this sense she is right. But why continue to disallow a critical practice which has been both transformative and transformed in the work of feminist writers, academics, and activists (compare with Paula A. Treichler's "Teaching Feminist Theory," in *Theory in the Classroom,* ed. Cary Nelson [Urbana: University of Illinois Press, 1986], 57–128)? And why discard the term "theory" just when women of color have begun to claim it (e.g., bell hooks, *Feminist Theory: From Margins to Center* [Boston: South End Press, 1984])? On the politics of location, see also Adrienne Rich, "Blood, Bread, and Poetry: The Location of the Poet," in her *Blood, Bread, and Poetry,* 167–87.

46. See Moraga and Anzaldúa, *This Bridge Called My Back*, 23.

47. Frye, "The Politics of Reality," 154.

48. Wittig, "One Is Not Born a Woman," 52.

49. Christine Delphy, *Close to Home: A Materialist Analysis of Women's Oppression*, trans. and ed. Diana Leonard (Amherst: University of Massachusetts Press, 1984), 217, 218.

50. "The Combahee River Collective Statement," in *Home Girls*, 274–78.

51. Christine Delphy, "A Materialist Feminism *Is* Possible," in *Close to Home*, 178–79.

52. Wittig, "One Is Not Born a Woman," 49.

53. See Wittig's "The Straight Mind."

54. Frye, "The Politics of Reality," 154.

55. Adrienne Rich, "Disloyal to Civilization: Feminism, Racism, Gynephobia," in *On Lies, Secrets, and Silences: Selected Prose, 1966–1978* (New York: W.W. Norton, 1979), 275–310.

56. Trinh T. Minh-ha, "Introduction," *Discourse* 6 (1986–87): 9.

57. Wittig, "One Is Not Born a Woman," 49.

58. Gayle Rubin, "The Traffic in Women: Notes on the 'Political Economy' of Sex," in *Toward an Anthropology of Women*, ed. Rayna Rapp Reiter (New York: Monthly Review Press, 1975), 157–210.

CHAPTER 8: UPPING THE ANTI [*SIC*] IN FEMINIST THEORY

Another version of this essay was published in *Differences: A Journal of Feminist Cultural Studies* 1.2 (Fall 1989) with the title "The Essence of the Triangle or, Taking the Risk of Essentialism Seriously: Feminist Theory in Italy, the U.S., and Britain," which was later reprinted in *The Essential Difference*, eds. Naomi Schor and Elizabeth Weed (Bloomington: Indiana University Press, 1994), 1–39. The two versions have in common the arguments set out in part I, but then, in parts II and III, present two quite distinct accounts of what I call the effective history of feminist theory and its specific, essential difference as a developing theory of the female-sexed or female-embodied social subject: there, an account, one possible history of feminist theory in Italy, here one account of feminist theory in North America.

1. For two very different historical views of feminism, see Rosalind Delmar, "What Is Feminism?" in *What Is Feminism? A Re-Examination.*, ed. Juliet Mitchell and Ann Oakley (New York: Pantheon Books, 1986), 8–33, and Karen Offen, "Defining Feminism: A Comparative Historical Approach," *Signs: Journal of Women in Culture and Society* 14.1 (Autumn 1988): 119–57.

2. The typological project is central to, for example, Alice Echols, "The New Feminism of Yin and Yang," in *Powers of Desire: The Politics of Sexual-*

ity, ed. Ann Snitow, Christine Stansell, and Sharon Thompson (New York: Monthly Review Press, 1983), 439–59, and "The Taming of the Id: Feminist Sexual Politics, 1968–83," in *Pleasure and Danger: Exploring Female Sexuality,* ed. Carole S. Vance (Boston: Routledge & Kegan Paul, 1984), 50–72; Hester Eisenstein, *Contemporary Feminist Thought* (Boston: G. K. Hall, 1983); Zillah Eisenstein, *The Radical Future of Liberal Feminism* (New York: Longman, 1981); Alison M. Jaggar and Paula S. Rothenberg, *Feminist Frameworks: Alternative Theoretical Accounts of the Relations Between Women and Men* (New York: McGraw-Hill, 1984); and more recently Chris Weedon, *Feminist Practice and Poststructuralist Theory* (Oxford: Basil Blackwell, 1987). In this proliferation of typologies, essentialism as the belief in "female nature" is associated with cultural feminism, "separatist" (read: lesbian) feminism, radical feminism (with qualifications), and occasionally liberal feminism, while socialist feminism and now poststructuralist or deconstructive feminism come out at the top of the scale. Third World feminism is also widely used as a term but seldom given official type status in the typologies. A notable exception is Jaggar and Rothenberg's anthology which, in its 1984 revised edition, adds the new category "Feminism and Women of Color" to the five categories of the 1978 edition of *Feminist Frameworks:* conservatism, liberalism, traditional Marxism, radical feminism, and socialist feminism. On their part, Black, Latina, Asian, and other U.S. Third World feminists have not participated in the making of such typologies, possibly because of their ongoing argument with and ambivalence toward the larger category of "white feminism." And hence, perhaps, Jaggar and Rothenberg's respectful labeling of the new category "Feminism *and* Women of Color," suggesting a distance between the two terms and avoiding judgment on the latter.

3. Marla C. Lugones and Elizabeth V. Spelman, "Have We Got a Theory for You! Feminist Theory, Cultural Imperialism and the Demand for 'the Woman's Voice,'" *Women's Studies International Forum* 6.6 (1983): 573–81.

4. *The New Feminist Criticism: Essays on Women, Literature, and Theory,* ed. Elaine Showalter (New York: Pantheon Books, 1985) includes Barbara Smith, "Toward a Black Feminist Criticism," first published in 1977, and Bonnie Zimmerman, "What Has Never Been: An Overview of Lesbian Feminist Criticism," first published in 1981.

5. Since Alcoff refers extensively to my own work, this essay is in a sense a dialogue with her and with myself—that dialogue in feminist critical writing which often works as a variation of consciousness raising or better, its transformation into a significant form of feminist cultural practice, and one not always reducible to "academic" activity.

6. Donna Haraway, "Situated Knowledges: The Science Question in Feminism and the Privilege of Partial Perspective," *Feminist Studies* 14.3 (Fall 1988): 575–99.

7. The quotation marks around "internal" and "external" are there to de-naturalize any notion of boundary between feminism and what is thought of as its outside, its other, non-feminism. For, even as we must speak of divisions within feminism, of a feminist political thought, a feminist discourse, a feminist consciousness, etc., we nonetheless well know that no permanent or stable boundary insulates feminist discourse and practices from those which are not feminist. In fact, as Ernesto Laclau and Chantal Mouffe argue in *Hegemony and Socialist Strategy: Towards a Radical Democratic Politics* (London: Verso, 1985), "the irresoluble interiority/exteriority tension is the condition of any social practice. . . . It is in this terrain, where neither a total interiority nor a total exteriority is possible, that the social is constituted" (111). In thinking through the relation of feminism to other social discourses and practices, I find very useful their notion of *articulation*. If we abandon the notion of "*'society'* as a sutured and self-defined totality," Laclau and Mouffe state, we may instead conceive of the social as a field of differences, where no single underlying principle fixes, and hence constitutes, the whole field of differences (111); but the "impossibility of an ultimate fixity of meaning implies that there have to be partial fixations—otherwise, the very flow of differences would be impossible. Even in order to differ, to subvert meaning, there has to be a meaning." Thus they define a "practice of articulation" as "the construction of nodal points which partially fix meaning," an attempt to arrest the flow of differences, to construct a center (112–13). In this sense, the history of feminist theory would be the history of a series of practices of articulation.

8. I am indebted to Kirstie McClure for pointing out to me that the opposition between theory and practice is a long-standing element of the Western intellectual tradition well before Marxism. One of the classic modern efforts to overcome that opposition, and an equally unsuccessful effort, is Kant's essay "On the Common Saying: 'This May Be True in Theory, but It Does Not Apply in Practice,'" in *Kant's Political Writings*, ed. Hans Reiss (Cambridge: Cambridge University Press, 1970), 61–92.

9. See, for example, Alice Walker, *In Search of Our Mothers' Gardens: Womanist Prose* (San Diego, Calif.: Harcourt Brace Jovanovich, 1983); bell hooks, *Feminist Theory: From Margin to Center* (Boston: South End Press, 1984); Audre Lorde, "An Open Letter to Mary Daly," in *Sister Outsider: Essays and Speeches* (Trumansburg, N.Y.: The Crossing Press, 1984), 66–71; and especially Chela Sandoval, "Oppositional Consciousness in the Postmodern World: United States Third World Feminism, Semiotics, and the Methodology of the Oppressed," (PhD diss., University of California, Santa Cruz, 1993).

10. See B. Ruby Rich, "Feminism and Sexuality in the 1980s," *Feminist Studies* 12.3 (Fall 1988): 525–61; Catharine A. MacKinnon, *Feminism Unmodified: Discourses on Life and Law* (Cambridge, Mass.: Harvard University Press, 1987); Nancy Hartsock, "The Feminist Standpoint: Developing the Ground for a Specifically Feminist Historical Materialism," in *Discovering Reality*, ed.

Sandra Harding and Merrill B. Hintikka (Dordrecht, Neth.: Reidel, 1983), 283–310; Donna Haraway, "A Manifesto for Cyborgs: Science, Technology and Socialist Feminism in the 1980s," *Socialist Review* 80 (1985): 65–107; Samois, *Coming to Power: Writings and Graphics on Lesbian S/M* (Boston: Alyson Publications, 1982); *Against Sadomasochism: A Radical Feminist Analysis*, ed. Robin Ruth Linden, Darlene R. Pagano, Diana E. H. Russell, and Susan Leigh Star (East Palo Alto, Calif.: Frog in the Well Press, 1982); Chris Bearchell, "Why I Am a Gay Liberationist: Thoughts on Sex, Freedom, the Family and the State," *Resources for Feminist Research/ Documentation sur la Recherche Féministe* [*RFR/DRF*] 12.1 (March/Mars 1983): 57–60; Wendy Clark, "The Dyke, the Feminist and the Devil," in *Sexuality: A Reader*, ed. Feminist Review (London: Virago, 1987), 201–15; Marilyn Frye, "Lesbian Feminism and the Gay Rights Movement: Another View of Male Supremacy, Another Separatism," in *The Politics of Reality: Essays in Feminist Theory* (Trumansburg, N.Y.: The Crossing Press, 1983), 128–50; Pat Califia, "Introduction," in *Macho Sluts: Erotic Fiction* (Boston: Alyson Publications, 1988), 9–27; Gayle Rubin, "Thinking Sex: Notes for a Radical Theory of the Politics of Sexuality," in *Pleasure and Danger*, 267–319; Jacqueline Rose, "Femininity and Its Discontents," *Feminist Review* 14 (Summer 1983); 5–21, a response to Elizabeth Wilson, "Psychoanalysis: Psychic Law and Order," *Feminist Review* 8 (Summer 1981).

11. Teresa de Lauretis, "The Essence of the Triangle or, Taking the Risk of Essentialism Seriously: Feminist Theory in Italy, the U.S., and Britain," *Differences: A Journal of Feminist Cultural Studies* 1, no. 2 (Summer 1989): 3–37. The text I discuss there is Libreria delle Donne di Milano, *Non credere di avere dei diritti: La generazione della libertà femminile nell' idea e nelle vicende di un gruppo di donne* ["Don't Think You Have Any Rights: The Engendering of Female Freedom in the Thought and Vicissitudes of a Women's Group"] (Turin: Rosenberg & Sellier, 1987). *Sexual Difference: A Theory of Social-Symbolic Practice* (Bloomington: Indiana University Press, 1990) is an English translation of this book.

12. Teresa de Lauretis, *Technologies of Gender: Essays on Theory, Film, and Fiction* (Bloomington: Indiana University Press, 1987), 26.

13. See, for example, Moira Gatens, "A Critique of the Sex/Gender Distinction," in *Beyond Marxism: Interventions after Marx*, ed. J. Allen and P. Patton (Sydney: Intervention Press, 1983), 143–60; B. Ruby Rich, "Anti-Porn: Soft Issue, Hard World," *The Village Voice*, July 20, 1982; Sue-Ellen Case, "Towards a Butch-Femme Aesthetic," *Discourse: Journal for Theoretical Studies in Media and Culture* 11.1 (Fall-Winter 1988–89): 55–73; and Mariana Valverde, "Beyond Gender Dangers and Private Pleasures: Theory and Ethics in the Sex Debates," *Feminist Studies* 15.2 (Summer 1989): 237–54.

14. For example, Jaggar and Rothenberg in *Feminist Frameworks*: "We believe that the feminist struggle must be guided by feminist theory, by a systematic analysis of the underlying nature and causes of women's oppression" (xii).

CHAPTER 9: HABIT CHANGES

1. Sigmund Freud, *The Interpretation of Dreams* (1900), *The Standard Edition of the Complete Psychological Works of Sigmund Freud* [hereinafter *Standard Edition*], trans. and ed. James Strachey, 24 vols. (London: Hogarth, 1953–74), 4–5:1–628.

2. Teresa de Lauretis, *The Practice of Love; Lesbian Sexuality and Perverse Desire* (Bloomington: Indiana University Press, 1994).

3. Teresa de Lauretis, special issue ed., "Queer Theory: Lesbian and Gay Sexualities," *differences* 3.2 (1991).

4. Judith Butler, *Bodies That Matter: On the Discursive Limits of "Sex"* (New York: Routledge, 1993), 15.

5. Sigmund Freud, *Three Essays on the Theory of Sexuality* (1905), *Standard Edition*, 7:123–246, 147–48.

6. Sigmund Freud, "Instincts and Their Vicissitudes" (1915), *Standard Edition*, 14:109–140, 122 (emphasis added).

7. Both disavowal and repression are defense mechanisms and both are operative in sexuality, in perversion and neurosis. See Alan Bass, "Fetishism, Reality, and 'The Snow Man,'" *American Imago* 48 (1991): 295–328, 321.

8. Sigmund Freud, *The Ego and the Id* (1923), *Standard Edition*, 19:1–66, 26–27.

9. See Jean Laplanche and Jean-Bertrand Pontalis, "Fantasy and the Origins of Sexuality," *Formations of Fantasy*, ed. Victor Burgin, James Donald, and Cora Kaplan (London: Methuen, 1986), 5–34.

10. See note 27, below.

11. Teresa de Lauretis, *Technologies of Gender: Essays on Theory, Film, and Fiction* (Bloomington: Indiana University Press, 1987), 1–30.

12. Richard Wollheim discusses Freud's notion of the bodily ego in relation to mental and corporeal representations or internal and external realities. Drawing on Melanie Klein, his discussion of internalization (introjection) in relation to the unconscious fantasy of incorporation is necessarily tied to the notion of developmental (progressive) stages; his argument is limited to and by a developmental perspective. See Richard Wollheim, "The Bodily Ego," *Philosophical Essays on Freud*, eds. Richard Wollheim and James Hopkins (Cambridge: Cambridge Univeristy Press, 1982), 124–38. My reading of the bodily ego draws on Jean Laplanche, who links fantasy to Freud's *Nachträglichkeit* (deferred action or, as Laplanche translates it, "afterwardness"), which makes the notion of fantasy more supple and conducive to a dynamic view of sexuality or sexual structuring. See Jean Laplanche, "The Freud Museum Seminar," *Seduction, Translation, Drives*, eds. John Fletcher and Martin Stanton (London: Institute of Contemporary Arts, 1992), 41–63.

13. Michel Foucault, *The Use of Pleasure*, trans. Robert Hurley, vol. 2 of *The History of Sexuality*, 3 vols. (New York: Random House, 1985), 4–6.

14. Sigmund Freud, *Interpretation of Dreams,* in *Standard Edition* 4:98–99.

15. Michel Foucault, *The Care of the Self,* trans. Robert Hurley, vol. 3 of *The History of Sexuality,* 3 vols. (New York: Random House, 1986), 238–40.

16. "Technologies of the Self," in *Technologies of the Self: A Seminar with Michel Foucault,* ed. Luther H. Martin, Huck Gutman, and Patrick H. Hutton (Amherst: University of Massachusetts Press, 1988): 16–49, 28.

17. Charles Sanders Peirce, *Collected Papers,* 8 vols. (Cambridge, Mass.: Harvard University Press, 1931–1958), 5:491; emphasis added.

18. Jessica Benjamin, "The Other Woman," *New York Times Book Review,* September 4, 1994, 15.

19. Ellen Brinks, "The Awesome Pull of Desire," *Lambda Book Report,* July-August 1994, 19.

20. With the exception of Anne Freadman, an Australian Peirce scholar, to whom I express my gratitude for her careful reading and generous suggestions in a personal communication.

21. Jean Laplanche *Life and Death in Psychoanalysis,* trans. Jeffrey Mehlman (Baltimore, Md.: Johns Hopkins University Press, 1976), 27.

22. Michel Foucault, *The History of Sexuality: An Introduction,* trans. Robert Hurley, vol. 1 of *The History of Sexuality,* 3 vols. (New York: Pantheon, 1978).

23. In others, the fetish is a writing hand, a femme's masquerade of femininity, a flower, or even a whole fantasy scenario—none of which makes reference to masculinity.

24. Sander Gilman, *The Case of Sigmund Freud: Medicine and Identity at the Fin de Siècle* (Baltimore, Md.: Johns Hopkins University Press, 1993).

25. Sigmund Freud, "On Narcissism: An Introduction" (1914), *Standard Edition,* 14:67–104, 88–89.

26. Biddy Martin, *Woman and Modernity: The (Life)Styles of Lou Andreas-Salome* (Ithaca, N.Y.: Cornell University Press, 1991), 207.

27. A similar point is argued in Whitney Davis's *Latent Images: Homosexuality and Visual Interpretation in Freud's "Wolf Man" Case* (Bloomington: Indiana University Press, 1995), a study of homosexuality and visual interpretation in Freud's "Wolf Man" case. I am indebted to Davis for the trope of the subject as permanently under construction.

CHAPTER 10: THE INTRACTABILITY
OF DESIRE

1. The first and most influential feminist work on gender, "The Traffic in Woman: Notes on the 'Political Economy' of Sex" by Gayle Rubin (in *Toward an Anthropology of Women,* ed. Rayna Reiter, [New York: Monthly Review Press, 1975]), used the term "sex/gender system" to designate "the set of arrangements by which a society transforms biological sexuality into products

of human activity, and in which these transformed sexual needs are satisfied" (159). Further demonstrating the synonymity of sex and gender typical of feminist thought in the 1970s, Rubin summarized Freud's theories on female sexuality with a now-surprising phrase: "psychoanalysis is a theory of gender" (198). Some ten years later, Rubin, in an equally influential essay, maintained the need to elaborate a theory and politics of sexuality autonomous from the critique of gender as a social structure of the oppression of women (Gayle Rubin, "Thinking Sex: Notes for a Radical Theory of the Politics of Sexuality" [1984], in *The Lesbian and Gay Studies Reader*, ed. Henry Abelove, Michele Aina Barale, and David M. Halperin [New York: Routledge, 1993], 309).

2. Teresa de Lauretis, *Sui generiS*, trans. Liliana Losi (Milan: Feltrinelli, 1996).

3. See Teresa de Lauretis, "Eccentric Subjects," *Feminist Studies* 16.1 (Spring 1990): 115–50, and in this volume (151–82).

4. "Adriana Cavarero in Dialogue with Rosi Braidott: The Decline of the Subject and the Dawn of Female Subjectivity," *DWF* (Donna Woman Femme) 4.20 (1993): 75. Further citations in the text.

5. de Lauretis, *Sui generiS*, 163. See also Teresa de Lauretis, *Technologies of Gender* (Bloomington: Indiana University Press, 1987), 26.

6. Donna J. Haraway, "Cyborg Manifesto," in Haraway, *Simians, Cyborgs and Women: the Reinvention of Nature* (London: Free Association, [1990], c. 1991); Sandy Stone, "The Empire Strikes Back: A Posttransexual Manifesto," in *Body Guards: The Cultural Politics of Gender Ambiguity*, ed. Julia Epstein and Kristina Straub (New York and London: Routledge, 1991), 280–304. Judith Butler's book, *Bodies That Matter: On the Discursive Limits of "Sex"* (New York: Routledge, 1993), provides another example of the contradiction between the negativity of theory and the positivity of politics: on the one hand, she maintains that the subject does not exist except as an effect of the very citationality of power; that the I acquires existence only through quoting, reiterating the law through "a reiterative or rearticulatory practice, immanent to power" (15), for which reason the I is always within power and complicit with it. On the other hand, however, Butler tells us that queer practices bring about a "reworking of abjection into political agency" (21), a politics that wants to give legitimacy to abject bodies, excluded from the social body, which is to say to homosexual bodies, and transform them into "bodies that matter," that is, bodies that are socially recognized as "lives . . . [that are] valuable, worthy of support." But how this politics of re-signification might take place if there are no subjects who practice it (given that, as Butler argues, the subject does not exist) remains an unresolved question that creates contradictions within her own theoretical discourse.

7. "Una, due, tre discussioni . . . tanto per cominciare," in *E l'ultima chiuda la porta. L'importanza di chiamarsi lesbiche, I quaderni viola* 4 (Milan: Nuove Edizioni Internazionali, 1996), 18–32.

8. On the difficult relations between lesbianism and feminism, see Simonetta Spinelli, "Il silenzio è perdita," *DWF* (Donna Woman Femme) 4 (Oct.-Dec. 1986): 72–8, and Bianca Pomeranzi, "Differenza lesbica e lesbofemminismo," *Memoria* 13 (1985): 72–78.

9. This is a problem analogous to the slippage of the term *homosexuality* from the meaning "lesbian sexuality" or "gay sexuality"—two different types of sexuality—to the meaning that can be indicated by Luce Irigaray's term *hom(m)osexuality*, that is homosexuality thought of as a simple variant of institutionalized heterosexuality (that is to say, the reproductive sexuality in which male and female are both necessary and complementary), a variant that is acted by two people of the same sex. I have analyzed the conceptual ambiguity of this term in *Differenza e indifferenza sessuale* [*Sexual Difference and Indifference*] (Florence: Estro, 1989), see "Sexual Indifference and Lesbian Representation," in chapter 2 of this volume.

10. The concept of heterosexual institution entered into Anglo-American feminist discourse, not without resistance on the part even of lesbian women, with a feminist text written by the collective Purple September Staff, "The Normative Status of Heterosexuality," in *Lesbianism and the Women's Movement*, ed. Charlotte Bunch and Nancy Myron (Baltimore: Diana Press, 1975), but the better-known text, whose title has passed into the Italian discourse, is by Adrienne Rich, *Compulsory Heterosexuality and Lesbian Existence* (1980), Italian translation by Maria Luisa Moretti, "Eterosessualità obbligatoria ed esistenza lesbica," *Nuova DWF*, 23–24 (1985): 5–40. I have written about the contribution of lesbian thought to North American feminism in "Eccentric Subjects."

11. Antonia Ciavarella, "O cambiamo politica o cambiamo vita!" [Either we change politics or we change our lives!], *I quaderni viola* 4, 43.

12. See Monique Wittig, *The Straight Mind and Other Essays* (Boston: Beacon Press, 1992) and Marilyn Frye, "Some Reflections on Separatism and Power," in Frye, *The Politics of Reality: Essays in Feminist Theory* (Trumansburg, N.Y.: The Crossing Press, 1983), 95–109.

13. Lea Melandri, *Migliaia di foglietti: Mineralogia del mondo interno* [*Thousands of Slips of Paper: Minerology of the Internal World*] (Faenza: Mobydick, 1996), 60.

14. Liana Borghi, "Apertura del Convegno" [Conference Opening Address], in *Da desiderio a desiderio. Donne, sessualità, progettualità lesbica* [*From Desire to Desire: Women, Sexuality, Lesbian Political Project-Making*], proceedings of the 5th National Lesbian Conference, Impruneta, 5–7 December 1987 (Florence: L'Amandorla, 1987), 9.

15. Lia Cigarini, "Il tempo, i mezzi, i luoghi" [The Time, the Means, the Places], *Sottosopra* December 1976, quoted by Ida Dominijanni in "Il desiderio di politica," introduction to Lia Cigarini, *La politico del desiderio*, ed. Luisa Muraro and Liliana Rampello (Parma: Nuova Pratiche Editrice, 1995), 12.

16. "È accaduto non per caso" [It Didn't Happen by Chance], *Sottosopra,* January 1996, 4–5.

17. Simonetta Spinelli, "Nell'insieme e nel dettaglio" [Altogether and in Detail], *DWF* (Donna Woman Femme) 15 (1991): 27–29. The quotation is from *Da desiderio a desiderio,* 125–28 (see note 14).

18. I have developed the thesis that sexuality is the place in which subjectivity is produced in relation to social signification and to material reality, in *Pratica d'amore* (Milan: La Tartaruga, 1997), chapter 7. See de Lauretis, *The Practice of Love* (Bloomington: Indiana University Press, 1994).

CHAPTER 11: FIGURES OF RESISTANCE

1. For this I thank Dr. Maryann Valiulis, Director of the Center for Gender and Women's Studies at Trinity College.

2. The UW-Madison Women's Studies Department was then under the direction of Elaine Marks, to whose memory I dedicate this chapter.

3. For this I thank Prof. Rosi Braidotti, Chair of the Utrecht Women's Studies Department. The first part of this chapter includes large sections of my 1991 inaugural lecture, later published as "Feminist Genealogies: A Personal Itinerary," *Women's Studies International Forum* 16.4 (1993): 393–403.

4. See Mons. Nicola Fusco, PA, *Elena Lucrezia Cornaro Piscopia* (Pittsburgh, 1978), 22. This is a commemorative volume under the auspices of the Hunt Foundation, the University of Pittsburgh, and the U.S. Committee for the Elena Lucrezia Cornaro Piscopia Tercentenary.

5. Or so reports her biographer (35–36). "In the second half of the twentieth century," explains Mons. Fusco, "the Roman Cathoic Church abolished its sweeping veto. Today, in Europe, there are many female Doctors of Theology. In Elena Piscopia's day, the Conventual Father Felice Rotondo, a teaching theologian at the University of Padua, remarked: 'If the women are permitted to study Theology, why must they be denied the doctorate in that subject?' As his supporters, he cited Duns Scotus (1266–1308), the Jesuit Alfonso Salmeron (1515–1596), and Cornelius a Lapide (1567–1637), Church luminaries. But Cardinal Barbarigo compromised with Father Rotondo's view, reluctantly. 'Woman,' he said, 'is made for motherhood, not for learning. However, if the Procurator of San Marco insists, I am willing to modify the point and let his daughter become a Doctor of Philosophy'." No textual reference is given for these words by Cardinal Barbarigo. In a letter, Mons. Fusco states that he is not writing a critical monography but "a Profile, that is, a short story" (Appendix, 95).

6. Shakespeare, *Romeo and Juliet,* 1.1.192. These questions seem to me central to Alicia Gaspar de Alba's wonderful "novel" on seventeenth-century Mexican poet and nun Juana Inés de la Cruz, *Sor Juana's Second Dream* (Albuquerque: University of New Mexico Press, 1999).

7. Ihab Hassan, "Passage from Egypt: Excerpt from an Imaginary Autobiography," *Sub-Stance*, 37/38 (1983): 192 and 211.

8. John Cody, *After Great Pain: The Inner Life of Emily Dickinson* (Cambridge, Mass.: Harvard University Press, 1971), cited in Sandra Gilbert and Susan Gubar, *Shakespeare's Sisters: Feminist Essays on Women Poets* (Bloomington: Indiana University Press, 1979), xix.

9. John Crowe Ransom, "Emily Dickinson: A Poem Restored," cited in Gilbert and Gubar, *Shakespeare's Sisters*, xix.

10. Alice Walker, *In Search of Our Mothers' Gardens* (San Diego: Harcourt Brace Jovanovich, 1983), 232–33.

11. Shoshana Felman, "Women and Madness: The Critical Phallacy," *Diacritics*, 5.4 (1975): 2–5.

12. Ibid., 10.

13. Virginia Woolf, *A Room of One's Own* (New York & London: Harcourt Brace Jovanovich, 1957), 3. Further references in the text.

14. The current understanding of gender as social construction dates back to the feminist critique of patriarchy in the 1970s and early 1980s. At that time, referring to this same text by Woolf, I suggested the term "experience" for the *process* of gender construction as it is subjectively lived. See Teresa de Lauretis, "Semiotics and Experience," in *Alice Doesn't: Feminism, Semiotics, Cinema* (Bloomington: Indiana University Press, 1984), 158–60.

15. Luce Irigaray, "La tâche aveugle d'un vieux rêve de symétrie," in *Speculum de l'autre femme* (Paris: Minuit, 1974), 7–162; Dale Spender, *Man Made Language* (London: Routledge & Kegan Paul, 1980).

16. "Being with him . . . saved her from the strain of responding to other boys or even noting the whole category of men. . . . This, then, was probably what sex meant to her; not pleasure, but a sanctuary in which her mind was freed of any consideration for all the other males in the universe who might want anything of her. It was resting from pursuit." Alice Walker, *Meridian* (New York: Pocket Books, 1976), 61–62.

17. Paul de Man, "The Rhetoric of Temporality," in *Blindness and Insight: Essays in the Rhetoric of Contemporary Criticism* (Minneapolis: University of Minnesota Press, 1983), 214 and 216. See also Hayden White's definition of irony: "The trope of irony, in which falsehood is presented as the truth, constitutes the limit of figurative characterizations of reality; for an ironic utterance is not merely a statement about reality, as metaphor, metonymy, and synecdoche are, but presupposes at least a tacit awareness of the disparity between a statement and the reality it is supposed to represent" (*Tropics of Discourse: Essays in Cultural Criticism* [Baltimore: Johns Hopkins University Press, 1978], 207–8).

18. Rosi Braidotti, *Patterns of Dissonance: A Study of Women in Contemporary Philosophy* (Cambridge: Polity Press, 1991), 150.

19. Angela Davis, *Women, Culture and Politics* (New York: Random House, 1990), xiii.

20. Paul de Man, *The Resistance to Theory*, foreword by Wlad Godzich (Minneapolis: University of Minnesota Press, 1986). Further references in the text.

21. Michel Foucault, *The Archaeology of Knowledge and the Discourse on Language*, trans. A. M. Sheridan Smith (New York: Pantheon Books, 1972), 37.

22. Roland Barthes, "From Work to Text," in *Image/Music/Text*, selected and trans. by Stephen Heath (New York: Hill and Wang, 1977), 157.

23. De Man, "Semiology and Rhetoric," in *Allegories of Reading* (New Haven, Conn.: Yale University Press, 1979), 10; emphasis added.

24. Sabina Spielrein, "Destruction as Cause of Becoming," quoted in Aldo Carotenuto, *A Secret Symmetry: Sabina Spielrein between Jung and Freud*, trans. by Arno Pomerans et al. (New York: Pantheon Books, 1982), 191–95. The original German paper was "Die Destruktion als Ursache des Werdens," *Jahrbuch für psychoanalytische und psychopathologische Forschungen* 4 (1912): 465–503.

25. I thank the following doctoral students in the departments of History of Consciousness and Literature at the University of California, Santa Cruz, for their contributions to the seminar and urge them to take to heart Woolf's exhortation that "so to work, even in poverty and obscurity, is worthwhile" (*Room*, 118): Felice Blake-Kleiven, Shannon Brownlee, Natalie Hansen, Timothy Koths, Isela Ocegueda, Anita Starosta, Christina Stevenson, Carra Stratton, Scott Thompson, Robin Tremblay-McGaw, and Kristina Valendinova.

26. Felman's reading of Balzac's novella "Adieu" is in her "Women and Madness: The Critical Phallacy," cited above.

27. One notable exception is the novel by the French writer Anne Garréta, *Sphinx* (Paris: Bernard Grasset, 1986). But, for example, when the Italian translation of *Written on the Body* (*Scritto sul corpo*), forced by grammatical rules to designate the gender of the narrator as either feminine or masculine, opts for the feminine, it necessarily resolves the ambiguity that makes Winterson's "I" the figure of a transgender subject: the "I" is read conventionally, as a lesbian, and the resistance to gender figured in the "I" is all but lost in translation.

28. For the former, see Esther Newton, "The Mythic Mannish Lesbian: Radclyffe Hall and the New Woman," *Signs* 9.4 (Summer 1984): 557–75 and Rebecca O'Rourke, *Reflecting on* The Well of Loneliness (London: Routledge, 1989); and for the latter, Jay Prosser, "'Some Primitive Thing Conceived in a Turbulent Age of Transition': The Invert, *The Well of Loneliness*, and the Narrative Origins of Transsexuality," *Second Skins: The Body Narratives of Transsexuality* (New York: Columbia University Press, 1998), 135–69.

29. The epistemological authority of referential language is most clearly asserted in this often cited passage: "To posit a materiality outside of language,

where that materiality is considered ontologically distinct from language, is to undermine the possibility that language might be able to indicate or correspond to that domain of radical alterity. Hence, the absolute distinction between language and materiality which was to secure the referential function of language undermines that function radically" (Judith Butler, *Bodies That Matter* [New York: Routledge, 1993], 68).

Name and Title Index

TERESA DE LAURETIS is a professor in the Department of History of Consciousness at the University of California, Santa Cruz, and is internationally recognized for her work in semiotics, psychoanalytic theory, literature, science fiction, film, film theory, and queer and feminist theory. She is author of over a dozen books, which have appeared in many languages, including the canonical *Alice Doesn't: Feminism, Semiotics, Cinema* and *Technologies of Gender: Essays on Theory, Film, and Fiction.*

PATRICIA WHITE is an associate professor and chair of the program in film and media studies at Swarthmore College. She is the coauthor with Timothy Corrigan of an introductory film studies textbook, *The Film Experience,* and the author of *Uninvited: Classical Hollywood Cinema and Lesbian Representability,* as well as of numerous articles on feminist and lesbian and gay film culture. She is a member of the editorial collective of the leading English-language journal of feminism and film, *Camera Obscura.*

The University of Illinois Press
is a founding member of the
Association of American University Presses.

Composed in 10/13 Sabon,
designed by Jan Tschichold
with Filosofia display,
designed by Zuzana Licko
Typeset by Barbara Evans
at the University of Illinois Press
Book designed by Copenhaver Cumpston
Manufactured by Sheridan Books, Inc.

» » »

UNIVERSITY OF ILLINOIS PRESS
1325 South Oak Street
Champaign, IL 61820-6903
www.press.uillinois.edu